Against Global Apartheid

South Africa meets the World Bank, IMF and International Finance

Patrick Bond

Second edition

University of Cape Town Press

Zed Books Ltd
London and New York

Against Global Apartheid:
South Africa meets the World Bank, IMF and International Finance 2nd edition was first
published by UCT Press (Pty) Ltd, PO Box 24309, Lansdowne 7779, South Africa and
outside South Africa by Zed Books Ltd, 7 Cynthia Street, London N1 9JF, UK and 175
Fifth Avenue, New York, NY 10010,USA in 2003.

Second edition 2003

ISBN 1 919 71382 4 UCT Press, limp
ISBN 1 842 77393 3 ZED Books, limp
ISBN 1 842 77392 5 ZED Books, Hb

Cataloging - in - Publication Data is Available from the British Library

US CIP has been applied for from the Library of Congress

Copy editing by Alex Potter of FPP Productions
Proofreading and indexing by Jan Schaafsma
Cover design by The Pumphaus Design Studio cc
Typesetting by RHT desktop publishing cc, Durbanville
Printed and bound in South Africa by Formeset Printers

Acknowledgements
Cover photograph of Jubilee protest courtesy of *Business Day.*
All other photographs courtesy of Ben Cashdan

Distributed in the USA exclusively by Palgrave, a division of St. Martin's Press LLC, 175 Fifth
Avenue New York, NY 10010
www.zedbooks.demon.co.uk

Contents

Preface

[Southern African countries] were pressured into implementing [IMF and World Bank] programmes with adverse effects on employment and standards of living ... The *RDP* must use foreign debt financing only for those elements of the programme that can potentially increase our capacity for earning foreign exchange. Relationships with international financial institutions such as the World Bank and International Monetary Fund must be conducted in such a way as to protect the integrity of domestic policy formulation and promote the interests of the South African population and the economy. Above all, we must pursue policies that enhance national self-sufficiency and enable us to reduce dependence on international financial institutions. (African National Congress *Reconstruction and Development Programme*, 1994)[1]

Introduction: International financial pressure points

The words above were amongst many in the first African National Congress (ANC) campaign platform, the *RDP* (Reconstruction and Development Programme), that conveyed progressive ambitions – infused with informed scepticism about global financial power – for South Africa's future. How quickly this particular promise was broken![2]

I recall distinctly entering into fierce debates in January–February 1994 with an ANC official based at party headquarters in Luthuli House, in the seedy Joubert Park section of central Johannesburg. The stony fellow responsible for banking/finance policy,[3] under the supervision of Trevor Manuel and Tito Mboweni, was terribly upset with our tortuous formulation on foreign debt, especially the idea of 'self-sufficiency', which was arrived at after many attempts by the *RDP* drafting team. Sensing trouble, leaders of the SA National Civic Organisation (SANCO), which I served as *RDP* editor, went back to their base for mandates. The word came back: the provision hostile to international finance could not be dropped. *RDP* representatives of the Congress of SA Trade Unions (Alec Erwin) and SA Communist Party (Jeremy Cronin) overrode the neo-liberal ANC official. The ANC's formal political representative (Max Sisulu) concurred.

But good *RDP* rhetoric could not disguise bad practice by those like Manuel and even Erwin, when they became intent upon international financial integration. (And in any case, the discursive victory was merely a symbolic – not decisive – incident.) Beginning in mid-1990, 'reconnaissance missions' from the Washington-based financial institutions were already undermining the integrity of domestic policy formulation, and ambitiously promoting the interests of international financial and corporate capital. This book tells that broader story, tracing it forward into the post-apartheid era. Indeed, by early 2001, George Soros confirmed during an interview with film-maker Ben Cashdan at the Davos World Economic Forum that, 'Today South Africa is very much in the hands of international capital.'[4]

But from illegitimate domination, resistance inevitably emerges. A few minutes prior to Soros' confession, on an international satellite transmission that linked Davos to Porto Alegre's World Social Forum, Soweto political activist Trevor Ngwane had, face to face, accused the financier of indirectly putting a massive squeeze on Pretoria's budget. In turn, fiscal austerity was the most proximate national cause of water cut-offs, a failure to install pipes to households without access, and a resulting cholera outbreak that, within ten months, infected more than 100 000 people, killing more than 200.

> I come from South Africa. We still had a hope that liberation would bring houses, jobs and good education for our people. But since our government got closer to the World Bank and people like George Soros, we have lost a million jobs. As I am talking we had an outbreak of cholera because the government was forced by the likes of Soros to introduce privatisation of basic services like water and electricity.

Ngwane 'actually has a point, because South Africa has to meet the requirements of international capital', acknowledged Soros.

> I think South Africa is following pretty sound macroeconomic policies, but is not able to generate sufficient growth to satisfy the legitimate aspirations of the people. And there is something wrong with this ... Because actually, the global market, as it functions, is really an uneven playing field. The centre is much better situated than the periphery countries. And it is better situated not just because it is wealthy, but also because it controls the system.

Ngwane, Soros and the politicians who sit uncomfortably in between will make further appearances in this book, as I document global uneven development, inequality, financial crisis and some of their implications for ordinary South Africans.

Soros, to his credit, has always spoken frankly of the threat that international capitalism poses to society. On occasion, Thabo Mbeki and his colleagues have said much the same. But repeatedly, the outcome has always appeared to any attentive observer as a case of 'talking left, acting right'.

The larger point of all this will become clearer in Parts 1–3 of this book. Put briefly, it is, simply, that the democratic transition in South Africa to an important degree hinged not only on pressures for *political liberation*. Just as crucial was acknowledgment by ANC deal-makers that the trade-off for the big business community's belated rejection of apartheid was *economic liberalisation* – i.e. release of local capital from apartheid's *laager*, whether through dramatically lower corporate taxes (down from 48% in 1994 to 30% by 1999), lower tariffs on imports, or the lifting of controls that had prevented capital flight.

Crudely put, big business basically said, '*You chaps can have the state, but let us get our money out of here!*' Not only did the financial looting of South Africa follow apace, but also the country's economic, social, cultural and policy environment was – and continues to be – enormously influenced by global economic processes and institutions.

Yet what is termed 'globalisation' brazenly contradicts society's strong motivation for more equitable development to redress the massive residual disparities of apartheid. The detrimental influence of international economic integration is most strongly felt through new financial, trade and investment vulnerabilities, but also in social policy that follows international norms, and to a certain extent in political-cultural subordination to the global markets. As President Mbeki himself put it in mid-2000, 'The globalization of the economy resulting among other things in rapid movements of huge volumes of capital across the globe, objectively also has the effect of limiting the possibility of states to take unilateral decisions.'[5]

The narrowing of national sovereignty is most evident when a country falls foul of the likes of George Soros. So let us take a quick look at what exactly happens.

In the hands of international capital

South Africans are repeatedly told that since 1994, 'sound macroeconomic policies', including rapid financial and trade liberalisation, ensured 'stability' and the highest international regard. It is as if by repeating the mantra often enough, the harsh underlying reality can be disregarded.

Yet many of us who served the ANC and South African government will never forget at least two moments during Nelson Mandela's 1994–9 presidency, moments of terrible panic that reflected both unique local frailties and – thanks to the vagaries of international finance – the more general brittleness of 'emerging market' economies.

In the first example, in February 1996, a decision to drop capital controls eleven months earlier suddenly proved disastrous. The two main macroeconomic managers, Reserve Bank governor Chris Stals and finance minister Chris Liebenberg, abolished the 'financial rand' exchange-control mechanism in March 1995. The finrand, a market-related dual exchange rate, had served as South Africa's main barrier to damaging global financial flows for nearly a decade. In August 1985, foreign banks fled immediately after PW Botha's finger-wagging 'Rubicon' speech, so the finrand substantially slowed subsequent capital flight by serving as a tax on outflows.[6] As a result of its 1995 demise, sufficient 'hot money' flowed into South African shares that year to fund half the trades on the Johannesburg Stock Exchange.[7]

But in early 1996, the hot money flooded back out, leading to a currency crash of more than a quarter of the rand's value over several months, set off by a 'sell' report emanating from Zurich bankers that was induced by a false rumour that Mandela was ill. The Reserve Bank quickly lost R5 billion of its hard-currency reserves, representing a drop in import coverage from two months' worth to less than one month's by mid-1996. The value of the rand slid from R3.60 to the US$ in January 1996 to R4.40/$ in March, to R4.70/$ in December. In order to stem the outflow and stabilise the rand, interest rates were hiked dramatically over a few weeks. In 'real' (after-inflation) terms, the prime interest rate paid by leading firms rose from 12% to nearly 15% in May 1996, a level only once surpassed in modern South African history (in mid-1998).

The adoption of the homegrown structural adjustment programme Growth, Employment and Redistribution (Gear) followed soon after, as a direct response to international investor demands. 'Just call me a Thatcherite', whimpered Mbeki at the Gear press conference on 14 June, begging the markets to stabilise. But self-humiliation was not enough, as the currency slide continued for several more months.

No matter the painful and surprising experience of 1996, South Africa's macroeconomic managers failed to learn from their experience. The second post-apartheid rand crash occurred over a few weeks beginning in April 1998. Global investors fled the 'emerging markets' following the East Asian and Russian collapses, and South Africa again faced financial crisis. Most spectacularly, Stals wasted more than R30 billion in hard currency reserves one weekend in June when he unsuccessfully tried to defend the rand from attack by local and foreign sellers.

The rand's fall continued, from R5.10/$ in May to R6.70/$ at its low point in July, before it stabilised at R6.20/$ in subsequent months. More so than in 1996, this badly affected the JSE, whose all-share index dropped nearly 40% from its April 1998 peak of 8 200, to a low of less than 5 000 in August. In addition, net bond purchases switched from an inflow of nearly R10 billion in the first quarter of 1998 to an outflow of nearly R16 billion in the third quarter. This was the key factor in the drop in Reserve Bank foreign reserves from an import cover of more than three months to just over two months from April to September 1998. To attract funds back to South Africa, Stals raised the Reserve Bank's main lending rate from 14.8% in April to 21.8% in August.

To break – or to shine – the chains of global apartheid?

These incidents were merely the two most important surface manifestations of South Africa's decline. There were many other economically suicidal exposures to global processes in the years immediately following democracy in 1994, leaving South Africa with an international competitiveness ranking of 43rd out of 49 major countries in the main Swiss business school's 2001 competitiveness survey.[8] And at a deeper level, as Chapter one will show, further damage was wrought by the general international economic slowdown that had begun around three decades earlier, amplified at the turn of the century by a massive glut in unutilised production capacity worse than at any other time since the 1930s.[9]

On the one hand, in this context, growing foreign trade amplified South Africa's own long-standing economic crisis – particularly deindustrialisation and job loss. On the other hand, a trade surplus with Africa reached an extreme level, causing untenable balance of payments problems and deindustrialisation in the region. The neo-liberal regional policy generated rising geopolitical tensions and lured economic refugees from neighbouring lands, in turn contributing to world-class xenophobia amongst South African workers.

There was, moreover, a net outflow of international direct investment from South Africa during the first five years after apartheid, while the uneven dribs and drabs of incoming foreign investment were largely of the merger/acquisition variety rather than long-term investments projects. Most of the country's biggest companies – Anglo American, Old Mutual, Gencor/Billiton, South African Breweries, Didata – took the gap, relisting to conduct their primary stock-market trading in London, or in the case of De Beers, delisting entirely in 2001. Simultaneously, economic advice from international financiers boiled down to persistent demands for macroeconomic policies conducive to South Africa's increased global vulnerability.

A regular declaration of 'impotence' was the response to these pressures from South Africa's political leaders, especially Mandela, Mbeki, Manuel, trade minister Alec Erwin and approximately a dozen others with key ideological and functionary responsibilities. (Manuel actually used the word, in an interview, when discussing state job creation capacity.)[10] Parts three and four of this book consider the debate over whether Pretoria had or has room for manoeuvre, and whether it was necessary to take the strategic turn towards neo-liberalism chosen by key state officials when confronted by the ever-tightening chains of the global economy.

I borrow here the metaphor that then Archbishop Desmond Tutu taught my fellow anti-apartheid activists at Johns Hopkins University in early 1986, when he encouraged us to increase the pressure for 'divestment' by universities (and other aspiring socially responsible shareholders) on companies with active South African operations. At the same time, a few miles up the I-95 highway in Philadelphia, an inner-city preacher, Rev. Leon Sullivan, was conducting an entirely different crusade: to help multinational corporations continue operating within South Africa, but under a half-hearted code of conduct committing them to conduct their own operations in a somewhat less explicitly racist manner. Tutu referred to Sullivan's gambit as 'shining the chains of apartheid', and confirmed that the demo-cratic forces would fight on until apartheid's chains were completely broken.

Thabo Mbeki unabashedly terms the international political-economic system 'global apartheid'. The next logical question is: are Mbeki, Manuel, Erwin and their colleagues aiming to 'break' the chains of 21st-century global apartheid, or merely to provide a glossy, New South Africa 'shine'?

Nixing not fixing global apartheid: A South African case study

According to Pretoria's critics, instead of fundamentally challenging global apartheid, the South African government has been lubricating the financial, trade and investment processes that are amongst the most damaging. Evidence is found not only in the enthusiastic local application of the Washington Consensus through the Gear strategy. In addition, key South African officials are lending legitimacy to the World Bank, International Monetary Fund (IMF), World Trade Organisation (WTO) and like-minded institutions. At home, the same officials persist in denying the need to roll back free-market processes, even in areas such as patent protection on HIV/AIDS drugs (discussed below in Part three) and capital controls (Part four), where there is an overwhelmingly case for breaking global apartheid's chains.

However, even if Parts one and two of *Against Global Apartheid* offer a profoundly pessimistic account of South African and international macro-economic management, this by no means implies that pandering to inter-national elites is a permanent affliction. On the contrary, there is evidence to suggest that the free-market Washington Consensus ideology began to ebb during the late 1990s, and that popular resistance is already affecting not just state policies, but also the international balance of forces.

Can the damage that has been done be reversed?

I think it can, and therefore most of the second half of the book is devoted to exploring ways in which popular pressure exerted from below can end, not perpetuate, global apartheid. By way of concluding this preface, I want to reflect, for a moment, on a single case of concrete activism that is indicative of broader potentials.

The university at which I teach, the University of the Witwatersrand ('Wits') in central Johannesburg, is presently the site of a 'World Bank

Bonds Boycott' campaign by students, staff and faculty. The short-run demand is simple: that university finance officials commit themselves never to buy bonds issued by the World Bank. (The World Bank gets 80% of its funding from investors like Wits.)

From 1995, Wits officials could move 15% of the university's R1 billion endowment offshore. Some of that money – the amount varies from day to day, depending on investment trends – is channeled into bonds issued by the World Bank and sold to Wits via international fund managers. The same is true of most major South African institutions, and indeed virtually all funds that have access to international capital markets buy at least a small share of internationally rated, top-grade World Bank securities.

As Part four argues, the strategy of closing – 'nixing' – the World Bank and IMF is not a faulty one. And to that end, the World Bank Bonds Boycott is an inspired tactic, since it allows activists and ordinary people to get involved in fighting global apartheid every day in their own communities (not just at major demonstrations in Seattle, Prague, Washington, Quebec City and so on).

As I will show in more detail in Chapter three, there are many reasons specific to South and Southern Africa why getting the World Bank to close up shop would be beneficial to local peoples. Borrowing the Wits activists' rhetoric, I lay out below some of the reasons for bond-boycotting the World Bank. Specific crimes committed by the World Bank and IMF during South Africa's apartheid era include:

n   *the World Bank's US$100 million in loans to Eskom from 1951 to 1967* that gave only white people electric power, but for which all South Africans paid the bill;

n   *the World Bank's point-blank refusal to heed a United Nations General Assembly instruction in 1966* not to lend to apartheid South Africa;

n   *IMF apartheid-supporting loans of more than $2 billion between the Soweto uprising in 1976 and 1983*, when the US Congress finally prohibited lending to Pretoria;

n   *a World Bank loan to build dams in Lesotho that was widely acknowledged to 'bust' sanctions against apartheid South Africa in 1986*, via a London trust; and

n   *IMF advice to Pretoria in 1991 to impose the regressive value-added tax (VAT)*, in opposition to which 3.5 million people went on a two-day stayaway.

Subsequently, neo-apartheid lending and policy advice by the Bretton Woods twins include:

n   *an $850 million IMF loan to South Africa in December 1993* that carried conditions of wage restraint and cuts in the budget deficit, which in turn hampered the transition to democracy;

n *World Bank promotion of 'market-oriented' land reform in 1993–94*,
   which established such onerous conditions (similar to the failed
   Zimbabwe policy) that instead of 30% land redistribution as mandated
   in the RDP, less than 1% of good land was redistributed;

n *the World Bank's endorsement of bank-centred housing policy in August
   1994*, with recommendations for smaller housing subsidies;

n *the World Bank's design of South African infrastructure policy in
   November 1994*, which provided the rural and urban poor with only pit
   latrines, no electricity connections, inadequate roads and communal
   taps instead of house or yard taps;

n *the World Bank's insistence that corrupt Lesotho Highlands Development
   Authority boss Masupha Sole stay in his job in December 1994* (six years
   after he began taking bribes from international construction companies), in a threatening letter to the Lesotho government;

n *the World Bank's promotion of water cut-offs for those unable to afford
   payments, its opposition to a free 'lifeline' water supply and its recommendations against irrigation subsidies for black South Africans in
   October 1995*, within a government water-pricing policy in which the
   World Bank claimed (in its 1999 *Country Assistance Review*) it played an
   'instrumental' role;

n *the World Bank's conservative role in the Lund Commission in 1996*,
   which recommended a 44% cut in the monthly grant to impoverished,
   dependent children, from R135 per month to R75;

n *the World Bank's participation in the failed Growth, Employment and
   Redistribution (Gear) policy in June 1996*, through contributing two staff
   economists and its economic model;

n *the World Bank and IMF's consistent message to South African workers
   that their wages are too high*, and that unemployment can only be cured
   through 'labour flexibility';

n *the World Bank's role in Egoli 2002*, including research support and
   encouragement of municipal privatisation;

n *the World Bank's repeated commitments to invest, through its subsidiary
   the International Finance Corporation, in privatised infrastructure,
   housing securities for high-income families, for-profit 'managed healthcare' schemes, and the now-bankrupt, US-owned Dominos Pizza franchise*;

n *the consistent failure of World Bank and IMF 'structural adjustment
   programmes' in Southern Africa since the 1980s*; and

n *the stubborn refusal by the World Bank and IMF to cancel debt owed by
   our impoverished neighbours since the mid-1990s*, except in tiny amounts
   and with brutal conditionality provisions.

There are, to be sure, people of good conscience who dispute 'nix-it' strategies and tactics. Some have made valiant efforts since the early 1980s to 'fix'

the IMF, World Bank, international financial markets and other manifestations of global apartheid. In fields like environmental regulation, gender
sensitivity, community participation, institutional transparency, corporate
accountability, and even the highlighting of poverty, the fixers can claim a
few victories.[11]

But simultaneously, broader social, environmental and economic conditions worsened dramatically. Reformers can claim less and less legitimacy
for their efforts, which often appear as merely shifting deck-chairs on a
Titanic-like global economy. So it is to a different group we will have to
turn, especially in Chapters ten to twelve, for a vision of a better future, to
what I term 'global justice movements'. In this group can be found organisations and people who have little or no faith in the initiatives advanced by
the small bloc of Third World nationalists and 'post-Washington
Consensus' reformers, and who see the need for deeper surgery.

Over the past fifteen years, I have been extremely privileged to have had
contact with inspiring global justice advocates, activists and intellectuals.
Whatever I may have written in the pages below that makes some sense is
due almost entirely to their input.

Notes

1 African National Congress (1994), *The Reconstruction and Development Programme*,
Johannesburg, Umanyano Publications, sections 1.4.17 and 6.5.16.
2 For a recounting of other promises and how they fared, see Bond, P. and Khosa, M.
(1999), *An RDP Policy Audit*, Pretoria, Human Sciences Research Council; and
Bond, P. (2000), *Elite Transition: From Apartheid to Neoliberalism in South Africa*,
London, Pluto and Pietermaritzburg, University of Natal Press, Chapter 3:
'Rumours, Dreams and Promises'.
3 Tellingly, a few weeks after the mid-1994 transition, after failing to get the top
Reserve Bank financial regulatory position he sought, Neil Morrison took a job with
a Johannesburg merchant bank to promote privatisation.
4 This and subsequent quotes come from Cashdan, B. (2001), *Globalisation: Whose
Side are We On?*, film, Johannesburg, recorded in January in Davos.
5 Mbeki, T. (2000), 'Keynote Address to the ANC National General Council', Port
Elizabeth, 12 July.
6 The premium paid by exporters of financial capital ranged from 10% to 50%,
depending on exchange rates and political circumstances. See Chapter twelve for
more on the finrand.
7 The finrand was dropped, inexplicably, in the immediate wake of a run on the
currencies of Mexico and other Latin American countries by investment speculators. Suddenly, as a result, purchases of South African bonds by non-residents
doubled from the average annual levels of the past decade. The inflow also led to a
rise in the monthly average share turnover from R5 billion to R10 billion within
a year, and the stock-market all-share index rose from 5 000 in early 1995 to 7 000 a
year later (using 1960 as the 100 index).
8 *Business Day*, 25 April 2001.
9 *The Economist*, 22 February 1999.
10 *Sunday Independent*, 9 January 2000.

11 Personally, I was party to several such campaigns to reform the World Bank, beginning in 1985 when I joined the national executive of the US Debt Crisis Network. Finally, in 1998, I gave up on this approach. The straw that broke the camel's back was the World Bank Inspection Panel's rejection of a formal, well-documented request to investigate the Lesotho Highlands Water Project scheme, as Chapter three describes, leaving Johannesburg township activists stunned at the World Bank's lack of accountability. The last gasp for reform was probably the effort by World Bank chief economist Joseph Stiglitz to introduce a 'Post-Washington Consensus' economic paradigm – but Stiglitz was fired in late 1999.

Acknowledgements

First, refer to endnote 2 of Chapter three for a list of extraordinary Southern Africans active in various campaigns against global apartheid at the turn of the 21st century. I honour these women and men for giving society so much raw material of praxis, upon which this book so often draws.

Let me recognise some other local and international influences. I regularly assert that the horrors of worsening uneven development in my adopted hometown – perhaps the world's most unsustainable city, though incongruously chosen to host the United Nations World Summit on Sustainable Development ('Rio+10') in September 2002 – are outweighed by Johannesburg's enormously rich political, social and cultural ambience. This is most explicit when progressive South Africans think about the lessons they have to share with the rest of the region and world.

These experiences are quite frequent. The Johannesburg/Pretoria nexus has been a great place from which to watch the world go by this last decade. In large part this is because a wide variety of internationalists regularly stop by and give seminars, hosted by Jubilee South Africa, the Campaign Against Neoliberalism in South Africa, my university and other organisations. In addition, I personally have been a very grateful beneficiary of a 'people's globalisation' that, in the form of frequent-flying conference-hopping, wreaks havoc on the environment (through jet-engine emissions), but that has allowed me to participate at some of the most exciting sites of conflict with global-apartheid institutions, and to also engage in careful reflection in more tranquil settings.[1] Affable hosts invariably motivated me to work my arguments into better shape.[2]

In the process, this book has benefitted enormously from a welcome stream of e-mails and from face-to-face discussions with dozens of other colleagues over these past three years,[3] not to mention advice from some tolerant housemates: Ben Cashdan, Darlene Miller and Greg Ruiters. This was a fine mix.

While Darlene and Greg kept me updated on international intellectual fads and scolded me, correctly but always with a smile, about the dangers of 'substitutionism', Ben made contributions that far transcend the photographs I have lifted from him. His persistent, humorous questioning of the world's most powerful men warrants the cult status that his documentaries are acquiring.

On the activist front, Dennis Brutus, George Dor, Trevor Ngwane and John Saul remain my heroes and closest comrades, for their tireless commitment to popular education and mobilisation. Archbishop Njongonkulu Ndungane and Fatima Meer have served as politico-moral compasses, with their mature but no less urgent intent to abolish global apartheid.

Back at the office, the director of the Wits Graduate School of Public and Development Management, Guy Mhone, established the ideal conditions for a footloose academic/activist, and all my colleagues have been broad-minded about their errant hallmate. My co-directors of the Municipal Services Project, David McDonald and Greg Ruiters, kept me thinking and researching locally. I have been lucky to labour within a milieu of enquiry at Wits where masters and doctoral students have taught me a great deal.[4] And I serve as a volunteer associate of two other institutions which are remarkably effective on shoestring budgets: the Alternative Information and Development Centre (Cape Town/Johannesburg) and Center for Economic Justice (Washington).

An old Argus Company desk at which I wrote most of the words that follow was a gift from my former neighbour Peter Wellman, who passed away a few days after the first draft of this book went to the publishers. Peter was a great iconoclast, an advocate of racial and social justice who wrote and edited unusually clearly and prolifically, a journalist with enormous commitment (though his employer never knew the risks he took for the ANC underground), an internationalist and regionalist whose socialist spine never bent, and a man who immediately understood the campaigning against global apartheid over which I enthused. He left us all with fondest memories, including tossing typewriters out of buildings in frustration!

And then there are abundant Johannesburg friends, including those in the *debate* journal and e-mail listserve, and patrons of the Workers Library and Museum, the Supper Club in Berea, Peg's jazz bistro in Troyeville, the Wits Post-Grad Pub, Cosatu House, the NGO ghetto of Braamfontein, Rockey Street, township shebeens and other motley hangouts.[5]

My publisher Solani Ngobeni at Juta/UCT Press encouraged me and forgave my quirky schedule, and I warmly thank his staff for hard work and forbearance. Additional gratitude is due to several editors, journals and publishing houses for permission to revise articles and chapters for inclusion below.[6] The Human Sciences Research Council funded an early investigation along these lines in 1997, and the International Development Research Centre and University of Natal Centre for Social and Development Studies were also benefactors. My son Jan was magnanimous with patience, rooting for me as best he could in the real world, and always asking the hardest questions.

And the numerous global justice movements kept us all focused, just as did the many institutions and people responsible for the continuation of global apartheid. Special thanks go to the World Bank and IMF for doing more to unite social change activists across the globe than anything since apartheid itself.

I have a feeling that all of those implicated above will be critical to our future: mine, yours, South Africa's and probably the world's.

Patrick Bond
Johannesburg, May 2001

Notes

1   Going backwards to the point in mid-1998 when I began putting together these arguments about resisting global apartheid for seminars, workshops and conferences, many open-minded audiences heard portions of this book, and all provided valuable feedback. In the first half of 2001, these included the Wits University Graduate School of Public and Development Management's seminar on Advanced Topics in Political Economy and several other P&DM classes; the Integrated Social Development Centre fora on development finance and water privatisation in Accra; the Southern and Eastern African Trade Information and Negotiations Initiative conference on Financing for Development in Geneva; Oxford University's School of Geography; the World Council of Churches' consultation on the Bretton Woods institutions, Geneva; the University of Natal/Durban Centre for Social and Development Studies; and in Windhoek, the Labour Research and Resources Initiative's Southern African Conference on Foreign Direct Investment.

During 2000, I attended the South African Graduates Development Association conference on student-worker alliances in Johannesburg; Kairos Europa's Financial Markets Consultation, Frankfurt; the NGO parallel session to the G-20 Finance Ministers Meeting in Montreal; Columbia University's Institute of African Studies academic seminar, New York; the University of Cape Town Graduate School of Business Seminar on Globalisation; the Southern African Regional Institute for Policy Studies Colloquium on Southern African Integration, Harare; the Ottawa Public Interest Research Group chapter meeting at Carleton University; the International Development Research Centre seminar on governance, Ottawa; the Brecht Forum, New York; Hofstra University's Department of Political Science, New York; the Rocky Mountain Peace and Justice Center, Boulder, Colorado; a seminar held by the Center for Economic Justice and the Center for Economic Policy Research, Washington; the University of Durban-Westville's inaugural Fanon Lecture; the African Network and Forum on Debt and Development Project on Regional Applications of the Tobin Tax, Harare; the Grahamstown Festival Wordfest; the Anglican Diocese conference on social and economic change, Cape Town; the Africa Centre, London; the Bretton Woods Reform Organisation, London; the United Nations University's World Institute of Development Economics Research, Helsinki; the Southern African Catholic Bishops' Conference Symposium on Strategies to Bridge the Gap Between Rich and Poor in South Africa, Gauteng; the 50 Years is Enough Network seminar on structural adjustment, Washington; the Departments of Sociology at Rhodes University, East London campus and Rand Afrikaans University, Johannesburg; the University of Port Elizabeth Department of Political Science; the SA National Economic Policy Research Institute seminar on macroeconomic policy,

ACKNOWLEDGEMENTS xix

Johannesburg; the University of California/Los Angeles Center for Social Theory and Comparative History colloquium on Causes and Consequences of Neoliberalism; gatherings at the Rainforest Action Network, Economic Justice Network, International Rivers Network, and Global Exchange in San Francisco; a Bank Information Center seminar, Washington; a York University conference on The Global Working Class at the Millennium, Toronto; and a *Monthly Review* lunchtime seminar in New York.

In 1999, I was invited to the Russian Academy of Sciences Institute of Comparative Political Studies conference on Globalisation and Alternatives to Neoliberalism in Moscow; Oxfam's Southern African Trade Union Council Workshop on Trade and Investment, Johannesburg; the Globalization Monitor Workshop's Seminar on Global Strategies and Tactics, Hong Kong; the Korean Association of Economic Geography Seminar on Global Economic Crisis, Seoul; the Taegu Round Global Forum, Towards a New International Financial Order, South Korea; the Sungkonghoe University's International Conference on Neoliberalism, Global Capitalism and Civil Alternatives, Seoul; a seminar of the Alliance for Global Justice, Preamble Center, Essential Information and Results at the US House of Representatives, Washington; the Union of Radical Political Economics Summer Conference on Political Economy, the Environment and the Economic Crisis, Connecticut; the Africa Council of Churches globalisation seminar in Manzini, Swaziland; Jubilee 2000's Africa Conference, Lusaka; Wits University's School of International Relations; Yokohama National University's Department of Economics masters course on globalisation and development; the Focus on the Global South Conference on Economic Sovereignty in a Globalized World at Chulalongkorn University, Bangkok; and Jubilee 2000's Southern Africa Conference at Wits University.

In 1998, I spoke at the Parliamentary Initiative on the Mozambican External Debt at the Assembly of the Republic, Maputo; a York University Department of Political Science seminar, Toronto; the NGO parallel conference to the IMF/World Bank Annual Meetings, Washington; the Halifax Initiative's parallel conference to the Commonwealth Finance Ministerial Meetings, Ottawa; a World Resources Institute, National Wildlife Federation and Friends of the Earth workshop on international financial regulation, Washington; the South African Parliamentary Committee on Foreign Affairs, Cape Town; and the Foundation for Global Dialogue, Department of Foreign Affairs and Department of Trade and Industry conference, Preparing for the Non-Aligned Movement, Pretoria.

2 In Africa, my hosts were Charles Abugre and Rudolf Amenga-Etego (Accra); Horacio Zandamela (Maputo); Peter Henriot and Chawe Mpanda (Lusaka); Tendai Biti, Joan Brickhill, Jonah Gokuva, Opa Kapijimpanga, Davie Malungisa, John Masimba Manyanya, Allast Mwanza, Sam Moyo, Tandeka Nkiwane, Helga Patrikios, Brian Raftopoulos, Richard Saunders, Yash Tandon and John van't Hoff (Harare); Herbert Jauch (Windhoek); Heinrich Boehmke, Lisa Bornstein, Ashwin Desai, Mary Galvin, David Moore, Percy More, Kiru Naidoo, Vishnu Padayachee, Richard Pithouse and Imraan Valoodia (Durban); Susan Booysens and Boyce Papu (Port Elizabeth); Azwell Banda, Russell Grinker, Sarah Hugow, Litha Mcwabeni and Derrick Mosenthal (East London); and Mercia Andrews, Brian Ashley, Carl Brecker, Mark Delene, Dot Keet, Thomas Koelble, Roger Ronnie, David Sanders and Anna Weekes (Cape Town).

In Europe, hospitality and assistance were offered by Hein Marais, Rogate Mshana and Bob Scott (Geneva); Niall Bond (Lyons); Ulrich Duchrow, Theo Kneifel, and Anya Osterhaus (Frankfurt); Boris Kagarlitsky and Vladimir Shubin

(Moscow); Mansoob Murshed (Helsinki); David Hall, Joe Hanlon, Alex Wilks, Angela Wood and Ellen Meiksins Wood (London); Karen Bakker, Tony Lemon and Eric Swyngedouw (Oxford); and Paul Cammack (Manchester).

In North America, I am indebted to George Caffentzis, Greg DeFreitas, Sylvia Federici, Doug Henwood, Vicki Larson, John Mage, Mzwanele Mayekiso, Andrew Nash, Rachel Neumann, Louis Proyect, Danny Schechter and Maliq Simone (New York); Steve Askin, Soren Ambrose, Moya Atkinson, Tony Avirgan, Jaron Bourke, Joanne Carter, Jim Cason, Fantu Cheru, Dana Clark, Carole Collins, Andrea Durbin, Bob Lenhard, Jon Liss, Lisa McGowan, Robert Naiman, Njoki Njehu, Graham Saul, Tom Schlesinger, Todd Tucker, Neil Watkins, Mark Weisbrot, Rob Weissman (Washington); David Barsamian, Denis Bond, David Martin and Julika Slaby (Colorado); Beverly Bell (Alburquerque); Robert Brenner, Eric Mann and Leanne Mann-Hurst (Los Angeles); Erick Brownstein, Kevin Danaher and Lori Pottinger (San Francisco); Greg Albo, Sam Ginden, Roger Kiel, Colin Leys, Leo Panitch, John and Pat Saul and Alan Zeuge (Toronto); Karen Emily, Pam Foster, Robin Round and Christina Zarowsky (Ottawa); and Michel Chossudofsky and Jaggi Singh (Montreal). In Mexico, Gustavo Castro, a masked Zapatista and Global Exchange were excellent guides to Chiapas.

In Asia, warmest thanks go to Walden Bello, Nicola Bullard, Shalmali Guttal and Kamal Malhotra (Bangkok); Kate Bond (Chiang Mai); Gerard Greenfield (Hong Kong); Ji-hoon Choi, Chan-geun Lee and Won Soon Park (Seoul); Byongdoo Choi, Chan Keun Lee and Serapina Cha Mi-Kyung (Taegu); and Keiichi Yamazaki (Yokohama).

3   Thanks for their time, interest and insights to Hans Abrahamsson, Christophe Aguiton, Katharine Ainger, Yilmaz Akyuz, Michael Albert, Samir Amin, Giovanni Arrighi, Andy Banks, David Barkin, Alejandro Bendana, Eve Bertelsen, Fred Bienefeld, Tom Bramble, Jeremy Brecher, Paul Burkett, Horace Campbell, John Cavanagh, Camille Chalmers, Chris Chase-Dunn, Noam Chomsky, Harry Cleaver, Alexander Cockburn, Jane D'Arista, Julie Davids, Paul Davis, Brad DeLong, Javes Devine, Norm Dixon, Peter Dorman, Michael Dorsey, Fiona Dove, John Dylan, Martina Egli, Ben Fine, Laura Flanders, Jonathan Fox, Susan George, John Gershman, Jayati Ghosh, Bill Greider, Sara Grusky, Vineeta Gupta, Tony and Eve Hall, Gillian Hart, Marty Hart-Landsberg, David Harvey, David Hemson, Joe Iosbaker, Jomo KS, Mark Jones, Josh Karliner, Naomi Klein, Martin Khor, Tom Kruse, Paul Kumar, Annie Leonard, Kari Polanyi Levitt, Jamie Love, Erin McCandless, Paddy McCully, George Monbiot, Martin Murray, Vicente Navarro, Anders Nielson, Leonce Ndikumana, Zar Ni, Jim O'Connor, Ezekiel Pajibo, Raj Patel, Medha Patkar, Michael Perelman, John Pilger, Erik Reinert, Ian Roberts, Max Sawicky, Art Serota, Anwar Shaikh, Jim Shultz, Jeff St. Clair, Carlos Vilas, Hilary Wainwright, Immanuel Wallerstein, Peter Waterman, John Williams, Daphne Wysham, Koh Young-joo and Iris Marion Young. All honed my line of argument, even if perhaps not yet to each of my counselors' satisfaction.

And in addition to books by writers listed in these notes, I gained a great deal from reading Harry Shutt's *The Trouble with Capitalism* (London, Zed, 1998), Michael Hardt and Toni Negri's *Empire* (Cambridge, Mass., Harvard University Press, 2000), and especially Robert Biel's *The New Imperialism* (London, Zed, 2000).

4   These include, amongst many, Tamara Braam, Peter Benjamin, Omano Edigheji, Sharon Edigheji, Patrick Flusk, Prathima Garbharran, Tony Hercules, Llanley Simpson, Tawanda Mutasah, Daniel Plaatjies, Horacio Zandamela, Langa Zita, and all the participants in a memorable March–April 2001 Sabi seminar on globalisation.

5   In addition to those listed already, I must mention Johannesburg lefties Glenn Adler, Peter Alexander, Matseleng Allais, Franco Barchiesi, Florencia Belvedere, Chris Bolsmann, Eddie Cottle, Molly Dhlamini, Nick Dieltens, Ann Eveleth, Sean Flynn, Bonnie Friedman, Steven Greenberg, Ferial Haffajee, Lisa Hoyos, Mazibuko Jara, Meshack Khosa, Bridget Kenney, Ulriche Kistner, Majbritt Fiil Laugesen, Sarah de Villiers Leach, Oupa Lehulere, Moses Majola, David Masondo, Dale Mckinley, Andile Mngxitama, Darrell Moellendorf, Sam Moiloa, John Molefinyane, Johny Mphou, Prishani Naidoo, Tebogo Phadu, Caroline Riley, Bobby Rodwell, Melanie Samson, Virginia Setshedi, Richard Sherman, Robyn Stein, Nicole Ulrich, Salim Vally, Lucien van der Walt, Maria van Driel and Ahmed Veriava.

6   Before sometimes quite extensive modification, the chapters below initially appeared in the following forms:

   • *Preface*: 'Globalisation, Economic Crisis and South African Vulnerabilities', in M. Khosa (ed.), *Empowerment through Economic Transformation*, Pretoria, Human Sciences Research Council, 2000.

   • *Chapter one*: 'Globalisation, African Economic Crisis and South African Vulnerabilities', *African Communist*, November 1999; and 'Sustaining US Hegemony: The Economic Factor', in *Solidarity for Social Progress* (Korea), February 2001.

   • *Chapter two*: 'The Southern African Working Class: Production, Reproduction and Politics', in L. Panitch and C. Leys (eds), *Socialist Register 2001: The Global Working Class at the Millennium*, London, Merlin and New York, Monthly Review Press, 2000; and 'Regionalism, Environment and the Southern African Proletariat', *Capitalism, Nature, Socialism*, 11(3), September 2000.

   • *Chapter three*: 'The IMF and World Bank Reconsidered', in J. Coetsee, J. Graaf, F. Hendricks and G. Wood (eds), *Development: Theory, Policy and Practice*, Cape Town, Oxford University Press, 2001.

   • *Chapter four*: 'Foreign Aid and Development: South Africa's Negative Experiences and Perceptions, 1994–99', *Transformation*, 45, 2001.

   • *Chapter five*: 'Global Economic Crisis: A View from South Africa', *Journal of World Systems Research*, 5(2), 1999; and 'Their Reforms and Ours: The Balance of Forces that Inform a New Global Financial Architecture', in W. Bello, K. Malhutra and N. Bullard (eds), *Cooling Down Capital: How to Regulate Financial Markets*, London, Zed Press, 2000.

   • *Chapter six*: 'Pretoria's Perspectives on Globalisation', *Politikon*, 28(1), 2001.

   • *Chapter seven*: 'Can Thabo Mbeki Change the World?', in R. Calland and S. Jacobs (eds), *Thabo Mbeki*, Cape Town, IDASA, and Pietermaritzburg, University of Natal Press, 2002.

   • *Chapter eight*: 'Globalisation, Pharmaceutical Pricing and South African Health Policy: Managing Confrontation with US Firms and Politicians', *International Journal of Health Services*, 29(4), 1999.

   • *Chapter nine*: 'The Political Economy of HIV/AIDS Treatment Policy in South Africa', *International Journal of Health Services*, 31(2), 2001.

   • *Chapter ten*: 'Strategy, Self-Activity and African Grassroots Roles in the "Anti-Globalisation" Movement', in G. Kohler and E. J. Chaves (eds), *Globalization: Critical Perspectives*, New York, Nova Press, 2001.

   • *Chapter eleven*: 'Defunding the Fund, Running on the Bank', *Monthly Review*, 52(1), 2000.

   • *Chapter twelve*: 'A History of Finance and Uneven Geographical Development in South Africa', *South African Geographical Journal*, 80(1), 1998.

In addition, a variety of popular publications have carried shorter versions of the arguments in the pages below. These include: *Against the Current, Americas Update, Business Day, Development Update, Focus on Trade, Global Dialogue, Green Left Weekly, Indicator SA, International Viewpoint, Land and Rural Policy Digest, Leadership, Left Business Observer, Lokayan Bulletin, Mail and Guardian, Mots Pluriel, Multinational Monitor, New Routes, Southern Africa Report, Sunday Independent, Sunday World, Third World Resurgence, Watching the World Bank in Southern Africa,* and *ZNet*.

Finally, it is of some amusement to me that two sections of the last chapter – 'Comparative capital controls' and 'Exchange control options for South Africa' – were accepted for publication by two reviewers of the *South African Journal of Economics* during a nine-month period in 1999–2000. But the piece was then rejected by a new editor and third reviewer, whose explanation in April 2001 suggests either the durability of market-Stalinism in the local economics profession, or – as the reviewer confesses below – a material self-interest in *not* igniting an informed debate on capital controls. Here are excerpts from the review:

> Should the SAJE publish a paper in favour of capital controls suited to a left-wing-, labour- or 'Keynesian' audience? Should the SAJE publish a paper in favour of financial market liberalisation targeted at a right-wing, business- or 'Neo-Classical' audience? I think it should not lend itself to publish either ...
>
> The vulnerability of SA's economy to international financial flows is actually a good thing. The reason is that it imposes constraints on macro and micro policies. Basically, it lowers domestic policy autonomy, because if these policies are bad they will be reflected in capital outflows and a weaker currency ...
>
> I strongly disagree that financial market liberalisation imposes inappropriate policy discipline on sovereign states. Rather, it is a blessing in disguise because it dishes out penalty points immediately to failing governments and policies such as is partly the case in SA (especially w.r.t. the labour market, product market and delays over privatisation) ...
>
> The US trade deficit is not unsustainable ... Following the 'Washington Consensus' has worked extremely well for the USA, Canada, Europe etc. Just do a plot of per capita GDP and free market institutions. Of course, interesting countries that did not follow the Washington Consensus are for example Tanzania and Zambia. Since independence they followed socialist policies. Where are they now? ...
>
> The unmotivated demand for just 'lower interest rates' doesn't make any sense nor does it inspire any confidence in the author's economics background ...
>
> I don't think it is feasible that SA takes a bold global leadership position on restoring domestic financial security ...
>
> The present 15 percent restriction of foreign portfolio investment should be seen as another 'tax' on residents. If I could, the larger share of my assets would be in the USA say, not in RSA.

At the same moment that the ostrich-like economists were blocking discussion of the merits of exchange controls in their professional journal, the South African government – with the approval of even *Business Day* newspaper columnists (27 February and 5 March 2001) – toughened existing controls in the 2001 budget.

Acronyms

ALF-CIO	American Federation of Labour-Congress of Industrial Organizations
ANC	African National Congress
BMS	Bristol-Myers Squibb
BoP	balance of payments
BSAC	British South Africa Company
CBO	community-based organisation
CHOGM	Commonwealth Heads of Government Meeting
CoNGO	co-opted NGO
Cosatu	Congress of South African Trade Unions
DTI	Department of Trade and Industry
EDL	essential drugs list
EPZ	export processing zone
ESAP	Economic Structural Adjustment Programme (in Zimbabwe)
EU	European Union
FAO	Food and Agriculture Organisation
FDI	foreign direct investment
FNB	First National Bank
Fosatu	Federation of South African Trade Unions
GATT	General Agreement on Tariffs and Trade
GDP	gross domestic product
Gear	Growth, Employment and Redistribution (policy)
HIPC	highly indebted poor country
ICU	Industrial and Commercial Union
IDASA	Institute for a Democratic South Africa
IFC	International Finance Corporation
IMF	International Monetary Fund
ISI	import substitution industrialisation
JSE	JSE Securities Exchange
LHWP	Lesotho Highlands Water Project
MDC	Movement for Democratic Change
MIGA	Multilateral Investment Guarantee Agency
NAL	Non-aligned Movement
NDA	National Development Agency

NIEP	National Institute of Economic Policy
NGO	non-governmental organisation
OECD	Organisation for Economic Cooperation and Development
PHC	primary health care
PhRMA	The Pharmaceutical Research Manufacturers of America
PRC	People's Republic of China
PRD	Party of Revolutionary Democracy
PRI	Party of Institutional Revolution
PRSP	poverty reduction strategy paper
R&D	research and development
RDP	Reconstruction and Development Programme
SACP	South African Communist Party
SADC	Southern African Development Community
SACTUCC	South African Trade Union Co-ordinating Council
Sangoco	South African Non-governmental Coalition
SAP	structural adjustment programme
SAPA	South African Press Association
SDI	spatial development initiative
Swapo	South West African People's Organisation
TAC	Treatment Action Campaign
TEC	Transitional Executive Council
TI	Transparency International
TNC	transnational corporation
TNDT	Transitional National Development Trust
TRIPS	trade in intellectual property rights
UDI	Unilateral Declaration of Independence
UN	United Nations
UNCTAD	United Nations Conference on Trade and Development
UNDP	United Nations Development Programme
UNICEF	United Nations Children's Emergency Relief Fund
USAID	United States Agency for International Development
USTR	United States Trade Representative
WTO	World Trade Organisation
ZANU	Zimbabwe African National Union
ZCTU	Zimbabwe Congress of Trade Unions

Top: Prof. Fatima Meer, official biographer of Nelson Mandela and leading social justice activist, Durban, March 2000.
Bottom: Archbishop of Cape Town, Njongonkulu Ndungane, and Truth and Reconciliation Commissioner, Yasmin Sooka, Davos, January 2001.

Top: Anti-apartheid poet Dennis Brutus, Prague, September 2000.
Bottom: Political activist Trevor Ngwane and Finance Minister
Trevor Manuel, Washington, April 2000.

PART ONE

Powers and vulnerabilities

Neville Gabriel of Jubilee, South Africa, debates Bretton Woods officials
Tom Dawson, Mamphela Ramphele and Mats Karlsson, Prague, September
2000.

Top: Davie Malungisa of the Zimbabwe Coalition on Debt and Development and Molly Dhlamini, Wits student leader, Washington, April 2000.
Bottom: IMF acting managing director Stanley Fischer and World Bank president James Wolfensohn, Washington, April 2000.

CHAPTER ONE

Global crisis, African oppression

1. Introduction

Rather than repeat the standard litany of pity and frustration over Africa's rock-bottom living standards and the minimal power and influence its states possess in the arena of international relationships, let's begin by examining the continent's problems in the context of the ongoing world-wide economic crisis – with the aim of explaining why the economic decay faced by South Africa and lower-income countries of the South reflect global, not merely Third World, chaos.

To do so, we turn first to the analysis of South Africa's current (2001) ruling party, the African National Congress (ANC), of the global economic crisis and its implications for South Africa.[1] This discussion document, which appeared in October 1998, was co-authored by Joel Netshitenzhe of the ANC and Jeremy Cronin of the South African Communist Party, along with the then-leader of one of the world's most dynamic trade union movements, Mbhazima Shilowa of the Congress of SA Trade Unions (Cosatu). These central players in what is known as the Tripartite Alliance (which is made up of the three organisations mentioned) were mandated to argue a case within the ruling coalition. They had no qualms about using the 'c' word in their argument (even if, as we will observe later, this was mainly bluster), so nor should we:

> The present crisis is, in fact, a global capitalist crisis, rooted in a classical crisis of overaccumulation and declining profitability. Declining profitability has been a general feature of the most developed economies over the last 25 years. It is precisely declining profitability in the most advanced economies that has spurred the last quarter of a century of intensified global-ization. These trends have resulted in the greatly increased dominance (and exponential growth in the sheer quantity) of speculative finance capital, ranging uncontrolled over the globe in pursuit of higher returns.[2]

Grating as it might sound to the uninitiated, the paragraph above is a helpful summary of three processes that will be examined below (in Section 2):

1) falling profits combined with systematic overproduction;
2) the geographical expansion by transnational corporations in response to stagnation in home markets; and
3) the simultaneous reach by capital across time and space, through a credit mechanism that permits consumption now, payment later.

In these ways, we will see, capital responds to crisis by *shifting and stalling* its problems.

If this still seems excessively abstract, it won't remain so once we track the deadly implications of the crisis. For Africa, they are multifaceted, and worthy of far more attention than I give them in Section 3 of this introductory chapter, which primarily considers aspects of trade and debt that follow from the long-term global economic crisis. Nevertheless, I will conclude in Section 4 that if current trends are very depressing, matters must soon change, potentially in progressive directions. For I believe that global crisis management will soon be exhausted, and with a break in power relations, even the most venal African political/economic relations can then be challenged from below, in a way that could lead us from the current stage of despondency to a higher one of strategic clarity and mass activism.

2. Global crisis, and crisis displacement

The term 'crisis' is understood in many ways. In the economic context, one of the ways in which people experience crisis is as a time when power gets exercised in brutally obvious ways on behalf of uncaring economic forces. At such times, the adoption of neo-liberal economic policies often represents the point at which the most powerful corporate and financial agents get their way in the given country. And with a shift of influence towards Washington's preferred ideology comes demands for dramatic cuts in local standards of living. Hence, one metaphor of the last quarter of a century of global economic change is of knots in the economic rope tied around the necks of ordinary people getting ever tighter and digging ever deeper, of which I give only a few key examples here:

■ the economic policies of disciples of Milton Friedman (i.e. young Chilean bureaucrats with doctorates in economics from the University of Chicago) strangling Chile from 1973, once Augusto Pinochet had killed democratically elected Salvador Allende and began imposing the first thorough-going neo-liberal strategy;
■ the resurgent International Monetary Fund (IMF) dictating British macroeconomic policy in 1976 at a point when the Labour Party was desperate for a loan, even prior to Thatcherism;
■ the brutal reign of Paul Volcker at the US Federal Reserve beginning in 1979, snuffing out inflation with dramatic interest rate increases (the catalyst for the Third World debt crisis), followed quickly by Ronald

Reagan's devastating attacks on US trade unions and the social wage, combined with military attacks on those few Third World states (Nicaragua, Grenada, Mozambique, etc.) that dared to be different;

- the IMF's hard-line reaction to Mexico's 1982 bankruptcy, which heralded Washington's capacity to impose 'structural adjustment' and simultaneously bail out the New York, London, Frankfurt, Zurich and Tokyo banks;
- the World Bank's shift from project funding alone to the imposition of structural adjustment and sectoral adjustment, done in the name of making countries more competitive and efficient, but in reality wiping out decades' worth of improvement in living standards;
- the series of crisis-management techniques (such as the Baker and Brady Plans) during the late 1980s and early 1990s, which helped get dangerous Third World debt off the books of Northern banks by socialising their losses through new IMF and World Bank loans, though not without heightened demands from the banks concerned for repayment by wretched borrowers; and
- the renewed austerity that accompanied the late-1990s 'emerging-markets crises', amidst further bailouts for investment bankers exposed in countries whose hard currency reserves were suddenly depleted by runs.

Yet the problems run far deeper than the particular instances in which sovereignty was ceded to financial markets, or neo-liberal ideology was adopted locally by home-grown structural adjusters, or stop-gap measures were imposed by Washington to redistribute resources from poor to rich, from producers to financiers, and from South to North. Instead, I believe the ANC Alliance's intellectual leaders were correct when in 1998 they identified the underlying issue as the 'overaccumulation of capital'. It is therefore to a discussion of this concept that we now turn.

A brief theory of crisis
The term 'overaccumulation' is classical Marxist jargon, but this should not in itself mean that the term is no longer relevant, now that most of the governments that once claimed to espouse Marxism no longer do so. I believe that if the concept of overaccumulation uniquely defines the root causes of the current economic crisis, it should not be dismissed as an outdated idea that no longer applies.

'Overaccumulation' refers to a condition combining too high a level of productive capacity, too many inventories, too great a proportion of capital invested in financial assets, and too many people without paid employment. Perhaps the best evidence that overaccumulation has in fact set in is a structural decline in the rate of profit in productive-sector economic activities, especially traditional manufacturing. This is typically caused by gluts of production, insufficient buying power or intensified class struggle.

Depending upon the state of class struggle, Marx described how a falling rate of profit could be reversed. In *Das Kapital*, he talked of the 'absolute' and 'relative' ways of increasing surplus value so as to restore profits.[3] The former refers to making workers toil longer and harder with the same technology, and the latter to the replacement of workers with capital-intensive machines in search of at least temporary efficiencies that might momentarily raise profits, in a competitive economic environment (prior to the generalised adoption of the technology by all producers). But these methods never work out so simply, and do not stave off structural declines in productive-sector profit rates for long. There is only so much 'absolute' exploitation that can be accomplished – through sweat-shop conditions, the speeding up of assembly lines, outsourcing to cheaper sites (typically with much lower wages and no benefits), and various ways of forcing workers to accept more 'flexible' work arrangements – before limits are reached. And as for 'relative' surplus value, after an initial boost, the substitution of machines for workers both lowers the capacity for exploitation of labour (because output is now increasingly a function of machinery and less of value-adding labour) and generates even more output – far more than can be readily consumed. The problem essentially is that capitalism generates accumulation of wealth for owners only because living labour is the source of added value. As labour's role in production recedes, the class power that capital enjoys over workers, from which profits are derived, also recedes. A productive capitalist doesn't enjoy the same class power over another capitalist (e.g. one who sells the machinery that replaces the workers), and so the system tends towards declining profitability.

While capitalism is inexorably overproductive, an outright 'crisis' sets in at a stage when the economy suffers such high overcapacity, such gluts of industrial and consumer goods, such heightened intercapitalist competition, such untenable levels of idle labour, and also such severe environmental damage and brutal exploitation of women and children, topped off by such extreme financial speculation, that the whole system starts to melt down. There have been numerous such examples throughout history, with the early part of the 21st century destined to follow the pattern of earlier international financial collapses (the mid-1810s, the late 1840s, the early 1870s, the mid-1890s, the late 1910s and the early 1930s).

Yet this destiny – capitalism's inner self-contradictory tendencies regularly coming to full fruition, in the way that Marx predicted – has been successfully postponed since the latest crisis began to unfold from the early 1970s, when the profit plunge and rise of gluts across many terrains of production became noticeable. The tactics used to achieve this process, i.e. the 'stalling and shifting' of the crisis, will be discussed below.

This is not to say that the crisis has not been apparent, particularly from Africa's perspective, as I will show below. Financial meltdowns have been visited upon a vast number of places and people across the globe since the 1970s, and have damaged the planet at a dramatic rate. The broader economic crisis even left the working class in the United States with a 20% collapse of per-worker wage-related income over a two-decade period (1975–95).

Overall, however, it is crucial to acknowledge that Washington has so far successfully co-ordinated the 'management' and 'displacement' of crisis conditions. These crisis-displacement techniques, and the growing resistance to them, are the subjects that occupy the rest of this book. But at the outset, it is important to identify some key patterns in this process.

Stalling and shifting the crisis
In the process of staving off a full-blown meltdown, elites employ a variety of response mechanisms to crisis. These responses can mainly be understood by considering their somewhat different philosophies and interests, which will be explained further in Chapter five. But in general, five factors associated with elite management have sustained the capitalist system during the current crisis: surprisingly creative economic crisis management; the large cushioning role of nation-state expenditure (compared to, say, the early 1930s); the unparalleled power of Washington's overall techno-military apparatus; the control of virtually all major nation states by business-oriented political parties (including the so-called 'Third Way' social-democratic parties of the late 1990s); and an extremely effective 'class war' against the working-class and poor. As a result, a 1929–33-style financial seizure and subsequent Great Depression has so far been avoided.

This can be expressed conceptually through the processes of 'shifting' and 'stalling'. In contrast to the last few troughs of the international economic cycle, which were characterised by generalised collapse, the contemporary crisis has been both *moved around geographically ('globalisation') and delayed (through credit and financial speculation)*. The thesis I will pursue is that at a deep-rooted level, two linked processes have drawn together the North and South (and demolished the East) in a unified process of *displacement* of overaccumulated capital. These two processes make up the way in which the financial and trading systems re-engineer space and time relations, i.e. the twinned processes of shifting and stalling.[4]

The new crisis-displacement processes entail more than simply standard 'countervailing tendencies against the falling profit rate' (Marx's reference to relative and absolute surplus value extraction). The notion of financial/commercial crisis-displacement hints at the capacity of the system's most powerful elements to retard devaluation of overaccumulated capital and move it around. Devaluation represents the final recognition that returns on specific overaccumulated capital cannot, ultimately, be realised. The capital – and likewise people, in the form of the unemployed masses – have to be written off, in ways that include defaults on financial obligations, bank failures, dramatic declines in living standards, structured inflation, recessions and depressions.

Throughout the history of capitalist boom-bust cycles, shifting and stalling the inevitable devaluation of overaccumulated capital has always been a matter of geopolitical power derived largely from financial control mechanisms.[5] Whether a particular geopolitical bloc can push the devaluation somewhere else depends upon who is controlling the switch-points of the financial and commercial circuits of capital. These circuits – understood as flows of finance and commodities across space – are always to be found where overaccumulation pressure is most rapidly and intensively transmitted, and also where uneven development is most actively generated, particularly in the periodic expansion and contraction of global debt and speculative bubbles.[6]

There are concrete reasons for these financial and trade dynamics. In part, exuberant financial activity can be traced to high returns from speculative markets and from high interest rates paid on financial assets, during a period in which private financiers gain the power to dictate monetary policy to allegedly 'independent' central banks.[7] Of the $1.5 trillion involved in daily currency-market activity across the world, a tiny fraction is used for trade- or investment-related transactions. The entire volume of global trade in 1998 – $6.5 trillion – could have been financed through merely 4.3 days worth of forex market turnover. The additional daily trade in derivatives (i.e. securities whose returns are based on movements in the price of other paper assets) was $973 billion in 1998. In contrast, the total official foreign reserves held by all central banks amounted to just $1.6 trillion.[8] Therefore, virtually no single country has the reserves to withstand a co-ordinated attack by financial speculators.

Who gains from this apparently parasitic financial activity? The volatility of global money markets in part reflects the self-interest that international commercial banks, investment banks, hedge funds and other financiers have in manipulating funds. The mere movement of money generates profits through price changes, as well as through trading commissions. The merits of such casino capitalism were expressed in the *Annual Report 1998* of Standard Chartered Bank (which was founded in Port Elizabeth in 1857, but which disinvested from South Africa 130 years later), in which forex trading profits were responsible for 'outstanding' results: 'We have built a world-class team and their ability to continue trading, during periods of high volatility in the foreign exchange markets, resulted in exceptional dealing profitability.'[9]

Table 1: US financial-asset profits: inflation-adjusted long-term interest rates and average annual returns on stocks and bonds, 1940s–90s[10]

Decade	Interest rates	Stocks	Bonds
1940s	−3.2	4.9	−1.1
1950s	1.0	14.2	−4.1
1960s	2.2	4.4	−2.7
1970s	−0.2	4.2	−7.4
1980s	4.8	10.2	7.4
1990s	4.1	11.0	9.2

Part of the attraction to such financial overexposure is that world interest rates hovered at historic highs from around 1980, both in the United States (see Table 1) and especially in emerging markets. As a result, corporations achieved much higher 'real' (i.e. inflation-adjusted) rates of return when they shifted resources from overaccumulated productive circuits into financial assets.

Here we arrive at a crucial point in the argument, as illustrated by the 'hollowing' of many major manufacturing firms, which found that their treasuries were making more money simply by reinvesting retained earnings in financial assets. As manufacturing-sector profits fell, therefore, new capital spending by US non-financial corporations declined from levels in excess of 8.5% of GDP during the 1950s–60s, to less than 7% during the 1970s, to 4.7% during the 1980s, before recovering slightly to 5.3% from 1990 to 1997.[11]

Meanwhile, profit rates plus salaries in the US financial, insurance and real-estate sectors, as a percentage of gross investment, soared from 20–30% returns during the 1950s–70s up to the 35–45% range during the 1980s–90s, and the 'rentier' share (i.e. interest plus dividends) of the US corporate surplus (i.e. pretax profits plus interest) rose from levels of 20–30% during the 1950s, to 30–40% during the 1960s–70s, to 50–70% during the 1980s–90s. In the trading arena, geopolitical power also assists those corporations based in strong states, because trade agreements are conducted from a position of strength, and because Washington-imposed structural adjustments force weaker states to lower tariff barriers.

In short, financial and commercial circuits of capital move the devaluation around *spatially* (remember that devaluation is the only way to address the problem of overaccumulation), so serving as the catalyst for much of the contemporary globalisation of capital. And simultaneously, overaccumulation is addressed *temporally*, through hastened speed-up processes and, crucially, by expanding a credit system which permits traded goods to be purchased today but paid for later, on the assumption that future streams of surplus value can be extracted and realised. So, as overaccumulation persists and the resultant devaluation is shifted, labour, women (as workers and in the labour-reproduction process) and the environment are more frenetically exploited. This happens more in the South than the North, thanks to territorial power differentials, though virtually no corner of the earth has been exempt. The contradictions intrinsic to capitalism are, however, not resolved in the process. They are instead moved, delayed, and ultimately amplified.

Financial power/fragility

Tracking the phenomenon of rising financial influence and volatility helps us understand and react to Washington's co-ordination of crisis 'management' (if it deserves that purposive term). The volatility of the international financial system since the mid-1970s stems from several factors:

- profound changes in the incentive structure of investments, including a decline in manufacturing profits during the late 1960s and a consequent switch by many major firms of productive reinvestment into financial assets;
- the rise of the information society and economy;
- institutional factors associated with financial sector concentration and centralisation;
- the diminishing power of nation states;
- shortened investor time horizons; and
- heightened geographic mobility, resulting in part from more rapid transport and communications and other revolutionary technological changes.

Several specific features are worth mentioning to provide a more detailed sense of how the fabric of contemporary international finance has been tearing at the edges. From the early 1970s, the destruction of the Bretton Woods system – i.e. fixed exchange rates anchored by the US dollar (as I will explain below) – the world economy has witnessed upheavals of a kind not experienced since the 1930s. Once President Richard Nixon delinked the dollar from gold (as a result of excessive pressure on US reserves subsequent to US overseas investment and the Vietnam War) – an action that amounted to an $80 billion default on US obligations – the dollar went into a steep decline (see Chapter 5 for more details). One result during the 1970s was a rise in the nominal price of gold from $35/oz in 1944–71 to $850/oz in 1981, as investors sought refuge from the dollar. (In inflation-adjusted terms, using 1998 as a base year, the rise was from $150/oz to $1 250/oz over that period.)

But gold then fell in value (to just over $250 at its low point in mid-1999) as interest rates were raised to very high levels by the US Federal Reserve Board from 1979, finally stabilising the US dollar and giving investors a better return on assets than they got by holding gold. Simultaneously, in spite of the disincentive of high interest rates, debt rose dramatically virtually everywhere, partly thanks to universal financial deregulation, which opened up more credit-related products to corporations and ordinary people.

In the US, for example, the ratio of all forms of credit-market debt to GDP was fairly stable, in the 130–150% range from 1950 to 1975. It then soared to 250% over the next two decades. As another reflection of financial/commercial turbulence, international commodity prices in general suffered enormous downward pressure, losing more than 80% of their value from a 1973 peak. At the same time, overinvestment in manufacturing began to result in growing gluts of products, which were exacerbated when East Asian products flooded global markets during the 1980s and 1990s.

In the context of such commotion, it wasn't long before various surface-level financial bubbles began bursting in increasingly spectacular ways: the Third World debt crisis (early 1980s for commercial lenders, but lasting up to the present for the countries and societies involved); energy finance shocks (mid-1980s); crashes of international stock markets (1987) and property markets (1991–3); crises in nearly all the large emerging markets (1995–2000); and even huge individual bankruptcies, which caused powerful international ripples. Examples from the late 1990s of financial/speculative gambles gone very sour in derivatives, exotic stock-market positions, currency trading and bad bets on commodity futures and interest rate futures include Long-Term Capital Management ($3.5 billion in 1998), the Sumitomo/London Metal Exchange (£1.6 billion in 1996), I.G. Metallgessellschaft ($2.2 billion in 1994), Kashima Oil ($1.57 billion in 1994), Orange County, California ($1.5 billion in 1994), Barings Bank (£900 million in 1995), the Belgian government ($1 billion in 1997) and Union Bank of Switzerland ($690 million in 1998).

Such financial shocks are likely to continue, for even the US economy has grown increasingly vulnerable to substantial corrections on the basis of unsustainable trade and debt imbalances (the current account deficit reached 4.5% by the end of 2000), consumer and corporate borrowing (an unprecedented 7% of GDP by the end of 2000), and stock-market overvaluation. The latter was only partially corrected by the crash in 2000–01 of most Nasdaq high-technology shares, exemplified by the destruction of half the paper value of companies like Intel and Apple Computer over the course of a few hours once they had issued profit warnings. In a few such cases, wealthy investors were hurt. But mainly the world's working-class and poor and vulnerable groups and environments have paid the bill for the financiers' problems. The middle-income emerging markets were hit in particularly acute ways during the late 1990s, with no end in sight to their predicament.

The emerging-markets crisis

Cases of emerging markets in crisis allow more specific consideration of what has gone wrong in global financial markets, and whether there are any proposals on the table that provide reasonable prospects for financial sustainability and efficiency. In the period following the first round of brutal austerity (1982–91), as Northern economies were slow to recover from the early 1990s recession, large flows of speculative money arrived in stock-markets and bond markets of those middle-income countries that promised exchange-rate liberalisation. Hundreds of billions of dollars poured into Asian, Latin American and even two African countries, South Africa and Zimbabwe, during the 1990s.

But this 'hot money' fled as quickly as it came in. Financial chaos then erupted in Mexico in late 1994 (just over a fortnight after Bill Clinton publicly welcomed that country to the 'First World' of developed nations), and quickly moved to other countries in Latin America and then South Africa (early 1996 and mid-1998), South-east Asia (1997–8), South Korea (early 1998), Russia (periodic, but especially mid-1998), Brazil and Ecuador (1999), and Turkey and Argentina (2000–1).

In virtually all cases, the damage included huge drops in local financial markets and currency values, runs on the foreign reserves held in central banks, massive economic dislocations, and social austerity imposed through draconian increases in interest rates and cuts in state budgetary allocations. Meanwhile, bailouts allowed those lucky investors (especially from the North) who could convert their funds into hard currency an escape route. In 1997–2000 alone, the bailouts consumed $250 billion in funds mainly gathered together by the US Treasury and IMF. The bailouts were not gifts, but instead raised Third World debt over the $2 trillion mark, and under-mined national sovereignty in a qualitatively new way.

As I will discuss in Chapter five, below, some countries did manage to avoid Washington-sourced macroeconomic policy advice more easily than others, mainly by regulating capital flows and their currencies. But while responses to global economic turbulence have differed, there is growing evidence to suggest that in the context of a series of 1980s–90s financial bubbles, the common feature of the ongoing emerging-markets crisis was that during the 1990s, most middle-income countries made themselves far too vulnerable to inflows of short-term portfolio investments. Those port-folio investments were not directed into sustainable production, but instead were attracted by high returns in purely financial/speculative terms. This fundamental problem is now widely acknowledged, even by leading financiers.

In his book *The Crisis of Global Capitalism*, George Soros conceded that 'market forces, if they are given complete authority even in the purely economic and financial arena, produce chaos and could ultimately lead to the downfall of the global capitalist system.'[12] In a *Financial Times* article penned during the worst period of East Asia's meltdown in 1997, Soros concluded:

> The private sector is ill-suited to allocate international credit. It provides either too little or too much. It does not have the information with which to form a balanced judgment. Moreover, it is not concerned with maintaining macroeconomic balance in the borrowing countries. Its goals are to maximise profit and minimise risk. This makes it move in a herd-like fashion in both directions. The excess always begins with overexpansion, and the correction is always associated with pain.[13]

The crisis resolved?

Yet in Washington, global authorities insisted that their self-acknowledged *ad hoc* solutions were indeed resolving international financial turbulence. Beginning with the first major emerging-market bailout ($57 billion to investors in Mexico in 1995), and increasing rapidly as the dangers of meltdown and deflation peaked in August 1998, when Russia defaulted on sovereign debt-repayment obligations, the 'Wall Street-Treasury Complex' – in the words of conservative Columbia University economist Jagdish Bhagwati[14] – found sufficient money and imposed adequate technical solutions to avert and even extinguish the most serious problems. According to this line of thinking, the following policy measures (and a large measure of good fortune) prevented a 1930s-style international financial panic:
- the successful public/private bailout of the Long-Term Capital Management hedge fund in September 1998;
- slightly looser Federal Reserve monetary policy adopted in September–October 1998;
- a new, $90 billion IMF Contingent Credit Line announced in October 1998 and formalised in May 1999;
- the convening of a forum on financial stability made up of key countries;
- the lack of financial contagion (contrary to expectations) in the wake of Brazil's currency meltdown in January 1999;
- the long-awaited revival, however tentative, of the Japanese economy (at present, in April 2001, this seems to have ground to a halt);
- new plans for somewhat more transparent budgetary and exchange-rate systems in emerging markets;

- a decision at the Cologne meeting of the G-8 in June 1999 to sell 10% of the IMF's gold to fund partial debt relief for the poorest Third World countries;
- statements by Britain's Gordon Brown – in his role as head of the IMF Interim Committee – indicating a desire to step up the IMF's existing capacities in areas of financial supervision and regulation;
- the assembly of a 'G-20' group in September 1999 – led by Canadian finance minister Paul Martin and including South African finance minister Manuel – that includes many major emerging-market finance ministers, to discuss further reform of global finance and other crisis-avoidance techniques;
- the proposal by President Bill Clinton at the IMF/World Bank meetings in 1999 to write off 100% of debt owed to the US by 36 of the world's poorest countries, adding to momentum towards a millennial 'gift' to avoid the extraordinary marginalisation of the 'Fourth World' that has been noted in countless recent reports (a proposal followed 14 months later by Britain);
- the emergence of sufficient confidence within the international financial system in late 1999 to allow Ecuador to default on its Brady Bond obligations;
- the successful interventions of the US and allied governments that shored up the value of the newly introduced, fast-falling European Union (EU) currency, the euro, in September 2000; and
- further bailouts of desperate countries in late 2000, especially Turkey and Argentina.

Ongoing financial insecurity

But can soothing words and interventions from Washington and elsewhere prevent the various financial bubbles from bursting, given that investor bailouts invariably cause new bubbles somewhere else? Alan Greenspan, chairman of the Federal Reserve, had tried repeatedly to persuade New York stock-market investors that their 'irrational exuberance' should be reconsidered, but this had no effect until the 50% crash of the Nasdaq index in 2000–1. For at the same time that the key Washington managers of international economics – Robert Rubin, Lawrence Summers, Stanley Fischer and their colleagues – insisted that matters were under control, evidence of much deeper and more dangerous tensions continued mounting. Even the much-celebrated US economy suffered vast, unprecedented trade and budget deficits, dramatically overindebted consumers and corporations, and a stock-market more overvalued than in 1929.

One indication of an underlying concern with ongoing financial crises was a new IMF plan revealed by IMF managing director Michel Camdessus in March 1999, to unite foreign bankers so as to avoid fracturing their power in forthcoming bankruptcy negotiations with sovereign states. Camdessus spoke behind the scenes to an Institute of International Bankers meeting in Washington of the parallel need for 'creditor councils' that discipline 'individual dissident creditors' who catalyse 'panic-stricken asset-destructive episodes' through overzealous foreclosure actions.[15] (Ignoring this warning, however, one such dissident creditor, in the form of a so-called 'vulture fund', bought Ecuador's secondary market debt very cheaply and in October 2000 acquired a New York City court order allowing it to attach Ecuadorian assets.)

But aside from the periodic stalling and shifting gambits, there was little or nothing done at a structural level to prevent the massive asset destruction associated with international speculative runs on the currencies of Third World countries, including South Africa. For a brief period in 1998, it appeared that some preventative measures might emerge from social-democratic politicians in Germany, France, Italy and Japan. However, as I discuss in more detail in Chapter five, the resignation of Oskar Lafontaine, German minister of finance, in March 1999 represented a profound setback for this possibility, and the Japanese failed on several occasions to establish an Asian Monetary Fund to provide country bailouts without extreme IMF-style austerity as a result of vetoes by the US Treasury Department.

Partly for political reasons related to the funding of congressional and presidential elections by financial institutions, and partly because financial markets have an inordinate power in their own right, it became apparent that Washington – i.e. the US Treasury Department, Federal Reserve and multilateral financial agencies that are subject to Washington's veto clout – was fundamentally opposed to interfering with the prerogatives of major banks and other international creditors. Even the often-suggested co-ordinated regulation of interest rates amongst the major powers is unlikely to happen. Although Washington conceded the need for greater transparency in international financial transactions, in a world of derivatives trading and private-private debt relationships, it was virtually impossible to track flows of funds and to establish an accurate picture of a given country's external assets and liabilities.

The only substantial step toward financial security taken by Washington since 1998, a global bailout fund for emerging-market countries that agree to pay a substantial interest premium for short-term credit, was conceptually no different from the existing *ad hoc* mechanisms that poured hundreds of billions of dollars into South-east Asia, Russia and Latin America from 1995. Moreover, no changes could reasonably be anticipated in the corresponding credit 'conditionality' – i.e. austerity as the basis for macroeconomic policy – required by Washington. In sum, because they reward the speculators and creditors – while the bulk of the pain was displaced onto low- and middle-income emerging-market citizens (especially vulnerable ones like women, children, the elderly and the disabled) – the bailouts simply would not prevent the conditions that caused the crises from re-emerging.[16]

Ebbs and flows of foreign direct investment[17]

As a response to financial crisis, the single orthodox theoretical proposition that bears consideration, finally, is that transnational corporations (TNCs) invest increasing amounts of fixed capital which, in turn, helps to undergird the speculative financial capital by ensuring a more sustained inflow of long-term foreign investment. And indeed there has been a large upsurge in foreign direct investment (FDI) since the 1980s. The point, however, is to consider it critically.

We might start with the push factors, recalling the ANC Alliance argument given at the beginning of this chapter that 'It is precisely declining profitability in the most advanced economies that has spurred the last quarter of a century of intensified globalization'. From levels in the $50–$100 billion range from the mid-1970s to the mid-1980s (as profits stagnated at post-war lows in the major industrialised countries), there was a huge boom once IMF, World Bank and World Trade Organisation (WTO) pressure succeeded in destroying local sovereignty and crashing many local currencies. Overseas investments by TNCs skyrocketed to $865 billion by 1999, getting fire-sale prices on existing assets in East Asia at the end of the century thanks to that region's financial collapse. From 1990 to 1999, global FDI rose by 314%, compared to an increase in world trade of 65% and world gross domestic product (GDP) growth of 40%.

However, FDI trends exemplified the uneven development of global capitalist activity. Just ten major developed countries account for 70% of FDI activity (Japan, Belgium/Luxembourg, Ireland, Canada, Germany, the Netherlands, France, Sweden, Britain and the United States). Still, a growing share of FDI can be found in the largest emerging markets, especially China, East Asia and the large Latin American countries. All developing countries attracted annual FDI flows of $175 billion during 1997–8 and $200 billion in 1999, up from just $25 billion in 1990. During the 1990s, annual loans by commercial banks rose from $20 billion to $100 billion in 1997, but dropped back down to $20 billion in 1999; portfolio investment rose from $5 billion to $50 billion in 1996, but fell to $25 billion in 1999; and official development assistance stayed relatively stagnant at around $50 billion over the period. So by 1999, FDI represented 67% of all North-South flows of resources.

Meanwhile, Africa's share of FDI fell from 25% of all TNC investments during the 1970s to less than 5% during the late 1990s. And even the tiny amounts of FDI in Sub-Saharan Africa in recent years can be attributed in large part to investments by oil companies in Angola ($1.8 billion in 1999) and Nigeria ($1.4 billion). In these cases, massive corruption and internal strife did not deter TNCs, even although these conditions were regularly highlighted and condemned by Transparency International (TI) and international agencies.

The only substantive FDI flows into Sub-Saharan Africa unrelated to extractive minerals by 1999 were into South Africa ($1.4 billion). But on a relative basis, that amounted to just $10 per $1 000 of GDP in South Africa, which was the same as Zimbabwe. As I will discuss below, South Africa's own outflows of FDI, from firms with their headquarters in SA, exceeded inflows, even before the repatriation of dividends/profits and the payments of patent/royalty fees. Worse, statistics have never picked up the durable problem of transfer pricing, whereby foreign investors steal money from developing countries by falsely invoicing inputs drawn from abroad (e.g. mining firms in South Africa through their offices in Switzerland). In any event, the bulk of FDI into South Africa was based on mergers and acquisitions, the most important of which was the partial privatisation of Telkom, a critique of which I will offer in Chapter six. Many thousands of jobs were lost in the process, and the transfer of inappropriate technology made South Africa all the more dependent and vulnerable. In all of this, FDI did not undergird the speculative financial flows with value-producing investments, but instead exacerbated them.

More evidence of the damage done not only by hot-money speculation and FDI, but more generally by global economic volatility and stagnation, can be seen by dissecting the central processes behind Africa's crisis. There are internal and external features to consider, and the latter include trade and financial markets, and neo-liberalism's failures.

3. The African crisis continues

To relate the global crisis to Africa's sustained socio-economic oppression entails exploration of the key mechanisms of domination, including trade and debt. But it is important first to forthrightly address the broader dynamic of Africa's apparent trajectory of self-destruction.

The starting point is, necessarily, the grounding in development politics gained by communities, women, youth, workforces and churches on the one hand, and on the other, by nationalist political parties that still rule or strongly influence most African states (albeit sometimes merely as the media for the transmission of Washington-think). The contemporary context is the brutal socio-economic, gender, ecological, youth, public-health and disability crises that rack Africa.

The rise and fall of nationalism

Widespread Afro-pessimism – exemplified by banal, victim-blaming argumentation in an issue of *The Economist*, which entitled a cover story in mid-2000 'The Hopeless Continent'[18] – should not allow the fading from memory of 1950s–90s struggles for national/racial/social justice. For in virtually all the anti-colonial projects of Southern Africa, and indeed the rest of the continent, could be found rhetorics of human dignity and promises that a fully fledged citizenship would be provided at independence. There was recognition of the simultaneous need to capture the state and nurture participatory democracy, of socialist (or, at the very least, Uhuru) development ideals, of ending racial (and sometimes gender) oppression and of the harmonious relations between states and civil societies that would make these visions a reality. The late Claude Ake summarised the discourse as follows:

> The language of the nationalist movement was the language of democracy, as is clear from: *I Speak of Freedom* (Nyerere), *Without Bitterness* (Orizu), *Facing Mount Kenya* (Kenyatta), *Not Yet Uhuru* (Odinga), *Freedom and Development* (Nyerere), *African Socialism* (Senghor), and *The Wretched of the Earth* (Fanon). It denounced the violation of dignity of the colonised, the denial of basic rights, the political disenfranchisement of the colonised, racial discrimination, lack of equal opportunity and equal access, and economic exploitation of the colonised. The people were mobilised according to these grievances and expectations of a more democratic dispensation.[19]

Of course, things went badly wrong in virtually all cases, and by the early 1980s, as crisis and repression set in, the subcontinent's few sites of developmental hope were in Southern Africa, especially Mozambique and Zimbabwe, and, from 1994, South Africa. In some ways, the malgovernance that emerged across Africa pointed to larger political/economic processes and geopolitical alignments associated with the Cold War – whose African battlegrounds were often extremely hot – and the simultaneous slowdown in economic growth – and hence demand for raw materials – in Northern and Eastern industrial countries. These factors culminated in a global political/economic environment that, during the last two decades of the 20th century, was simply not conducive to African development.

There are internal and external reasons for the problems Sub-Saharan Africa has suffered for the past quarter of a century. Socio-economically, standards of living fell to 1950s levels in many countries. And militarily, many countries witnessed extraordinary social, civil and regional conflicts, ranging from genocide to attempted coups, during the 1980s–90s: Angola, Benin, Burkina Faso, Burundi, Cameroon, Chad, Congo, Cote d'Ivoire, the Democratic Republic of Congo, Ethiopia, Gabon, Ghana, Guinea-Bissau, Kenya, Lesotho, Liberia, Malawi, Mali, Mozambique, Namibia, Niger, Nigeria, Rwanda, Senegal, Sierra Leone, Somalia, South Africa, Sudan, Togo, Uganda, Western Sahara and Zambia.

The internal reasons for Africa's late-20th-century economic problems vary, but included inherited colonial legacies (including the illogicality of many borders) and the transition from colonialism to undemocratic and often corrupt, militarised, neo-colonial regimes. Many had adopted economic strategies that benefited a few urban elites at the expense of peasants, especially women producers, workers and even local manufacturers. The continent's civil wars and adverse climatic conditions (droughts and floods) are increasingly identified with structural political/economic problems, ranging from post-Cold War geopolitical fragility to global warming. But domestic economic policies, especially in settler-colonial societies, dating to World War II – when global linkages were at their weakest – were often inappropriate. The inward-looking import-substitution industrialisation (ISI) strategy typically did not foster linkages between mass consumption and mass production (which would have led to greater balance and sustainability), but rather was aimed at establishing local production of luxury goods for a small, wealthy elite, especially in South Africa and Zimbabwe, the economies with the most advanced manufacturing sectors. Ironically, as specialisation increased, the ISI approach ultimately made these countries even more dependent on external sources of sophisticated machinery, parts and raw materials than they had been earlier. Subsequent export-led growth strategies were typically promoted as a central component of 'macroeconomic reforms' imposed on countries by lenders and Northern governments, notwithstanding the declining, glutted character of world markets associated with the main goods produced in Southern Africa.

In virtually no cases, in Africa or elsewhere, were power relations optimal to develop an economy to meet the basic needs of all a country's citizens, even though such a strategy would have provided far greater 'multipliers' (economic spin-offs) than multinational corporate investments or the prestige projects of African post-colonial rulers. Aside from Cold War military and political interference, there were, moreover, two main external factors associated with Africa's economic crisis: falling international commodity prices since the mid-1970s and rising real interest rates since 1979 in a context of massive external debt.

Trade traps

In international markets, Africa has suffered unfair terms of trade (i.e. the difference between prices paid for exports in relation to prices paid for imports) since the peak of demand for its raw materials and before synthetic substitutes were invented during World War II. From the mid-1970s, terms of trade worsened, in part because of export-oriented policies, discussed below, which most African countries were compelled to adopt once they experienced a debt crisis.

The decline in the price index for the main (non-fuel) commodities dropped especially dramatically from 1977 to 1982, while the export prices of developed countries increased steadily. During the 1982–90 global expansion, the terms of trade of Third World countries still fell markedly, by 4% per year. Much of the decline was due to the drop in oil prices that began in earnest in 1986, but non-oil-producing Third World countries also witnessed a negative 1.5% annual deterioration in the prices of their exports relative to imports. This trend continued after the 1990–2 global recession, leaving 1998 commodity prices at their lowest levels since the Great Depression.[20]

In broader historical terms, the prices of primary commodities other than fuels have risen and fallen according to a deeper rhythm. Exporters of primary commodities, for example, have fared particularly badly when financiers have been most powerful. The cycle typically includes falling commodity prices, rising foreign debt, dramatic increases in interest rates, a desperate intensification of exports which lowers prices yet further, and bankruptcy. From around 1973, this process impoverished the non-industrialised Third World, with occasional, erratic exceptions in oil-producing regions.

For Africa, the trend of declining terms of trade was especially devastating because of the continent's extraordinary dependence upon a few export commodities. The following countries suffer from reliance upon a single product for at least 75% of their export earnings: Angola, Botswana, Burundi, Congo, Gabon, Guinea, Niger, Nigeria, Somalia, Uganda and Zambia. The only countries that diversified their exports, so making at least 25% of their export earnings from more than four products, are the Gambia, Lesotho, South Africa, Swaziland, Tanzania and Zimbabwe. Generally, across Africa, four or fewer products make up three-quarters of export revenues. More than three-quarters of all Africa's trade is with developed countries.

Export-led growth strategies adopted since the 1970s by virtually all Third World countries meant that Africa's market share of world commodity prices also shrank drastically. In the 1970s and 1980s alone, the African market share of coca fell from 75% to 58%, of palm oil from 58% to 18%, of sisal from 48% to 36%, of coffee from 35% to 20%, of crude petroleum from 15% to 8%, of cotton from 12% to 7%, and of copper from 10% to 6%.[21] The most far-ranging study of terms of trade (by Elbadawi and Ndulu) put the income loss during the 1970s and 1980s at nearly 4% of GDP, about twice as high as that of other countries.[22] Virtually no African economies made the necessary switch from reliance on primary export commodities. One reason was that state marketing boards were mandated to conduct trade at extremely low prices, even at a loss, simply to acquire the foreign currency needed to service large debts.

Debt crisis
Rising debt is the second formidable external aspect of economic crisis in Africa (Chapter 3 includes a lengthier discussion of its causes and conse-

quences in Southern Africa). The continent was drawn into a debt trap in ways that in retrospect appear entirely unjustified. The two most obvious problems were the use to which borrowed money was put, and the variable rate at which most foreign debt was contracted during the 1970s. While some of the debt originated in a need to cope with the increase in global oil prices in 1973, much of the rest of the borrowed hard currency was unnecessary, destined for white-elephant projects, for arms expenditure and for the import of luxury goods. The banks that lent the money were obviously at fault for 'loan-pushing'. Some of the money was understood to be lining the pockets of corrupt elites, but international banks, the IMF and World Bank ignored the moral implications of lending to a Mobutu, a Banda or a Botha.

Moreover, during the initial rise in African foreign debt during most of the 1970s, the interest rates on dollar-denominated loans were negative in real terms (i.e. once inflation was discounted, it cost less to repay the loans than they were initially worth). Then, in 1979, the interest payments suddenly increased dramatically when the US Federal Reserve implemented a 'monetarist' – i.e. high-interest-rate – policy. From negative rates in the 1970s, inflation-adjusted interest rates averaged 2% above the average annual growth of the world economy (which was 3%) during the 1980s. A related issue was the 'collateral' – i.e. security – for such loans. Such security was thought not to be an issue, since sovereign countries in the post-war era were not supposed to default. To this end, the IMF was used during the first part of the 1980s as a vehicle for ensuring that African countries repaid loans from Northern commercial banks, in exchange for the IMF gaining the power over those countries to impose austere macroeconomic policies which emphasised liberalisation, export orientation and an end to social subsidies.

The World Bank also stepped in, expanding beyond individual project and sector loans so as to finance fully fledged structural adjustment. All of this represented little more than a bailout by Northern taxpayers of Northern commercial banks through the IMF and World Bank. But incoming funds continued to decline, and, by 1984, net financial-resource transfers to the Third World were negative for the first time, as countries spent more on interest payments than they gained in new loans. By the end of the decade, the net South–North transfer had reached $50 billion a year, which reflected the success of financiers in shifting the repayment burden not only to Northern taxpayers but also to Third World citizens.

As a result, the Third World debt crisis was considered 'solved' by the early 1990s, as most Northern banks had by then either received their Third World loan money back through IMF/World Bank bailouts; or sold the bad loans at a discount on 'secondary markets' of sovereign debt; or, quite commonly, declared the loans as unrepayable for local tax purposes but continued to demand repayment by Third World countries. But effectively the debt crisis no longer threatened the Northern banks (see Chapter three for more details).

However, in contrast, developing countries found that by 1997 they still had more than $2 trillion in foreign debt to repay (up from $1.3 trillion during the early 1980s, when the debt crisis broke out, and $1.4 trillion in 1990). In 1997, the debtor countries paid the North $270 billion in debt service, up from $160 billion in 1990. In net terms, African countries paid $162 billion more than they received in new loans in 1997, up from $60 billion in 1990.[23]

Beginning with Mexico in 1982, the untenable character of the debt caused a series of Third World defaults. Sometimes the defaults were delayed by virtue of the IMF and World Bank arranging an urgent credit for the purpose of paying debts coming due. Occasionally, governments stood up to international pressure by declaring a partial repayment moratorium. This attracted enormous political pressure, as in the cases of Zambia under Kenneth Kaunda, Brazil following its temporary default in 1987, Peru under the populist Alain Garcia and Nicaragua under the Sandinistas. (South Africa in 1985-7 may be the most successful counter-example, when Pretoria successfully negotiated a repayment 'standstill' with Northern banks.)

The debt is particularly onerous for the poorest African countries, which defaulted *en masse* during the early 1980s, but were simply given new loans to pay off old loans. As a result, although between 1984 and 1996 the lowest-income African countries paid $1.5 billion in repayments – a sum 1.5 times greater than the amount owed in 1980, as a result of compounded interest payments – they still owe far more today. Repayment averaged 16% of the spending of African governments during the 1980s, as compared to 12% on education, 10% on defence and 4% on health.

There is convincing documentation that women and vulnerable children, the elderly and disabled people are the main victims of debt repayment pressure, as they are expected to survive with less social subsidy, with more pressure on the fabric of the family during economic crisis, and with HIV/AIDS closely correlated to structural adjustment. The economic policies imposed on Southern African countries as a result of their trade and debt vulnerabilities are therefore worth yet more consideration.

Africa 'reforms' for Washington's benefit

Based on the 1981 *Berg Report*, most of the macroeconomic reforms that IMF and World Bank teams insisted African countries pursue have been relatively uniform. The programmes, subsequently known as the 'Washington Consensus', nearly always involve the following components, most of which are extremely detrimental to state social policies:

- government budget cuts, increases in user fees for public services, and privatisation of state enterprises (including even municipal services);
- the lifting of price controls, subsidies and any other distortions of market forces;
- the liberalisation of currency controls and currency devaluation;
- higher interest rates and deregulation of local finance;
- the removal of import barriers (trade tariffs and quotas); and
- an emphasis on the promotion of exports, above all other economic priorities.

The effects of these policies have been quite consistent. Budget cuts depressed the effective demand of African economies, leading to declining growth. Often the alleged 'crowding out' of productive investment by government spending was not actually the reason for lack of investment, so the budget cuts were not compensated for by private-sector growth. The implementation of privatisation often did not distinguish which state enterprises may have been strategic in nature, was too often accompanied by corruption, and often suffered from the foreign takeover of domestic industry with scant regard for maintaining local employment or production levels (the incentive for this takeover was sometimes simply gaining access to markets).

Moreover, there were no attempts by IMF and World Bank economists to determine how state agencies could supply services that enhanced 'public goods' and merit goods. For example, the positive effects of water supply on public health, environmental protection, local economic activity and gender equality were never calculated. In this way, all state services were reduced to mere commodities, requiring of their recipients full cost-recovery through the elimination of subsidies.

A poignant example is water, which the World Bank has been pushing many municipal governments in Africa to privatise. In a context in which public-good effects of water supply were not factored into a World Bank-designed national infrastructure policy, South Africa faced an outbreak of cholera in August 2000 that led to scores of deaths and tens of thousands of infections, costing tens of millions of rands, because low-income people were not able to pay full cost-recovery on systems that then either broke down or suffered cut-offs by municipal officials (saving a few tens of thousands of rands). At the same time, the World Bank was circulating a document entitled *Sourcebook on Community Driven Development in the African Region*, which warned other World Bank staff that 'work is still needed with political leaders in some national governments to move away from the concept of free water for all'. As for project work on water, these staff were instructed to 'Ensure 100% recovery of operation and maintenance costs'.[24]

Another central reason for declining economic growth under structural adjustment was the tendency for interest rates to jump to very high levels once financial controls were released, or when a foreign-currency crisis emerged. Hardest hit were often small businesses. Likewise, the lifting of price controls along with foreign-currency liberalisation and currency devaluation often created a generalised inflationary tendency, accompanying a surge of imports of luxury goods. While this made more goods available, especially in elite urban shops, they were often so far out of range of most consumers that the benefits of liberalisation never trickled down.

The emphasis on liberalising imports and promoting exports did virtually nothing to improve the balance of trade, and in fact, in most cases, liberalisation caused trade surpluses to rapidly become deficits. Austerity usually killed formal-sector jobs, deindustrialised weak manufacturing sectors, rewarded the financial sector, and in the process worsened social inequality. At the end of the 1990s, the continent recorded somewhat higher growth, off a very low base in some countries. Yet such growth self-evidently failed to trickle down to most people, as poverty worsened and inequality rose sharply. And already meagre state services simply collapsed in many parts of the continent.

Structural adjustment not only worsened economic conditions. It never grappled with the real causes of the disempowerment of the mass of producers. Without being 'Afro-pessimistic' by 'reducing the past to a one-dimensional reality ... [through] a roots of crisis literature', Mahmood Mamdani nevertheless argues that much of Africa's local-level state administration in rural settings amounted to 'decentralised despotism', even prior to the crisis of the 1980s and 1990s. Virtually all attempts to reform colonial-era administration and its equivalent ethnic-based systems failed. Even in the best case, Museveni's Uganda, where local-level power relations inherited from centralised despotic rule had to be thoroughly broken, there remained a 'bifurcated' duality of power between a centrally located modern state (sometimes directly responsible for urban order in primate capital cities) and a 'tribal authority which dispensed customary law to those living within the territory of the tribe'.[25] With this observation, Mamdani addresses global-national-local processes:

> In the absence of democratisation, development became a top-down agenda enforced on the peasantry. Without thorough-going democratisation, there could be no development of a home market. The latter failure opened wide what was a crevice at Independence. With every downturn in the international economy, the crevice turned into an opportunity for an externally defined structural adjustment that combined a narrowly defined programme of privatisation with a broadly defined programme of globalization.[26]

Futile Washington spin control

It was soon evident that neo-liberal medicine was killing the African patient. By the late 1980s, after about a decade's experience in approximately three dozen African countries, critics more forcefully questioned macroeconomic reform. A debate raged about whether two World Bank reports (*Africa's Adjustment and Growth in the 1980s* and *Sub-Saharan Africa: From Crisis to Sustainable Growth*, both published in 1989) adequately explained the continent's dramatic declines in standards of living, terms of trade and ability to service debt. There was great doubt about the truth of a World Bank claim that during the late 1980s countries which adopted orthodox macroeconomic reforms grew more quickly.

Arguing in favour of structural adjustment, the World Bank was joined by many African leaders who probably felt they had no other choice in the matter. Their adoption of structural adjustment as (cynically named) 'home-grown' programmes can only be understood against the need the World Bank expressed, by the late 1980s, for legitimacy.[27] In the same spirit, the World Bank and its allies at the US Agency for International Development even argued, for a brief period in 1994, that structural adjustment was not harmful to the poor:

> In African countries that have undertaken some reforms and achieved some increase in growth, the majority of the poor are probably better off and almost certainly no worse off. The poor are mostly rural, and as producers, they tend to benefit from agricultural, trade and exchange rate reforms and from the demonopolisation of important commercial activities. As consumers, both the urban and the rural poor tend to be hurt by rising food prices. But adjustment measures have seldom had a major impact on food prices in either the open market or the parallel market, which supplies most of the poor.[28]

A variety of rebuttals and corrections of adjustment/poverty data followed.[29] For notwithstanding social programmes sometimes added so as to mitigate the effects of structural adjustment, the adverse effects were indeed concentrated on the poorest, least-organised groups in society. Imposition of user fees, especially, led to a decline in utilisation rates for health and educational services, which in turn substantially reduced 'human capital formation', with women suffering disproportionately.

Notwithstanding the attraction of 'sustainable development' concepts – particularly the need to 'internalise externalities'[30] (i.e. draw in other factors left out in market exchanges, such as pollution) – the rhetoric to this end was rarely matched by action. Virtually no attempts were made by the IMF, World Bank donors or domestic policy-makers to determine how state agencies could supply services that enhanced positive externalities. The effects of water supply on public health, environmental protection, local economic activity and gender equality were the subject of some World Bank research (e.g. in the World Bank *World Development Report: Infrastructure for Development* in 1994). But, as was noted above, public services were often reduced to mere commodities, requiring of consumers payment to equate with full cost-recovery, resulting in the elimination of cross-subsidies (rising block tariffs and lifeline supplies) that would favour the poor. (The point, typically, was to attract private investors in joint ventures, outsourcing or outright privatisation of state services, as World Bank personnel readily admitted.)[31] To the extent that social subsidies were still permitted, they were targeted through 'means-testing' in an ineffectual manner. Nearly all social programmes introduced to mitigate adjustment performed poorly.[32]

Evidence has grown of the social cost of the orthodox 'neo-liberal' (free-market) development plan. In three Southern African countries (Malawi, Zambia and Zimbabwe), per capita daily protein consumption, for example, fell 20–25% during the period 1970–95. In the health sector, conditions across the whole of the Southern African Development Community (SADC) deteriorated during the mid-1990s to levels amongst the world's worst for under-five mortality (140 per 1 000 children); maternal mortality (888 per 100 000 live births); life expectancy (52); malnutrition (20% of children under five underweight, and 36% suffering stunting); measles immunisation (just 68% of one-year-olds); contraceptive use (just 28% of women of 15–45 years of age); and the incidence of such deadly diseases as malaria (5 550 per 100 000 people), tuberculosis (149 per 100 000 people), and HIV/AIDS (30 AIDS cases per 100 000 people and a 12% prevalence for adults under 49 years of age in 1995, worsening dramatically by the end of the decade as the pandemic spread through South Africa).[33]

While social suffering worsened, the capacity of nation states to increase health and education expenditures declined. Given that social and economic policy-making for Third World countries was increasingly shifted from national capitals to Washington, on behalf of the financial markets, it is perhaps not surprising that an entire generation of nationalist leaders diverted course from populist mandates towards implementing ineffectual structural adjustment programmes (which in turn generally destroyed their popularity). So too did once-'communist' governments in Mozambique and Angola endorse a crude material-oriented and export-led strategy. This was a global problem, affecting all ex-communist, social-democratic and labour parties virtually everywhere. But in Sub-Saharan Africa, the stripping away of national sovereignty was most pronounced, leading in some cases in the Horn and in West Africa, to the collapse of state structures, of legal frameworks, of monetary systems and of any semblance of order.

The limits of Washington's line
Naturally, many Africans firmly resisted structural adjustment, in circumstances ranging from 'IMF riots' in urban shanty towns, to more obscure,

often religious-based, 'silent revolutions' through barter and other exit options in rural areas, to growing linkages being made between human rights violations and debt social movements (even middle-class church congregations), to formal critiques by an ever-smaller, beleaguered group of African intellectuals and progressive technical officials.

For example, the United Nations Economic Commission on Africa, led by Adebayo Adedeji, had offered two important rebuttals by the time structural adjustment became generalised, during the late 1980s: *Statistics and Policies: ECA Preliminary Observations on the World Bank Report* and the *African Alternative Framework to Structural Adjustment Programmes* (AAF-SAP). Further critiques emerged from case studies by independent observers, as well as in social statistics and reports from the UN Conference on Trade and Development (UNCTAD), the UN Children's Emergency Relief Fund (UNICEF)and the Food and Agricultural Organisation (FAO).

Remember that the economic problems discussed above were, at root, premised on the slowdown in economic growth in the major industrial countries beginning during the 1970s. Therefore the power of finance over the Third World during the 1980s represented not so much a true 'solution' in terms of more open trade and investment prospects (and hence higher TNC profits and lower global wages than would have been the case otherwise), but rather *a deepening of the problem*, as the limits of the strategy of draining the Third World were felt by even the most powerful of the world's banks. Indeed, the Third World debt crisis contributed significantly to international financial turmoil.

Yet unlike the 1930s, the Northern creditors have not yet suffered the kind of generalised financial collapse that gave so many other countries the ability to default, without facing serious political ramifications. (Those earlier creditors were mainly individual bondholders, not centralised, powerful commercial banks and Washington financial institutions.) Instead, the debt has been rolled over and meagre amounts of 'debt relief' have been ladled out to countries which continue to play by Washington's rules.

Given the obscene inequality and suffering associated with declining terms of trade, rising debt and structural adjustment programmes, some African countries were chosen by the IMF and World Bank as beneficiaries of the 'Highly-Indebted Poor Country' (HIPC) initiative. Most importantly, HIPC allows merely a write-off of *unserviceable* debt, which no one ever expects the poorest countries to repay. (Chapter 3 considers the Mozambique case, a sham that strengthened Washington's grip around Maputo's throat.)

HIPC is now widely condemned for merely prolonging Africa's debt misery. There is emerging, both from within Africa and from Northern (and other Southern) solidarity activists, a vibrant social movement whose objective is the full cancellation of Third World debt by next year. The movement – 'Jubilee 2000' (named after a statement in the Old Testament's Leviticus that debts should be periodically cleared to give debtors a chance to recover) – played an effective role in bringing the issue to international public attention. Though right-wing 'allies' – the Pope and economist Jeffrey Sachs – endorsed a weak version of the Jubilee call, a more durable 'Jubilee South' movement grew, holding summits in Johannesburg in late 1999 and Senegal a year later.[34]

The tradeoff that the Jubilee movement posits is simple. Sub-Saharan Africa paid the developed world $13.4 billion to service foreign debt in 1996, in part by borrowing $9.5 billion in new funds and using $2.6 billion of aid payments from Northern countries. By way of contrast, the cost of meeting basic goals in Africa for universal healthcare, nutrition, education and family planning is estimated at about $9 billion a year. This kind of money will not become available until the debt is cleared; but Africa's many leaders allied to Washington will never challenge the Washington-imposed status quo of power relations on their own.

Consider the assessment by Southern Africa's main debt negotiator during the 1980s, Zimbabwean finance minister Bernard Chidzero, discussing the IMF/World Bank annual meeting in 1989 at which he chaired the misnamed 'Joint Ministerial Committee on the Transfer of Real Resources to Developing Countries': 'Curiously enough, debt was not the central issue. It was at the back of everyone's mind. But those who are primarily concerned with the debt issue have been saying: "Look, the game is being played. Don't upset the applecart too much".'[35]

The most important problem that arises from these experiences is whether Africans can muster a *combination* of robust democratic activism, protest around socio-economic grievances, technical critiques and proposals, counterhegemonic local-level development strategies and national-policy advocacy. I will take this subject up again in Chapter eleven. First, however, it is useful to change the focus from global and continental issues, to regional and national issues (Chapters two to four), and explore the extent to which the South African state is preparing a challenge to the system (Part two), using the HIV/AIDS case as an example (Part three), before moving on to a discussion of international activism (Part four).

Notes

1 For the full reference, see endnote 2, below. I provide a context for understanding this document in Bond, P. (2000), *Elite Transition*, London, Pluto Press and Pietermaritzburg, University of Natal Press, Chapter 6. In essence, the radical tone reflected not only the deteriorating objective conditions of the country, but also, subjectively, the need for rhetorical turns of phrase that would allow the previously spurned left wing of the Tripartite Alliance back into the 'National Liberation Movement' fold prior to the 1999 national election.

2 ANC Alliance (1998), 'The Global Economic Crisis and its Implications for South Africa', ANC Alliance discussion document, October, Johannesburg, reprinted in *The African Communist*, 4th quarter.

3 Marx, K. (1967 edn) *Capital*, New York, International Publishers, vol. 1, parts 3 & 4.

4 See especially Harvey, D. (ed.) (1999), *Limits to Capital*, London, Verso, for the underlying theory of crisis formation and spatio-temporal displacement through the financial and commercial circuits of capital. Robert Brenner's more recent (2001) statement of the evidence is based on careful study of intensified inter-core-capitalist competition (see *Turbulence in the World Economy*, London, Verso). Other diverse, although at this level perhaps not irreconcilable, analyses of the 1970s–80s stage of overaccumulation include Clarke, S. (1988), *Keynesianism, Monetarism and the Crisis of the State*, Aldershot, Edward Elgar, pp. 279–360; Harvey, D. (1989), *The Condition of Postmodernity*, Oxford, Basil Blackwell, pp. 180–97; Mandel, E. (1989), 'Theories of Crisis: An Explanation of the 1974–82 Cycle', in M. Gottdiener and N. Komninos (eds), *Capitalist Development and Crisis Theory: Accumulation, Regulation and Spatial Restructuring*, London, Macmillan, pp. 30–58; Shutt, H. (1999), *The Trouble with Capitalism*, London, Zed, pp. 34–45; and Biel, R. (2000), *The New Imperialism*, London, Zed, pp. 131–89.

5 Arrighi, G. (1994), *The Long Twentieth Century: Money, Power and the Origins of Our Times*, London, Verso.

6 I expand on this argument in a case study: Bond, P. (1998), *Uneven Zimbabwe: A Study of Finance, Development and Underdevelopment*, Trenton, Africa World Press. Further theory can be found in Bond, P. (1999), the entries entitled 'Uneven Development' and 'Finance Capital' in P. O'Hara (ed.), *Encyclopaedia of Political Economy*, London, Routledge.

7 Henwood, D. (ed.) (1998), *Wall Street*, London, Verso.

8 Bank for International Settlements (1999), *Central Bank Survey of Foreign Exchange and Derivative Market Activity 1998*, Basle.

9 Standard Chartered Bank (1999), *Annual Report 1998*, London, p. 7.

10 Henwood, *op. cit.*, pp. 324–7.

11 These US data and others below are from Henwood, *op. cit.*, pp. 73–7 and 59.

12 Soros, G. (1998), *The Crisis of Global Capitalism: The Open Society Endangered*, New York, Public Affairs.

13 Soros, G. (1997), 'Avoiding a Global Breakdown', *Financial Times*, 31 December 1997.

14 Bhagwati, J. (1998), 'The Capital Myth: The Difference between Trade in Widgets and Trade in Dollars', *Foreign Affairs,* 77(3).

15 Camdessus, M. (1999), 'Capital Flows, Crises and the Private Sector', remarks to the Institute of International Bankers, Washington, DC, 1 March, p. 9.

16 This latter point is made by Stiglitz, J. (1998), 'Towards a New Paradigm for Development: Strategies, Policies, and Processes', Prebisch Lecture, UN Conference on Trade and Development, Geneva, 19 October.

17 Statistics below come from UNCTAD (2000), *World Investment Report*, Geneva, and Business Map (whose database often fails to distinguish between intended and actual investments). Typically, an investment by a non-domestic source is formally considered to be 'foreign direct investment' if the foreign ownership stake in a venture is at least 10% and if there is a tangible influence on management of that venture. This kind of subjectivity that even a major UN agency must resort to in its measurement of FDI is obviously a major problem. Moreover, in part because of UNCTAD's strong ideological tilt towards neo-liberalism during the late 1990s (under the presidency of South Africa's trade and industry minister, Alec Erwin), the

figures below should be treated with extreme caution. To illustrate, UNCTAD measured $1.8 billion of FDI in Angola, while Business Map measured $0 in the SADC energy and oil sector in the same year.

18 The subtitle (13 May 2000) explained, 'Africa's biggest problems stem from its present leaders. But they were created by African society and history'.

19 Ake, C. (2000), *The Feasibility of Democracy in Africa*, Dakar, Codesria, p. 46.

20 Barratt-Brown, M. and Tiffen, P. (1992), *Short Changed: Africa and World Trade*, London, Pluto Press, p. 3.

21 UNCTAD (1991), *Commodity Yearbook*, Geneva.

22 Elbadawi, A. and Ndulu, B. (1996), 'Long-run Development and Sustainable Growth in Sub-Saharan Africa', in M. Lundahl and B. Ndulu (eds), *New Directions in Development Economics: Growth, Environmental Concerns and Governments in the 1990s*, London, Routledge.

23 Jubilee 2000 (1997), 'Free Africa of Debt', London.

24 World Bank (2000), *Sourcebook on Community Driven Development in the Africa Region: Community Action Programs*, Africa Region, Washington, DC, 17 March (signatories: Calisto Madavo and Jean-Louis Sarbib), Annex 2.

25 Mamdani, M. (1996), *Citizen and Subject: Contemporary Africa and the Legacy of Late Colonialism*, Princeton, Princeton University Press, pp. 111.

26 *Ibid*, p. 287.

27 This was the obvious function of the key paper on this topic by former South African Communist Party activist Geoffrey Lamb, who by the 1980s became influential in the World Bank. At one point he warned that World Bank 'support for technocratic policy elites' should not be tempered by plausible deniability (on their part), so as to 'not too drastically compromise the recipients' influence'. See Lamb, G. (1987), 'Managing Economic Policy Change: Institutional Dimensions', Washington, DC, World Bank, p. 10.

28 World Bank (1994), *Adjustment in Africa: Reforms, Results and the Road Ahead*, New York, Oxford University Press, p. 7.

29 For contrary evidence of the effects of adjustment on the rural poor, see, amongst others, Ali, A. (1998), 'Structural Adjustment and Poverty in Sub-Saharan Africa', in T. Mkandawire and C. Soludo (eds), *African Perspectives on Structural Adjustment*, Ottawa, IDRC; and Costello, A., Watson, F. and Woodward, D. (1994), *Human Face or Human Facade? Adjustment and the Health of Mothers and Children*, London, Centre for International Child Health.

30 See, for example, World Bank (1994), *World Development Report 1994: Infrastructure for Development*, Washington, World Bank.

31 The debate is covered in Bond, P. (2000), *Cities of Gold, Townships of Coal: Essays on South Africa's New Urban Crisis*, Trenton, Africa World Press, Chapters 3–4.

32 Mkandawire, T. and Soludo, C. (1999), *Our Continent, Our Future*, Ottawa, IDRC, Trenton, Africa World Press and London, James Currey, pp. 74–5.

33 Southern African Political Economic Series (1998), *SADC Regional Human Development Report*, Harare.

34 Links to Jubilee South can be found at http://aidc.org.za.

35 *Southern African Economist*, November 1989.

CHAPTER TWO

Southern African socio-economic conflict
(Coauthored with Darlene Miller and Greg Ruiters)

1. Introduction

Southern Africa is probably the world's most extreme site of uneven capitalist development.[1] Inequality within and between the region's countries is severe, with race and gender domination largely undisturbed by the post-colonial experience, with the environment taking enormous strain, and with South Africa – and its 40 million of the region's 102 million citizens – responsible for $130 billion of Southern Africa's $160 billion formal-sector economic output in 1998.

It is logical to anticipate, as well, an uneven, fragmented evolution of working-class power and political strategy, given the area's different modes of class struggle, levels of consciousness, organisational capacity, militancy, and relations with political parties and other social forces. Yet as we shall see here and in Chapter eleven, developments in one country act as major reference points for others. And yet while Southern Africa's rich radical traditions – including once-avowed 'Marxist-Leninist' governments in Mozambique, Zimbabwe and Angola, mass-movements and powerful unions – owe much to revolutionary socialism and nationalism, this has not so far given rise to an explicit regional class project.

The question that ultimately has to be posed, then, is whether a coherent, cross-border vision can emerge to counteract the unevenness. Will 'globalisation' provide an opportunity for this, through rising international working-class consciousness in reaction to the multinational corporate agenda? Might the catalyst be a new round of parasitic South African corporate investment in the region? Or will fragmentation prevail, as was already reflected in the upsurge in South African working-class xenophobia in the late 1990s?

To address these strategic political problems, as I have attempted to do in Part four of this book, requires concrete, historical investigations linking particular situations to general trends. Certain aspects of working-class experience are, of course, regionally universal or at least comparable, in part reflecting the importance and homogenising effect of cross-border migrant labour. The counterpart of the current regeneration of rural-urban linkages caused by the desperation of many unemployed workers – including more than a million laid off during the 1990s – is the rural drift to rapidly growing urban slums.

Also common to all these countries are issues of perpetual concern to workers: the HIV/AIDS pandemic; the prevalence of child labour; ongoing farm-labour/tenant exploitation; low skills levels and inadequate training; rising privatisation pressures and controversies over other public-sector restructuring measures; periodic refugee inflows and debates over immigration policy; the emerging Export-Processing Zone threat to occupational safety, health and wages (based on prototypes in Botswana, Lesotho and Swaziland); and mass poverty. These broader social concerns, and other reflections of daily struggle, benefit little from traditional 'corporatist' (i.e. big government + big business + big labour) relationships still favoured by some of the region's union leaders.

Yet the concentration and centralisation of Southern African capital – from a geographical base in Johannesburg – is providing the whole region's workers with opportunities to challenge the same employers through cross-border solidarity. A 'free-trade' agreement (dominated by South African multinational corporate interests) is under way, and aims to eliminate inter-regional barriers to trade and investment in 2006. If it is brought to fruition, a gradual homogenisation of regional economic conditions can be predicted. But the deal could just as easily intensify the region's polarising tendencies, given the parallel process of South African capital's expansion and the linkage of the region to Europe and North America through unfavourable free-trade pacts.

A variety of other compelling reasons have also emerged since the end of apartheid for action on a regional scale to be taken up more enthusiastically by workers and their allies. Cross-border social and cultural connections have intensified; long-term migration patterns have begun to solidify since permanent residence was granted to long-term guestworkers by the South African government in 1995; controlling arms, drugs and other illicit traffic needs regional co-operation, as does the management of regional resources such as water; the artificiality of nation states sired at the colonial-Africa-carve-up conference in Berlin in 1885 is more readily questioned as post-colonial nationalism fades; and there is wider recognition of the worsening unevenness of development and related ethnic tensions between the rich and poor areas of the region.

Our scan of harsh regional realities – and progressive prospects driven not by Washington and its proxies, but instead by popular forces in the region – necessarily begins in the core industrial sites, i.e. mainly in the large cities of South Africa and Zimbabwe, as well as their now-declining mining regions. There, black workers established the first organisational roots of class power as early as the 1920s, often in the face of opposition from higher-skilled white workers and artisans.

The ebb and flow of black working-class power was heightened by impressive industrial unrest during the 1940s, followed by a downturn associated with intensified state repression, the formal establishment of apartheid in 1948 and the banning of trade unions or their leaders in many of the colonial regimes. Later, from the 1950s, working-class power was overlaid by the rise of national political movements. As these movements gained progressively greater access to state power across Southern Africa – and yet soon proved themselves hostile to working-class interests and ambitions – workers had to decide whether and how to strive for a post-colonial, post-nationalist and post-neo-liberal future.

In the immediate future, as Southern Africa remains mired in sustained economic crisis, the logic of neo-liberalism will have to be contested not only through defensive protest, but through both a new regionalism and more effective international solidarity, to serve working-class interests and those of poor people, and to protect regional ecology from corporate plunder. There exists a broad framework for this line of argument, namely a United Nations World Institute for Development Economics research project, whose leading African proponent, Samir Amin, advocates 'regionalisation aiming at the building of a polycentric world', in part grounded in 'grassroots labour-popular social hegemonies'.[2] It is with this potential project in mind that I will attempt to document lines of cleavage between and within the region's working classes and state-capital alliances.

Hence the main sections of this chapter interrelate: Section 2 deals with the historical colonial-capitalist origins of the region and the genesis of its proletariats; Section 3 with the contemporary economic crisis; Section 4 with working-class responses to crisis conditions; and Section 5 with divergent opportunities for regional class formation. At the site where these come together – in the potential contestation of regionalism between workers and the region's states/capitals (dominated as they tend to be by South African bureaucrats and corporations) – I will assess existing regional and even global strategies and tactics in Part four, and propose new ones.

2. Origins of the regional proletariat

To understand the region and its working class in the 21st century requires us to consider, however briefly, its formation in the late 19th. There we find durable aspects of class/race/gender/environmental power serving a process of capital accumulation in more than a dozen major urban centres, with capital ultimately flowing to London, New York and Lisbon. Over the course of the past century or so, diverse international and intraregional connections were forged through trade, transport and communications links, customs unions, the regional investment strategies of South African corporations, conflict over natural resources (especially water), and labour migration. Early commercial imperialism during the so-called 'Scramble for Africa' was codified by the Berlin conference of 1885, at which colonial boundaries (which would in the 20th century become the national boundaries of newly independent African states) were demarcated by Britain, Portugal, France, Germany and Belgium.

The region's partial, disarticulated proletarianisation occurred initially through mining and related industries, not only on the Johannesburg reef, but also in patches of Zimbabwe (which was called 'Southern Rhodesia' until 1965 and then 'Rhodesia' until 1979) and the copper fields of Zambia ('Northern Rhodesia' until independence in 1964). Of greatest interest, of course, is the fate of indigenous black African people under the compulsion of new wage/labour disciplines.

Yet even earlier, many white workers in and around the Kimberley diamond mines, the Johannesburg gold fields and the railways imported European traditions of trade unionism and mutual aid (e.g. building societies) as early as the 1880s. By the 1910s a brand of imported 'communism' (which was imbued with racism and sexism) flared brightly prior to the famous 1922 white mineworkers' strike (with the egregious slogan 'Workers of the world, unite for a white South Africa!'). In the wake of effective state repression, a co-opted white Labour Party then allied itself with other disaffected social layers within the South African government, as did a similar group of unionised white artisanal populists in Southern Rhodesia just to the north. In both of these rapidly industrialising places during the 1930s, there emerged from white capital-labour alliances a 'whites-only' welfare state generous with job-creation programmes, pension schemes, health benefits, housing and the like (especially for rural Afrikaners displaced to cities, who made up 'the poor-white problem'). With the impressive rise of inward-oriented manufacturing and development/finance systems, many white workers evolved into middle-class managerialism. Meanwhile in South Africa, black workers found labour markets increasingly attractive as local growth raised black wages in relation to white wages by an unprecedented (before or since) 50% during the 1930s–40s.

Worker power(lessness)

How, in this process, were indigenous African people disenfranchised and (partially) proletarianised? Once the colonial spoils were divided at Berlin, the British government mandated the Cape prime minister Cecil John Rhodes and his British South Africa Company (BSAC) to seize a vast area stretching north from Lesotho (then called Basutoland). The British military beat back resistance from the region's Africans (most decisively in Southern Rhodesia during the 1890s) and from Afrikaners (in the Anglo-Boer War of

1899–1902). British settlers therefore gave birth to the socio-political construct of Southern Africa. Using traditional techniques to strip land from indigenous peoples – 'hut taxes', debt peonage systems and fees for cattle-dipping and grazing, as well as other more direct forms of compulsion – the settlers drew African men from the fields, into the mines and emerging factories.[3] But it took more than geopolitical influence and investment to form a regional working class. Racialised capitalism throughout Southern Africa also came to depend heavily upon extraordinarily 'cheap' migrant labour and various forms of extra-economic coercion. The Johannesburg mining houses soon organised a Chamber of Mines in order to establish recruitment offices in far-flung parts of the region. Northern Rhodesia's copper mines and various Southern Rhodesian enterprises also followed the migrant labour model.

The system's profitability and durability relied initially upon a social subsidy – from household production by the families of the migrant workers back home on the land – that allowed wages to be set well below the cost of reproduction of labour power. In short, white capital and white-ruled states in the region spent next to nothing on black education in rural areas, on black workers' and their families' healthcare, or on black workers' pensions. The subsidy came partly from exhausting the ecology of the 'bantustan' (homeland) labour reserves, where land and water were degraded over time by overpopulation pressure, millions of people having been forcibly removed from 'white' parts of South Africa and Rhodesia. But the subsidy was mainly provided by the household production of rural women. Without jobs, they were denied pass-books, and without pass-books, they were denied access to the white settlers' major cities, even for conjugal visits to their partners working there. To find male workers at home in the rural areas for only a couple of weeks a year was not uncommon.

Migrant labour remains a core element of the surplus extraction process today, but with cash remittances from the cities now balancing the rural-urban subsidy. One indication of how badly South African capital required cheap immigrant workers was the reversal in 1986 of the decision by P.W. Botha, president of apartheid-ruled South Africa, to expel several hundred thousand Mozambican workers (as part of his regional destabilisation initiative), following pressure from the Chamber of Mines, whose members require 200 000 foreign workers for gold production alone even in the wake of dramatic downsizing in the 1990s.[4]

Worker power
Over the course of a century, resistance by black workers to this diabolical system was often violent and decisive, but sporadic. Sometimes, every-day survival strategies generated defensive mutual-aid societies, such as the 'burial' societies and social clubs (especially based on dancing, and oriented

to 'homeboy' networks) which emerged at the turn of the century. Yet militancy was not far away, and under the difficult conditions of the 1920s – inflation, stagnant incomes, tightening racial restrictions and increasing hardship – the Industrial and Commercial Union (ICU) flourished as a general-workers' union straddling urban and rural workers across the region, and drawing members from as far afield as Rhodesia and Nyasaland (now Malawi). The ICU called for defiance of the pass laws, negotiated with municipalities over worker grievances and campaigned for minimum wages. But ultimately the movement failed to match its fiery rhetoric with action. Formed during a 1919–20 dock-workers' strike, over time the ICU, with its 250 000 members, became demoralised as internal strategic differences widened. White communists were expelled in 1926, and because of leadership conservatism – exemplified in the slogan 'hamba kahle' (go carefully) – various provincial branches seceded, until during the early 1930s the ICU faced its demise.[5]

Likewise, the Communist Party of South Africa fell into a deep internal ideological crisis during the 1930s over the race/class debate, and even vibrant new 'red unions' could not sustain strikes. Revolutionary socialists led by Max Gordon (a close associate of Leon Trotsky) were somewhat more successful, grouping six unions with a combined membership of 15 700 into a Joint Committee. But the black political field was left mainly to the African National Congress, which from its founding in 1912 until the mid-1950s was dominated by *petit-bourgeois* leaders championing extremely moderate strategies.[6]

During the high-growth period of the late 1930s and early 1940s, black worker militancy increased (in 1942, for example, 58 strikes involved over 13 000 workers). Communists helped launch the Congress of Non-European Trade Unions, yet neither they nor the ANC gave effective support to the crucial African mineworkers' strike of 1946. Though nearly 100 000 black miners struck for five days, it ended in bitter defeat, with 13 of their number killed and 1 000 arrested. The whites-only election of 1948 introduced formal apartheid. During the same year a general strike in Bulawayo and Salisbury (now Harare) also surprised Southern Rhodesia's nationalist and communist movements, but was also severely repressed by a powerful white state.

In the 1940s and 1950s, even the region's poorest white families had graduated from 'poor-white' status to being masters of a 'house-girl' or 'house-boy'. But even with over half a million African women servants by the 1940s, all attempts to organise domestic workers failed, even in South Africa. Women were associated in the white media with illegal beer-brewing, hawking and prostitution. 'Surplus' women in urban areas were hounded by the state, and whether 'illegal', deserted, widowed or unmarried, found security only in squatter communities on the peripheries of towns. Township social movements like Soweto's Sofasonke and Alexandra's bus boycotts grew strong and gave rise to successful land invasions, thanks to the solidarity and desperation of women activists.

Labour, community and politics

Yet labour and community struggles seldom overlapped during the 1950s and 1960s, for South Africa's shanty-town struggles were abandoned or diffused by middle-class leaders. However, the ANC became progressively radicalised by the youth wing, led by Nelson Mandela, Oliver Tambo and Walter Sisulu. ANC leaders encouraged workers to join the South African Congress of Trade Unions (SACTU), but moulded the unions to fit the nationalist agenda. Banned along with black liberation movements during the early 1960s, SACTU lost most of its leading activists to ANC underground work, demoralisation or exile. Moreover, the rapid growth of mass-production industry changed the relative weight, numerical power and locations of black workers.[7] A similar process unfolded in Southern Rhodesia, with numerous bannings of parties interspersed by the rise of important links between trade unions and nationalists, illustrated by the rapid rise to the status of 'father of the nation' of Joshua Nkomo, a railroad union organiser.[8]

The deepening of proletarian class formation changed the character of politics, but only once a new round of more general anti-apartheid protest was kickstarted across the region during the 1970s. Between 1950 and 1980, the number of black workers in South Africa's manufacturing sector rose from 360 000 to 1 103 000, and in mining from 450 000 to 768 000. Increasingly strident forms of worker organisation were catalysed by the 1973 dockworkers' strikes in Durban. By 1976, trade unionism paralleled Steve Biko's Black Consciousness Movement and the student-led revolts that began in Soweto that year.

At the time of the launch of the Congress of South African Trade Unions (Cosatu) in 1985, some 12 000 black shop stewards represented an advanced guard of self-sacrificing militants, combining action within work-places, schools, townships and cities. In contrast to the sterile organising of the 1950s, the mid-1980s witnessed the metamorphosis of trade unions into nerve centres of informal resistance across the political spectrum.

For example, at the height of P W Botha's state of emergency in 1987–9, commuter trains in Johannesburg's industrial heartland became trans-mission belts of political mobilisation and education. Industrial Area Committees sprouted up and workers occupied factories in a rash of sleep-in strikes. Anti-apartheid political mobilisation found new channels of expression.[9]

The unprecedented growth in Cosatu's membership and power in the 1980s was not an isolated phenomenon. Similar processes were evident across the whole semi-periphery, from Brazil and the Philippines to Poland and South Korea, besides other Southern African countries. Cosatu served as a regional role model and gave direct assistance to unions in Namibia, Zambia, Zimbabwe and Swaziland.

In Namibia, a decade after the severe repression of the 1970s, unionism made a comeback when mass stayaways won the support of 70% of workers (in sympathy with school boycotts and opposition to South Africa's role in the country). But relations between nationalists and the unions were often tense, as the former feared that too successful a union movement would displace the national liberation movement. Ben Ulenga, leader of Namibian mineworkers, faced bruising encounters with the South West Africa People's Organisation (Swapo), which summoned him to Europe during a strike at Rössing Uranium mine to tell him that workers had no right to decide when strikes should be called.[10]

Across the region during the 1960s–90s, nationalist politics dictated that workers tone down or repress class demands, in the process undermining internal democracy.[11] During the early 1980s, 'workerists' within the South African labour left – the Federation of South African Trade Unions (Fosatu, later to become Cosatu) – saw their movement not only in terms of trade unionism but also as a potential political alternative to the ANC's 'populism'. According to the Fosatu general secretary, Joe Foster, nationalists 'would destroy the unity of worker organisation. Our concern is with the very essence of politics and that is the relation between the major classes in South Africa, being capital and labour. We should not hesitate to attack those who are impeding the development of a working class movement'.[12]

Conversely, the ANC writer known as Mzala contended: 'It is actually impossible for South Africa to advance to socialism before the national liberation of the black oppressed nation.'[13] Under pressure by the mid-1980s, key workerists quietly made peace with nationalists, whose township and rural prestige was immensely greater. Yet throughout the region, powerful tensions between nationalism and socialism remained. When a unified Marxist-Leninist-nationalist project (e.g. Zimbabwe, Mozambique and Angola) graduated from oppositional to state power, the working classes were inevitably disappointed.

Nationalism was not the only challenge to working-class politics. The sensibility of Southern African labour transcends the boundaries of factories, fields and mines, merging with broader social movements to spawn a host of popular protest activities. Another challenge faced by workers comes from market ideologues who have regularly blamed labour militancy for stagnation. Yet working-class organisation and political orientation are hardly responsible for the region's structural social, economic and environmental problems. For those, we must remind ourselves of the very logic of capitalist crisis formation.

3. Structural socio-economic and environmental decline

The systemic class exploitation and race/gender domination outlined above generated very high profits until the last quarter of the 20th century. Then a long-term crisis began. During the two decades from 1960 to 1980, black nationalist movements north of South Africa intensified the momentum of liberation, but then presided over a degeneration into debt, dependency and neo-colonial subjugation. As I discussed in the previous chapter, terms of trade moved decisively against non-petroleum mineral and agriculture mono-exports and real international interest rates on borrowed money soared during the 1980s. Soon enough, 'globalisation' revealed most of the region's manufacturing to be uncompetitive, particularly after 1990.

From such economic crisis and material desperation follow many of the geopolitical dilemmas of the 1980s–90s, including violent regional conflicts (manifesting themselves in civil war and strife in Angola, the Democratic Republic of the Congo, Lesotho, Mozambique, Namibia, South Africa, Zambia and Zimbabwe, which killed as many as two million people and set nationalist rulers against each other), and growing arms traffic.

With a few exceptions – namely Mauritius and Botswana, for very specific, non-reproducible reasons – Southern African economic conditions have been depressed since the mid-1970s, especially since the early 1980s in gold-producing countries (as the price of an ounce of gold fell from a high of $850 in 1981 to just above $250 in mid-1999). Dividing the most recent period for which reliable data are available into an immediate post-colonial 'developmental' era (1965–80), followed by generalised 'structural adjustment' (1980–95), even official statistics reveal the decay.

If we add to the ten core Southern African countries high-growth Mauritius and Seychelles on the one hand, and declining Tanzania and the DRC on the other (the two pairs offsetting each other) – we find that the SADC 14-country average annual per-capita GDP growth – corrected for currency fluctuations through the 'Purchasing Power Parity' measure[14] – was 3.0% from 1965 to 1980 and –0.7% from 1980 to 1995. The latter period saw foreign debt servicing double from 5% to 10% of export earnings, with Zambia, Mozambique, Zimbabwe and Malawi paying more than 20% by 1995. The largest economy, South Africa, declined from 3.2% per-capita annual GDP growth in the first period to –1.0% in the second.

Historical precedent

Southern African economic prospects were perhaps most adversely affected by South Africa's skewed 20th-century industrialisation process and more recent experiences of deindustrialisation. South Africa's economy is itself characterised by severe disarticulations. A 'minerals-energy complex' still comprises the core quarter of the economy, encompassing gold, coal, petrochemicals, electricity generation, processed-metals products, mining

Table 2: Southern African socio-economic and labour-market conditions: Various indicators, mid-1990s–2000[15]

Country	GDP per capita (PPP US$)	Agric. as % of GDP	Indus. as % of GDP	Gini Coefficient	Human Devel. Index	Population ('000s)	Lab. Force ('000s) [% fem.]	Formal jobs [civ. serv.]	Union members ('000s)	Density (%)
Angola	1 839	12	59	n.a.	.344	11 099	5 103 [46]	n.a. [138]	n.a.	n.a.
Botswana	5 611	5	56	53.7	.678	1 533	528 [46]	288 [98]	59	20
Lesotho	1 290	10	46	56.0	.469	2 023	825 [37]	250 [n.a.]	36	14
Malawi	773	42	27	62.0	.334	10 016	4 848 [49]	558 [48]	75	14
Mozam.	959	33	12	n.a.	.281	18 028	9 145 [49]	450 [63]	190	42
Namibia	4 054	14	30	70.0	.644	1 584	435 [41]	260 [67]	106	41
S. Africa	4 334	5	31	58.4	.717	37 859	9 787 [37]	5 708 [1 562]	3 202	56
Swazi.	2 954	14	45	n.a.	.597	926	327 [37]	57 [n.a.]	21	44
Zambia	986	22	40	46.2	.378	8 275	3 854 [45]	469 [151]	280	60
Zimbab.	2 135	15	36	56.8	.507	11 247	4 948 [45]	1 497 [175]	350	23

Most years 1995 (consistency ensured in SADC Regional Human Development Report); PPP = Purchasing Power Parity; Industry includes mining, energy and manufacturing; Density = union members as a % of formal sector jobs.

machinery and some other, closely related manufactured outputs.[16] Intermediate capital goods, especially machines that make other machines, remain underdeveloped, while luxury goods are produced locally at close to world standards (if not prices), thanks to high relative levels of (traditionally white) consumer demand based on extreme income inequality, decades of protective tariffs and the presence of major multinational corporate branch plants. Meanwhile, basic-needs industries are extremely sparse, as witnessed by the inadequate output of low-cost housing, dangerous and relatively costly transport, and the underproduction of cheap, simple appliances and clothing (which are increasingly imported), at the same time that social services and the social wage have been set at extremely low levels for the majority.

Reflecting the local overaccumulation crisis, South African manufacturing average profit rates fell steadily from 40% during the 1950s to less than 15% during the 1980s, and reinvestment dropped by 2% each year during the 1980s. By the trough of the 1989–93 depression, net fixed capital investment was down to just 1% of GDP, compared with 16% during the 1970s. From 1994 to 1996, fixed investment picked up, but then settled back into malaise, and the country consistently recorded bottom-tenth rankings in World Economic Forum competitiveness surveys. Post-apartheid trade liberalisation demolished several key South African industries, including electronics, appliances, footwear, clothing and textiles.[17]

The regional situation was even worse. Between 1992 and 1994 alone, Zimbabwe's largest textile company and more than 60 clothing firms collapsed.[18] The country became little more than a re-export platform for what were technically 'dumped' South and East Asian textiles and second-hand clothes from European aid agencies. Zambia's clothing and textile industries likewise suffered dramatically during the trade liberalisation of the early 1990s, with 90% of garment and more than a quarter of weaving jobs lost.

Regional deindustrialisation and degradation

Accompanying and contributing to the structural decline in the regional economy was the simultaneous failure of orthodox structural adjustment policies. Notwithstanding vocal labour protest, South Africa adopted its Growth, Employment and Redistribution (Gear) strategy in 1996. But from 1996 to 1999, virtually all Gear's targets were missed. To illustrate, formal-sector non-agricultural net job *losses* from 1996 to 1999 amounted to 500 000, instead of the net employment gains Gear anticipated of 950 000 new jobs.

Zimbabwe suffered similarly at the hands of a 1991–5 'Economic Structural Adjustment Programme' (ESAP) which, against all evidence to the contrary, the World Bank's *Project Completion Report* gave the best possible final grade: 'highly satisfactory'.[19] All of Zimbabwe's macro-economic objectives failed, e.g. the share of manufacturing in GDP dropped from a peak of 32% in 1992 to 17% in 1998.

The same was true of virtually every structural adjustment programme in the region. Dramatic changes in consumption norms followed currency crashes, the lifting of subsidies and price controls and the destruction of local manufacturing by import liberalisation, reducing even the small middle class, mainly found in the African civil service, to poverty. Officially set minimum wages dropped far below the starvation line in most countries in the region.

Even if a tiny group of state elites, merchants, financiers, compradors (i.e. local people who have allied themselves with global capitalism) and other *'rentier'* types benefited from regional economic restructuring, the vulnerable in Southern African societies paid most for the stagnation and decline of the past quarter of a century. State services could not keep up, whether in a country as wealthy as South Africa (the site of the world's first-ever heart transplant, but where most rural black people still have no primary healthcare) or one as poor as Mozambique. Indeed, in the latter country, World Bank conditionality for meagre debt relief in 1998 included a quintupling of user charges for public-health services and 'sharp' increases in water prices (as will be discussed in Chapter three). However, the rot didn't stop in society, but spread to the natural environment.

The structural decay of nature
There are many crucial intersections of class formation (and also of class destruction) and ecological exploitation, some of which occur explicitly at a regional scale between dominant global circuits of capital and denuded nation states. To facilitate higher profits and larger volumes of foreign investment, those states have simultaneously externalised environmental costs and, in the process, became hostile to social change. As individual units contested by populist-nationalists and a new generation of post-nationalist political parties, the region's states remain unappealing, even where post-nationalist parties are grounded in trade unions.

We must therefore consider whether, in turn, workers can potentially draw for their 21st-century consciousness upon a legacy of regional class formation and struggle that dates to the establishment of migrant labour systems for mines, plantations and manufacturing in the late 19th century. Can, in short, a more coherent Southern Africa eco-socialist vision emerge to counteract uneven capitalist development, transcend nationalist ideology, extinguish deep-burning xenophobic fires (which have scorched potential working-class solidarity) and establish economies of scale sufficient for a delinked contribution to polycentrism along the lines Samir Amin recommends (see endnote 2) some time in the future?

Regional water wars

It may well be that radical environmentalism can provide part of an impetus to this political project, given the need for far-reaching changes in eco-social power relations in each country. In relation to water, for example, all South Africa's neighboring countries are affected by Pretoria's mismanaged systems of cross-border water acquisition and consumption (especially Namibia and Lesotho), flood-control (proven lethally inadequate to Mozambicans in early 2000 and again in 2001), persistent pollution, limited downstream availability and related legal arrangements. The excess control of water-rights allocations by South African white farming capital is particularly obnoxious when most local black rural people are deprived of even the 60 litres per person per day promised in the 1994 Reconstruction and Development Programme (RDP).

Intense struggles over access to border rivers break out regularly between South Africa, Namibia, Botswana, Zimbabwe and Angola. Debates rage over the implications of the proposed transmission of water through pipelines from the Victoria Falls on the Zambezi River to major industrial conurbations to the south, as well as from the Democratic Republic of the Congo to desperately dry Namibian towns.

Further dam-building will exacerbate evaporation, yet the revelation that hydro-electric power contributes more to global warming than the region's huge coal-fired thermal plants is not likely to dampen the enthusiasm of Mozambican officials for another three huge dams on the Zambezi. Two other large World Bank dams – the ongoing Lesotho Highlands Water Project and the Kariba Dam (built on the Zambezi in 1956 as the world's then-largest artificial lake) – each displaced tens of thousands of indigenous people.

Working-class movements have arisen in South Africa recently to oppose cross-catchment water transfers (using large dams, and at the expense of the poor), water contamination, the hedonistic use of water and its corporatisation and privatisation. Free lifeline supplies and higher standards of infrastructure are part of a rights-based discourse adopted by key South African trade unions and civic and women's groups, while many white, middle-class environmentalists have joined the campaigns. A victory was won in late 2000, when the ANC promised free lifeline water and other municipal services as part of its municipal electoral pledges. But sabotage-minded bureaucrats and weak politicians could easily ensure that this becomes another set of 'rumours, dreams and promises' (as the RDP has been cynically retitled).

In Zimbabwe, not only have social movements recently made similar rights-based claims to water access (in the broad-based National Constitutional Assembly's popular draft constitution), but consciousness has also grown over excessively generous colonial-era irrigation arrangements for white farmers, especially in the tobacco sector. Water-rights allocations between Zimbabwe and Zambia on the Zambezi River's Lake Kariba have been hotly contested in class conflicts between lake- and river-side peasants and industrialists dependent upon both hydro-electric power and water for industrial use (mainly in Bulawayo).

In addition, as I will discuss in Chapter three, controversies have arisen over the privatisation of municipal and rural water systems – and 'dramatic' retail-price increases – as a central World Bank condition for Mozambican debt relief. In Namibia, the indigenous Himba people and environmentalist allies have nearly halted a major dam project, Epupa, despite the fact that it was strongly supported by President Sam Nujoma. In the interests of unifying such struggles, a Southern African network of environmental and community activists working on water issues came together in 1999, facilitated by the International Rivers Network and its local partners.

In most of these cases, there are not only local agents fouling the regional environment, but also a global network of neo-liberal institutions aiming to commodify water and nature more generally: the World Bank, the World Bank/UN Development Programme (UNDP) World Water Forum, and behind these, transnational construction firms, for-profit French and British water corporations, and privatisation-pushing merchant banks. In this situation, the possibility for increasing regional unity amongst workers and allied working-class social movements is necessarily also the possibility for decommodified, destratified and ultimately non-capitalist forms of the relationship between humans and nature. In this way, regionalism through eco-socialist politics offers a significant way forward for the Southern African working class.

Naturally, however, there will be opponents who remain far more committed to the maintenance of capital accumulation and existing class relations. Their role in the inter-related health, environment and water crises, as well as other aspects of social and economic decline, contributed to the growing sense of desperation of regional workers – and in some cases to their willingness to organise not only for immediate economic demands, but also to change society, or at the very least, the government.

4. Workers, organisations and class politics

In what condition have these multiple and interlocking economic and social crises left Southern African workers? For the sake of brevity, I will focus on the concentrated sites of commodity production, both formal and informal, in which workers come into contact with each other, and with the direct surplus-extraction system.

Across Africa, organised labour's reactions have in part flowed directly from the crisis conditions discussed above.[20] Yet even in the advanced South African economy, workplace trends incorporating greater flexibility, the outsourcing of labour and the subcontracting of union jobs have together made the documentation of class relations very difficult. In general, conflict and consent do not correspond directly and easily with the contours of core and periphery. Permanent workforces are not necessarily more militant or co-opted than contingent workforces, despite these inequalities in material conditions.

The numbers tell at least some of this story (see Table 2, above). Of around 100 million people living in the ten core countries of Southern Africa, the potential 'labour force' is estimated at less than one-third (32 million). But, more importantly, only about one in every ten people is 'formally' employed. Approximately 40% of these are now organised, however. Although employment in non-agricultural sectors has been declining since the mid-1980s, Southern African trade unions have claimed growing membership over the past decade, contrary to waning unionisation rates in most parts of the world.

In some sectors, the organising of workers only became legal over the past two decades, so that, for example, domestic and commercial agricultural workers are having some success with nascent unions. Namibia, South Africa, Swaziland and Zimbabwe are recording impressive increases in union membership, although extensive privatisation in Zambia has led to a contraction. Continuous organising drives amongst the region's stronger unions maintain membership at high levels, withstanding the effects of even mass retrenchments. These figures show substantial union power.

Post-nationalism?
Working classes are also increasingly adopting political positions in opposition to their governments. As Namibian labour researcher Herbert Jauch puts it, 'With the SADC divided along political lines, trade unions have achieved a higher degree of unity than ruling nationalist parties.'[21] A regional perspective and discourse may, indeed, override a variety of national limitations. Fred Cooper argues that 'The tension between workers' claims to globally defined entitlements and Africans' assertions of political rights as Africans was, during the 1940s and early 1950s, a creative and empowering one.'[22] In contemporary struggles, though, a regional and more universalist paradigm potentially allows workers to raise demands for higher standards of socio-economic rights more forcefully. In contrast, the trap of nationalist corporatism, within a framework that supports competitiveness, was a questionable labour strategy, once liberation movements moved sharply right.[23]

Politically, Southern African unions spent some hard years in the post-independence era breaking away from ruling-party tutelage and explicit state repression (although Mozambican and Malawian unions are still heavily influenced by their governments). In countries with relatively robust political-party divisions that take place in the electoral sphere (or, as in Angola, on the battleground), the political alliances of trade unions become an issue, e.g. in Botswana, Mozambique, Namibia, South Africa and Zimbabwe. But party politics and union politics are uneasy bedfellows. In Zambia, for example, a trade unionist, Frederick Chiluba, was elected president as leader of the multiclass Movement for Multiparty Democracy in 1991 following 27 years of Kenneth Kaunda's nationalist misrule – and then even more forcefully implemented structural adjustment during the 1990s.

In contrast, in Zimbabwe, the ruling Zimbabwe African National Union (ZANU) regime, led interminably by the autocratic Robert Mugabe, continued to give lip-service to socialism while carrying out unrelenting neo-liberal policies during most of the 1990s. Political opposition rallied around left-leaning trade-union leaders, Morgan Tsvangirai and Gibson Sibanda, whose Movement for Democratic Change took half the vote in the parliamentary elections in June 2000, albeit only after a dramatic shift to the right, through endorsing neo-liberal economic precepts, so as, opportunistically, to attract approximately $2 million in campaign funds from white businesses and conservative international allies.

Likewise in Namibia, where autocratic control by President Sam Nujoma prevents serious internal party debate, the Swapo-affiliated National Union of Namibian Workers charged that the ruling party had scant regard for workers: 'if reconciliation is understood as the perpetuation of apartheid and is equated with exploitation, then workers will no longer tolerate this.'[24] A post-nationalist political movement, the Congress of Democrats, led by a former trade unionist, Ben Ulenga, became an important opposition force after the national elections in 1999, and several individual unions expressed a desire to end their affiliation with Swapo.[25] However, several more years of neo-liberalism may be required before the frustrations of union leaders overwhelm their nationalist loyalties.

In South Africa, more durable left-leaning politics were generally associated with trade unions, but by the late 1990s debates raged about whether an alliance with the ruling ANC liberation movement, which was decidedly neo-liberal in terms of its economic policy, was helping workers or stunting their further mobilisation and development. In practice, however, the union movement increasingly lost its internal vibrancy. Periodic public-sector strikes against job cuts and inadequate pay, added to large-scale anti-privatisation demonstrations by municipal workers, reflected widespread grassroots antipathy to ANC policies.

But in the absence of alternative political parties or a credible set of options, workers still placed pragmatic value on the Tripartite Alliance as a means of pressuring the ANC, even if so far, according to Glenn Adler and Eddie Webster, such 'pressure has objectively eroded the position of workers'.[26] In late 1999, Cosatu leaders condemned the ANC government – specifically, the minister of public administration, Geraldine Fraser-Moleketi (who was also deputy-chairperson of the SA Communist Party) – for

> trying to isolate and undermine workers demands by posing the dispute as being about 'general' interest versus 'sectoral' ('selfish', 'economist') interests of public sector workers. The 'dirty tricks' campaign [entailed] disinformation, and statements released to the press without consulting with the unions, and conducting the dispute in the media. The actions of the government are not in accord with spirit of the Tripartite Alliance, and indicate a greater concern to appease international capital than to enhance workers rights and speed up delivery.[27]

Corporatism and state control

Cosatu is also a part of the National Economic Development Council, a corporatist arrangement in which business, state and labour jointly formulate policy on labour and economic issues. But nearly two-thirds of workers surveyed during the late 1990s had no knowledge of this council.[28] Cosatu became increasingly vulnerable to both bureaucracy and careerism, as leaders successfully sought paths to more lucrative government jobs. On the other hand, this was a process reserved for a few, as many local-level corporatist efforts in the same vein – 'workplace forums' mandated under the post-apartheid Labour Relations Act, aimed at edging unions into local co-determination of productivity – failed to take off.

The story did not advance this far elsewhere. In Botswana and especially Swaziland, labour became the basis for progressive political-party and pro-democracy activism, which may pose substantial challenges for neo-colonial governments, while in Malawi, trade unions played a role in unseating a neo-colonial dictator, President Hastings Kamuzu Banda, during the 1990s, but did not replace him with a leader of their own. In Mozambique, nascent unions were showing a capacity for militancy by the late 1990s. Working-class movements in Lesotho (drawing on traditions of mine labour) and Angola (still bedeviled by war) were slow to gather pace.

The point, perhaps, is that a major breakthrough for workers cannot occur in one country without the rest of the regional working class seeing some possibility of also gaining power in their own respective states, and also simultaneously developing a regional perspective that transcends the artificial boundaries drawn up by colonialists. We will return to this possibility in Part four.

Regional unionism?

However, simply counting union membership and estimating labour influence over local politics is only the beginning. The ability of federations and individual unions to embark upon major strike action is just as vital an indicator of strength. In Zimbabwe, autonomous, shopfloor-based actions outran the ability of national union bureaucrats to control or direct the membership, and the corporatist strategy mistakenly pursued during the mid-1990s by the Zimbabwe Congress of Trade Unions (ZCTU) quickly became irrelevant. And in South Africa, despite the country's deep economic woes, union militancy increased as the state's attack on public-sector workers intensified.

Regionally co-ordinated actions and growing class-consciousness also reflect progress. In Swaziland, for example, an 11-day general strike in 1996 and further strikes in 1997 led to solidarity in the form of a border blockade organised by sister unions in South Africa and Mozambique, which forced the anachronistic monarchy to concede worker rights. Indeed, new sections of workers across the region are demanding similar rights to those won by South African unions.

International and regional solidarity is probably the only real hope for many of the less-resourced union movements, as well as the relatively dormant Southern African Trade Union Co-ordinating Council (SATUCC) itself. But given the difficult material conditions faced by regional unions and the enormous tactical and strategic differences over international economic policy (see Chapter eleven), it is vital first to enquire whether there exists a basis for a regional working-class consciousness (as opposed to retaining ties with nationalist allies).

5. Capital accumulation and regional visions

Can workers establish a regional class-consciousness in coming years? Notwithstanding cross-border solidarities associated with three decades of anti-colonial and nationalist liberation struggles from 1960 to 1990, notions of Southern Africa remain for the most part contained within dominant global conceptions of regionalism, namely a sub-imperial South Africa as the gateway for capital accumulation in Africa as a whole, but organised on a regional scale between Pretoria and the global institutions (using Thabo Mbeki's notion of an 'African Renaissance' as cover). This has required new, post-apartheid institutional processes that take for granted a conception of the Southern African region as a neo-liberal site of ever-amplifying, uneven development. It remains to be seen whether there can be an alternative, working-class regional vision, and whether class practices may emerge to turn Southern African workers into agents for historical change.

What would a potential working-class regional solidarity have to contend with? At least two main aspects of contemporary politics and economics threaten the universal class interests of Southern African workers. The first is the power of the multinational corporate/banking/free-trade/finance agenda. But as I will discuss in Part four, the apparent power of US-centred neo-liberalism is also pock-marked with vulnerabilities, even if the international working class remains confused over whether to try 'fixing' or 'nixing' neo-liberalism's core institutions.

Secondly, elite-nationalists are contemplating an interlocking of South-South interests, with workers left out of the equation. This is not merely a matter of Robert Mugabe's often-stated envy of the Malaysian exit option from volatile international currency speculation (late 1999 saw Mahathir bin Mohamad, prime minister of Malaysia, giving seminars to Southern African leaders not only in a resort near Kuala Lumpur, but also, at Mugabe's insistence, at Victoria Falls). As I will consider in more detail in Chapters seven and ten, South Africa has opened discussions about trade and investment with a range of countries that variously included Algeria, Brazil, China, Egypt, India, Indonesia, Mexico, Nigeria and South Korea. Many such discussions focused on the prospects for unifying Southern countries when bargaining with the G-7 powers over reform of an international financial and trading system that many workers and social movements were concluding needed to be 'nixed', not 'fixed'.

Sites of regional capitalist-class unity
But looking beyond occasional statements of Southern African and South-South interstate solidarity to where capital is actually flowing, we may see a hint of a more realistic regionalism, and also of worker resistance. Sub-Saharan Africa has witnessed a renewed ebb and flow of South African corporate penetration since around 1993. Privatisation and liberalisation of African parastatal firms were critical points of contact, as were banking, services, retail activity and mining firms.[29]

What are the implications? To consider one example hyped loudly and regularly by Pretoria, it now transpires that 'public-private partnerships' in geographically concentrated, 'corridor'-aligned infrastructure projects between South African investors and the region's states are unprofitable, for the primary reason that affordable state finance is virtually unavailable, given Southern Africa's huge residual liabilities to Northern creditors. Thus Erwin castigated the North for its 'criminal, just criminal' lack of substantive debt relief shortly after the 1999 G-8 summit in Cologne. (That this public outburst against a lower-level US trade official occurred at the primary site where the region's elite meet to plan their economic strategies, the Davos-based World Economic Forum's Southern Africa conference, was all the more telling.)

Under Erwin, after all, South Africa's Department of Trade and Industry (DTI) had taken practical responsibility for the regional restructuring required for a particularly neo-liberal, export-oriented, accumulation process. Behind the DTI strategy is faith that 'Spatial Development Initiatives' (SDIs) will add a rich fabric of 'development' along and within a corridor linking key nodes of accumulation, e.g. Johannesburg–Maputo, which embody features of 'Export Processing Zones' (EPZs).[30] The DTI project methodology seeks first to identify potential port/rail/EPZ complexes in an underdeveloped target area that might be of interest to investors, and then help local stakeholders plan and promote infrastructural investments which improve access.[31] After the ANC's first term of office, only two of the 14 proposed SDIs were operative. But the official consensus around the merits of an SDI strategy – no matter the lack of theoretical basis in economic geography, the environmental destruction, the capital-intensive orientation and the lack of backward-forward linkages to generate other economic activities[32] – shows how far a regional version of the Washington vision of export-led globalisation enjoys hegemony amongst Southern African policy-makers.

Such a regional strategy requires institutional frameworks, such as SADC, an institution initiated by Northern donor governments during the 1980s to help combat apartheid, which changed uneasily – with a major hiccup in 1999 resulting from staff corruption, requiring an entirely new secretariat – into an organisation for free-trade deals under the rubric of regional integration, co-operation and harmonisation. As early as 1989, SADC committed the region to becoming a free-trade area by 2006, but progress was slow, including steps backward when during the mid-1990s Zimbabwe and Zambia imposed tariffs on imported South African manufactures that were threatening entire domestic industries. In August 2000, finally, in the wake of the retirement of Zimbabwean trade minister Nathan Shamuyarira (whose replacement, banker Nkosana Moyo, was classically neo-liberal in matters of principle), a free-trade deal for Southern Africa was signed by SADC members.

Aside from SADC, other parallel and occasionally competing institutional arrangements for the region (most of which will probably be merged or fade over time) include the Common Market of Eastern and Southern Africa (from which, tellingly, Tanzania and Mozambique resigned because of fear of domination by Egyptian producers), the South African Customs Union (a long-standing free-trade deal between SA, Lesotho, Botswana, Swaziland and Namibia) and the Common Monetary Union, while WTO membership will open up other regional and bilateral relationships, e.g. bringing in Angola and Mozambique, which otherwise are not involved in non-SADC free-trade arrangements.

An alternative working-class regionalism

But all such bilateral and multilateral deals are premised, it is clear, upon export orientation, not inward industrialisation, and upon increasingly 'flexible' and competitive labour markets. Southern African labour understands this, implicitly, even if SATUCC and the federations of each country have not yet established an alternative vision. To this end, SATUCC advisor Dot Keet has proposed that to 'deglobalize' from neo-liberal, multinational corporate and financial influence requires not only alliances with those in the North seeking 'innovative alternatives to over-producing/consuming capitalism,' but also a proactive, internally oriented regionalism.[33]

As I will argue in Part four, the elaboration of such an alternative regional-global strategy is in the interests of poor and working people in Southern Africa, and could also be the basis for a global working-class strategy. Such a strategy would ultimately entail not only regional delinking from neo-liberal imperialism (in alliance with Northern social and labour movements, which would simultaneously weaken the grip of imperialism), but also relinking along South-South axes. However, such a strategy must first confront some extremely serious contradictions within the local and international labour movements themselves, and in their relations with national governments. These I will take up again in Part four.

Notes

1 To establish our boundaries, the Southern African Development Community (SADC) comprises both strong and frail nation states: Angola, Botswana, the Democratic Republic of the Congo (DRC), Lesotho, Malawi, Mauritius, Mozambique, Namibia, South Africa, Seychelles, Swaziland, Tanzania, Zambia and Zimbabwe. The large, well-populated but impoverished island of Madagascar also belongs, geographically, but is generally excluded because of its isolation and Francophone heritage. For the purposes of this chapter, I will mainly consider the capital flows, labour movements and regional linkages within the ten most-southern, mainland countries, i.e. omitting the DRC, Mauritius, Seychelles and Tanzania.

2 Amin, S. (1999), 'Regionalization in Response to Polarizing Globalization', in Bjorn Hettne, Andras Inotai and Osvaldo Sunkel (eds), *Globalism and the New Regionalism*, London, Macmillan, p. 77.

3 Similar imperatives were introduced in Portuguese-controlled Mozambique and Angola, and in Namibia (the German-run former South West Africa until South Africa took over after World War I. South Africa retained the name 'South West Africa', then changed it to 'South West Africa/Namibia a few years before independence. For the sake of simplicity, I have called it 'Namibia' throughout.). But such accumulation was mainly based upon extractive rather than settler-oriented economics, through control of plantation labour.

4 Torres, L. (ed.) (1998), *One out of Ten: The Labour Market in Southern Africa*, Oslo, Fafo, p. 56. Nearly half of these workers are from Lesotho, with another third from Mozambique and the balance from Swaziland and Botswana. The definitive work on migrancy is McDonald, D. (ed.) (2000), *On Borders: Perspectives on International Migration in Southern Africa*, New York, St. Martin's Press.

5 Roux, R. (1964), *Time Longer than Rope*, Madison, University of Wisconsin Press.

6 McKinley, D. (1997), *The ANC: A Political Biography*, London, Pluto Press.

7 Fine, R. and Davies, D. (1991), *Beyond Apartheid*, London, Pluto Press.

8 Raftopoulos, B. and Phimister, I. (eds) (1998), *Keep on Knocking: A History of the Labour Movement in Zimbabwe, 1990–97*, Harare, Baobab.

9 Mayekiso, M. (1996), *Township Politics*, New York, Monthly Review Press; Ruiters, G. (2000), 'Urban Struggles and Urban Defeats in the 1980s', *Urban Forum*, 11(1).

10 Leys, C. and Saul, J. (1995), *Namibia's Liberation Struggle: A Two-edged Sword*, London, James Currey, p. 84.
11 Saul, J. (1999), 'Liberation without Democracy', in Jonathan Hyslop (ed.), *African Democracy*, Johannesburg, Witwatersrand University Press, p. 167.
12 *Fosatu Workers News*, April 1982, p. 2. See also Lewis, D. (1986), 'Capital, Trade Unions and Liberation', *South Africa Labour Bulletin*, 11(4), p. 35.
13 Cited in Saul, J. (1988), 'Class, Race and the Future of Socialism', in W. Cobbett and R. Cohen (eds), *Popular Struggles in South Africa*, London, James Currey, p. 216.
14 Without such corrections, the collapse in per-capita GDP is enormous, leaving Southern Africa with six of the world's 16 poorest countries: the DRC ($110), Mozambique ($140), Malawi ($210), Tanzania ($210), Madagascar ($250) and Angola ($260), according to *The World Bank Atlas*, Washington, DC, 1999.
15 Sources: *UNDP Human Development Report 1998*, New York; *SADC Regional Human Development Report 1998*, Southern African Political and Economic Series, Harare; Torres, *op. cit.*; *World Labour Report 1997/98*, ILO, Geneva; *Trade Unions of the World 1996*, ILO, Geneva; *Africa Competitiveness Report 1998*, Davos.
16 Fine, B. and Rustomjee, Z. (1996), *The Political Economy of South Africa: From Minerals-Energy Complex to Industrialisation*, London, Christopher Hurst and Johannesburg, Witwatersrand University Press.
17 Bond, P. (2000), *Elite Transition: From Apartheid to Neoliberalism in South Africa*, London, Pluto Press and Pietermaritzburg, University of Natal Press, Chapter 1.
18 Zimbabwe Congress of Trade Unions (1996), *Beyond ESAP*, Harare, p. 48.
19 World Bank (1995), *Project Completion Report: Zimbabwe: Structural Adjustment Program*, Country Operations Division, Washington, DC, p. 23.
20 Callaghy, T. and Ravenhill, J. (eds) (1993), *Hemmed In: Responses to Africa's Economic Decline*, New York, Columbia University Press.
21 Jauch, H. (1999), 'Building a Regional Labour Movement', *South African Labour Bulletin*, 23(1), p. 85.
22 Cooper, F. (1996), *Decolonization and African Society: The Labour Question in French and British Africa*, Cambridge, Cambridge University Press, p. 468.
23 Bassett, C. and Clarke, M. (2000), 'Class Struggle', *Southern African Report*, March.
24 Leys and Saul, *op. cit.,* p. 167.
25 Nyman, R. (1998), 'An Overview of Namibian Unions', in Torres, *op. cit.*, p. 162.
26 Adler, G. and Webster, E. (2000), 'South Africa: Class Compromise', *Southern Africa Report*, March.
27 Cosatu press statement on public-sector strike, December 1999, http://www.cosatu.org.za.
28 Satgar, V. and Jardine, C. (1999), 'Cosatu and the Tripartite Alliance', *South African Labour Bulletin*, 23(3), p. 8.
29 Ahwireng-Obeng, F. and McGowan, P. (1998), 'Partner or Hegemon? South Africa in Africa', *Journal of Contemporary African Studies*, 16(1).
30 Jauch, H. and Keet, D. (1996), *A SATUCC Study on Export Processing Zones in Southern Africa: Economic, Social and Political Implications*, Cape Town, International Labour Research and Information Group.
31 Jourdan, P., Gordhan, K., Arkwright, D. and De Beer, G. (1996), 'Spatial Development Initiatives (Development Corridors): Their Potential Contribution to Investment and Employment Creation', working paper, Development Bank of Southern Africa, Midrand, October.
32 Emblematic is the Coega SDI, as described in Bond, P. (2000), 'Economic Growth, Ecological Modernization, or Environmental Justice?: Conflicting Discourses in Post-Apartheid South Africa', *Capitalism, Nature, Socialism*, (11)1.

33 Keet, D. (1999), 'Globalization or Regionalisation: Contradictory Tendencies? Counteractive Tactics? Or Strategic Possibilities?', working paper, Institute for Global Dialogue, Johannesburg, June.

CHAPTER THREE

Bretton Woods bankruptcies in Southern Africa

1. Introduction
The International Monetary Fund (IMF) and World Bank are exceptional institutions, both for their size and for the international financial flows that they influence. The World Bank together with three affiliated development-bank institutions in Asia, Africa and Latin America employ 17 000 staff in 170 offices, with $500 billion in capital and $50 billion in annual lending (more than two-thirds of which is directed to just 11 large countries). The IMF is even more influential.

The IMF and World Bank have played decisive roles in various facets of South and Southern African development since the 1950s. Their influence has ranged from the way in which particular very large projects were financed, to the design of national programmes and policies under the influence of the agencies' neo-liberal 'Washington Consensus' ideology, to the reshaping of the global economy under conditions of extreme financial volatility. Most Southern African countries know the phenomenon of IMF and World Bank 'missions' jetting in, often for as little as two weeks, to draft *'aides memoire'* (often suspiciously similar to those of the countries previously visited). Sometimes with fanfare, sometimes without, they pronounce on macroeconomic and social policies, establish huge development schemes and gain the ears of the most important state and business elites, simply because of the institutional prestige they carry.

This prestige is meant to translate into access to international financial markets for otherwise unattractive debtor nations. Indeed, without an IMF 'seal of approval' in the form of a structural adjustment programme, it is virtually impossible for countries to borrow on a medium- or long-term basis from commercial markets. The visiting missions are also able to marshall the very best data available and hire the best local consultants. Regardless, therefore, of whether one approves or disapproves of IMF/World Bank ideology, methods and results, they cannot be ignored.

But the lack of socio-economic and environmental progress in Southern African economies since the IMF and World Bank became qualitatively more powerful in the early 1980s has generated some fierce debates amongst intellectuals. Three competing lines of argument usually emerge:

1) The IMF/World Bank perspective in Southern Africa aims to establish 'sound macroeconomic policy'; to follow market processes rather than resisting them; to halt *'rentier'* (parasitic) activity by bureaucrats; to promote sensible investments and policies that alleviate poverty, enhance the role of women in development, and promote environmental sustainability; and thereby contribute to efficient, effective governance.

2) IMF/World Bank interventions are typically necessary, *if insufficient*, for helping Southern Africa to engage the global economy; for utilising regulated markets to achieve 'sustainable' financial and environmental development; and for sending signals to the international community that foreign investment is welcome. However, IMF/World Bank policy, programmes and projects sometimes are badly phased; appear to be 'one-size-fits-all' in character (because they fail to take local conditions into account); and cause social and environmental problems which must then be mitigated through additional programmes.

3) The IMF/World Bank agenda has been – and continues to be – disastrous for Southern Africa, for it imposes eurocentric notions of development and modernity; downgrades democracy by propping up friendly authoritarian regimes; serves transnational corporate and banking interests above all else; values people and nature less than (narrowly defined) economic growth; hurts women, disabled people and the vulnerable in society far more than other social sectors; amplifies an already exceptionally unequal distribution of wealth; and often leads to economic disaster, even on its own limited terms.

Contrasting these three positions is important at the outset of the 21st century, in part because the possibility of a world state has become more important as a subject for debate than ever before. The IMF and World Bank are the most important embryos of global government, by all accounts, and – along with the World Trade Organisation (WTO) – they have come under withering attack by critics from both left and right (as I will show in Chapter five and Part four). Important movements from both ends of the spectrum have called for the abolition of these institutions.

Evidence from Southern Africa of IMF/World Bank help and hindrance has already been influential in the global debates. However, several interesting local personalities have influenced the IMF and World Bank in turn. In recent years, these have included the following people:[1]

- *Stanley Fischer*: born in Zambia, raised in Bulawayo and Cape Town, former World Bank chief economist and IMF deputy-managing director associated with 1980s structural adjustment design and late 1990s financial crisis management;

- *Bernard Chidzero*: Zimbabwean finance minister during the 1980s and early 1990s, main promoter of Zimbabwean structural adjustment, and suave chairperson of the IMF/World Bank development committee (ironically called 'The Committee on the Transfer of Real Resources to the Developing Countries') during the late 1980s period when North-South net funding-flows were reversed;

- *Geoffrey Lamb*: former SA Communist Party intellectual and University of Sussex radical academic, then key advisor to World Bank presidents on making African structural adjustment appear 'homegrown', and subsequently the main World Bank representative in Europe;

- *Caroline Moser*: as an academic at the University of London, the main World Bank gender critic, founder of 'Gender and Development' strategies to replace World Bank 'Women in Development' theory, and then, as World Bank staffperson in the 1990s, a key inside promoter of 'social capital' investment;

- *Trevor Manuel*: once advocate of anti-apartheid financial sanctions and strong critic of the IMF/World Bank, then SA minister of finance and sponsor of Bank involvement in SA macroeconomic policy, and then chairperson of the IMF/World Bank board of governors at the controversial meetings held in 2000 (including in Prague, where two days of sessions had to be truncated to one because of protests outside);

- *Ian Goldin*: former anti-draft activist during apartheid, and later chief economist of the European Bank for Reconstruction and Development and managing director of the Development Bank of Southern Africa (where, notoriously, he refused a key municipality a loan for expanded water supply but lent a private company a much larger amount, apparently to push the privatisation agenda), prior to becoming senior policy advisor to the World Bank's chief economist in 2001; and

- *Mamphela Ramphele*: former vice-chancellor at the University of Cape Town (where she successfully broke the National Education, Health and Allied Workers Union in the process of cutting the wages of menial workers in half), and from mid-2000 the World Bank's managing director responsible for human development.

On the other side of the global class struggle at the turn of the century were leaders like poet Dennis Brutus, Anglican Archbishop Njongonkulu Ndungane, former Soweto city councillor Trevor Ngwane (fired from the ANC for opposing a World Bank-influenced municipal privatisation programme), sociologist Fatima Meer (the first official biographer of Nelson Mandela), liberation theologian Molefe Tsele, and student leader

Molly Dhlamini.[2] All were anti-apartheid activists, subsequently associated with Jubilee South Africa. During the late 1990s, they quickly gained status as amongst the most respected international voices arguing for an end to debt, to structural adjustment and even to the IMF and World Bank as determinants of Southern African development.

Given the diversity of experiences, views and strategies amongst the contending forces, there is no short-term hope of resolving Southern African debates on the merits of the IMF, the World Bank and the foreign debt that invariably accompanies them. Nevertheless, these topics offer us an outstanding window on broader problems of development, and on debating perspectives that are increasingly becoming universal. This chapter considers first the basic historical and institutional characteristics of the IMF and World Bank, and puts their huge increase in power into the context of rising Third World debt since the 1970s. I will then consider examples of controversial World Bank project lending, using the examples of huge dams at Kariba in Zimbabwe/Zambia (1950s) and Lesotho (1980s-present). During the 1980s–90s, the IMF/World Bank's more general influence over economic development strategies grew dramatically, as recent Southern African experiences demonstrate.

2. From Bretton Woods to the debt crisis

The Bretton Woods institutions were founded in mid-1944, at the hotel of the same name in rural New Hampshire, in the north-eastern US, where representatives of 44 Western-oriented countries, including South Africa, met to establish global economic rules for the post-war era. The deal was brokered by Harry Dexter White from the US Treasury and British economist John Maynard Keynes (who later wrote of his extreme disappointment that the US won so many concessions). The World Bank was designed to provide reconstruction support to war-damaged Europe and subsequently to other countries, while the IMF was mandated to smooth disruptions in international financial relations between countries. (A few years later in fascist-ruled Cuba, the General Agreement on Tariffs and Trade [GATT] was initiated, and in 1995 was renamed the World Trade Organisation.)[3]

Financial crisis and clout

The shift in global political and economic power that elevated the IMF and World Bank to their present exalted status occurred, as I discussed in Chapter one, in the immediate aftermath of the Third World debt crisis (specifically, the Mexican near-default of 1982), but the roots of global financial turbulence are found in the 1960s, when national controls on banking were eroded.[4] The geographical expansion of finance in the 1960s was ratified by further internationalisation of productive capital led by transnational corporations. Although some researchers argue that international financiers merely follow TNCs into new markets, banks exert strong influence over TNCs in the normal course of business, in part through a wide range of services: the financing of foreign subsidiaries; the placing of medium-term Eurocredits and Eurobonds; the international management of liquid assets and foreign exchange risks; leasing services; consultation on finance and computing; and maintaining teams of industrial experts capable of making technical assessments of investment projects.[5] Indeed, by 1978, through such services and other command mechanisms, banks 'controlled' 125 of the 487 leading companies in the world, up from 64 in 1965, according to one scholar.[6] As the recessions of the 1970s affected more and more economies, geographic shifts of funds followed the higher profitability of larger TNCs relative to smaller firms in what had become a unitary global economy.

As I discussed in Chapter one, the 'overaccumulation' of productive capital had become a global phenomenon by this stage, as excessive capital intensity in production had generated far more output than could be absorbed through regular market channels. Corporate resources were rein-vested less in overproductive manufacturing firms, given rising excess capacity and declining rates of profit in the G-7 countries (from 20–30% levels during the 1960s–70s to 5–15% during the 1970s–90s).[7] Instead, they were increasingly funnelled into the financial circuit of capital through a variety of new international routes. The world's two-dozen largest banks controlled most of the action, granting three-quarters of the total amount of loans to Third World borrowers. It was convenient that concentration existed on the borrowing side as well: three-quarters of the credit of all lenders went to fewer than a dozen large Third World and newly indus-trialised countries. The Eurodollar market hence grew from $50 billion in 1973 to more than $2 trillion 15 years later, and in addition to European banking centres, was increasingly located in unregulated hot-money centres, e.g. the Cayman Islands, Hong Kong and the Bahamas. Along with 'petrodollars' centralised in New York banks mainly from Arab oil-produc-ing states, the Eurodollars required an outlet, hence new explorations for borrowers further afield, including in the Third World.[8]

If part of the pressure to free global financial flows from national controls came from the internationalisation of productive capital, of equal importance were changing monetary conditions in the US. Consistent prob-lems with the US balance of payments (BoP) followed expenditures on the Vietnam War and the Great Society (the BoP deficit tripled from 1957 to 1970), and left foreign traders less willing to hold dollars – previously the currency to which all others were pegged – and to turn to gold instead. As a result, US gold stocks fell from $24.6 billion – 70% of the world's supply – in 1949, to $20.6 billion in 1958 and to $10 billion in 1971. Justifying President Richard Nixon's decision to withdraw from the Bretton Woods system of fixed exchange rates in 1971 (which cost foreign holders of dollars an estimated $80 billion), John Connally, Nixon's treasury secretary, commented, 'We had a problem and we are sharing it with the world just like we shared our prosperity ... That's what friends are for.'

Sharing the problem

As a result, the dollar devalued steadily. A US BoP deficit of $6.9 billion for 1972, up from $2.7 billion in 1971, caused a great stir, and the dollar collapsed when that (now-seemingly trivial) deficit was announced in March 1973. Having decisively broken arrangements for international monetary stability, the US installed the 'flexible exchange rate system' still in place today. As a result, in monetary struggles against other advanced capitalist countries, Washington found ways of keeping the gold price relatively low, forcing instead an upward revaluation of the currencies of other countries.[9]

In this way, a correcting mechanism for the US trade imbalance was temporarily found to ease the first major global monetary crisis in four decades. The revaluation of other currencies – resulting from what the US called its 'Passive Strategy for the Balance of Payments' – moved the inflationary implications of the US deficit to other countries.[10] The struggle over which relatively weaker parts of the world would bear the pain of devaluation was in large part played out in important IMF policy changes.

Along with Eastern Europe, which also took on massive debt from 1975–95, the Third World was the weakest part of the global system. Because the petrodollar deposits were generally short-term and thus cost-sensitive, the banks insisted that the Third World sovereign loans be taken on a floating-rate basis. From late 1979, as world interest rates soared, this became an enormous predicament for the Third World. Still, some commercial banks found ways to profit from the crisis.

Profiting from pain and corruption

Borrowers had been offered loans during the 1970s at a premium (often 2%) far above the London Interbank Offering Rate, the rate at which international banks lend each other short-term funds. The banks charged syndication fees as well as high fees (typically 1–2%) when, after the repayment burden became unmanageable in the early 1980s, debt rescheduling was necessary. The banks also gained from the rebound of funds, popularly known as 'capital flight', to the same banks' VIP deposit accounts. Finally, the ability of the US banks to take advantage of their foreign branches, which were beyond the reach of bank regulators, brought a higher profit rate. Had the banks been lending the foreign deposits to domestic US customers, they would have had to keep 12% of the assets in a reserve fund for liquidity purposes. Not having to do so meant another 0.5% on their profit margins. So in fact, prior to expensive increases in loan-loss reserve funds in mid-1987, the banks actually gained from the disaster of the Third World debt crisis.[11]

Then the threat of mass default suddenly emerged, as 33 countries found themselves in need of foreign-debt rescheduling during the early 1980s.[12] To this end, the IMF financed the repayment of commercial bank loans in exchange for a change in development strategy demanding an export orientation and an end to various state subsidies, especially in social spending.[13] The World Bank stepped in later in the decade when the IMF's credibility ran out and its funding became temporarily scarce, expanding from individual project loans to fully fledged structural-adjustment financing using 25% of its resources. The funds of the two institutions were regularly topped up by member governments, which allowed the borrowing countries to repay the commercial banks and hence shift the costs of devaluing the overaccumulated financial capital from New York, London, Frankfurt, Zurich and Tokyo onto both taxpayers of the advanced capitalist countries and Third World peasants, workers and environments.

How did all of this look from the perspective of Third World borrowers? Commercial banks didn't mind how the money was spent, and as a result, corruption was an integral component of Third World borrowing. Examples include Haiti, where the Duvallier family's estimated theft was $500 million; Zaire (since renamed the Democratic Republic of the Congo), where Mobutu Sese Seko is thought to have been illegitimately worth $5 billion; the Philippines, where Cory Aquino accused Ferdinand Marcos of having stolen tens of billions of dollars, while her government inherited a foreign debt of $36 billion; and Mexico, where even the liberal President Lopez Portillo apparently took $1 billion with him in 1982 to his retirement in Italy.[14]

But even where the borrowers included relatively more democratic governments, economic calculations associated with debt quickly went askew. The dollar's depreciation and generalised inflation made interest rates on international loans appear negative in real terms (i.e. after inflation) throughout the 1970s. Most Third World countries outside East Asia were suffering from a slow-down in investment, as a function of their own local overaccumulation crises. In order to industrialise or otherwise cope with problems of underdevelopment, many national leaders saw loans as a way out of dependency on the First World. Various earlier development paths – especially those based on direct foreign investment and import substitution – had not proven successful even on their own limited terms.

The main reason was slowing demand in the world economy, as a result of global overaccumulation and conservative policy responses in advanced economies under the Thatcher, Reagan and Kohl governments that were aimed at weakening organised labour through the imposition of austerity.

One overarching strategy – 'monetarism' – emerged to support currencies, to rid economies of inflation and in the process to lower costs associated with First World labour – by increasing unemployment rates – and Third World commodities. Extremely high interest rates were introduced by the Labour government in Britain under IMF influence in 1976, and fully cemented on a global scale by the US Federal Reserve Board in late 1979.[15] The interest-rate increase raised the repayment burden of Third World debtor nations to impossible levels. The fragility of the advanced capitalist banking system was thus exposed and exacerbated. Accumulation was pushed into spatial and temporal outlets which would prove untenable.[16]

The implications of crisis displacement
The next step was for Third World borrowers to confront the limits of their earning capacities. This was not purely a function of the limits of Third World accumulation, but can be traced to the continuing crisis in the advanced industrial world. Following a bout of extreme commodity-price inflation in the early 1970s, a series of recessions in advanced industrial economies led to a reorganisation in the cost structures, and sometimes the industrial compositions themselves, of the primary exports of the beleaguered debtor nations. This resulted in a 77% decline in world prices of non-petroleum commodities from 1973 to 1988 (which was the key period of crisis formation), while global real interest rates rose from –4% to 4%.[17]

By the 1980s, the policies of the IMF and World Bank had exacerbated these structural changes, as all countries were not only compelled to shift towards export-led growth strategies (which exacerbated the global commodity gluts in the process), but also to adopt a standard range of neo-liberal structural adjustment policies: fiscal constraints – especially social-subsidy cuts – privatisation, trade and financial liberalisation, the deregulation of their labour markets and higher interest rates. Prior to investigating the application of these policies in selected Southern Africa cases (South Africa, Zimbabwe and Mozambique), we should consider the other key role of the World Bank in Third World development, namely project finance. Two large dam complexes – Kariba and the Lesotho Highlands Water Project (LHWP) – illustrate the problems.

3. Shaping Southern African development
While the IMF was, until the 1970s, largely a technical agency whose aim was to keep the international balance sheets of individual countries in sync, in contrast the World Bank looked far and wide for opportunities to provide project loans. Initially the World Bank confined itself to European reconstruction, but during the 1950s it became the largest foreign financier to several Southern African colonies then still under minority rule, including the Central African Federation of the Rhodesias and Nyasaland (later

renamed Zimbabwe, Zambia and Malawi), South Africa and Portuguese-ruled Angola and Mozambique. By all accounts, World Bank projects were not aimed at furthering the causes of racial equality, economic justice and ecological sustainability but, on the contrary, promoted white-controlled infrastructure for the benefit of extractive, exploitative white economic interests and relatively wealthy white consumers. Witness the two huge dam complexes financed by the World Bank on the Zambezi River and in the Lesotho Highlands.[18]

Kariba power

During the mid-1950s, the then-largest World Bank project (at a total cost of $80 million) was the huge Kariba hydro-electric dam on the Zambezi River border between Zambia and Zimbabwe. Because of its size, complexity and the controversy associated with its development, Kariba deserves some specific consideration.[19] The dam created one of the world's largest inland bodies of water, generated massive amounts of hydro-electricity, and spawned the birth of major tourism and fishing industries in what previously had been an undeveloped area. But in the process, 56 000 Tonga (Batonka) people were summarily displaced from ancestral lands and lost their livelihoods without compensation, and many of them died because of degraded resettlement conditions.

One source of electricity demand in colonial Zimbabwe was white business and suburban consumption, which was enhanced by the World Bank's earlier $28-million electrification loan in 1952. But far greater demand for Kariba energy was emerging from Zambian copper-field expansion by South African, British and US multinational mining corporations. 'Their role in the (regional) economy' was, according to historian Colin Leys, 'in itself decisive and it is not too much to say that the meetings of their boards of directors can be as important for the inhabitants of the Federation as those of the Federal cabinet.'[20] Hence the World Bank's Kariba loan catered for these interests, instead of those of the vast majority of Zimbabweans and Zambians.

However, when the World Bank underestimated (by 50%) the money that would be required to build Kariba, the two main beneficiaries – Anglo American and Roan Selection Trust, together with their allied financiers the British South Africa Co., Standard Chartered World Bank and Barclays Bank – were approached by the Federation governor to provide a substantial top-up loan to the project, on the grounds that with copper prices soaring during the mid-1950s, the firms were enjoying a windfall they should share. The resulting credit was nearly as large as the World Bank's contribution, and had the effect of diverting revenues that would have at least partially been available for use in Zambia, causing severe strains in intra-Federation relations. According to a World Commission on Dams investigation into Kariba in 1999, the top-up loan 'stole funds from the Zambian government ... Zambia was seeking funding for a large rural development programme long discussed and promised to reverse the accelerated flow of rural people into the mining towns and along the line of rail', which the copper companies subsequently refused to support because they had extended the Kariba credit.[21]

Another financing-related criticism of Kariba emerged in an official expert-committee report in 1962, which noted the government's over-reliance on foreign-denominated loans from the World Bank, the US Export-Import World Bank and the Commonwealth Development Corporation. This financing method had generated 'special problems in the negotiation and amortisation of such loans, which may make them an unsuitable vehicle for financing projects promising a return only in the distant future. In the case of such capital expenditures, the obligation of paying interest and the repayment of capital may become too burdensome'.[22]

Indeed, the danger of foreign-currency loans for developmental purposes was made by Rhodesian economist John Handford: 'One of the loans that had helped to build Kariba – that by the British Commonwealth Development Corporation – proved somewhat expensive, because the interest payable on it was linked to the price of money by being 1% higher than the British Bank Rate. Thus, when recurring financial crises in Britain led to raising of the Bank Rate, the cost of the loan also rose.'[23]

The mismatch of lending – namely, foreign-currency obligations to pay for local-currency assets – bedeviled not only Kariba, but became one of the most important factors in the subsequent Third World debt crisis when global interest rates soared, and continues to raise questions as to the merits of large project-financing deals to pay for inputs such as dam cement, steel and locally remunerated labour that can be acquired using domestic currency.

Even where the World Bank was more inclined to consider the developmental condition of indigenous majority populations, it again readily adopted the colonial point of view, such as in Zimbabwe, where another major loan, again denominated in hard currency, was aimed at implementing the Native Land Husbandry Act of 1959. This law imposed alien individual-ownership title systems on African communal lands, thus generating sufficient peasant protest to halt the process. Displacement appeared under colonial logic as a means of accelerating economic development: 'We do not want native peasants', Garfield Todd (a future prime minister) told parliament during the early 1950s, 'We want the bulk of them working in the mines and farms and in the European areas and we could absorb them and their families.'[24] Cheryl Payer concluded that the World Bank-funded law 'was designed in part to provide white industrialists with a captive labour force by denying migrant labour the right to return to land in the reserves'.[25]

Notwithstanding the technical, social and environmental problems caused by loans for Kariba, rural land tenure and other projects, the underlying rationale for the World Bank's involvement in what was then Southern Rhodesia and the rest of the region was to integrate Southern Africa into world financial circuits. After a two-week visit by a World Bank public-relations officer in 1956, a leading business journal observed that, 'The two note-books full of notes which he had made on the trip would be used both internally by the World Bank, and as a source of information for use by Swiss, USA and other financial interests.'[26]

Lesotho water[27]

In South Africa, the World Bank's history was just as controversial, for it began developing business plans just two years after apartheid was formally introduced in 1948, and the World Bank's first loans – $30 million to Eskom and $20 million for railways and harbours – were granted in 1951. Follow-up loans of $162 million for both projects continued until 1968. Indeed, in the wake of the Sharpeville massacre in 1960, when the sanctions movement gathered steam, the World Bank granted loans worth $45 million to Pretoria, including $20 million in 1966 after then-ANC president Albert Luthuli and Rev. Martin Luther King, Jr. had called for financial sanctions against apartheid. There was no direct benefit for black consumers who, because of apartheid, were denied Eskom power that had been financed by the World Bank and whose prospects of rail transport were mainly linked to their employment – if they possessed a pass-book – in urban centres. The World Bank discontinued lending to South Africa when the last Eskom loan (for a coal-fired power station) was repaid, because per capita GDP rose to levels that disqualified access by Pretoria.[28]

However, the World Bank still contributed to apartheid through the Lesotho Highlands Water Project, which dammed rivers and tunnelled through mountains to supply water to thirsty Johannesburg customers – mainly wealthy households, white-owned farms and white-owned mines – notwithstanding huge social and environmental costs. The loan was signed in October 1986, following a Pretoria-sponsored coup which ousted Lesotho prime minister Leabua Jonathan. This was at a time of harsh repression in South Africa, after the foreign debt repayment 'standstill' of September 1985, when there was little chance of South Africa getting access to fresh foreign funds.[29] Lesotho – with its $600 per-capita income and its reliance on foreign aid for 20% of its GDP – was granted a World Bank loan of $110 million, solely because of South Africa's ability to stand surety.

(In fact, the only financial risk analysis in the World Bank's initial report was concerned with whether Pretoria would default.) The LHWP loan came to be described as 'sanctions busting' by the first ANC water minister, Kader Asmal (though he later expanded the project, in the face of strong community protest).[30]

As with Kariba, the LHWP was Sub-Saharan Africa's largest-ever public-works project. The first phase alone, costing $4 billion, involved construction of two dams and cross-catchment tunnels which will supply an additional billion cubic metres of water to Johannesburg (for which annual royalties of $50 million will be paid), as well as hydro-electricity to Lesotho. Water ordinarily draining into the Orange River catchment area is now being diverted through the mountains to the Vaal River in order to supply the continent's largest industrial complex, raising important social, environmental and economic concerns. Indigenous communities in Lesotho are witnessing large-scale displacement affecting 20 000 people, loss of common resources like grazing land, topsoil and woodlots, loss of income through land submersion, and flooding of ancestral burial grounds (for which reimbursement and resettlement schemes were considered unsatisfactory by a majority of residents, according to surveys in the late 1990s). There was also an increase in social problems consequent to dam construction, including a dramatic increase in AIDS, alcohol abuse and livestock theft. Under pressure from local church groups and international NGOs, the World Bank and South African officials have been involved in resettlement and compensation. But rural development programmes were mired in corruption, as was the management of the Lesotho side of the project (it was alleged that the Basothu chief executive officer of the LHWP, Musapha Sole, was provided with bribes from some of the largest construction companies in the world, including ABB of Switzerland, Impregilio of Italy and Dumez of France, over a ten-year period).[31]

The environmentalist critique has also been difficult to resolve. The LHWP exacerbates Lesotho's scarcity of cultivated land (only 9% of the country can be used for farming), hence pushing peasants onto soil more vulnerable to erosion. The dams also destroy crucial habitats of the Maluti minnow (an endangered species), the bearded vulture and four other species considered 'globally threatened'. Moreover, early LHWP feasibility studies failed to include an environmental-impact assessment; linings for tunnels were inadequate and had to be cemented; reservoir-induced earthquakes were far worse than anticipated; and soil erosion and sedimentation – which typically lower dam capacity by 1% per year and silt up intake areas – were not initially taken into account. Lesotho's own access to water has also become a matter of concern, with experts now certain that there is insufficient water in the country to share with South Africa beyond the still-planned LHWP Phase 2, and within ten to thirty years, Lesotho would itself probably face a condition of water scarcity.[32] The capital city, Maseru, suffered a serious water shortage in late 1999, for example.

There was also a consumer critique of the LHWP, especially the World Bank's role, from Soweto and Alexandra township residents, who argued that the financing of the project makes water provision to low-income black residents of Johannesburg more, not less, difficult. The World Bank's estimates in the mid-1980s of anticipated demand in the Witwatersrand area (now Gauteng Province) were, by task manager John Roome's own estimation, higher by 40% than actual consumption in the late 1990s, which meant that the first Lesotho water destined for the Vaal in early 1998 had to be redirected back to the Lesotho lowlands. In 1995, approximately 1.5 million residents of Gauteng did not have direct access to water, and to supply them with 50 litres per person per day would have required only 22 million cubic metres of additional supply annually, representing a small fraction of the water that middle- and upper-income consumers used to water gardens and fill swimming pools. The LHWP's first two phases will supply a billion more cubic meters of water to Gauteng each year.[33]

Furthermore, in addition to hedonistic water use by wealthy consumers, a vast proportion of incoming water – approximately half in most townships – leaks out of Gauteng's apartheid-era infrastructure, which black households are expected to pay for. The possibilities for conservation not only from fixing infrastructure but imposing limits on suburban household and industrial consumption were estimated by some credible officials at 40%. But the LHWP water-distribution structure meant that the main catchment-area intermediary (the Rand Water Board), which should have been in a position to fix leaks and promote conservation through 'demand side management', had the reverse incentive, namely to charge municipalities for high-level consumption in order to make payments on LHWP interest charges. Therefore, given limited municipal resources, the expectation was that the leaks would not be fixed. As a result, for consumers to pay for the LHWP would mean raising the marginal price of water dramatically (the World Bank suggested by a factor of five once Phase 1B is complete, to accurately reflect cost increases). Moreover, while bulk-water charges to municipalities rose by 35% between 1995 and 1998 mainly because of the LHWP, the levy for the first block of the Johannesburg block tariff, i.e. the lowest block, increased by 55%, indicating that, relatively speaking, first-block consumers paid a higher proportion of the increase than did consumers who used more water.[34]

For Gauteng township consumers who could not pay their bills, water cut-offs soon began to occur, following Roome's suggestion made in 1995 that a 'credible threat of cutting service' was needed to discipline residents who continued the municipal payments boycotts begun during the 1980s.[35] In contrast to the apartheid era, in which water cut-offs were extremely rare – in part because of strong opposition from civic movements – 1997 witnessed more than a ten-fold increase in water cut-offs in Gauteng, and a decline from 50% to 20% in the proportion of those who were cut off who subsequently reconnected. The rate of water cut-offs intensified further in 1998, with entire townships disconnected in some cases, including individual house-holds who had paid their bills. The LHWP-related increases in the price of water were the main cause of the inability to pay, but when Alexandra residents went to the World Bank Inspection Panel to object that the burden of LHWP financing fell on low-income people, it rejected the complaint.[36]

Nevertheless, the communities continued struggling, and were vindi-cated in late 2000 when the World Commission on Dams analysed problems associated with big dams in much the same way that they did. The LHWP violated so many of the commission's recommendations that Lesotho peasant representatives and Gauteng township leaders together called for a moratorium on further LHWP construction (a call which was ignored in both Pretoria and Washington).

The Kariba and LHWP projects are revealing because of their size, the enhancement of inegalitarian status-quo power relations that result from them, and their enormous impact on the relationship between society and nature. But the Bretton Woods institutions were most decisive in Southern Africa when it came to Washington Consensus economic policies. These reflected leverage enjoyed through financing relationships, ranging from particular project credits to more general structural/sectoral adjustment loans.

4. From projects to policy in Southern Africa

As the Third World debt crisis became more difficult to manage, and as the efficacy of major project loans began to be questioned, the IMF and World Bank shifted their attention to macroeconomic management aimed first at ensuring repayment of external debts. Although political relationships with newly liberated countries, with sometimes radical-sounding nationalist governments, were not easy, the role of the Bretton Woods institutions in Southern Africa was not qualitatively different than elsewhere in the world. Most importantly, increasing IMF/World Bank funding and influence did not solve debt and economic crises, but often deepened them. Even countries that did not agree to externally imposed adjustment policies, like war-torn Angola, relatively prosperous Botswana and South Africa, still gave the IMF 'policy undertakings' – under the threat of losing inter-national credit-worthiness, and therefore access to hard currency, without the IMF's seal of approval.

The widespread failure of IMF/World Bank structural adjustment programmes across Southern Africa, and indeed across the world, is not disputed. As I have indicated above, central to the global crisis was the

IMF/ World Bank strategy of pushing every Third World country to export more, resulting in declining prices and rising debt burdens. But the particular way in which Southern African economies – Mozambique, Zimbabwe and South Africa, for example – were restructured during the 1980s–90s deserves brief attention.

South Africa turns neo-liberal

The wealthiest country in the region, South Africa, reflects a profound contradiction in its relations with the IMF and World Bank. Without a substantial lending relationship, the Bretton Woods institutions have nevertheless been extremely influential in determining South Africa's economic and social policies.[37] To consider the IMF first, its advisors had a central role during annual visits in the apartheid government's shift in the late 1980s towards neo-liberal economic strategies, resulting in very high real interest rates (from –7% in 1987 to +6% in 1989), privatisation (Iscor), export-oriented growth strategies and the implementation of the regressive Value Added Tax (which led to a two-day strike by 3.5 million workers).

In previous years, the IMF had ignored international condemnations of apartheid and the financial sanctions campaign. During the late 1970s and early 1980s, in the wake of the Soweto uprising, the IMF lent $2 billion to Pretoria just as international anti-apartheid activists began persuading commercial banks to boycott Pretoria. In 1983, the US Congress forbade further IMF loans to the apartheid regime after anti-apartheid pressure increased.

Despite this history, leading economists of the African National Congress believed that the legitimacy associated with the IMF was required for a democratic South Africa to access international financial markets. In December 1993, the first act of the Transitional Executive Committee (a government-in-waiting combining the ANC and the ruling National Party) was to borrow $850 million from the IMF, ostensibly for drought relief, although the drought had ended 18 months earlier. The loan's secret conditions were leaked to *Business Day* in March 1994, presumably to establish confidence in financial markets that the election in April 1994 and the subsequent transfer of power would be characterised by continuity in economic policy. These conditions included not only items from the classic structural-adjustment menu (lower import tariffs, cuts in state spending, large cuts in public-sector wages, etc.), but also informal but intense pressure by IMF managing director Michel Camdessus to reappoint both finance minister Derek Keys and Reserve Bank governor Chris Stals, the two main stalwarts of National Party neo-liberalism.

The World Bank's re-entry into South Africa was far more subtle. In May 1990, shortly after F. W. de Klerk unbanned the ANC, World Bank staff began to woo critics both from the internal Mass Democratic Movement and those from within the exiled ANC. The World Bank conceded its 'strongly negative image, particularly among ANC cadres who viewed the World Bank through the lens of their experience in other African countries undergoing structural adjustment'.[38] Sensitivities were initially addressed by World Bank team leader Geoffrey Lamb (the former SA Communist Party intellectual), who set up specialist teams to analyse conditions and generate policy options in macroeconomics, industry, health, education, housing and land reform from 1991 to 1994.

The World Bank agreed, apparently reluctantly, that there would be no loans to the De Klerk government.[39] The World Bank earnestly desired legitimacy from working with the incoming ANC government (Nelson Mandela was periodically fêted in Washington during the early and mid-1990s by World Bank and IMF leaders), and it saw South Africa as an ideal place to establish the function now termed the 'Knowledge Bank'.[40] Indeed, the sole World Bank loan to the first democratic South African government – worth just R340 million (although in fact only around half that amount was actually used) – was only granted in 1997, for the purpose of making small and medium enterprises more globally competitive.[41] This reflected, in part, the power of social movements and Pretoria's difficulty in justifying foreign-sourced financing for development in a context of highly liquid domestic financial sources.

The real impact of the World Bank in post-apartheid South Africa was therefore witnessed not through lending, but in policy advice: land reform, housing, healthcare, public works, child-welfare finance, infrastructure, industrial development and macroeconomic policy. There were no doubt others, but as the World Bank itself said in 1999, 'several successful initiatives had no formal outputs or public recognition of our role'.[42] The most high-profile initiative, however, was the Growth, Employment and Redistribution strategy. But this became a severe embarrassment to World Bank macroeconomic modellers (one of whom, Richard Ketley, subsequently left the World Bank to play a crucial role in the Department of Finance, before continuing, in 2000, to another well-remunerated position at the Deutsche Bank).[43]

In addition to World Bank policy advice, two far lower-profile World Bank subsidiaries – the International Finance Corporation (IFC), its investment-ownership arm and the Multilateral Investment Guarantee Agency (MIGA) – were active in South Africa. From 1996, IFC investments soon topped $100 million (in financial services, pulp and paper, cement/construction, privatisation of municipal infrastructure, private healthcare and a Domino's Pizza franchise, though the latter went bankrupt in late 2000). MIGA provided tens of millions of dollars in investment guarantees, as well as supporting SA corporate investment in the controversial Mozal aluminium smelter in Maputo.[44]

The World Bank and IMF role in South Africa was obviously highly controversial, and the effects of structural adjustment were hotly debated between proponents with widely divergent ideologies. Of the three discourses about the Bretton Woods institutions noted in the introductory section earlier in this chapter, the first and third were most in evidence in South Africa. But experiences in Zimbabwe and Mozambique provide additional perspectives.

Zimbabwe's plunge

In Zimbabwe, matters were both more blunt – IMF/ World Bank structural-adjustment conditionality was not in the least disguised, as I will show below, particularly when Zimbabwe became desperate for foreign exchange in 1999 – and far more complicated. Indeed, a full interpretation of IMF and World Bank policy roles entails not only an assessment of the failed structural adjustment programme of the 1990s, but also of a variety of other sectoral- and project-loan interventions dating back to the early 1980s. But the main lesson to be learned from Zimbabwe relates to the second of the three discourses noted at the outset: the origins of the view that IMF/World Bank structural-adjustment policies are 'necessary but insufficient'.

In its oppositional statement about an alternative to adjustment, even the Zimbabwe Congress of Trade Unions (ZCTU) posed a crucial limitation on its own future strategies, namely that 'there can be no return to pre-ESAP policies, partly because of the stranglehold that foreign creditors have on policy through the substantial debt that has accumulated, paradoxically, because of the failure of the policy'. As ZCTU leader Morgan Tsvangirai put it in his preface to the ZCTU publication, *Beyond ESAP*: 'While acknowledging that SAPs are necessary, the study shows that they are insufficient in fostering development.'[45] (A more traditional labour discourse would have generated the affirmation that ESAP was *un*necessary and indeed that it *under*developed Zimbabwe during the 1990s.)

To comprehend this apparent concession to orthodox ideology, and the overwhelming material and financial power of the IMF/World Bank which it reflects, some background is necessary. For two decades after independence in 1980, Zimbabwe suffered an unusual mix of populist government rhetoric from a nominally 'Marxist-Leninist' ruling party; white corporate domination of the industrial, agricultural, financial and services sectors; and an inability to break into global markets. President Robert Mugabe steadily condoned an ever-greater role for the private sector in Zimbabwe's development, in the process taking on vast quantities of international debt.

One reason was the role played by finance minister Bernard Chidzero, who advocated borrowing massively at the outset, in the belief that repayments – which consumed 16% of export earnings in 1983 – would 'decline sharply until we estimate it will be about 4% within the next few years'.[46]

The World Bank, which lent $700 million to Harare during the 1980s and made Chidzero head of its 'Development Committee', concurred: 'The debt service ratios should begin to decline after 1984 even with large amounts of additional external borrowing.'[47] In reality, Zimbabwe's debt servicing spiralled up to an untenable 35% of export earnings by 1987.

Loan conditions quickly emerged. By 1985, the IMF pressured Mugabe to cut education and health spending, and in 1986 food subsidies fell to two-thirds of their levels in 1981. Similarly, land reform was stymied not only by the 1979 Lancaster House constitution's 'willing-seller, willing-buyer' compromise, but by the World Bank's alternative to redistribution, i.e. showering peasants with unaffordable microloans. From a tiny base in 1980, the World Bank's main partner agency granted 94 000 loans by 1987. But without structural change in agricultural markets, the strategy floundered, as 80% of borrowers defaulted in 1988 (good rains notwithstanding).[48]

Chidzero then persuaded Mugabe to ditch Rhodesian-era regulatory controls on prices and foreign-trade/financial flows. The Economic Structural Adjustment Programme, which ran from 1991 to 1995, was heavily promoted by the World Bank and IMF. The programme failed decisively, not simply because of two bad droughts in 1992 and 1995. The overall structure of Zimbabwe's economy and society left it ill-suited for rapid liberalisation and its resultant extremely high real interest rates, a dramatic upsurge in inflation associated with the lifting of price controls and devastating cuts in social-welfare spending.

Worse, social policy went into reverse gear. As a direct result of funding cuts and cost-recovery policies, exacerbated by the AIDS pandemic, Zimbabwe's brief rise in literacy and health indicators in the 1980s was dramatically reversed. In contrast, the stock-market reached extraordinary peaks in mid-1991 and mid-1997, but these were followed by crashes of more than 50% within a few months, along with massive hikes in interest rates. Although growth was finally recorded in 1996–97, it quickly expired when international financial markets and local investors battered Zimbabwe's currency from November 1997 onwards, ultimately shrinking the value of a Z$ from $0.09 to $0.025 over the course of a year. As a result, unprecedented inflation was imported, leading in January and October 1998 to urban riots over maize and fuel-price hikes.[49]

As Mugabe stumbled, as economic grievances intensified, as public-sector employees and other workers increasingly went on strike, and as evidence of political unaccountability mounted, the ZCTU became more political. In early 1999, the National Working People's Convention gave a strong civil-society endorsement to the formation of an opposition party, which was formed in September 1999 and was known as the Movement for Democratic Change (MDC).

Meanwhile, the IMF sent a high-level team to negotiate the disbursement of a $53 million loan (which in turn was to release another $800 million from other donors and lenders). The team's objectives were straight-forward. Mugabe was told in August 1998 to reverse the only three progressive things he had done in recent years, namely a ban on holding foreign exchange accounts in local banks, an import tax imposed on luxuries in 1997 and price controls imposed on staple foods in mid-1998 in the wake of riots.

Mugabe soon conceded the first point (although he reversed it again in February 2001 when a forex shortage and petrol crisis compelled the seizure of forex accounts, for conversion to local currency at an artificially low rate). As for the second and third points, by March 1999 the IMF assistant director for Africa, Michael Nowak, was publicly insisting that Mugabe must 'reduce the tariffs slapped on luxury goods … and we also want the government to give us a clear timetable as to when and how they will remove the price controls they have imposed on some goods'.[50]

In mid-1999, Nowak agreed to increase the loan amount to $200 million. But there now new conditions, reflecting general public outrage at the apparently corrupt use of 12 000 Zimbabwe army troops as a proto-mercenary force in the Democratic Republic of the Congo, through which Mugabe's cronies were accumulating vast wealth by protecting diamond mines from Ugandan-backed rebels. An IMF representative revealed the character of the negotiations to international journalists: 'The Zimbabweans felt offended, shocked, but they all the same agreed to give us the information, we got all the clarification we wanted. They had no choice … We have had assurances [that] if there is budgetary overspending, *there will be cuts in other budget sectors.*' (My emphasis.)[51]

Mugabe's own confused and confusing reaction included agreeing to the regressive economic conditions associated with the loan (which he soon violated, leading to a cut-off of the next tranch). But he also regularly lambasted the 'imperialist' role of the IMF, once telling them to 'shut up!'. However, again and again throughout ZANU's history, Mugabe had reserved his most revolutionary sounding rhetoric for those occasions when left-wing political threats appeared (namely, the National Working People's Convention and an emerging opposition party). As a US banker observed as early as 1982, 'I feel it is a political pattern that Mugabe give radical, anti-business speeches before government makes pro-business decisions or announcements.'[52]

Mugabe's defeat by Tsvangirai's movement in a referendum on constitutional reform in February 2000, together with another forex crisis and petrol shortage, amplified his desperation. To save forex, Mugabe autho-rised finance minister Herbert Murewa not to repay bank loans in February 2000. Moreover, anxious to retain rural votes in the parliamentary election scheduled for June 2000, Mugabe condoned and encouraged land invasions of more than 20% of Zimbabwe's white-owned farms. The situation degenerated into deeper economic crisis and sustained conflict verging on anarchy.

By October 2000, Zimbabwe had accumulated six months of World Bank arrears and, desperate to regain access to hard currency, Mugabe authorised the new technocrat finance minister, Simba Makoni, to begin paying the World Bank. By paying $50 million, Mugabe hoped for $140 million in new loans, but this was quite a gamble. Indeed, Zimbabwe had joined the list of countries like Iraq, Yemen and the Democratic Republic of the Congo considered to be basket cases. Confusingly, the opposition MDC spent 2000 calling for both the Zimbabwe Democracy Act to be passed on Capitol Hill (sponsored mainly by white, conservative Republicans), which would prohibit new IMF/World Bank loans to Zimbabwe, and for more IMF/World Bank-type economic programmes. The contradictions will perhaps be resolved by the presidential election in 2002, but whether the MDC will turn left or right on economic policy if they win it is still up in the air.[53]

In sum, Zimbabwe's post-1997 plunge can, at a superficial level, be traced to the problems Mugabe himself caused with one political blunder after another. But it is also more generally a direct outcome of the context of the early 1990s in which, structurally, his government's power and his own decisions were repeatedly limited, conditioned and ultimately reversed by Washington.[54]

Mozambique under Washington's thumb

The ability of the IMF and the World Bank to wield such power becomes even more obvious when one considers other Southern African countries. Impoverished Mozambique provides a third example of the way IMF and World Bank influence is felt in the region, especially in relation to debt relief, because it was considered to be one of the star pupils of Washington during the late 1990s, following rigidly conservative monetary policies and privatising large sections of the economy.[55]

Mozambique was plunged into deep depression throughout the 1980s, in part because of ineffective development policies, but mainly because of a devastating civil war sponsored by first Rhodesia and then Pretoria, costing approximately one million lives and at least $20 billion in physical destruction. Facing debt service obligations to international creditors (initially the Eastern Bloc, and later Western governments and commercial suppliers) that consumed 93% of export earnings by 1991, Mozambique could typically afford to repay only a small proportion of the loans (making up only around 25% of trade inflows), but still far more than the health and education budgets combined. So the foreign debt of $5.6 billion was 'rolled over' periodically. In 1998, for example, Mozambique repaid only $110 million that year.

In 1996, the IMF and World Bank launched their 'Highly-Indebted Poor Countries' initiative, and Mozambique was a high-profile pilot project. But harsh conditions were attached to the paltry debt relief, as expressed in a letter sent to President Joaqim Chissano of Mozambique by James Wolfensohn, president of the World Bank, in March 1998. These conditions involved:

- the privatisation of municipal water (which required, in a classic public-squeeze-prior-to-private-profiteering policy, the 'sharp' rise in water tariffs, which were 'to be increased even further prior to the signing of management contracts');
- the quintupling of patient fees for public-health services over a five-year period; and
- the privatisation and simultaneous liberalisation of the important cashew-nut processing industry (which led to the collapse of most factories and 10 000 job losses – mainly of women – until finally, after vibrant national debate, the Mozambique parliament reversed the policy in January 2001).[56]

A year later, more than 70 new conditions emerged in the next IMF debt-relief package, including a recommendation that parliament make the tax structure more regressive (i.e. so that the rich would pay a decreasing share of their income). At this stage, the IMF used new jargon in applying its neo-liberal conditionality to the rural water sector, stating that the aim of its programme was that of 'transforming the planning and delivery of rural water and sanitation services from a supply-driven model to a sustained demand responsive model, characterised by community management, cost recovery, and the involvement of the private sector'.[57] Trendy language cannot disguise the fact that such a 'demand responsive model' was an increasingly discredited development strategy, having failed dramatically when applied to rural water projects in far wealthier countries like South Africa (leading in 2000–01 to tens of thousands of cholera cases). Such cost-recovery strategies simply don't work in a country in which 70% of the population live below the poverty line. Still, for mainly ideological reasons, the World Bank continued pushing 100% cost-recovery policies on water projects across Africa, while lobbying African governments 'to move away from the concept of free water for all'.[58]

In 1999, however, increased public pressure against the IMF and World Bank – including Chissano's own public frustration over HIPC – led to slightly greater concessions for Mozambique, and repayments fell to $73 million and then to $58 million by 2001. Nevertheless, the IMF and World Bank remained crudely callous towards Mozambique's grinding poverty, and were unmoved even by the floods that devastated Mozambique in January and February 2000. Instead of providing more debt cancellation, Washington offered only to reschedule repayment by adding the amount due that year to the end of the amortisation schedule.

So, for one of the world's poorest countries, the experience of HIPC debt relief shows how the combination of international financial power, unrepayable debt and the Washington Consensus economic philosophy can be a lethal combination. In part because of experiences such as Mozambique's, and in part because the implications of the financial volatility experienced by Zimbabwe and South Africa were so threatening, an international movement arose during the 1990s to contest the Bretton Woods institutions, aiming not only for reforms, but for their complete closure.

We investigate that social movement in Part four, following discussions of the South African government's strategy for reforming the Bretton Woods twins and the world economy, and the tragic failure to make headway against the global apartheid implicit in differential access to HIV-AIDS treatment. However, a final example of dominance over South Africa by Washington and its allies should first be considered, namely overseas development aid.

Notes

1 A key Zimbabwean was Callisto Madavo, who became World Bank vice-president for Africa. Other South Africans included Hennie van Greuning (former registrar of banks at the Reserve Bank in Pretoria during a crucial period of deregulation and financial chaos in the early 1990s), Kam Chetty (once a left-wing Cape Town NGO activist, then a civil-society fixer for the World Bank's Pretoria office), Roland White (former anti-apartheid student leader, later responsible for many of the worst neo-liberal processes in municipal infrastructure when he worked for the Department of Finance in Pretoria during the late 1990s), Alan Gelb, a pro-liberalisation trade economist, and Jeff Rackie, an urban planner, all of whom played damaging roles in South Africa's socio-economic development processes in the 1990s. An interesting exception was that of Ismail Lagardien, former executive committee member of the Azanian People's Organisation, then main assistant to Trevor Manuel when he was SA minister of trade and industry, and then speechwriter for Joseph Stiglitz when as World Bank chief economist he unveiled the 'Post-Washington Consensus' critique of the IMF.

2 Amongst other Southern Africans who were highly regarded in the international activist community were Bishop Bernadino Mandlate from Maputo, Jonah Gokova and Davie Malungisa from the Zimbabwe Coalition on Debt and Development, Godfrey Kinyenze of the Zimbabwe Congress of Trade Unions, Mauritian activists Rajni Lallah and Alain Ah-Vee, Zambian economist Opa Kapijimpanga from the Harare-based African Debt and Development Network, Rosemary Nyerere Mwamakula and Rogate Mshana from the Tanzania Debt and Development Coalition and World Council of Churches, and Francis N'Gambi and Michael Nyirenda of the Malawi Debt and Development Coalition.

In South Africa, other key global-issue activists/strategists included Jubilee 2000's Neville Gabriel, community/women's activists Mercia Andrews and

Lindelwe Nxu, NGO leader Abie Ditlhake, Jubilee South co-ordinator Donna Andrews, Johannesburg media activist Ashraf Patel, SA Municipal Worker Union staffers Roger Ronnie, Lance Viotte and Anna Weekes, environmentalists Bobby Peek, Chris Albertyn, Richard Sherman, Tebogo Phadu, Jessica Wilson and Liane Greeff, health activist Zackie Achmat and several Alternative Information and Development Centre associates (Trevor Ngwane, Andrews, Carl Brecker, Brian Ashley, Dot Keet, Jeff Rudin and George Dor).

Combatting the WTO with extraordinary effectiveness were Mohau Pheko of the Africa Trade Network in Johannesburg, Kato Lambrechts of the Institute for Global Dialogue (subsequently Christian Aid), and the brilliant Ugandan political economist Yash Tandon, based in Harare. Amongst South African labour activists with international influence were Cosatu's Zwelinzima Vavi and Ibrahim Patel (although their role at the WTO Seattle protests was severely compromised by their collaboration with the controversial South African delegation).

Many other South African militants not only thought globally but worked locally, concentrating on building opposition to the IMF/World Bank at local level (with marches and events on 26 September 2000 in Johannesburg, Durban, Cape Town, Pietersburg and East London), including Campaign Against Neoliberalism in South Africa, the SA Non-Governmental Organisations Coalition, the SA Communist Party, the 'Keep Left' collective, the Anti-Privatisation Forum, the Treatment Action Campaign, the Northern Province's Movement for Delivery, the Soweto Electricity Crisis Committee, Jubilee chapters in KwaZulu-Natal, Western Cape, Eastern Cape, Northern Province and Gauteng, a few other progressive thinktanks (such as the International Labour Research and Information Group, the National Institute for Economic Policy, the National Labour and Economic Development Institute, and the Institute for Global Dialogue), environmental groups (Environmental Monitoring Group, Earthlife Africa, Group for Environmental Monitoring and GroundWork) and the more advanced trade unions in Cosatu (especially the SA Municipal Workers Union, the SA Democratic Teachers Union and the National Education, Health and Allied Workers Union).

The main activist perspectives are analysed in Part four.

3 For background, see Block, F. (1977), *The Origins of International Economic Disorder*, Berkeley, University of California Press; Parboni, R. (1981), *The Dollar and its Rivals*, London, Verso; Wachtel, H. (1986), *The Money Mandarins*, New York, Pantheon; Wood, R. (1988), *From Marshall Plan to Debt Crisis*, Berkeley, University of California Press; and Caufield, C. (1997), *Masters of Illusion: The World Bank and the Poverty of Nations*, London, Macmillan.

4 For example, during the Great Depression, when the previous excesses of financiers were addressed in US legislation, strict regulatory constraints affected the domestic operations of American banks – including bans on interstate banking, harsh restrictions on the scope of banking activities, and severe limits on the amount of interest that banks could pay depositors. This led to increasing pressure to explore foreign markets. An 'interest equalization tax' was imposed in the hope of making capital flight more costly, but actually encouraged it in the long run by providing an unprecedented incentive to US banks to set up foreign branches immune from the regulation. Under such domestic constraints, major US banks spent the 1960s rapidly expanding their international branch networks in search of new markets. Eleven US banks had 181 foreign branches in 1964; by 1974, 129 US banks operated 737 foreign branches. For details, see Mayer, M. (1984), *The Money Bazaars*, New York, Simon & Schuster.

5 Andreff, W. (1984), 'The International Centralization of Capital and the Reordering of World Capitalism', *Capital and Class*, 22, p. 62.
6 Grou, P. (1985), *The Financial Structure of Multinational Capitalism*, Leamington Spa, Berg, p. 198.
7 Brenner, R. (2001), *Turbulence in the World Economy*, London, Verso.
8 Hawley, J. (1984), 'Protecting Capital from Itself: U.S. Attempts to Regulate the Eurocurrency System', *International Organization*, 38(4). Eurodollars are unregulated dollar deposits that are held in banks outside the US; they were first created by the Chinese and Soviets in the 1950s to guard against US government confiscation, but only became important as a source of funds in international financial markets in the mid-1960s.
9 Van der Pijl, K. (1984), *The Making of an Atlantic Ruling Class*, London, Verso, pp. 254–71.
10 Evans, T. (1985), 'Money Makes the World Go Round', *Capital and Class*, 24.
11 MacEwan, A. (1986), 'International Debt and Banking: Rising Instability within the General Crisis', *Science and Society,* 50(2); Watkins, A. (1987), *Till Debt do us Part*, Washington, DC, Carnegie Foundation.
12 Whereas 20–25 countries were in default each year during the 1930s, that number never exceeded eight during the 1950s and 1960s. Suter, C. (1992), *Debt Cycles in the World Economy*, Boulder, Westview Press, p. 63.
13 Phillips, R. (1983), 'The Role of the International Monetary Fund in the Post-Bretton Woods Era', *Review of Radical Political Economics*, 15(2).
14 Morgan Guarantee World Bank (1986), *World Financial Markets*, New York, Morgan Guarantee; Henry, J. S. (1986), 'Where the Money Went', *New Republic*, 14 April.
15 Clarke, S. (1988), *Keynesianism, Monetarism and the Crisis of the State*, Aldergate, Edward Elgar.
16 MacEwan, A. (1990), *Debt and Disorder: International Economic Instability and US Imperial Decline*, New York, Monthly Review Press.
17 Gulhati, R. (1987), 'Recent Reforms in Africa: A Preliminary Political Economy Perspective', Washington, DC, World Bank.
18 More details are found in Bond, P. (2001), 'Do Dams Mainly Serve the Rich?: Lessons from Southern Africa', in C. Miller (ed.), *History in Dispute: Water*, Farmington Hills, Gale Publishing.
19 The Kariba loan entailed a major innovation in international-infrastructure project-finance packaging: World Bank – £28.6 million; Central African Federation (loan raised from copper companies) – £28 million; Commonwealth Development Corporation – £15 million; and Commonwealth Development Finance Co. Ltd. – £3 million. Details can be found in Bond, P. (1999), 'Paying for Southern African Dams: The Social Financing Gap', paper presented by the Group for Environmental Monitoring, International Rivers Network and Environmental Monitoring Group, to the World Commission on Dams Africa Regional Conference, Cairo, 23 November.
20 Leys, C. (1959), *European Politics in Southern Rhodesia*, Oxford, Oxford University Press, p. 111.
21 Reynolds, N., Masundire, H., Mwinga, D., Offord, R. and Siamwiza, B. (1999), 'Kariba Dam Case Study: Scoping Paper: Final Report', submission to the World Commission on Dams, Cape Town, August.
22 Advisory Committee (J. Phillips, J. Hammond, L. H. Samuels, and R. J. M. Swynnerton) (1962), *Report of the Advisory Committee: The Development of the Economic Resources of Southern Rhodesia with Particular Reference to the*

Role of African Agriculture, Salisbury, Southern Rhodesia Ministry of Native Affairs, p. 87.

23 Handford, J. (1976), *Portrait of an Economy Under Sanctions, 1965–1975*, Salisbury, Mercury Press, p. 148. When the illegal Unilateral Declaration of Independence was announced by Ian Smith in 1965, he also defaulted on World Bank loan repayments amounting to several million pounds.

24 Cited in Arrighi, G. (1973), 'The Political Economy of Rhodesia', in G. Arrighi and J. Saul, *Essays on the Political Economy of Africa*, New York, Monthly Review Press, p. 362.

25 Payer, C. (1982), *The World Bank*, New York, Monthly Review Press, pp. 239–40.

26 *Property and Finance*, May 1956.

27 See Bond, P. (2001), 'A Political Economy of Dam Building and Water Supply in Lesotho and South Africa', in D. McDonald (ed.), *Environmental Justice in South Africa*, London, James Currey and Columbus, University of Ohio Press.

28 World Bank (1999), *South Africa: Country Assistance Strategy*, Washington, DC, 2 March.

29 Pretoria's unbalanced military relationship with Lesotho revived in September 1998, when, in order to rescue a friendly government threatened by popular unrest and a coup, SA National Defense Force troops flew by helicopter to the first LHWP dam, Katse, and killed 17 Lesotho army troops in order to secure the area, while the capital city Maseru was burned and looted.

30 See Horta, K. (1995), 'The Mountain Kingdom's White Oil: The Lesotho Highlands Water Project', *The Ecologist*, 25(6) and (1996) 'Making the Earth Rumble: The Lesotho-South Africa Water Connection', *Multinational Monitor*, May; Potts, M. (1996), 'Presentation by the DBSA to the Lesotho Highlands Water Workshop', in Group for Environmental Monitoring (ed.), *Record of Proceedings: Lesotho Highlands Water Workshop*, Johannesburg, 29–30 August 1996; Bond, P. (1997), 'Lesotho Dammed', *Multinational Monitor*, January–February.

31 *Business Day*, 5 August 1999; *Washington Post*, 13 September 1999.

32 Addison, G. (1998), 'Dam It, Let's Pour Concrete', *The Saturday Star*, 3 November.

33 Archer, R. (1996), *Trust in Construction? The Lesotho Highlands Water Project*, London, Christian Aid and Maseru, Christian Council of Lesotho, pp. 58–9.

34 World Bank Inspection Panel (1998), *Lesotho/South Africa: Phase 1B of Lesotho Highlands Water Project: Panel Report and Recommendation*, Washington, DC, 19 August, p. 81.

35 Roome, J. (1995), 'Water Pricing and Management: World Bank Presentation to the SA Water Conservation Conference', unpublished power-point presentation, South Africa, 2 October, p. 51. The World Bank (1999), *South Africa: Country Assistance Strategy*, Annex C, p. 5 declared that Roome's 'power-point presentation to Department of Water Affairs' was 'instrumental in facilitating a radical revision in South Africa's approach to bulk water management'. The World Bank was also instrumental in retail water-related infrastructure investment, through its lead authorship of the 1994–5 *Urban Infrastructure Investment Framework* commissioned by then-RDP minister Jay Naidoo.

36 Details are to be found in Letsie, D. and Bond, P. (2000), 'Debating Supply and Demand Features of Bulk Infrastructure: Lesotho-Johannesburg Water Transfer', in M. Khosa (ed.), *Empowerment through Service Delivery*, Pretoria, Human Sciences Research Council.

37 Details are provided in Bond, P. (2000), *Elite Transition: From Apartheid to Neoliberalism in South Africa*, London, Pluto Press, Chapter 5.

38 World Bank, *op. cit.*, p. 18.

39 Tellingly, rural mission leader Robert Christiansen and the director of a local World Bank-aligned research NGO (the Land and Agricultural Policy Centre) flagged 'a suspicion on the part of many South Africans that the focus of the World Bank's program in any country was the need to lend and to dictate policy as a precondition to that lending'. Christiansen, R. and Cooper, D. (1994), 'Presentation to 14th Symposium on Agriculture in Liberalizing Economies', Washington, DC.

40 See World Bank (1998) World Development Report: Knowledge and Development, Washington, DC.

41 World Bank (1997), 'South Africa: Industrial Competitiveness and Job Creation Project', Washington, DC, Africa Regional Office.

42 World Bank, South Africa: Country Assistance Strategy, p.18.

43 Virtually all Gear's targets were missed by vast margins. National Institute for Economic Policy, NGQO: An Economic Bulletin, 1(1), http://www.niep.org.za, pp. 1–3.

44 World Bank, South Africa: Country Assistance Strategy, pp. 19, 35 and 43.

45 Zimbabwe Congress of Trade Unions (1996), Beyond ESAP, Harare, pp. 61 and i.

46 Herald, 22 February 1983.

47 World Bank (1992), Zimbabwe: Power Project, Washington, DC, Energy Division, Eastern African Regional Office, Report #3884-ZIM, p. 3.

48 Bond, P. (1998), Uneven Zimbabwe, Trenton, Africa World Press, Chapter 10.

49 Bond, P. (1999), 'Zimbabwe's Political Reawakening', Monthly Review, 50(11).

50 Financial Gazette, 12 March 1999.

51 Agence France-Presse, 20 July 1999.

52 Hanlon, J. (1988), Beggar Thy Neighbour, London, James Currey, p. 35.

53 I have laid out more detailed arguments along these lines in Bond, P. (2000), 'Movement for Democratic Change at the Eddie Crossroads', Southern Africa Report, second quarter; (2001), 'Radical Rhetoric and the Working Class during Zimbabwean Nationalism's Dying Days', Journal of World Systems Research, May; and (2001), 'Inward versus Outward Orientation in Post-Nationalist Zimbabwe', Labour, Capital and Society.

54 As I argue in Uneven Zimbabwe, the economic crisis dates back further, to the mid-1970s, when overaccumulation became a severe problem.

55 More background on the destructive role of the IMF in Mozambique can be found in Hanlon, J. (1997), Peace without Profit, London, James Currey.

56 Details provided in Bond, P. (1998), 'Mozambican Parliament Questions Debt Management', Sunday Independent, 21 December; and see rebuttal letters from the World Bank's Mozambique officer Phyllis Pomerantz on 24 January 1999, and from myself and Joe Hanlon on 7 February 1999 and 11 July 1999. See also Denny, C. and Elliott, L. (1999), 'Fund Admits Debt Plans will Fail Poor', Guardian, 19 April.

57 International Monetary Fund (1999), Mozambique: Enhanced Structural Adjustment Facility Framework Paper for April 1999–March 2002, Washington, DC.

58 World Bank (2000), Sourcebook on Community Driven Development in the Africa Region: Community Action Programs, Washington, DC, Africa Regional Office, 17 March (signatories: Calisto Madavo and Jean-Louis Sarbib), Annex 2.

CHAPTER FOUR

Foreign aid, development and underdevelopment

1. Introduction

The ongoing global economic crisis is unevenly experienced, as Chapter one has shown. Washington's capacity to stall and shift the crisis generated a degree of relative prosperity during the 1990s within the advanced capitalist countries of the Organisation for Economic Co-operation and Development (OECD). Yet donor aid by OECD member states accounted for less than a quarter of 1% of their GDP in 1998, the lowest figure since statistics began in 1950 (and far lower than the 0.7% agreed to at the Rio Earth Summit in 1992). As persistent development-aid failures and corruption led to alleged public-opinion 'aid fatigue', the real value of North-South aid fell during the 1990s by a third.[1] Already by January 1995, President Nelson Mandela had famously criticised President Clinton for his three-year, $600 million aid package through the US Agency for International Development (USAID): 'It's peanuts. We would have expected from the United States far more than that.'[2]

Yet even in declining amounts, aid remains a vital determinant of the political and economic conditions of many recipient countries. For increasingly dependent recipients in Sub-Saharan Africa (aside from South Africa), aid/GDP ratios soared from 6% from 1975–84 to 13% by the early 1990s. Relations between aid and development also reveal a great deal about international and local power structures and struggles.

South Africa was pledged approximately $5 billion in foreign development-related aid from 1994 to 1999, an enormous sum compared to other, more desperate, African countries. The grants and loans that were 'pledged' – though not fully committed, disbursed or implemented – to Pretoria in this period included vast funds from the European Union ($1.75 billion), United States ($800 million) and Japan ($550 million). The degree to which funding actually reached beneficiaries was highly variable, with 'delivery' areas like rural water or roads recording very low levels. One report judged that the aid record of the largest donor, the EU, was 'abysmal', in part because its ratio of money actually committed to that pledged was just

51%, and the amount disbursed compared to that committed was only 13%.[3] Even by mid-1999, fully two-thirds of the previous five-years' worth of EU pledges had not been spent.[4] Yet while government could not disburse its own development-related monies in housing, infrastructure, land reform and many other fields, due to lack of capacity, foreign donors simultaneously shifted from funding civil society to funding the state, as I will describe below.

Although it is small in comparison to the wide variety of state spending programmes, at just 2% of the national budget, aid contributes a substantial share to South African development funding, particularly of capital projects. Given that the state spends a large amount of its budget (90%) on recurrent costs, foreign aid can be decisive in shifting capital expenditure into areas donors decide – although sometimes without much reference to sustainability, maintenance and infrastructure. It was presumed that many aid missions would end their work after 1999, once democratic development policies were established and implementation got under way, but most have continued to justify a presence on the basis of unfulfilled programme and project implementation.

Studies of post-1994 aid to South Africa are only now beginning in earnest.[5] Donors, state officials and civil society recipients are reliant for assessments upon popular perceptions sometimes captured in the media, and upon hidden consultancy reports. The largely negative character of the former and apolitical nature of the latter are themselves of interest. Until a more comprehensive investigation into donor activity is published,[6] this chapter merely captures some of the main debating points that have arisen in both popular and behind-the-scenes analysis. Three key issues that emerge from even an initial review of the aid industry include aid as a tool of foreign policy leverage, the appropriateness of hard-currency loans for development and the uneven impact of donor aid on civil society. I will consider each below.

2. Dependency and leverage
The incentives for donors to give aid are diverse. Amsterdam-based aid critic David Sogge argues that the economic agenda behind much aid includes access to markets, commercial rivalry and acquisition of local primary products. Beneficiaries include

> agribusinesses; purveyors of arms, aircraft, vehicles, pharmaceuticals and engineering services; and universities, which accepted African bursary holders ... Consultants and other bearers of technical assistance for SSA have accounted for about one-third of all aid flows ... [As a result,] public sector management is weakened, due to national policies being segmented into discreet projects designed by and for the aid system; internal brain-drain to agencies from the public service; and aid agencies developing 'kingdoms' in

specified provinces, cities or 'development corridors', thus distorting internal relationships and blocking coherent national policy development ... The
aid system has shifted accountability toward foreign funders and away from
voters and taxpayers, undermining citizen-state reciprocity.[7]

Concerns over dependency and increasing donor leverage remain widespread. Less than a year after South Africa's first democratic election, the
then-president of the National Union of Mineworkers, James Motlatsi,
pronounced, 'South Africa must be independent of foreign aid ... Then we
will be able to get on with our independence without having to look continually over our shoulders in case we are being destabilised.'[8]

Policy destabilisation

The degree to which aid influences policy in South Africa is hotly debated.
The influential advisory role of the World Bank, often through 'donor co-
ordination' projects, has tended to reinforce the perception that aid is
tightly bound up with the broader neo-liberal agenda of shrinking the state.
Although virtually no loans were requested by South Africa, there have
been many other means of World Bank policy persuasion, including 'just-
in-time policy availability', training sessions and strategic visits by South
Africans to World Bank headquarters. World Bank teams have successfully
introduced neo-liberal policy advice in areas such as macroeconomic policy,
the basic housing and infrastructure programme, land reform, national
water pricing, welfare-programme cuts and the like. In even a policy matter
as obscure (yet as vital) as bulk-water pricing, the World Bank describes its
advisory role as 'instrumental'.[9]

Yet while there is usually some motivation by donors to induce policy
changes, this is not always successful. Foreign aid 'has had no net effect on
the recipients' growth rate or the quality of their economic policies',
according to World Bank aid researchers David Dollar and Craig Burnside,
in a study of post-1970 donations that attempts to shift blame for ineffectual neo-liberalism to aid recipients: 'We got into thinking we could induce
countries to reform. But it turns out this was wrong.'[10] The occasional unre-
liability of foreign aid as policy leverage is reflected in the case of Taiwanese
donations to South Africa. In 1994, these were apparently aimed initially at
currying political favour with the ANC – a donation of $10 million to the
party prior to the first election was cited as one basis for retaining official
SA recognition of Taiwan instead of the People's Republic of China (PRC)[11]
– and later at influencing government policy for the same reason by the
supply or withholding of development aid. Thus, when in 1996 South
Africa reversed its position by recognising the PRC, the furious Taiwanese
foreign minister, John Chang, suspended grants to South Africa worth $80
million and loans worth $50 million.

FOREIGN AID, DEVELOPMENT AND UNDERDEVELOPMENT   83

Debate has also raged over the European Union's interests in South Africa, particularly in relation to the EU-SA free-trade agreement in March 1999, to which continued grant aid is integrally tied. The 12-year deal allows South Africa slightly more time than EU firms for adaptation to declining import protection. But extremely severe competition from European imports is anticipated in sectors as diverse as clothing and automobiles. The free-trade agreement was controversial in part because at the last moment, in April 1999, Germany and Holland requested a brand new and seemingly unrelated repatriation clause for illegal aliens from South Africa, and because southern European countries demanded greater agricultural protection, particularly against SA use of traditional brand names of alcohol.[12]

US strings attached
Tied service contracts represent a highly visible way in which foreign aid supports donor constituencies. These are not unlike the tied commodity-import programmes that are popular amongst aid agencies so as to assure donor-country sales of farm and related equipment to aid recipients. Even conservative commentator Simon Barber of *Business Day* newspaper alleged that Clinton's $600 million aid package to South Africa for 1994–6 was a 'sleight of hand', because $72 million were for US export promotion and at least $75 million were not in grants, but rather loan guarantees on housing loans.[13] US donor programmes came under further suspicion as Republican Party pressure emerged in 1995 to cut the US government aid budget, for defenders argued that they benefitted Americans as much as South Africans.

As Andrew Young, former US representative to the United Nations, noted when organising his 'Constituency for Africa' against the 1995 Republican Party threat to cut aid, 'We get a five to one return on investment in Africa, through our trade, investment, finance and aid. Don't you see, we're not aiding Africa by sending them aid, Africa's aiding us.' At the same Constituency for Africa meeting, Washington-based aid consultant Joseph Szlavik warned African aid recipients: 'Pay more attention to their voting in the United Nations, trying to meet the US position more often than they currently do. By moving forward, African countries will be able to "win friends and influence people" as the saying goes.'[14]

Most evidently, this was the case when in early 1997 President Clinton threatened to withdraw aid shortly after the South African cabinet approved arms sales to Syria in December 1996, which the US considers a terrorist state. According to one press report, 'In the toughest public warning it has ever issued to President Nelson Mandela's government, the Clinton administration said yesterday it was "deeply concerned" by cabinet's provisional approval of a R3bn arms sale (aim-enhancing gear for

Soviet-made tanks) to Syria, and might be obliged under US law to suspend aid to SA.'[15] Although Mandela replied in March 1997 that it was immoral to abandon countries that had supported the ANC in the anti-apartheid fight 'on the advice of countries that were friends of the apartheid regime' (i.e. the US), defence minister Joe Modise confirmed that a marketing permit was issued for the arms, but that, in the wake of the US warning, 'We did not tender, as no documentation was received from Syria.'[16]

Later, South Africa's Medicines and Related Substances Control Amendment Act of 1997 (especially Section 15c) raised a major controversy because it threatened the interests of US, and to some extent European, pharmaceutical companies by promoting cheaper imports of generic drugs.[17] In response, the companies used congressional allies to (unsuccessfully) pressure the US government in 1998 to 'prohibit aid to the SA government until Congress receives a report containing the plan of action to negotiate the repeal, suspension or termination of section 15c'.[18] As Chapter 9 will show, only pressure from grassroots activists was sufficient to reverse the US strategy.

What sometimes appears as overt US involvement in South African politics is also widely condemned. At the 50th conference of the ANC in December 1997, Mandela harshly criticised USAID policies for having a political agenda, especially in support of NGO opposition groups.[19] As *Business Day* stated, 'When government first voiced its concern about NGOs receiving foreign donor support, fears were heightened that Pretoria wanted to undermine the independence of NGOs – a crucial feature of these organisations.' Still, editorialised *Business Day*, 'SA needs to be careful of unnecessarily alienating foreign donors. Aid agencies should not be confused with charities. Whether one likes it or not, they are instruments of foreign policy, designed to further their governments' political and commercial interests.'[20]

In 1998, a confidential internal US government report more explicitly accused USAID officials of 'extreme and unqualified meddling' in SA policy-making.[21] Rev. Frank Chikane, a key Mbeki advisor, commented at the time that donors must 'loosen aid strings, including the use of foreign nationals', who should be 'a last resort in development projects. If the necessary expertise is not available in SA, it will be sourced from anywhere in the world, not necessarily from the donor nation as is now currently the practice.'[22]

3. Currency risk on loans

A major trend in the aid industry is the evolution of donor grants into loans. The most active aid-related lenders were the EU and Japan (whose grant/loan ratios were $740/$675 million and $40/$500 million, respectively). Should South Africa take foreign aid in the form of hard currency loans? According to the Reconstruction and Development

Programme, 'The RDP must use foreign debt financing only for those elements of the programme that can potentially increase our capacity for foreign earnings.'[23] As the SA National Civic Organisation explained in 1994 in its report, *Making People-Driven Development Work,*

> The reason for the hard line on foreign borrowing is three-fold. First, South Africa is awash with capital, and at least in the short term does not need to borrow abroad. Second, and more important, is the much reported foreign debt trap. Foreign loans are denominated in foreign currency – dollars, yen, ecu, etc. During the coming years, the Rand will continue to devalue against those currencies, so that even if the interest rate is very low in dollar terms the effective cost in Rand may be much higher. This, in turn, is cyclic – if foreign borrowing is high then international financial institutions such as the IMF push for further devaluation, which further increases the Rand repayments. Thus, the more foreign debt South Africa takes, the more onerous become the repayment conditions. Many countries – including industrialising ones like South Africa – have been caught in this trap and found that supposedly soft loans became a millstone around their neck. Third, no foreign loan is truly unconditional – there are always restrictions on the use of the loan or on government economic policy, and these impose a substantial hidden cost (pp. 60–1).

Mixed signals

The RDP foreign-loan provision was widely accepted, even in the business press.[24] Thus in 1998, South Africa turned down $75 million worth of Japanese loans for KwaZulu-Natal bulk-water development and the upgrading of Eastern Cape rural roads because, as one report noted, 'the requirement to provide only yen-denominated loans was making Japanese loans only marginally cheaper. This signals an increasingly cautious approach to foreign aid by government.' The Department of Finance itself explained, 'Due to exchange rate risks, and increased costs associated with taking out forward cover, the landed cost of the loans is only marginally cheaper than loan facilities on the local market.'[25]

However, foreign development lending still continues, particularly to South Africa's major foreign parastatal borrowers, such as the Development Bank of Southern Africa. With the currency suffering periodic declines, including two bouts of 30% nominal devaluation over a few weeks in early 1996 and mid-1998, as well as a 25% drop during 2000, repaying such loans in cases where there are no offsetting hard-currency income sources is bound to be prohibitively expensive. For many years, South Africa avoided a World Bank loan estimated in the range of $750 million for basic infrastructure. As Kgalema Motlanthe put it, 'Once you start taking loans from the World Bank and IMF, they can tell you even who your finance minister must be.'[26] Yet rumours continually resurfaced of that loan's resurrection in the Departments of Provincial and Local Government, and Finance.

4. Civil society expectations

The most debilitating experience for many civil society organisations since 1994 was being unceremoniously dumped by donors, at a time when donor funding for government was going unspent. According to the South African NGO Coalition (Sangoco, an advocacy group with 3 000 member organisations that include both NGOs and community-based organisations or CBOs):

> Despite the commitment signalled by Government in the *Reconstruction and Development Programme* (RDP), NGOs and CBOs in South Africa have come to experience a massive crisis of unparalleled proportion in the present transition. The root of the crisis lies in the major funding squeeze that the sector is experiencing. Major international donors, corporate and other donors, anticipating the new government would step in to fund this sector have reprioritised their allocation of development finance, withdrawn or claim that they are putting their money in government for the RDP. This has resulted in the sector experiencing a major funding drain and many organisations collapsing.[27]

Yet at the same time, a proliferation of Northern-based NGOs and donor agencies appeared in South Africa, with some taking on functions of support to community development once performed by organic South African NGOs. As a result, South African civil-society organisations have lobbied strenuously for an indigenous donor agency. The main vehicle chosen by the government to channel foreign aid to NGOs (including CBOs, other development organisations and the labour movement) is the National Development Agency (NDA), formerly known as the Transitional National Development Trust (TNDT). The TNDT emerged, in a bureaucratic and tardy manner, during the intensifying funding crisis immediately following the first democratic elections in 1994. It is generally accepted that the establishment of the TNDT and NDA represented belated and inadequate responses to the decline in funding.

Strangling civil society

Perhaps the two most widely held concerns on the establishment of a conduit of funding from government to civil society are the long delays in these structures becoming operational, resulting in lengthy 'funding gaps', and the small amounts of money assigned to these institutions. The two funding gaps occurred between 1994 and 1997 and from 1998 until 2000, when, after many delays, the NDA became operational. Even as late as mid-2000, however, many TNDT recipients were denied NDA funds, and collapsed.[28]

The South African government promised to fund the NDA to the tune of R50 million in its first year of operation, R165 million in the second year and R265 million in the third, which represents an increased commitment. This is nevertheless still well short of the amount required to provide adequate support to the sector. The Independent Development Trust's promised contribution of R100 million was well short of the support it could provide, given its reserves in excess of R1 billion. There were interminable delays experienced in the Department of Trade and Industry in disbursal of lottery monies to NGOs and charities. The EU, as the only major contributor to the TNDT aside from government, played an important role, yet the contribution of R70 million during the late 1990s represents an average of a mere R15 million a year. A further EU promise of 30 million euros over three years represents a declining ratio of EU funding compared to government funding.[29]

Moreover, debate has raged over which sectors should be funded and which shouldn't. In 1997, for example, the Nedlac Community Constituency attacked the NDA Advisory Committee's *Final Report*: 'It fails to recognise the potential problems and pitfalls of a body which engages in both funding and determining development policy, that is, determining what is to be funded. It is inadvertently assigning a gatekeeper role to the organisation.' Sangoco, in a report on the proposed funder, added: 'The principal role of the NDA should be that of being a conduit for development grant finance to NGOs and CBOs, who should be the implementing agents of development projects and the recipient beneficiaries of grant funds.'[30]

5. Attributing blame

Are the complaints about foreign development aid recorded above convincing? They must be tempered by the South African government's own enormous shortcomings in managing aid. The ANC had, after all, promised to 'introduce measures to ensure that foreign governmental and non-governmental aid supports the RDP',[31] but, in fact, failed to do so, in part because its own policies often directly violated the RDP.[32]

To some extent, contradictory policies, weak programmes and unsustainable projects were major factors in the failure of foreign funded development. Financial sustainability was a perennial problem, for typically once capital spending has generated some form of physical infrastructure, donors have achieved what they want and move on to the next project, without sufficient concern about the recipients' ability to afford the recurrent operating and maintenance costs of the project. This was remarked upon by finance minister Chris Liebenberg: 'Donors often insist that aid is used to build something like a hospital or township but forget that the government is left to put in the infrastructure and maintenance which puts a tremendous strain on the budget which is struggling to meet basic needs.'[33]

Moreover, the South African government's own oversight of donor activity has left much to be desired. The representative responsible for managing aid – in the case of the EU's $1.75 billion, for example – was the deputy-minister of finance (from 1994 to 1996, Alec Erwin, and from 1996 to 1999, Gill Marcus). As the EU's *South Africa Country Review* put it, however, 'there is no real involvement [by the deputy-minister of finance] … in terms of policy dialogue on national priorities and the main focus of EU support. As far as coordination is concerned, no framework has been set up for dialogue between government and the donor community as a whole; the dialogue is organised at bilateral level between SA and the donor concerned.'[34]

Moreover, in fields like education and health, according to the same EU report, there was 'no real institutional framework for donor coordination; it is the case with the Ministry of Education, to a lesser extent with the Ministry of Health, and this has a negative influence on the implementation of the programme'. Although this was partly due to the provincial responsibility for implementation in these areas, the Department of Trade and Industry was also criticised by the EU for 'weak capacities at technical and administrative level'.[35]

It may be possible to conclude, therefore, that there are extremely good – and some bad – reasons for foreign aid to have generated negative perceptions in the post-apartheid era. Many of these reasons can, ultimately, be located at the levels of specific policies, programmes and projects within the South African state. However, enough additional concerns about the agendas and *modus operandi* of donors are raised by these experiences to suggest the need for a fundamental rethink.

This was also the conclusion arrived at from a balanced analysis of aid across Africa, conducted during 2000 by the Harare-based African Network on Debt and Development. Citing a World Bank study that acknowledges that 'a typical poor country receives 90% of GDP through Aid but the poorest quartile of the population consume only 4% of the GDP', Opa Kapijimpanga concluded that 'aid is a tool to serve the commercial, political, economic and strategic interests of donor countries'. As a result, 'The donor creditor countries must keep all their aid and against it write off all the debt owed by poor African countries … The bottom line would be elimination of both aid and debt because they reinforce the power relations that are contributing to the imbalances in the world.'[36]

Ultimately, the use of aid – and possibly debt cancellation and reparations payments, if channelled through the state – depends on whether increased pressure can be put on Pretoria and other regional state capitals to serve the needs of the citizenry. As we will see in Part two, there are many reasons to question whether meeting the needs of the citizenry is indeed the agenda of the South African government, in the context of worsening global apartheid.

Notes

1 *Financial Times*, 11 November 1998.
2 *Business Day*, 14 January 1995.
3 Commitments failed to translate into disbursements and implementation for several reasons: an overly bureaucratic RDP Office (which initially funded aid-related projects on a reimbursement basis, not up-front, and had excessively complex requirements for project business plans); a requirement to direct funding through the general revenue fund; parliamentary oversight; project tendering requirements; the imposition of VAT on aid; complex donor procedures; conflicts with government; and an increasingly demobilised civil society. See Bratton, M. and Landsberg, C. (1998), 'Trends in Aid to South Africa', *Indicator SA*, 15(4).
4 Montes, C., Migliorisi, S. and Wolfe, T. (1999), 'Evaluation of EC Country Strategy: South Africa, 1996–99', Paris, Investment Development Consultancy and Rome, Development Strategy, p. v.
5 See, for example, Bratton, M. and Landsberg, C. (1998), 'From Promise to Delivery: Official Development Assistance to South Africa, 1994–98', Johannesburg, Centre for Policy Studies; Budlender, D. (1999), 'Donor Funding Poses Questions for South Africa', *Budget Watch*, IDASA Budget Information Service, August; Budlender, D. and Dube, N. (1999), 'Gender and Official Development Assistance in South Africa', in D. Budlender (ed.), *The Fourth Women's Budget*, Cape Town, IDASA; Heard, J. (1999), 'Foreign Aid, Democratisation and Civil Society in Southern Africa: A Study of South Africa, Ghana and Uganda', *IDS Discussion Paper* 368; and Love, R. (1999), 'Changing Aid Patterns in Southern Africa', *Development in Practice*, 9(3).
6 Such research is under way in the Department of Finance and the University of Natal-Durban's Centre for Social and Development Studies. A good model is the study of Lesotho aid by James Ferguson (1994), *The Anti-Politics Machine*, Minneapolis, University of Minnesota Press.
7 Sogge, D. (1998), 'Misgivings: Aid to Africa', *Indicator SA*, 15(4). See also Sogge, D. (ed.) (1996), *Compassion and Calculation: The Politics of Private Foreign Aid*, London, Pluto Press.
8 SAPA, 19 January 1995.
9 For an accounting of such influence from within, see the World Bank (1999), *South Africa Country Assistance Strategy*, Washington, DC; for a more critical account, see Chapter three, above, and Bond, P. (2000), *Elite Transition: From Apartheid to Neoliberalism in South Africa*, London, Pluto Press and Pietermaritzburg, University of Natal Press, Chapter 5.
10 *Financial Times*, 14 April 1997. See these authors' 1997 summary, 'Aid Spurs Growth – In a Sound Policy Environment', *Finance and Development*, 34(4) and their 1998 book, *Assessing Aid: What Works, What Doesn't and Why*, Washington, DC, World Bank.
11 Tony Leon, leader of the opposition Democratic Party, concluded, 'Our whole foreign policy is based on the electoral debts of the ANC. When the ANC is short of cash it runs off to the Gulf states or to Morocco for help.' (*Mail and Guardian*, 8 December 1995.)

12 Just as importantly, the deal has been criticised by regional policy-makers for lack of transparency and for its potentially devastating impact on (non-SA) regional manufacturing firms (in view of far more competitive European firms using SA as a trading base to penetrate into the region). Zimbabwe and Zambia even imposed new protectionist barriers against SA imports, in the wake of 40% of Zimbabwe's manufacturing output disappearing between 1991 and 1995, and 75% of Zambia's formal-sector jobs evaporating during the same period.
13 *Business Day*, 24 May 1994.
14 Bond, P. (1995), 'A Five to One Return', *African Agenda*, 1(2), March.
15 *Business Day*, 16 January 1997.
16 *The Star*, 19 March 1997.
17 Bond, P. (1999), 'Globalization, Pharmaceutical Pricing and South African Health Policy: Managing Confrontation with US Firms and Politicians', *International Journal of Health Policy*, 29(4).
18 *Business Day*, 20 July 1998.
19 *Business Day*, 16 December 1997.
20 *Business Day*, 16 March 1998.
21 *Business Day*, 19 February 1998.
22 *Business Day*, 19 February 1998.
23 African National Congress (1994), *Reconstruction and Development Programme*, Johannesburg, Umanyano Publications, sec. 6.5.16.
24 See the discussion in Bond, P. (2000), *Elite Transition*, pp. 174–5.
25 *Business Day*, 2 March 1998.
26 *Business Day*, 6 June 2000.
27 Submission of the South African NGO Coalition to the Advisory Committee Investigating the Feasibility of the Establishment of a National Development Agency, undated.
28 *Sunday Independent Reconstruct*, 21 May 2000.
29 Concerns were articulated, off the record, that the EU insisted on micromanaging TNDT development priorities, as a result of a regular insistence on its right to give the go-ahead on individual projects to be funded from the EU contribution to the TNDT.
30 *The Star*, 11 July 2000.
31 African National Congress, *op. cit.,* sec. 6.5.16.
32 Bond, P. and Khosa, M. (1999), *An RDP Policy Audit*, Pretoria, Human Sciences Research Council.
33 *Mail and Guardian*, 21 July 1995.
34 European Union South Africa Mission (1999), *South Africa Country Review*, Pretoria.
35 *Ibid.*
36 Kapijimpanga, O. (2001), 'An Aid/Debt Trade-Off the Best Option', in G. Ostravik (ed.), *The Reality of Aid Reality Check 2001*, Oslo, Norwegian Peoples Aid.

PART TWO

Elite contestation of global governance

Thabo Mbeki addresses the World Economic Forum 'Backlash against Globalisation' plenary, Davos, January 2001.

Top: Chair of the IMF/World Bank Board of Governors, Trevor Manuel, Washington, April 2000 (with James Wolfensohn, far right).
Bottom: Trevor Ngwane (from the World Social Forum in Porto Alegre) debates George Soros, Davos, January 2001.

CHAPTER FIVE

The global balance of forces

1. Introduction

South Africa has been contesting the terrain of international economics with increasing vigour since the late 1990s. In Part one, I examined that terrain using a simplistic dichotomy as our conceptual map, i.e. struggles between those promoting what we can call 'global apartheid', and those fighting for social justice. But by the turn of the 21st century, a more accurate reading of the balance of forces required examination of at least five major currents of argumentation and activism. From those currents follow different analyses, strategies, tactics and alliances.

What forces have been working on the fragile architecture of the international financial system, and what is the likelihood of their success in achieving their aims? By examining both ideological and material positions related to crisis management, we can identify three of these five tendencies, all located in Washington, which aim to bolster the architecture in the interests of the North (see Section 2). In contrast, two other tendencies are much more critical of the status quo, even though they differ about 'fixing' or 'nixing' the international financial, investment and trade system (see Section 3). The five positions, from left to right on the political spectrum, can be labelled as follows:
1) 'Global justice movements';
2) 'Third World nationalism';
3) the 'Post-Washington Consensus';
4) the 'Washington Consensus'; and
5) the 'Resurgent right wing' (see Table 3).[1]

The balance of these forces shifts constantly, with no durable alliances in sight (see Section 4). Even the fluidity with which key individuals move between two or more camps is disconcerting. Thabo Mbeki, President George W. Bush, US labour leaders, financier George Soros and many others often appear in more than one of the camps within very short periods of time, depending upon circumstances and perceived opportunities. But the philosophical positions appear ever more clearly delineated. Getting a

Table 3: Five reactions to the global crisis

	Global justice movements	Third World nationalism	Post-Washington Consensus	Washington Consensus	Resurgent right wing
Main argument	Against globalisation of *capital* (not *people*), for 'people-centred development'	Join the system, but on much fairer terms	Reform 'imperfect markets'; achieve 'sustainable development'	Slightly adjust the status quo (transparency, supervision and regulation)	Restore US isolationism; punish banks' mistakes
Key institutions	Social/labour movements; environment-advocacy groups; radical-activist networks; regional and national coalitions;	Self-selecting Third World nation states (Algeria, Argentina, Brazil, China, Cuba, Egypt, Haiti, India, Malaysia, Mexico,	Most UN agencies; governments of France and Japan; [SA government?]	US agencies (Treasury, Federal Reserve, USAID); Bretton Woods institutions; WTO; centrist Washington think-tanks;	Populist and libertarian wings of Republican Party; American Enterprise Institute; Cato Institute; Manhattan Institute;

	left-wing think-tanks; academic settings; [many SA groups]	Pakistan, Russia, Venezuela, Zimbabwe); [SA government?]		British and German governments; [SA government?]	Heritage Foundation
Key proponents	Amin Bello, Bendana, Bordieu, Bove, Brutus, Chalmers, Chomsky, Danaher, Galeano, George, Kagarlitsky, Khor, Klein, Lula, Maathai, Marcos, Nader, Ndungane, Njehu, Patkar, Pilger, Shiva, Trumka?	Aristide, Castro, Chavez, Mahathir, Mbeki?, Mugabe, Obasanjo, Putin	Annan, Jospin, Lafontaine?, Krugman, Sachs, Soros, Stiglitz	Baker?, Blair, Brown, Bush?, Camdessus, Clinton, Fischer, Greenspan, Koehler, Moore, O'Neill?, Rubin, Schroeder, Summers, Wolfensohn	Buchanan, Bush?, Haider, Helms, Le Pen, Lindsay?, Lott, Kissinger, Meltzer?, Shultz

handle on those positions is crucial, to set the stage for strategic considerations of the elite-reform gambit of South African government leaders, as I
will discuss in the two subsequent chapters.

2. The pro-status-quo forces

The Washington Consensus

I will consider, firstly, the most powerful force: the pro-status-quo
Washington Consensus, which has dogmatically promoted free trade, financial liberalisation and foreign investment incentives, business deregulation,
low taxes, fiscal austerity and privatisation, high real interest rates, and
flexible labour markets.[2] If there were problems outstanding in the world
economy, they would always merely be temporary, according to this grouping, to be overcome by more IMF bailouts (embarrassingly generous to
New York bankers though they were), intensified application of 'sound'
macroeconomic policies, augmented by greater transparency, a touch more
financial sector supervision and regulation, and less Asian cronyism. (An
IMF attempt in early 1999 to go a bit further and establish a Washington
Consensus 'lender of last resort' was discredited, for it was seen as a naked
power play.)

Personalities are important here, even if we are sometimes confused by
their erratic, opportunistic twists and turns, and by their habit of telling lies
about their underlying agenda. Providing political cover for the status quo
at the end of the century were Bill Clinton and Tony Blair (with no objec-
tion from Gerhard Schroeder of Germany). Providing operational support
were US treasury secretary Robert Rubin and the man who replaced him in
1999, Lawrence Summers, US Federal Reserve chairperson Alan Greenspan, and IMF managing director Michel Camdessus and his 2000 replacement Horst Koehler, ably supported by deputy MD Stanley Fischer.
Gordon Brown, Britain's Chancellor of the Exchequer, chaired a key IMF
committee which coerced consent from the lowlier member states, and
Canadian finance minister Paul Martin served much the same function with
the G-20 group of finance ministers (including some nationalists). Offering
periodic intellectual justification were Fischer and Summers. World Bank
president James Wolfensohn was very much a Washington man, even if he
sometimes had to pretend he wasn't.[3] WTO secretary Michael Moore regularly pretended he was a New Zealand labour leftist, but in reality proved
(together with Clinton's US trade representative Charlene Barshefsky) that
he was prepared to defend Washington's corporate sponsors no matter the
shame involved.

The Bush administration has given mixed signals, as we see below, but
the likely orientation was in the old establishment mould set by James Baker
and Nicholas Brady during George Bush Sr.'s presidency in 1989–93. (Paul

O'Neill as treasury secretary would represent corporate interests with no qualms, having served as chief executive of International Paper and the Aluminum Corporation of America, two of that country's worst polluters and right-wing firms.)

A variety of bank and corporate-sponsored Washington think-tanks echoed the party line, while allies were found in the World Trade Organisation, the Bank for International Settlements, the Organisation for Economic Cooperation and Development, and numerous academic economic departments that followed the University of Chicago's lead. But even if free-marketeers could be found in every country (and when in government, mostly in central banks and finance ministries), the accent was always Washington's. Given Japan's decline during the 1990s, most of the main beneficiaries of the Washington Consensus were firms with their headquarters in the US. As conservative economist Rudiger Dornbusch conceded in 1998, 'The IMF is a toy of the United States to pursue its economic policy offshore.'[4]

Aside from Third World nationalists and leftists who were critical of US-centric economic policy, two other positions emerged as threats to the Washington Consensus during the late 1990s. Neither fundamentally questioned the profit system, nor the prerogative of US-based corporations to dominate the world. The most important, thanks to their control of key committees of the US Congress and their influence in the Bush administration were the right-wing libertarians, populists and establishment politicos crossed with liberal internationalism; while the apparent Post-Washington Consensus successors to the Washington Consensus appeared in 1998–99, then quickly faded. I will consider each in turn.

The resurgent US right wing

Amongst those scornful of the Washington Consensus were conservatives, largely based in reactionary pockets of the US. But it was a mistake to discount congressional heavyweights like Senators Jesse Helms and Trent Lott (with House of Representatives allies Dennis Hastert and Dick Armey), or loud-mouthed populists like Pat Buchanan and their kind as mere rednecks. Jean Marie le Pen of France and Jörg Haider of Austria would represent the neo fascist movements – with their traditional anti-semitic hatred of bankers – giving the right wing an international flavour. Moreover, the right-wing critique of public bailouts for New York financiers was backed by think-tanks like the stalwartly conservative Heritage Foundation and the libertarian but very influential Cato Institute in Washington.

Surprisingly, their disgust of Bretton Woods interventionism was closely paralleled by elite conservative concerns, notably those of Henry Kissinger and George Shultz, geopoliticians who lost dear friends like President

Suharto of Indonesia in the 1997–8 financial turmoil. (Others from the Republican elite who revolted against Washington financial managers were Nixon's treasury secretary William Simon, former Citibank boss Walter Wriston and former Reagan administration chief economist Martin Feldstein.) Together, by 1998, these resurgent rightists had mounted both a formidable attack on IMF policies as unworkable, and opposition to the US Treasury Department's request for $18 billion in further IMF funding.[5]

The Bush administration has economic tendencies towards the resurgent right, thanks in part to the powerful advisory role of Lawrence Lindsay, a critic of bank bailouts, the key appointment of John Taylor, who once called for the IMF's abolition, as under-secretary of the Treasury[6] and the anti-cipated renewal of the agenda proposed by the Republican right's Meltzer Commission. Carnegie Mellon University economist Alan Meltzer's report in 2000 recommended substantial downsizing of the IMF and World Bank; in the same spirit in October 1998, the Republican-controlled Congress demanded that higher interest rates and faster payback periods be imposed on IMF borrowers, before finally approving the $18 billion in new appro-priations the IMF insisted was required to keep its bailout fund topped up.[7]

The most interesting problem for Washington analysts is deciphering the occasional tactical alliances between, say, a Buchanan and left-wing populist movements, such as the Ralph Nader networks and Friends of the Earth, a point that will be taken up again in Chapter 10.[8] Political strategies that unite right and left, as inter-war Germany showed, do most damage to the latter. While the right-wing challenge appears formidable at times, it is also subject to co-option (as Clinton achieved with the 1998 recapitalisation). Xenophobia and isolationism are also logical political threats from this political stance, and economically it wouldn't be hard to envisage latter-day Smoot Hawley-style protective tariffs kicking off a downward spiral of trade degeneration reminiscent of the early 1930s, if resurgent right-wing advocates had their way.

The Post-Washington Consensus

The third pro-status-quo position was termed the 'Post-Washington Consensus' by former World Bank chief economist Joseph Stiglitz.[9] Aimed at perfecting the capitalist system's 'imperfect markets', Stiglitz cited organic problems like asymmetric information in market transactions (espe-cially finance) and anti-competitive behaviour by firms as key contributors to the current instability. However, by advocating somewhat more substan-tive national regulatory interventions (tougher anti-trust measures, and even 'speedbumps' or dual exchange rates to slow hot money) and more attention to social development and employment, Stiglitz was as reluctant to tamper with underlying dynamics as was George Soros, whose call for a global banking insurance fund looked suspiciously self-interested, in particular since it came at a time, in August 1998, when he lost several billion dollars of his Russian investments because of Boris Yeltsin's default on state debt.[10] Similarly, Soros played a pro-Washington role at Prague when on a panel that was challenged by left-wing critics.

Others from a neo-liberal economic background who jumped the Washington Consensus ship include Massachusetts Institute of Technology economist Paul Krugman, who claimed both a temporary fondness for capital controls to halt speculative runs and responsibility for Mahathir bin Mohamad's restrictions on trading the Malaysian ringgit in September 1998.[11] (Further analysis of Krugman's views on capital controls can be found in Chapter twelve.) Similarly, Jeffrey Sachs, director of the Harvard Institute for International Development, offered such vociferous critiques of IMF austerity economics as to (nearly) disguise his own previous advocacy of deregulatory 'shock therapy' from Latin America to Eastern Europe and his continuing promotion of sweatshops.[12]

Slightly more durable than the growing chorus of reform-oriented neo-liberals were the institutions which have an actual material stake in promoting human welfare, such as several key United Nations agencies. Some of the main ones -- the UN Conference on Trade and Development, the International Labour Organisation, the World Health Organisation and UNICEF – made regular appeals for state intervention and social entitlements contrary to Washington's gospel. But Kofi Annan did enormous damage to his reputation, both through appointing a Washington-oriented advisory team on international finance (chaired by Mexico's controversial ex-president Ernesto Zedillo and including Citibank co-chairperson Robert Rubin), and through the UN's 'Global Compact' with 50 of the world's largest companies.

In addition, the World Water Forum – a joint venture of the World Bank and the United Nations Development Programme (itself run by Mark Malloch Brown, Wolfensohn's mid-1990s public relations man) – transparently promoted the commodification/privatisation agenda at its key meeting in March 2000 in the Hague. Without Ted Turner's bailouts, the UN would have even less capacity to withstand the varying pressures from Washington – one day isolationist, but the next humanitarian-imperialist – in any case. 'Can the UN be salvaged?' asked the International Forum on Globalisation grouping of leading international left-liberals during the Millennium Summit in September 2000, and failed to answer conclusively in the affirmative.

More potentially significant than any of the above were the shifting political sands of social-democratic and Green or otherwise left-leaning party politics in Germany, France, Italy and Japan.[13] Still, when Oskar Lafontaine, the reform-minded social democrat, resigned his finance ministry post in disgust in early 1999,[14] Schroeder realigned Germany away from Paris – at least, away from Lionel Jospin's wing of socialism – and towards London, and hence Washington. At the same time, Tokyo, led by Miyazawa, was prevented from establishing the Asian Monetary Fund it wanted during the late 1990s because of Rubin/Summers vetoes.[15] Whether Japan and Europe would rise again to challenge Washington probably depended mostly upon whether a US-led global recession would change the balance of forces and reduce dependence upon Washington's economic dictates.

All of the forces and ideologies cited above were, however, fundamentally guided by an acceptance of Western consumption norms and habits, a hostility (sometimes verging on the lunatic) to socialist values and a tendency to paint economics in the narrowest and most technical terms. So any rearrangement of personnel by the Bush administration or potential minor reforms – even slight downsizing – of the Washington institutions would not make much difference. The pro-status-quo forces had no plan to restore either international financial stability or Third World prospects for capital accumulation envisaged at the original Bretton Woods conference in 1944.

Meanwhile, the US economy continued to suffer unprecedented trade and debt imbalances, unprecedented consumer and corporate borrowing, and persistent stock-market overvaluation (on the NY Stock Exchange, if not Nasdaq, which crashed violently from March 2000). Japan's apparent break from its decade-long stagnation in early 1999 was brief, with a downturn soon returning. The rapid recovery of the East Asian countries from system-threatening crisis contributed yet further to the more durable trade and investment imbalances, with no sign of the more balanced character of capital accumulation so desperately required. Were there, in this dangerous context, *any* feasible systematic reforms worth promoting by intelligent progressives, or would the powers-that-be in Washington and other financial capitals necessarily drive the financial system off the economic cliff early in the 21st century?

What might work

The lack of a sufficient international political will for a more durable antidote – such as a revival of what has been termed 'global Keynesianism' – was disturbing and somewhat surprising, given how much was at stake. George Soros predicted in early 2001: 'The last crisis [1997–9] was the product of a boom of investments in emerging markets, followed by a very steep fall. Now the problem that the world faces is inadequate capital flows from countries at the center to countries on the periphery. It is going to be a chronic, not a temporary crisis, and I believe it is already underway.'[16]

Under not dissimilar circumstances during the Great Depression, Keynes offered a philosophically grounded economic diagnosis in his 1936

General Theory, based on the disjuncture between savings and investment that recurs periodically under capitalism. He also suggested a remedy to depression-ridden capitalism that, from the early 1940s, revolutionised economic thinking for a period of more than three, relatively high-growth, relatively less-unequal decades. He considered that remedy to lie in fiscal expansion, but just as crucial for him was the proper control of flows of financial capital. Keynes insisted that a footloose flow of capital 'assumes that it is right and desirable to have an equalisation of interest rates in all parts of the world. In my view the whole management of the domestic economy depends upon being free to have the appropriate interest rate without reference to the rates prevailing in the rest of the world. Capital controls is a corollary to this.'[17]

Thanks largely to Keynes, who argued in 1944 against the American negotiating team at Bretton Woods, the IMF Articles of Agreement still allow member countries to 'exercise such controls as are necessary to regulate international capital movements'. As recently as 1990, 35 countries retained capital controls. I will look at this matter again in Chapter twelve. But from the early 1990s, the US Treasury Department led a formidable attack on this provision, and not only forced South Korea's financial doors open as a condition for it joining the Organisation for Economic Cooperation and Development, but even attempted to change the IMF Articles of Agreement to ensure that all member states agreed to full financial liberalisation.

At the global level, meanwhile, Washington continued to ward off any systematic protective measures against the dangers of financial speculation and contagion, notwithstanding a series of calls by respected economists for crucial technical interventions. One remedy for global crisis contagion – endorsed in March 1999 by a two-thirds majority in the Canadian parliament – is the application by the major countries of a 'Tobin Tax' (bearing the name of Nobel Prize laureate James Tobin) of 0.05–0.50% on cross-border financial transactions.[18] Noted futurist Hazel Henderson has also suggested creative means to prevent currency 'bear raids' by focusing on electronic funds transfers and a transparent transaction-reporting system.[19]

To concerns that money would flee the major countries for off-shore centres (the Bahamas, Jersey, Guernsey, the Cayman Islands, Panama, etc.), advocates of the Tobin Tax insist that any funds flowing to or from such sites could be penalised by concerted G-8 country action.[20] To concerns that the rise of trade in derivatives and other financial innovations would make a Tobin Tax difficult to apply,[21] advocates suggest taxing profits or losses through a 'contract for differences' payment mechanism, realised as a result of movements of the exchange rate relative to the notional principal amounts traded. In other words, logistical hurdles can be overcome. Establishing the European Union's common currency was, after all, a far more difficult technical exercise, yet was accomplished with few problems because there was sufficient political will. (It is, however, widely recognised that a Tobin Tax is simply defensive, and that other investment measures are needed to assure a more appropriate flow of finance to areas of potential economic – not merely speculative – return.)

Similarly, other proposals for international financial regulation, ideally co-ordinated by a United Nations system agency, have gone unheeded. Sir John Eatwell and Lance Taylor advocated the establishment of a World Financial Authority.[22] The 'post-Keynesian' economist Paul Davidson proposed an international clearing union providing for capital controls.[23] The leading UNCTAD economist, Yilmaz Akyuz, made similar calls.[24] Other far-sighted US economists – Jane D'Arista, James Galbraith, William Darity and Dean Baker of the Financial Markets Center in Washington – suggested a new international public bank and regulatory framework.[25]

In addition, in view not only of further currency crashes that compel interest-rate increases that in turn bankrupt many local borrowers, but also of a legitimate fear of continuing sovereign defaults (like Russia's of August 1998, as well as South Africa's standstill of September 1985 and Brazil's of 1987), UNCTAD suggested extending some form of national bankruptcy procedure (along the lines of the US Bankruptcy Code, Chapters 9 and 11) on the international level.[26] Fears remained, however, that if a bankruptcy arbitration panel is influenced by the IMF, serious conflicts of interest would arise, given that the IMF itself is typically a central creditor in all such cases. And the question of whether the UN system could generate such a panel cannot be answered in the affirmative unless there is a dramatic shift in power balances and an increase in political will.

Reflecting the concern among at least a few left-leaning Northern parliamentarians that existing financial regulatory measures at the national and international levels are insufficient, a motion tabled in the German Bundestag in May 1999 by the Party of Democratic Socialism called upon the government to take measures that included the following:

1) within the G8 framework, to take steps to curb short-term speculation on the financial markets, *inter alia* through a combination of the following measures:
   - by introducing a currency exchange transactions tax (Tobin Tax). All transactions which result in an immediate exchange of currency must be taxed at a standard proportional rate of 0.25% on the full volume of their monetary value;
   - by introducing special compulsory minimum reserves for non-project-specific bank credits, i.e. for bank loans which are not earmarked for specific purposes (e.g. the purchase of consumer goods, investments, trade finance etc.). As speculation is generally undertaken with

borrowed rather than own funds, it may be assumed that these credits – especially to hedge and investment funds – are used primarily for short-term financial speculation. The banks will pass on the costs of holding the reserves to borrowers, thereby pushing up the price of the financial commitment and reducing the investment;

■ imposing a charge on non-interest-bearing or low-interest cash deposits when importing or exporting capital, thus adding more to the cost of such transactions than the percentage levied by a Tobin Tax. A sliding scale of charges may be imposed in line with the type and/or the term of capital flows: high rates would apply to short-term, high-risk accounts, while low rates would be charged on long-term, lower-risk investments.

2) with the objective of improving banking supervision, to take initiatives:

■ to enhance transparency by ensuring that off-balance sheet transactions (especially with derivatives) are identified and included in risk calculations;

■ to tighten the own capital regulations for banks and extend them to all types of financial institution. The assessment and calculation of credit risks must no longer be left to these institutions – as has hitherto been the case – as this reduces the own capital security of the credit operation. The own capital regulations for credit institutions must be applied more rigorously to derivatives transactions, and risk-weighted minimum reserves must be introduced for transactions by investment funds;

■ to introduce compulsory insurance for international loans, so that private risks are insured on a private basis and losses are no longer passed on to the tax payer, as is the current practice;

■ to abolish offshore finance centres, or to penalize banks and financial institutions which do business with these offshore centres.[27]

Related areas of nation-state intervention, such as prohibiting certain kinds of deregulated financial market activity, would also be appropriate. Indeed, a gathering of left-wing reformers at the Institute for Policy Studies in Washington in December 1998 established a variety of other approaches, such as proposed regional-crisis funds belonging to a manageable set of countries with similar norms, values and practices, and domestic redirection of locally raised monies (hence 'soft currency' in many cases, intermediated by worker-influenced pension funds or mutual funds), along with progressive national taxation.[28]

Perhaps surprisingly, proposals for national and supranational interventions against cross-border financial flows are not terribly controversial in the economics profession, given the damage done over the past quarter

of a century. To a lesser degree, such intervention has been endorsed by the
three most active Washington economists of the late 1990s: Summers,
Fischer and Stiglitz. Most notably, Summers even co-authored an academic
article recommending a tax on global financial speculation.[29] Fischer
argued as recently as 1991 that 'domestic firms should not be given un-
restricted access to foreign borrowing, particularly non-equity financing'.[30]
Likewise, Stiglitz once advocated a tax-based approach to cooling hot
money.[31] So the idea that both Washington and Post-Washington
Consensusites could imagine the reforms required to at least stabilise global
capitalism was in no way outlandish.

However, there is a vast distance between obscure articles destined for
audiences of economists and the professional requirements associated with
maintaining imperialist financial interests. Given the enormous hostility of
Wall Street, the City of London and other European financial centres, the
prospect of any global regulatory agency emerging to gain control of financial flows in the manner that Keynes envisaged is remote.

If this is true, then it is the nation state that must intervene to assure
domestic financial security, in an increasingly dangerous world in which
global financial management is simply inadequate and power relations
are unlikely to change to bring international finance to heel. But the
question that arises next is whether Third World nationalists are
prepared to take such steps, or whether radical social movements have to
push them. South Africa is a case in point, as we will observe in the next
two chapters.

3. Forces for change (?)

Third World nationalism
The fourth of the five groups under discussion, Third World nationalists,
cannot claim to share traditions in any respect. Some nationalists have been
effective in keeping international financial pressure at bay during the 1990s.
China and India forthrightly resisted financial liberalisation. The Chinese-
ruled statelet of Hong Kong controversially prohibited the short selling of
local stock-market shares in September 1998, and also bought $14 billion
in shares to prop up the Hang Seng index. At the same time, Taiwan
outlawed what were described as illegal funds-trades by Soros hedge funds.
All of these countries survived the Asian financial crisis of 1997–9. And
though his economy was being put through the wringer, Boris Yeltsin
formally defaulted on $40 billion worth of domestic Russian state debt
(30-day bonds carrying triple-digit interest rates) held to a large extent by
foreigners in August 1998.[32]

But it was in rather different nationalist regimes in Asia, Africa and Latin
America that more radical discourses of opposition to the Washington

Consensus were heard at the turn of the century. From Malaysia (Mahathir)[33] to Zimbabwe (Robert Mugabe),[34] to Venezuela (Hugo Chavez),[35] IMF-bashing was back in style, even if the rhetorical flourishes had different origins, i.e. one Muslim, one self-described socialist, one simply populist. Other interesting – if flawed – Third World leaders included Haiti's Jean-Bertrand Aristide, Nigeria's Olusegun Obasanjo, Russia's Vladimir Putin and South Africa's elite economic team, whose ideas and agenda are discussed in the next two chapters.[36]

Could these diverse forces find a way to build unity against Washington? Fidel Castro's hosting of the G-77 South Summit in April 2000 generated a quite progressive 'Havana Programme of Action' (Castro even called for the closure of the IMF), but its approach was clearly in the spirit that 'we want in' to global financial capitalism. 'We emphasize the importance of the effective and beneficial integration of the LDCs into the global economy and the multilateral trading system as its main driving force', said the G-77 communiqué, through 'reform of the international financial architecture that addresses issues of financing for development and stability of the international financial system including the need for regulation of hedge funds and highly leveraged institutions and strengthening of the early warning system to provide for improved response capabilities to help countries deal with the emergencies and spread of financial crises.'[37]

The approach chosen in these cases amounts mainly to attempting to join the system, to play by its rules and, having discovered that the game is set up unfairly, to adjust these rules somewhat in the Third World's favour. Recall in contrast the demand in the 1970s by the governments of these same countries for a 'New International Economic Order'. This strain of politics faded badly over the subsequent two decades. And in the cases of Mahathir, Mugabe and others, 'talking left' also entailed repression of opposition parties, public interest groups, trade unions, women and gay-rights movements, which was less publicised but just as chilling to democratic processes as the arrest of a high-ranking Malaysian politician who supported the Washington Consensus, and the terrorising of Zimbabwean journalists and white commercial farmers.[38]

Not just a problem of Third World nationalism, selling out the poor and working classes on behalf of international finance was also the general fate of so many labour and social-democratic parties in Western Europe, Canada and Australia. Even where once-revolutionary parties remained in control of the nation state – in China, Vietnam, Angola and Mozambique, for example – ideologies wandered over to hard, raw capitalism. And yet, too, the very universality of financial crisis would necessarily allow counter-hegemonic voices to emerge. Thus there was still talk within the African National Congress of potential interlocking interests of many nations – Algeria, Argentina, Brazil, China, Cuba, Egypt, India, Mexico, Pakistan,

Russia – which would potentially reflect renewed muscle in the Non-Aligned Movement, Group of 77 and various other forums of revived nationalisms.

Global justice movements

Finally, a variety of radical social movements adopted a relatively harmonious goal (which I will consider in much greater detail in Chapters ten and eleven), namely *to promote the globalisation of people and halt or at least radically modify the globalisation of capital.* These movements spanned Old Left forces (many labour movements and some ex-Stalinist communist parties),[39] other newer political parties,[40] progressive churches, human-rights and disarmament movements, democracy activists, urban/rural-community and indigenous-peoples movements, organisations of women, youth and the elderly, HIV and health activists, disability-rights lobbyists, consumer advocates and environmentalists who work on both the local and global levels (Greenpeace and Friends of the Earth in the latter group, along with international environmental-justice networks).

Naturally, these movements are all extremely diverse in all aspects of their existence. Were there any discourses that could combine the mass-based movements and the NGOs, the proletarian (or often lumpen) activists and *petit-bourgeois* intellectuals, the women and the men, the environmentalists and the workers? In both strategic and tactical respects, achieving a synthesis of particularist struggles is always difficult, not least in the simple matter of movement leaders and activists even finding common and mutually supportive discourses. Nevertheless, by the turn of the century, virtually all countries provided evidence of coalitions and networks of anti-globalisation activists, many of which were fairly well-grounded in mass democratic organisations that acted locally but thought globally.[41]

Some localised efforts were already having inspiring results, such as anti-dam struggles in parts of South Asia and the unveiling of Chile's repressive legacy as part of an international campaign to bring General Pinochet to justice. But it was always vital to question whether these sorts of organisations could forge links, so as not only to think globally and act locally, but also act globally.[42] The most successful of these groups during the late 1990s tackled three global issues: landmines (nearly victoriously were it not for the United States), the Multilateral Agreement on Investment (where several stunning stalemates were won, mainly in European settings) and Third World debt. Indeed, it was possible to locate within the Jubilee 2000 debt-cancellation movement a campaigning spirit that attracted celebrities ranging from the Pope, to singer Bono of the group U2, to Bob Geldoff, to Muhamad Ali, but also drew tens of thousands of ordinary activists to protest at G-8 meetings in Birmingham in 1998, Cologne in 1999 and Okinawa in 2000.[43]

Not only did social movements show that in some settings they could move from marginal sideline protest to shake ruling-class confidence in major neo-liberal initiatives, e.g. the North American Free Trade Agreement and US support for the General Agreement on Tariffs and Trade were threatened more by radical US farmer and labour activists than by the Republican right-populists. They also claimed quite substantial resources for future struggles, including effective advocacy networks[44] and a few progressive nerve centres in sites of power, particularly Washington, DC.[45] There were, in addition, several radical economic think-tanks associated with the social movements,[46] university allies,[47] and a handful of accessible international activist-oriented periodicals[48] and publishing houses,[49] not to mention world-class spokespeople and luminaries from the new movements who easily outwit conservative debating opponents.[50]

However, the global balance of forces is very clearly weighted against Third World nationalists and the global justice movements, and there appears little real basis for any forms of alliance between the two, given the former's penchant for authoritarianism and patriarchy. There is also a variety of other important, organised social forces such as Muslim fundamentalist oppositionists, Andean guerrillas or still-stodgy US trade unionists[51] that don't fit neatly into any camp as yet, but which may influence matters to some degree.

4. Alliances falter

Between the full-blown emergence of the international financial crisis around mid-1997 (although the full extent of contagion was only felt a year later) and the onset of a US recession in early 2001, roughly 40 months transpired of give-and-take, mass protests, negotiating sessions and production of reams of paper (and even more kilobytes of cyberspace argument), all devoted to making the case that only one camp had it right. Although a few momentary initiatives were made to explore alliances – or at least non-aggression pacts – these petered out, and the five competing blocks grew more divided than ever.

Not that there weren't interesting possibilities for co-operation between the camps, and, as we shall see in Chapters ten and eleven, perpetual internecine conflict amongst organisations representing the oppressed. But the opportunities for truly uniting forces were few and far between, and the best that various groups could hope for was a temporary non-aggression pact here or there.[52]

Washington makes no deals, takes no prisoners

Powerful and influential Washington Consensus exponents, for example, practically exterminated their intellectual opponents on the Post-Washington Consensus left, beginning in September 1999. After Stiglitz raved at IMF incompetence in Russia, he was effectively dismissed – as Jagdish Bhagwati put it in the *Financial Times* – 'with a fig leaf, a sorry episode'.[53] Wolfensohn first censured and then censored Stiglitz in October, weakly rebutting his critique of the IMF and then apparently prohibiting him from press comment, according to the *Washington Post*. Ironically, perhaps as an epitaph, Stiglitz's disciplinary credentials were endorsed in the *New York Times* by Nobel laureate Kenneth Arrow (Summers' father-in-law): 'The Stiglitz group represents one of the most important innovations in economics in the last 100 years.' Soon thereafter, Ravi Kanbur – the World Bank's redistribution-minded consultant who was to be lead author of *World Development Report: Poverty 2000* – also resigned because of explicit censorship by Summers.

Camdessus' resignation in early 2000 also reflected institutional embarrassment ('I never signed a Washington Consensus',[54] he cried in Bangkok, shortly after receiving a creampuff pie in his face from a leading global-justice-movement veteran, Robert Naiman). As one reflection of tensions within the international movement, Jubilee 2000 UK sought the approval of the Pope for its (limited) anti-debt campaigning, while the Pope sought Camdessus as an advisor. Jubilee's UK and US chapters also called for help to Sachs on a regular basis, notwithstanding the Russian financial scandal that festered at his Harvard institute and his tendency to still preach the virtues of sweatshops in Third World countries. In a similar reflection of untenable alliance-building, Bono met Wolfensohn at the meeting in Prague in September 2000 and inexplicably rewarded the World Bank president with the title 'the Elvis of economics'.[55] But there was no apparent benefit to Jubilee, just more World Bank stonewalling on debt.

Washington's hegemony continued. Minor reforms to global financial-market regulation announced at the G-8 meeting in Cologne and the IMF/World Bank annual meetings held in 1999 were not, by virtually all accounts, sufficient to prevent a future wave of financial panics. Debt relief promised in Cologne was simply ignored by most of the G-8 finance ministers. Only the right-wing threat forced an occasional modification here or there, especially when Sachs temporarily allied with conservative populists on the Meltzer Commission, instead of with the commission's corporate liberals, who the Democratic Party had deployed to win the arguments.

Other alliances?

Meanwhile, the conservative members of the US Congress and right-wing populists everywhere enviously realised that when it came to mass mobilisation around international financial and trade matters, the Right had nothing like the capacity shown by the Left in Seattle, Washington and Prague. One deal that brought the protesters' Washington technocrats together with creative Republicans was a successful effort in October 2000 to prevent the World Bank and IMF from imposing user fees on healthcare and education in future loan conditions.

The global justice movements did earn occasional acknowledgement from the elite. On the verge of leaving the World Bank in early April 2000, Stiglitz praised the street protesters. But that too was a stillborn friendship, as Stiglitz was quickly sucked into an elite-intellectual exercise on 'the alternative' (funded, predictably, by Ford) at Brookings, Stanford and Ottawa's North-South Institute, which didn't give the global justice movements a second thought. But likewise, few on the Left saw Stiglitz's contorted rebuilding of neo-classical economics through 'information-theoretic' augmentations as a worthwhile exercise, when their champion was so obviously now out of the power loop.

Some leftists tried reaching out a bit to the nationalists, with Noam Chomsky praising the Havana Summit,[56] and internationalist activists – from Global Exchange, Ruckus Society and other groups, organised by a small group with excellent e-mail contacts, United Peoples – concluding in mid-2000 that alliances with Southern rulers are possible: 'With regard to the fundamental debt cancellation and fair trade issues, the G77 summit in Havana once again confirmed the accordance between the views of the G77 and the new worldwide anti-globalization movement that protested WTO/IMF/World Bank in Seattle and Washington. A cooperation between the two parties therefore would seem appropriate in order to achieve our common goals in the most efficient and speedy way.'[57]

Again, this came to nothing as nationalists looked for relief instead to sites of power, not to disruptive left-wing groups with which they too experienced regular friction. Some Third Worldists were heartened by grudging elite acknowledgements in September 1999, led by Stiglitz but joined too by IMF researchers, that the previous year's Malaysian currency controls were effective medicine. But efforts by Mahathir to gather like-minded world leaders both at home and, by invitation of Mugabe, at Zimbabwe's Victoria Falls, had no apparent success in expanding the nationalist current. (South Africa, for example, was distinctly uninterested in nationalist-type financial boat-rocking.)

And looming still, as potentially a denouement to financial power – and in turn as the creator of space required to re-establish national economic sover-eignty – was the likelihood of a further financial 'correction'. The next time, all observers either feared (or hoped), the epicentre would be the US, whose capacity to suck in foreign goods on credit gave the appearance of superficial glitter, while economic fundamentals were in fact rotting underneath. As I discussed in Chapter one, that country's trade deficit, foreign debt, domestic corporate and consumer debt, and asset inflation all stood at unprecedented levels at the turn of the century. The buildup of financial stresses in the global economy – and the balance of forces that accommodated these stresses – could surely not be sustained forever. It would then be a matter of shifting the alliances and mobilising the activists to confront an extraordinary combination of financial power and vulnerability.

But does the South African government see it this way?

Notes

1   In an important overview of the debate over global financial reform, Walden Bello, Kamal Malhotra, Nicola Bullard and Marco Mezzera argue (in 'Notes on the Ascendancy and Regulation of Speculative Capital,' paper presented to the conference on 'Economic Sovereignty in a Globalized World', Bangkok, 24 March 1999) that there are three tendencies of global financial reform: 'It's the wiring, not the architecture' (the Washington Consensus plus Group of 22); 'Back to Bretton Woods' (a strong version of the Post-Washington Consensus); and 'It's the development model, stupid!' (global justice movements) – ignoring the resurgent US right-wing critique, and also collapsing nationalists and Post-Washington Consensus economists into the second category.

2   The term 'Washington Consensus' comes from John Williamson (1990), 'The Progress of Policy Reform in Latin America', *Policy Analyses in International Economics*, Washington, DC, Institute for International Economics. As one minor personal indication of the awesome power invested in Washington Consensus leaders, *Time* magazine (15 February 1999) anointed Rubin, Summers and Greenspan the 'Three Marketeers' who could save the world from depression.

The arrogance of Consensus-think was evident in Camdessus' description of the Asian crisis as a 'blessing in disguise' (*Wall Street Journal*, 24 September 1998). Illustrative of crisis-era justifications are articles and speeches by Robert Rubin (1998), 'Strengthening the Architecture of the International Financial System', remarks to the Brookings Institution, Washington, DC, 14 April; by Laurence Summers (1998), 'The Global Economic Situation and What it Means for the United States', remarks to the National Governors' Association, Milwaukee, Wisconsin, 4 August; by Stanley Fischer (1997), 'IMF – The Right Stuff', *Financial Times*, 17 December; (1998), 'In Defence of the IMF: Specialized Tools for a Specialized Task', *Foreign Affairs*, July-August, and (1999), 'On the Need for an International Lender of Last Resort', IMF mimeo, Washington, DC, 3 January; and by Michel Camdessus (1998), 'The IMF and its Programs in Asia', remarks to the Council on Foreign Relations, New York, 6 February. See also the Organisation for Economic Cooperation and Development (1998), *Report of the Working Group on International Financial Crises*, Paris.

It is tempting to place South Africa's government in the Washington Consensus grouping, given the evidence of how much elites like Mbeki, Manuel and Erwin celebrated their homegrown adoption of Washington-friendly austerity policies. But this would be to jump ahead of evidence to the contrary, as I will discuss below.

3   Wolfensohn, J. (1999), 'A Proposal for a Comprehensive Development Framework (A Discussion Draft)', Washington, DC, World Bank, 29 January.

4   Dornbush, cited in Doug Henwood (1999), 'Marxing up the Millennium', paper presented to the 'Marx at the Millennium' conference, University of Florida, 19 March.

5   For a good description, see Leaver, R. (1999), 'Moral (and Other) Hazards: The IMF and the Systematic Asian Crisis', paper presented to the conference on 'Economic Sovereignty in a Globalizing World', Bangkok, 24 March. For their own words, see Cato Institute, http://www.cato.org/research/glob-st.html; Henry Kissinger (1998), 'IMF no Longer Able to Deal with Economic Crises', *Los Angeles Times*, 4 October;

Shultz, G., Simon, W. and Wriston, W. (1998), 'Who Needs the IMF?', *Wall Street Journal*, 3 February.

6 Yonan, A. (2000), 'Bush seen Pushing IMF toward less Interventionist Role', Dow Jones newswires, December 20.

7 *Wall Street Journal*, 20 March 2000.

8 Franke-Ruta, G. (1998), 'The IMF Gets a Left and a Right', *The National Journal*, 30(3).

9 Stiglitz, J. (1998), 'More Instruments and Broader Goals: Moving Toward a Post-Washington Consensus', WIDER Annual Lecture, Helsinki, 7 January.

10 In a perceptive review of the 1998 book, Doug Henwood ('Let George Do It', *Left Business Observer*, 88, February 1999) argues that Soros has lifted unattributed arguments about financial-market disequilibrium ('nonergodicity') from Paul Davidson, the post-Keynesian economist, and that his analysis is far less convincing in these matters than Keynes, Joan Robinson, Karl Polanyi and Hyman Minsky, who pioneered theories of imperfect financial markets long before Stiglitz. (Stiglitz told me personally that he did not take Soros' ideas terribly seriously, for he saw Soros mainly as a practitioner with insufficient intellectual distance; interview, 1 October 1998, Ottawa.)

Most tellingly, Soros' solutions wilt when it comes to national exchange controls, at a time when honest economists were reviewing this once widely practiced technique as part of the solution to financial market turbulence – and at a time when Stiglitz, who initially worried that the Malaysian exchange controls of September 1998 represented 'too much of a backlash', prepared to endorse Malaysia's controls. (He told me three weeks later that he preferred dual-currency controls like South Africa's finrand of 1985–95.) After all, Stiglitz conceded in mid-1999, 'There was no adverse effect on direct foreign investment ... there may even have been a slight upsurge at some point' (Agence France-Presse, 23 June 1999). Soros, whose famous tiff with an evidently anti-semitic Mohamad bin Mahathir in 1997–8 may have influenced matters (*Economist*, 27 September 1997), shied well away from exchange controls, for if widespread, these would end his speculating days. And as Henwood (*op. cit.*) concludes of Soros' insurance proposal, 'Making creditors bear the risk of lending beyond sanctioned limits might not do all that much' to cool down hot money flows in any event.

11 Krugman, P. (1998), 'Saving Asia: It's Time to get RADICAL', *Fortune*, 7 September.

12 Sachs, J. (1997), 'The IMF is a Power unto Itself', *Financial Times*, 11 December; (1998), 'The IMF and the Asian Flu', *The American Prospect*, March-April.

13 With its own occasional Post-Washington Consensus rhetoric, South Africa, too, watched and waited, as I will show in the next two chapters. Sweden and Chile were meant to be new-and-improved social-democratic allies, though there was little real evidence of any practical application of such a grouping.

14 Lafontaine was also Old Left, and possibly belongs not in the Post-Washington category, but rather amongst global justice movements, in part because a key advisor was the Berlin Free University's famous Marxist economist, Elmar Altvater. See Lafontaine O. and Mueller, C. (1998), *Keine Angst vor der Globalisierung: Wohlstand und Arbeit für Alle*, Bonn, Dietz Verlag.

15 Hitoshi, H. (1999), 'The Asian Monetary Fund and the Miyazawa Initiative', paper presented to the conference on 'Economic Sovereignty in a Globalizing World', Bangkok, 24 March.

16 Reuters, 2 January 2001.

17 See D. Moggeridge (ed.), *The Collected Works of J. M. Keynes*, vol. 25, London, Macmillan, p. 149.

18 Tobin, J. (1978), 'A Proposal for International Monetary Reform', *The Eastern Economic Journal*, 4, July/October; Eichengreen, B., Tobin J. and Wyplosz, C. (1995), 'Two Cases for Sand in the Wheels of International Finance', *Economic Journal*, 105; and Tobin, J. (1996) in M. ul Haq, I. Kaul and I. Grunberg (eds), *The Tobin Tax: Coping with Financial Volatility*, New York, Oxford University Press. See also Felix, D. (1995), 'Financial Globalization vs. Free Trade: The Case for the Tobin Tax', Geneva, United Nations Conference on Trade and Development discussion paper no. 108.
19 Henderson, H. (1996), *Building a Win-Win World*, San Francisco, Berrett-Koehler.
20 In 1990, the Bank for International Settlements Committee on Interbank Netting Schemes of the Central Banks of the Group of Ten Countries agreed on the 'Lamfalussy Minimum Standards' for regulation of such flows, for example, by taxing transactions that are registered through the Society for Worldwide Interbank Financial Telecommunications (SWIFT, the primary commercial bank clearing mechanism), which now incorporates netting done through the Exchange Clearing House Organization and Multinet International Bank. See Bank for International Settlements (1990), *The Lamfalussy Report: Report of the Committee on Interbank Netting Schemes of the Central Banks of the Group of Ten Countries*, Basle.
21 Garber, P. and Taylor, M. (1995), 'Sand in the Wheels of Foreign Exchange Markets: A Sceptical Note', *The Economic Journal*, 105; Garber, P. (1998), 'Derivatives in International Capital Flow', National Bureau of Economic Research working paper no. 6623, New York.
22 Eatwell, J. and Taylor, L. (1998), 'International Capital Markets and the Future of Economic Policy', *CEPA Working Paper Series III*, working paper no. 9, New School for Social Research, New York, September.
23 Davidson, P. (1997), 'Are Grains of Sand in the Wheels of International Finance Sufficient to do the Job when Boulders are often Required?' *The Economic Journal*, 107, and (1998), 'The Case for Regulating International Capital Flows', paper presented at the Social Market Foundation Seminar on Regulation of Capital Movements, 17 November.
24 Akyuz, Y. (1995), 'Taming International Finance,' in J. Michie and J. G. Smith (eds), *Managing the Global Economy*, Oxford, Oxford University Press, and (1998), 'The East Asian Financial Crisis: Back to the Future', in K. S. Jomo (ed.), *Tigers in Trouble*, London, Zed.
25 See http://www.fmcenter.org.
26 Instead of shutting down municipalities and companies or bankrupting consumers who have liquidity problems, such procedures attempt to resolve the problems through restructuring. This makes them relevant to foreign debt negotiations. In its *1998 Trade and Development Report*, UNCTAD proposed the establishment of an independent panel to determine when a country under attack by speculators can be permitted to impose exchange or capital controls (including debt standstills), consistent with the IMF's Article VIII, section 2(b).
27 PDS Parliamentary Group (1999), 'A social and democratic world economic system in place of neo-liberal globalization', printed paper 14/954, German Bundestag, Bonn, 4 May.
28 For details, see Anderson, S., Cavanagh, J. and Lee, T. (1999), *Field Guide to the World Economy*, New York, The Free Press.
29 Summers, L. (1989), 'When Financial Markets Work Too Well: A Cautious Case for a Securities Transactions Tax', *Journal of Financial Services*, 3.
30 Fischer, S. (1991), *Issues in International Economic Integration*, Bangkok, p. 20.

31 Stiglitz, J. (1989), 'Using Tax Policy to Curb Speculative Short-Term Trading', *Journal of Financial Services*, 3.
32 In addition, trade negotiations witnessed periodic upsurges of Third World nationalism, especially in behind-the-scenes maneuvering at Seattle by the Organisation of African Unity's more nationalist trade ministers (mainly from Zimbabwe, Uganda and Kenya, working directly against South Africa). The denial of consensus of these ministers blocked the WTO in December 1999. Again, a year later at a meeting of African trade ministers in Libreville, permission was denied Alec Erwin and WTO officials to proceed with a new 'comprehensive' round. The main source of information and support for the more nationalist-inclined African ministers was a Harare-based NGO, Southern and Eastern African Trade, Information and Negotitations Initiative, based at the UNDP, led by Yash Tandon, former Ugandan minister of culture.
33 Mahathir, M. (1998), 'The Future of Asia in a Globalized and Deregulated World', speech to the conference 'The Future of Asia', Tokyo, 4 June.
34 There was a confused flurry in early 1999 when Mugabe sought funding elsewhere than the IMF. See, for example, 'Zimbabwe Severs Ties with the IMF', *Wall Street Journal*, 12, April 1999 and AP Worldstream, '"We Won't Cut Ties with IMF, World Bank," says Zimbabwe', 12 April 1999. See also Chapter three, above.
35 The main controversies associated with the honeymoon period following his impressive electoral victory in 1998 – on an anti-poverty campaign platform – were whether the falling world oil price (leading to an estimated 4% decline in Venezuelan GDP in 1999) would force budget and real wage cuts, and how quickly Chavez would carry out his threat to impose a state of emergency. Within a month of taking office, he cut the budget by 11% while denying he was already an IMF devotee, notwithstanding some extra spending on public works programmes. While unions demanded a 50% wage increase to keep pace with inflation, Chavez offered only 20% in a national tripartite bargaining forum, and, when that broke down, imposed the negative real-wage deal on public-sector workers (see Reuters, 'Venezuela not Negotiating, just Talking to IMF', 3 March 1999; Associated Press, 'Venezuela faces Severe Recession', 4 March 1999).
36 There were occasional hints that the South African government could potentially join progressive nationalists, were any to rise in protest at Washington economics. But as I noted above, just as many other hints suggested that Mbeki, Manuel and Erwin belonged with their Washington friends, and others gave the impression that the ANC leaned more logically towards a Post-Washington Consensus ideology. The only constant here, as we will see in the subsequent two chapters, was systematic confusion and mixed signalling.
37 Group of 77 South Summit (2000), 'Havana Programme of Action', Havana, 10–14 April, http://www.g-77.org.
38 My forthcoming book analysing Mugabe's degeneration is tentatively entitled *Zimbabwe's Plunge: Catastrophic Combinations of Nationalism and Neoliberalism*.
39 Some extent of popular backing was found amongst communist parties in the Philippines, South Africa, Germany, parts of Eastern Europe and Cuba.
40 The most important of such parties were the Brazilian Workers Party, the Nicaraguan Sandinistas and their allies of the São Paulo Forum in Latin America.
41 To cite only a few such mass movements which apparently worked well with other local and global anti-neo-liberal initiatives – simply to give a flavour of this position – there are Mexico's Zapatistas (both the retreating army and the emerging peasant and worker civil-society organisations, as I will describe in Chapter eleven), Brazil's Movement of the Landless, India's National Alliance of People's

Movements, Thailand's Forum of the Poor and the Korean Confederation of Trade Unions.

42 Again, by way of example, local struggles to make housing and food social entitlements – expanding the sphere of human rights discourse beyond 'first generation' liberal political rights into more radical socio-economic spheres – were aggregated into the Habitat International Coalition and FoodFirst International Action Network. Other international networks had successes in banning the dumping and incineration of toxic waste (Health Care without Harm). The Zapatista 'Intergalactic Encounters for Humanity, Against Neoliberalism' planted more visionary seeds, as have growing anarchist-inspired networking and activism – epitomised by the civil disobedience of the impressive network inspired by Zapatismo known as 'Peoples' Global Action' – in London, Paris, Geneva, Davos, San Francisco and other sites of Northern power. The most impressive activist movement in the US is Direct Action Network, augmented by the Independent Media Centers in various cities.

43 Admittedly, as I will discuss in more detail in Chapter eleven, classic South-versus-North sentiments arose not only in Jubilee 2000 critiques of the Washington Consensus and the highly-conditional debt relief schemes on offer from Washington, but also in Jubilee South critiques of their Northern advocacy counterparts, who often appeared extremely pliant to the gambits of Northern politicians. For an excellent article on this topic, see Dot Keet, 'The International Anti-Debt Campaign: An Activists' View from the South, to Activists in the North', AIDC discussion document, http://www.aidc.org.za.

44 Again a handful of examples will suffice, e.g. the Third World Network based in Penang and Accra, the environmental group Greenpeace and the International Rivers Network in Berkeley.

45 Worth citing are the Nader organisations, the Alliance for Global Justice, the Center for Economic Justice and the Center for International Environmental Law.

46 For example, Focus on the Global South in Bangkok, the Center for Economic Policy and Research and Institute for Policy Studies in Washington, DC, Amsterdam's Transnational Institute and International Institute for Research and Education.

47 Critical masses of radical political economists had amassed at Toronto's York University, London's School of Oriental and African Studies, the University of Massachusetts/Amherst, and American University in Washington.

48 In English, these included *The Ecologist, Green-Left Weekly, International Socialism, International Viewpoint, Left Business Observer, Links, Monthly Review, Multinational Monitor, New Internationalist, Red Pepper, Third World Resurgence* and *Z*.

49 These included Pluto, Zed, Monthly Review Press, South End and Verso, amongst just the English-language presses.

50 In the same illustrative spirit, some of the leading anti-neo-liberal spokespeople, activist-leaders and leftist luminaries of the late 1990s deserve mention: Subcommandante Marcos of the Zapatistas, Lula (Luis Ignacio da Silva) of the Brazilian Workers Party, President Fidel Castro of Cuba, Urugayan writer Eduardo Galeano, ex-diplomat Alejandro Bendana of Nicaragua, Camille Chalmers of the Haitian anti-neo-liberal movement, Samir Amin of the World Forum for Alternatives in Dakar, Kenyan environmentalist Wangari Maathai, Kenyan leader of the 50 Years is Enough coalition Njoki Njehu, South African poet Dennis Brutus of the debt cancellation movement and Archbishop Njongonkulu Ndungane of Cape Town, Indian anti-dams and social movement campaigner Medha Patkar and her ally, writer Arundhati Roy, Martin Khor of Third World Network in Penang, Indian

feminist-scientist-environmentalist Vandana Shiva, Walden Bello of Focus on the Global South, Australian journalist John Pilger, Russian intellectual Boris Kagarlitsky, Susan George of the Transnational Institute, French intellectual Pierre Bordieu and radical farmer Pierre Bove, Canadian anti-corporate writer Naomi Klein, US consumer activist Ralph Nader, movement-builder Kevin Danaher and US intellectual Noam Chomsky.

51 Within the AFL-CIO, the balance of forces was fluid, between right-wing populist Jimmy Hoffa, Jr. of the teamsters and left-leaning former mineworker leader Rich Trumka, with overall leader John Sweeney tending to conservatism and corporatism.

52 For example, Jeffrey Sachs promised Stiglitz and his World Bank colleagues a breather from criticism. But not long after the latter's departure, Sachs used the *Financial Times* to call Wolfensohn a 'master of deceit' (12 October 2000).

53 This quotation, and the following one by Kenneth Arrow, appeared in the *Left Business Observer*, February 2000.

54 See Bretton Woods Project newsletter at http://www.brettonwoodsproject.org/update.

55 *Ibid.* This accolade referred, presumably, to the bloated, vain, self-destructive and hallucinatory state in which the singer found himself not long before his death.

56 Chomsky, N. (2000), 'Summits', *ZNet* commentary, 17 July, http://www.zmag.org/.

57 http://www.unitedpeoples.net.

CHAPTER SIX

Ideology and global governance

1. Introduction

In *The Wretched of the Earth*, Frantz Fanon concluded, 'For my part, the deeper I enter into the culture and political circles the surer I am that the great danger that threatens Africa is the absence of ideology.'[1] So the question to be asked is surely, Is there a coherent explanation and ideological posture in relation to globalisation – indeed to 'global apartheid' – to be found within the top echelons of the South African state and ruling party?

I pose the question because President Thabo Mbeki has made explicit arguments to this effect. At a social-democratic youth gathering in July 2000 in Sweden, for example, he exhorted his listeners that:

> Fundamental to the labour, social democratic, socialist and national libera-
> tion movements from their very inception, is the adherence to the view that
> the people must be their own liberators. These movements have therefore
> always fought for democracy and, more than this, for the empowering of the
> people to represent their own interests through their political parties and
> through mass struggle ... Democracy is about the exercise of political power
> by the people themselves. As the organised representative of these masses,
> the progressive movement cannot, on the basis that the market will decide
> these issues, as [*New York Times* columnist Thomas] Friedman asserts,
> abandon the struggle for the all-round and sustained betterment of the lives
> of the people and the attainment of social justice. Accordingly, we have to
> continue to treat the struggle against poverty, national and social exclusion
> and marginalisation as fundamental to the objectives of socialist movement.[2]

Mbeki's long-term objective in relation to globalisation may not, therefore, appear to differ much from the project of 'National Democratic Revolution' established by the African National Congress at home. Yet both in South African and on the international terrain, complexities and contradictions quickly appear. South Africa has offered two major initiatives within the global political-economic arena: reforming the embryonic world-state system, and lending South African prestige and concrete assistance to alleviating the plight of the African continent.

The first challenge, upon which all else hinges (and hence upon which this analysis dwells at greatest length), has at least three component strategies:

1) leading the launch of a new WTO round, in co-operation with select semi-peripheral allies (such as Algeria, Brazil, China, Egypt, India, Mexico, Nigeria and South Korea), to contest Northern protectionism;

2) promoting the revitalisation of the IMF and World Bank by advocating more democratic functioning (especially a higher voting share for Africa), invoking a modified Post-Washington Consensus approach to development, and demanding a larger volume of debt relief; and

3) rejuvenating the UN – apparently through seeking a permanent seat on the Security Council – and associated agencies in key areas of international influence.

The second challenge entails the assertion of South Africa's politico-economic-military-diplomatic might in Africa, in at least six debates over:

1) the merits of interventions within Southern African countries to prop up contested allied governments (unjustified when Zimbabwe enters the Democratic Republic of the Congo but justified by Pretoria when South Africa intervenes in Lesotho);

2) whether residual nationalist alliances should determine South Africa's posture towards Zimbabwe (for in spite of qualms from within the ANC, Pretoria was ultimately extremely supportive of the Mugabe regime);

3) the maximisation of South Africa's formidable comparative advantages of scale in manufactured exports to Africa (notwithstanding a serious backlash by SADC partners);

4) the costs of African immigration to South Africa (a process still strongly opposed and viciously punished by Pretoria);

5) the diminishing role of human rights in the making of foreign policy, as witnessed in arms sales and both African and international deal-making; and

6) the leadership of Mbeki, along with Nigeria's Olusegun Obasanjo and Algeria's Abdelaziz Bouteflika, in a proposed Millennium Africa Programme concerning development, debt, investment and trade, through the Davos World Economic Forum (first) and the Organisation of African Unity, which aims to raise higher levels of aid, debt cancellation and market access in exchange for governance-related conditionality.

Although it is beyond my immediate scope to address these extremely complex issues, a prerequisite query can be posed: Is ideology required to make sense of, and ultimately to justify, these interrelated tasks? After all, the late 1990s witnessed a general global rethink of the neo-liberal free-market philosophy, as a result of crises of international economic regulation and growing global inequality. Even if it is still sometimes termed 'social democracy', the modified 'Third Way' neo-liberalism practised by the ruling parties of the United States from 1993 to 2000, Britain from 1997 and Germany from 1998 was virtually indistinguishable from the policies of conservative predecessors – Reagan, Thatcher and Kohl – who launched the global resurgence of corporate rule and attack on the social wage during the 1980s.

Alan Zuege puts it in a way that is strikingly applicable to South Africa's own socio-economic strategy, which, in common with the Third Way,

> seeks to adapt not just industrial and political structures, but social struc-
> tures as well, to the imperative to compete and win in global markets. In
> pursuit of this agenda, the so-called modernising left asks workers to trade
> away what remains of their post-war entitlements of the chimerical promise
> of participation in a global knowledge economy, and to buy into the new
> industrial, distributional, and civic accords which purport to make it possi-
> ble. But with the legacy of overaccumulation still unravelling and the ravages
> of international competition unyielding, these reformist 'bargains' amount to
> little more than a 'negotiated' path to austerity.[3]

Of course, no matter the similarity between ANC policy and this descrip-tion, from ANC headquarters would come a robust denial that the ANC is in lockstep with the neo-liberal economics and Third Way politics of Clinton, Blair and Schroeder. Instead, Mbeki's primary personal and political-party challenge has been to ally with regimes like those in Sweden and Chile that wear a post-neo-liberal face, and to project a new compas-sion for marginalised people and countries that transcends the market. In his Swedish speech, Mbeki clarified the ideological starting point of a revived social democracy: 'I believe that the question we should all ask ourselves is whether it is the *vox populi* – the voice of the people – that is the voice of God, or is it the voice of the market, that is the voice of God!'[4]

The voice of the people, or the voice of the market? Matters become infi-nitely more nuanced once we consider not merely rhetorical claims, but explanations and ideological underpinnings (see Section 2). To the extent that an apolitical, technocratic reading is possible, Mbeki provides one (see Section 3). The conclusion (Section 4) therefore enquires into aspects of solidarity that follow from a modernisationist view of globalisation together with a techno-economic ideology. In combination, these belie Mbeki's talk of 'sustained betterment of the lives of the people and the attainment of social justice' – and, predictably, what we ultimately discover to be at stake in the ideological debate over globalisation is merely vulgar self-interest.

2. Explaining globalisation

At the July 1998 Mercosur meetings of South American nations, Nelson Mandela was heard to announce: 'Globalization is a phenomenon that we cannot deny. All we can do is accept it.'[5] But just weeks later, the mood within the highest circles of the ANC seemed to shift quite dramatically in the opposite direction. (However, as I explain below, the 'inevitability thesis' – and its corollary, the excuse that 'globalisation made me do it!' – is still trotted out regularly when learned-helplessness posturing is required.)

Both Mbeki and then Mandela had scolded a major SA Communist Party congress and a Cosatu executive committee in June–July of that year for opposition to neo-liberalism. But whether because of the national elections pending in 1999 (requiring Tripartite Alliance reconciliation) or a genuine change of heart, some flaps on the left of the broad ANC tent were reopened within months, and communists and trade unionists streamed back in.

The market as cannibal?

One of the catalysts was the elevation of South Africa to lead the Non-Aligned Movement in September 1998. Mbeki's plenary address to the heads of state assembled in Durban that month included the comment that 'the message that comes across is that the market is a cannibal which feeds on its own offspring ... we are showered with accolades for cooperating in the effort to fatten ourselves for the kill'.[6] The next month, a leading ANC intellectual, Joel Netshitenzhe, complained in an official ruling-party document entitled 'The State, Property Relations and Social Transformation' that South Africa was not attracting the foreign investment anticipated to correspond with the requisite 'sound' economic policies:

> If in the past the bourgeois state blatantly represented the interests of private capital, today its enslavement is even the more pronounced, with its policies and actions beholden to the whims of owners of stupendously large amounts of capital which is in constant flight across stocks, currencies and state boundaries. More often than not, governments even in the most advance countries assert their role in the economy merely by 'sending signals to the markets', which they can only second-guess. If in the past, the Bretton Woods Institutions (the IMF and World Bank) and the World Trade Organisation pursued the same interests as these powerful corporations and governments, today their prescriptions are turned on their heads as 'the animal spirits' sway moods in a set of motions that have no apparent rhythm or logic. Yet there is rhythm and logic. It is the logic of unbridled pursuit of profit which has little direct bearing to production ...
>
> What this in fact means is that, in terms of the broad array of economic and social policy, information and even political integrity, the state has lost

much of its national sovereignty. This applies more so to developing countries.[7]

The market's damage could be understood not merely in moral terms, but also as a self-destructive force, according to the Tripartite Alliance:

> As the depth and relative durability of the crisis have become apparent, the dominant economic paradigm (the neoliberal 'Washington Consensus') has fallen into increasing disrepute ... The dominant assumption in the 1990s has been that alignment with globalization would guarantee economies more or less uninterrupted growth. The paradigm of an endlessly expanding global freeway, in which, to benefit, individual (and particularly developing) economies simply had to take the standard macro-economic on-ramp (liberalisation, privatisation, deregulation, flexibility and a 3% budget deficit) is now in crisis.[8]

Indeed, at that stage, the East Asian collapse was acute; financial-crisis 'contagion' had spread to Russia and then South Africa; controversial Malaysian nationalist Mahathir bin Mohamad shocked the world by successfully imposing exchange controls; and IMF and World Bank legitimacy had sunk to unprecedented lows.[9] A bit of cheekiness was surely justified, even if the attack implicated South Africa's *own* macroeconomic managers?

Development ideology

But to gain the requisite scepticism about the durability of the ANC leadership's attack on the global market requires a look at the underlying philosophy Mbeki brings to development. For in his argumentation, Mbeki carefully avoids drawing the obvious *causal* linkages between growing wealth in one part of the world and growing poverty elsewhere. (Never is such causality debated, and only rarely is it mentioned, but an unusual example was trade and industry minister Alec Erwin's throwaway comment to parliament, just prior to the WTO debacle in Seattle, that 'the mobility of [financial] capital acts to further set back economic growth in the developing countries'.)[10]

When Mbeki does invoke arguments reminiscent of so-called 'dependency theory' – i.e. that economic integration under conditions of global corporate and financial domination entails the *development of underdevelopment* – so as to more explicitly challenge global elites, economic variables are quickly obscured. The *modus operandi* becomes, simply, helplessness, of the kind he expressed in a speech in May 2000 to the US foreign policy establishment at Georgetown University in Washington:

> Many of our countries, including all those on our Continent, do not have and are unlikely to have in the foreseeable future, the strength themselves to

determine on their own what should happen to their economies. The more they get integrated into the world economy, the further will this capacity be reduced, making them more dependent on the rest of the world economy with regard to meeting the challenge of ending poverty within their countries.[11]

'[M]ore dependent on ... the world economy' – but by definition, in Mbeki's post-communist, pragmatic leadership dictionary, *that shouldn't be a bad thing*, and is certainly a *necessary* process. Indeed, in a speech at the White House, Mbeki warmly endorsed the amplification of US-dominated, corporate rule: 'We are particularly pleased that the African Growth and Opportunity Act has been signed.'[12] But, looking carefully, there is never to be found in Mbeki's repertoire of explanations the notion, dangerous to the neo-liberal stance, that the gulf between rich and poor widens *precisely because Northern capital enjoys an ever-growing capacity to source inputs ever more cheaply from the South*, thanks to asymmetric trade relations, debt peonage and currency crashes generated by regular bouts of speculative financial raiding.

That possibility, and the policy implications it suggests, can never be considered, much less stated, in polite discourse. On the contrary, judging from the Georgetown speech, Mbeki appears to have backpedaled from a University of Sussex-era interest in dependency theory to 'modernisation-theory' principles, by way of the notion of development 'take-off' pioneered by US imperialist planner W. W. Rostow, and long ridiculed by the Left: 'Relative to the needs of these countries, including our own, the world economy disposes of sufficient capital resources whose injection into our countries as long-term investment, would succeed to take us to the "take-off stage" once spoken of in textbooks on development economics.'[13]

But to take off, under current global circumstances, requires access to new technology. And to justify the freedom given to South African businesses since 1994 to import job-killing, capital-intensive machinery in a context in which a vast number of South Africans still lack not only gainful employment but also access to goods to fulfil their basic needs, in turn requires a techno-economic perspective on globalisation.

3. Globalisation's techno-economic fix?

There are diverse discourses in Mbeki's circles about globalisation, as was demonstrated in the paper entitled 'The Global Economic Crisis and its Implications for South Africa' of October 1998 (see the opening paragraphs of Chapter one). Recall the explanation that 'it is precisely declining profitability in the most advanced economies that has spurred the last quarter of a century of intensified globalization'. Thus instead of the strength and vitality of international capitalism that is to blame for globalisation's march, it is the system's 'overaccumulation crisis' and its resulting desperate attempt to reach out beyond stagnant home markets.

Joining the IT revolution

In contrast, a rather less-threatening strand of explanation seems to have prevailed at least up to mid-2000. For Alec Erwin, speaking in February 2000 to the UN Conference on Trade and Development (the international organisation over which he presided during the late 1990s), the motive force was the power not of increasingly footloose corporate capital, but the magic of IT:

> In a sense to say the world is global is a trite proposition. There is a new essence that we seek in the term globalization. It must surely be that we increasingly experience our globe in a common real time. This emerges as information technology links us. Knowledge of every type begins to flow so that we can know each other instantaneously.
>
> As a result everything else begins to move in a more rapid way. This movement of knowledge has powerfully inserted itself into production processes so that they move faster, with more precision, responding to immense complexity in nanoseconds. Surely it is this complex real time interaction that is the qualitatively new characteristic of globalization.
>
> If this is the case then it cannot be reversed. To think this is possible is like trying to prevent the spread of electricity because we fear being shocked when we don't take care.[14]

The same tone of inevitability was adopted in September 2000 by Nelson Mandela, speaking to the British Labour Party's convention:

> Those who are saying they are not going to prepare for this phenomenon are like saying 'I don't recognise winter, therefore I'm not going to buy clothing for winter'.
>
> We have our reservations about globalisation. We must certainly not be afraid to condemn those aspects of globalisation which lead to more poverty in the world. All human beings are born equal. They must be treated equally. We would argue that the shrinking of the globe through the advances in communications and information technology has made it even more incumbent upon us to become once more the keepers of our brothers and sisters.[15]

If globalisation is thus based on technological advance and not capitalist crisis tendencies, harnessing IT for development must then become a central objective. The G-8 meeting in Okinawa in July 2000 certainly advanced this thesis. Mbeki warmly accepted the bona fides of the world leaders, notwithstanding enormous disappointment expressed universally that, quite evidently, substantial debt relief was off the G-8 agenda. To illustrate, argued Mbeki to a gathering of young civil-service leaders the same month: 'Technology by itself, will not necessarily eradicate poverty, nor will it end underdevelopment. Yet, the availability of technology and its dissemination amongst many sectors of society, is a critically necessary condition for economic and social development.'[16]

The most poignant reference to the globalisation high road Mbeki regularly makes is to 'telemedicine' (i.e. interventions by specialists at a great geographical distance). As he put it in a speech to a corporate San Francisco audience, up the road from Silicon Valley, in May 2000:

> Few amongst us will disagree when we assert that a global society presents us with the opportunities to collapse both time and space, so that a village health worker in Uganda could perform some of the most difficult medical procedures with the assistance of a surgeon sitting in her office in San Francisco. To be able to do this, it requires of the people in a poor country such as Uganda to have access to education, to have access to satellite technology, and for the doctor and nurse in Uganda to be up to speed with the latest telemedicine technology.[17]

Yet telemedicine also requires something else that Uganda has a very hard time acquiring, given the fluctuating prices of its main agricultural exports and its extreme burden of foreign-debt repayment: hard currency. This vital barrier is obviously the main constraint behind the integration of Africa into the New Economy, yet paradoxically it also offers neo-liberal policy advocates a rationale – even an imperative – for intensifying further Africa's self-defeating, export-oriented development strategy.

Hunting for foreign exchange
The need to earn forex is always at the back of Mbeki's mind, and the last quarter of a century of declining prices of primary commodities weighs just as heavily. As he explained to the ANC National General Council in July 2000,

> You are aware of the fact that a central objective of our economic policy is and has been the expansion and modernisation of the manufacturing sector of our economy and the shifting of our export mix in favour of manufactured goods. Given our strong resource base, this must mean, among other things, that we add value to the resources we produce, so that we supply highly sophisticated intermediate products to the world industrial economy.[18]

But from this technological fix – the implications of which are to enter the world economy through greater 'beneficiation' of raw materials – there arises some profound dilemmas. Mbeki's best case for a pragmatic engagement with the world economy was close at hand when, at the meeting of the ANC leadership in Port Elizabeth, he sang the praises of a newly established factory to produce catalytic converters for cars:

To simplify this proposition, let me cite just one example of a new manufacturing facility that has been established in this city. I refer to a catalytic converter plant which produces such converters which, as you know, are used to reduce carbon dioxide emissions from motor vehicles, to promote a better environment. Again as you know, these converters use platinum, of which we stand out as one of the world's largest producers. The catalytic converter plant to which I refer, which is here in Port Elizabeth, was established by a foreign company and is therefore part of the foreign investment we constantly seek to attract to our country. Its establishment has made an important contribution to the struggle we continue to wage to transform ours into a modern manufacturing economy, with a relative reduction of our dependence on the export of raw materials. To be economically viable, this plant has to export a large part of its output. It must therefore respond to the world market in a way that ensures that it is able to compete against other plants, wherever they are located in the world, with regard to such factors as consistency in quality, delivery on time and cost. Among other things, the management must therefore ensure that the staff at the plant has the necessary skills to produce the converters and meet these requirements. To put the matter plainly, in the event that the plant experiences repeated work stoppages so that it is unable to address these requirements, the motor manufacturing will switch to other plants located outside our country. Accordingly the PE plant would then have to close down, with the inevitable job losses and our regression to the larger exports of raw platinum ... The story we have told is not a tale of fiction. It describes what we as a movement, a government and a country are trying to do, and the demands imposed on all of us by the modern, global economy.[19]

Costs and benefits of converters

Setting aside Mbeki's obvious attempt to discipline labour, several equally obvious critical questions are begged. Who profits from production of catalytic converters, what rate of return is expected, and how much of the surplus leaves South Africa forever, as opposed to remaining for reinvestment? What transfer-pricing problems might arise? Is the production process as labour-intensive as local conditions should dictate (as is the case for the leather-seat component sector)? Why didn't a South African capitalist, or even the state, not establish that investment? What backward-forward linkages, aside from platinum inputs, does South Africa gain from the investment? What other costs are there to South Africa, such as the generous (and expensive) Motor Industry Development Plan incentives (and could these have been used elsewhere to greater socio-economic benefit)?

Why, indeed, are catalytic converters themselves not required in South Africa's own fleet of motor vehicles? The answer, we know, is the added

IDEOLOGY AND GLOBAL GOVERNANCE 125

cost per vehicle, in a country where transport is already prohibitively expensive for the majority of people. Yet is affordability truly an acceptable constraint, in view of the hedonistic consumer-profile of the new-car market? What additional amount would a catalytic converter add to the price of a new Mercedes or BWM, the output of which for rich South Africans has barely faltered over the past quarter of a century of national economic stagnation? Moreover, why have there been no efforts to adjust the pricing mechanism within the domestic auto market – using, for instance, a consumption tax on local and imported luxury cars to pay not only for environmentally friendly accessories and unleaded petrol, but for a dramatic change in transport patterns – so that cleaner, more efficient, more equitable and more appropriate motor vehicles are produced? (The public transport recapitalisation of private taxis hardly qualifies as a substantial state intervention, given the sector's deadly contradictions.)

Likewise, another question begged in Mbeki's praise for catalytic-converter production concerns South Africa's broader responsibility for reducing its own per-capita emissions of carbon dioxide, which are nearly as high as Japan's. Indeed, the other major export-oriented, beneficiation strategy that Mbeki could easily have mentioned in Port Elizabeth is that city's local Spatial Development Initiative (SDI) pilot project: the proposed Coega stainless steel plant. Its initial formulation was as a zinc smelter, but when that failed because of a global oversupply of zinc, the proposed huge deep-water port and steel plant at Coega were justified as offsets for a purchase of submarines through a German firm. However, Coega – like Mozal in Maputo – is an electricity-guzzling, pollution-intensive, export-oriented, heavily-subsidised project which, as *Business Day* newspaper points out regularly, should not go forward without a clear demonstration of economic sustainability. Such sustainability is questionable, as the deal boils down to a face-saving device for the government's claim that R30 billion in arms purchases would generate R100 billion in matching investments.[20] Worse, the number of permanent jobs created is only around 1 000, with the cost per job roughly 1 000 times higher than traditional public works or even employment in small, medium and micro enterprises. In this case, funding the project from state coffers – covering a variety of SDI incentives plus a large Portnet subsidy for a questionable new deep-water port – will have the effect of diminishing Port Elizabeth's own potential to subsidise electricity for low-income households, as cross-subsidies from big firms to poor people are out of the question.[21]

A top official has already expressed great resistance to raising the price of heavily-polluting, electricity-intensive, export-oriented projects: 'If we increase the price of electricity to users like Alusaf, their products will become uncompetitive and that will affect our balance of payments … It's a fact that international capital holds sway as we come to the end of the

20th century.'[22] Mbeki could not be unaware of the massive socio-ecological injustice associated with South Africa's ultra-cheap energy prices for corporations like Alusaf, Columbus, Highveld and Iscor (which together consume more than a quarter of South African coal-generated electricity). He firmly endorsed the 'Berlin Communiqué' in June 2000, with its concern over global warming: 'The global environment must be handed on safely to future generations. Sustainable development is an important orientation for modern governance.' Yet in the next sentence is, once again, a resort to Washington Consensus-think: 'We support the commitments in the Kyoto Protocol and want to use new mechanisms, like emissions trading, to create common interest between the developing and developed world.'[23] Even setting aside the US government's attempt in November 2000 to sabotage the Kyoto agreement at a follow-up session in The Hague, the 'commodification of everything' proceeds apace, extending even to air.

Water wars
Similarly, South African water has also been subject to globalisation's techno-economic fix, in at least two ways. British and French water privatisers have been welcomed with open arms, notwithstanding convincing documentation of consumer exploitation, worker disempowerment and political corruption. And the World Bank has entered the debate over the pricing of water, strongly inveighing against the free 'lifeline' supply mandated in the RDP.[24]

Why shouldn't water, electricity and telephones be provided by international firms? According to finance minister Trevor Manuel, after all, 'foreign investment in state-owned enterprises allows for access to cutting-edge technologies and increases the effectiveness with which these entities can deliver on the rollout of essential services'.[25]

Yet on closer examination, the two most important pilots associated with 'public-private partnerships' in basic services had already proved Manuel wrong by the end of the 1990s. The role of Suez Lyonnais des Eaux in several Eastern Cape towns after five years left the black townships increasingly subject not just to water cut-offs for non-payment of bills, but even to curtailment of the 'bucket system' of excrement collection as well (contrary to the firm's promise in 1994 that it would urgently upgrade the sanitation system from the prevailing 19th-century standards).[26] The enduring use of the bucket system gives the lie to Manuel's belief that foreign investment brings effective delivery of essential services.

Telephone tag
Likewise, the most important partial privatisation to date, of Telkom, generated two scandalous dynamics that reflect the charlatan character of

such partnerships. Firstly, the Texan and Malaysian partners who in 1997 bought 30% of Telkom have not only retrenched tens of thousands of workers (for which the state must carry the burden of associated social costs), but have attacked the cross-subsidisation of telephone calls. Previously, a local call received a large subsidy, paid for by long-distance users. That cross-subsidy evaporated because it detracted from the US-Malaysian consortium's profitability (as do all such cross-subsidies). Secondly, the rollout of telephone lines is thus hampered not only by un-affordability, but by the phenomenon known as 'churning', i.e. in order to prove to government it has connected sufficient lines to warrant continuation of its monopoly status, Telkom simply reuses old connections, raises its prices for local calls, cuts off customers when they can't pay, and reconnects them (usually under another name), only to disconnect them all over again. The lack of sustainability in telephone rollout, as in the cases of water and electricity, is hence amplified by the role of the for-profit private sector.[27]

It is only fair to ask whether instead of attracting elusive foreign investment, more attention should not have been given to forcing local capital into a developmental mode (through mechanisms like prescribed asset requirements for institutional investors and community-reinvestment legislation against banks). Mbeki and his team spurned such RDP mandates, in favour of directing enormous efforts to petition foreign privatisers, whose demands for 30–35% US-dollar-denominated rates of return on investments did not, apparently, faze Pretoria.[28] And instead of promoting developmental investment by local firms, Mbeki gave them the opposite signal, leading even *Business Day* editorialists to comment 'with alarm and despondency' upon the 'flight of corporate SA abroad'. In the case of the second-largest conversion of a publicly listed company (De Beers) into private hands (Oppenheimer) in international history, which in turn denuded the Johannesburg Stock Exchange (JSE), the conservative editorialists blamed 'the speed with which the finance minister has approved the Anglo-De Beers deal (what odds on De Beers relisting in some form in London in the next two years?) and the ease with which Billiton, Old Mutual, Dimension Data and Anglo itself have slipped their local chains ...'[29]

4. Ideology and self-interest

By mid-2000, after having done all in his power to attract foreign direct investment, to little effect, Mbeki finally appeared ready to concede the futility of his efforts (in this case to US corporate representatives at the San Francisco gathering):

> Notwithstanding some specific problems in some developing countries and especially African countries, there are many among these countries that have

and continue to have stability and are at peace with themselves, countries that have responded positively, even under very difficult circumstances, to the prescriptions of both the prospective investors as well as the multi-lateral institutions. Many of these countries have created the necessary climate conducive to investment, for example by liberalising their trade, privatising state-owned enterprises, reforming their tax system and generally adhering to the prescribed injunctions, all done in an attempt to attract the necessary investments. The response from the developed countries, to these attempts by especially many African countries to stay within the confines of the rules, has been to treat the African continent as one country, and therefore, to punish a country on the one end of the continent for the deeds of another on the other end. In our own country, we have been assured that our economic fundamentals are correct and sound. We have developed a stable and effective financial and fiscal system. We have reduced tariffs to levels that are comparable to the advanced industrial countries. We have reformed agriculture to make it the least subsidised of all the major agricultural trading nations. We have restructured our public sector through privatisation, strategic partners and regulation. We have an equitable and sophisticated system of labour relations that is continually adjusting to new developments. We play an active role in all multilateral agencies in the world. Yet, the flow of investment into South Africa has not met our expectations while the levels of poverty and unemployment remain high.[30]

Likewise at Georgetown, Mbeki spoke of 'the many heroic efforts the governments and peoples of Africa have made and are making to correct past wrongs, encompassing ... the sustained effort in many countries to introduce new economic and social policies consistent with many elements of the so-called Washington Consensus'.[31]

Resisting change
Recognising the futility of adopting the Washington Consensus in expectation of economic rewards logically leads to two options: rethinking the strategy (including the assessment of friends and enemies), or sinking into a deepening malaise. Mbeki is certainly capable of a vigorous defence of national self-interest. But as witnessed by his failure to take advantage of successful activist pressure against transnational pharmaceutical corporations in the pricing of anti-retroviral drugs (see Chapter 9), economic policy-makers continued the failed neo-liberal strategy.

This reflects how Mbeki's analysis, strategy and tactics leave much to be desired. What about alliances? Unfortunately, instead of uniting with those who could fight international corporate power, Mbeki sought pity and a contentless 'solidarity' from global elites. At even a gathering so portentous as the G-77 'South Summit' in Havana, Cuba in April 2000, Mbeki invoked the words of none other than Michel Camdessus, the ex-managing director of the IMF:

> The global solidarity required does not simply mean offering something superfluous; it means dealing with vested interests, certain lifestyles and models of consumption, and the entrenched power structures in countries. I am certain that none of us present at this Summit would gainsay the importance of the observation Mr Camdessus made, that there needs to evolve a global solidarity that is more than just an adjunct of national policies. The relevance of this has just been demonstrated in our region of Southern Africa. Various countries of the North came to Mozambique to help the government and people of that sister country to cope with a very serious flood disaster. A week after they had arrived to demonstrate this global solidarity, they refused to do the most obvious thing to express solidarity with the suffering Mozambican people, namely to cancel Mozambique's debt. Presumably, such a humane decision would have been inconsistent with their national policies, to use Mr Camdessus's expression.[32]

Yet here we must immediately remark upon some substantial hypocrisy. After apartheid ended, South Africa made loans to Mozambique to resettle disgruntled Afrikaners and to refurbish electricity-generation lines that apartheid-backed Renamo rebels had sabotaged. These loans have not been forgiven by the Development Bank of Southern Africa and Eskom.

Changing the world would surely, for South Africa, begin within the region, by forthrightly addressing various Southern African dilemmas. Moreover, Mbeki and many of his closest colleagues were the beneficiaries of support from allied regional nationalist governments during the 1960s–80s. That this translated mainly into public soothing of a desperate Robert Mugabe, and not concern for the welfare of ordinary people, is clear from evidence of South African sub-imperialism reviewed in Chapter two.

Other friends?
Even if it were in better economic shape, the Southern African region would remain fragmented and war-torn. And even if Southern Africa one day provides a platform for a renewal of strident Third World nationalism – witness Mbeki's ally Robert Mugabe, who with his currency peg in 1999–2000 sought a Malaysian-style exit option from volatile international currency speculation – South Africa will still have to stitch together much stronger alliances. As the 1998 Tripartite Alliance discussion document cited earlier asked so pointedly, 'Can we forge a Brasilia-Pretoria-Delhi-Beijing Consensus in the absence of any Washington Consensus?'[33] There is a faint possibility, at the time of writing, of a G-5 bloc of semi-peripheral states: Brazil, Nigeria, Egypt, India and South Africa, plus potentially Mexico and

South Korea in future. But as always, the barriers not only of language and culture, but also of divergent material interests and ideology intervene.

There are, as well, at least a few G-8 ruling parties who Mbeki can consider as formal allies, especially the British Labour Party and German Social Democrats. As he told the ANC meeting, 'less than a year ago, we were admitted as members of the Socialist International. This is the biggest of all the international political associations and contains the most progressive political parties from all countries.'[34] In reality, those 'most progressive ... parties' within Europe turned out – at Okinawa, in the EU trade negotiations, in international sports negotiations, and in so many other settings – to sport a deadly punch. As a result, Mbeki turned in 2000 to the rulers of Sweden and Chile as potential *real* (not Third Way) social-democratic comrades, but whether this generates a sustainable ideology for the 21st century or is simply another gambit to faintly challenge the global power centres remains to be seen.

Aside from other governments, international businesses are also imagined and sometimes actual allies of Mbeki (as I note at the outset of the next chapter). While as late as December 1999, Erwin entertained Cosatu's proposal that trade agreements and the WTO specifically be modified with so-called 'Social Clauses' that invoke labour, social and environmental protections, Mbeki had apparently jettisoned any reform along these lines by the time of the Commonwealth Heads of Government Meeting (CHOGM) a few weeks earlier:

> We are pleased that the Commonwealth Business Council has made its own submission to CHOGM on this critical matter. Indeed we agree with your view that affirms the role of the WTO as an organisation that should be solely concerned with fair and efficient conduct and regulation of international trade. Accordingly, we also agree that it should not become an instrument for bringing extra-territorial policy changes outside the realm of the WTO or, more important, an institution for introducing new and discriminatory barriers to trade.[35]

For Erwin and Cosatu, the attempt to reform international trade through Social Clauses was, arguably, also misguided. Partly, it relied upon a corporatist arrangement: the National Economic Development and Labour Council in Johannesburg allowed big government, big business and big labour to fashion a joint negotiating position. But, more generally, Social Clauses violate fundamental principles of labour internationalism, namely the need to avoid promoting the material interests of an oppressor nation over those of an oppressed nation, above all when the wishes of the people most affected have not been consulted.

To be sure, it is certainly appropriate to support boycotts against apartheid-era South Africa and contemporary Burma – for whom sanctions called for by popular, democratic movements translate into a strategic attack on local oppressors – but impossible to justify 'humanitarian' interventions in the sphere of trade through Social Clauses enforced by the WTO, where economic interests are imperialist or at best narrowly protectionist, and where status-quo power relations are exacerbated.[36] Erwin eventually gave up on advocating Social Clauses, because in Seattle he found he was the only proponent amongst developing countries: internationalist solidarity on the basis of joint interests between Cosatu and the Mbeki government was clearly off to a bad start.

And that is indeed a fitting conclusion to this exploration of ideological debate surrounding the opportunities of globalisation and the threats of global apartheid. Less important than a vision of rehashed social democracy that veers slightly left of New Labour's Third Way is an understanding of material interests. South Africa is no different than any other country in that regard. Yet as we will see in the next chapter, Mbeki's initial prestige as Mandela's successor permitted him the luxury of making a fundamental (mis)impression, namely that with the requisite political will, he and his senior economics team could make a dent in international economic institutions. In this way, trying to change the world became itself an ideological ploy.

Notes

1 Fanon, F. (ed.) (1967), *The Wretched of the Earth*, Harmondsworth, Penguin, p. 186.
2 Mbeki, T. (2000), 'Vox Populi – Is it Real?' speech at the International Union of Socialist Youth Festival, Stockholm, 28 July. This and all the following citations here and in Chapter 7 attributed to Mbeki were published on the presidental website at http://www.gov.za/
3 Zuege, A. (1999), 'The Chimera of the Third Way', in L. Panitch and C. Leys (eds), *Necessary and Unnecessary Utopias: Socialist Register 2000*, London, Merlin and New York, Monthly Review Press, p. 106.
4 Mbeki, *op. cit.*
5 Cited in Bond, P. (1998), 'Global Financial Crisis: Why we should Care, What we should Do', *Indicator SA*, 15(3).
6 Mbeki, T. (1999), 'Statement at the XII Summit Meeting of Heads of State and Governments of the Non-Aligned Movement', Durban, 3 September.
7 ANC, 'The State, Property Relations and Social Transformation', ANC discussion document (mimeo) reprinted in the *African Communist*, fourth quarter 1998, pp. 13–14.
8 ANC Alliance (1998), 'The Global Economic Crisis and its Implications for South Africa', ANC Alliance discussion document, October, Johannesburg, reprinted in *The African Communist*, 4th quarter.
9 Bond, P. (1999), 'Global Economic Crisis: A View from South Africa', *Journal of World Systems Research*, 5(2).
10 Erwin, A. (1999), 'Address to Parliament on the Challenges of Globalization at the "Millennium" Debate Occasion', Cape Town, 19 November.
11 Mbeki, T. (2000), 'Lecture at Georgetown University', Washington, DC, 23 May.

12 In early 1998, during Clinton's visit to Cape Town, Nelson Mandela, SA president at the time, expressed enormous dissatisfaction with the same legislation. A period of severe US arm-twisting of African ambassadors to the US followed, and official SA scepticism was reversed.
13 Mbeki, 'Lecture at Georgetown University'.
14 Erwin, *op. cit.*
15 Cited in McSmith, A. (2000), 'Mandela Pleads for the Funds to Fight Aids, Pokes Fun at Demonstrators Protesting the Effects of Globalization', *Daily Telegraph*, 29 September.
16 Mbeki, T. (2000), 'Speech at the launch of the Presidential Strategic Leadership Development Programme', Pretoria, 23 July.
17 Mbeki, T. (2000), 'Address to the Commonwealth Club, World Affairs Council and US/SA Business Council Conference', San Francisco, 24 May.
18 Mbeki, T. (2000), 'Keynote address to the ANC National General Council', Port Elizabeth, 12 July.
19 *Ibid.*
20 See, for example, *Business Day*, 4 May 2000. The actual cost of the arms escalated to R43 billion in mid-2000, with some independent estimates at R60 billion.
21 Hosking, S. and Bond, P. (2000), 'Infrastructure for Spatial Development Initiatives or for Basic Needs? Port Elizabeth's Prioritisation of the Coega Port/IDZ over Municipal Services', in M. Khosa (ed.), *Empowerment through Service Delivery*, Pretoria, Human Sciences Research Council.
22 Dr Chippy Olver, quoted in the *Mail and Guardian*, 22 November 1996.
23 Mbeki, T. (2000), 'Berlin Communiqué: Progressive Governance of the 21st Century', Berlin, 23 May.
24 Details are provided in Bond, P., Dor, G. and Ruiters, G. (2000), 'Transformation in Infrastructure Policy from Apartheid to Democracy: Mandates for Change, Continuities in Ideology, Frictions in Delivery', in M. Khosa (ed.), *Infrastructure Mandates for Change, 1994–99*, Pretoria, Human Sciences Research Council; and Bond, P. and Ruiters, G. (2000), 'Droughts and Floods: Water Shortages and Surpluses in Post-Apartheid South Africa', in Y. Muthien, M. Khosa and B. Magubane (eds), *Economic Transformation in South Africa: Democracy and Governance Review*, Pretoria, Human Sciences Research Council.
25 Manuel, T. (1999), 'Address to the US-South Africa Business and Finance Forum', 24 September.
26 See Ruiters, G. and Bond, P. (1999) 'Contradictions in Municipal Transformation from Apartheid to Democracy: The Battle over Local Water Privatization in South Africa', *Working Papers in Local Governance and Democracy*, 99(1).
27 This is common knowledge amidst industry professionals: interview, Ashraf Patel, Wits P&DM LINK Centre.
28 See Bond, P. (2000), *Cities of Gold, Townships of Coal*, Trenton, Africa World Press, Chapter 4, for more details.
29 *Business Day*, 19 February 2001.
30 Mbeki, 'Address to the Commonwealth Club, World Affairs Council and US/SA Business Council Conference'.
31 Mbeki, 'Lecture at Georgetown University'.
32 Mbeki, T. (2000), 'Address of the Chairperson of the Non-Aligned Movement at the opening of the South Summit', Havana, 12 April.
33 For the reference, see Chapter one, endnote 2.
34 Mbeki, 'Keynote address to the ANC National General Council'.

35 Mbeki, T. (1999), 'Address at the Commonwealth Business Forum', Johannesburg, 9 November.
36 See Bond, P. (2000), 'Workers of the World, Transcend the Wedge!', *Z Magazine*, 24 February, http://www.zmag.org; for more on the Social Clause debate, see http://www.aidc.org.za.

CHAPTER SEVEN

Pretoria's global governance strategy

1. Introduction

Can Thabo Mbeki change the world? It's a fair question.

'We will succeed in the struggle to end poverty and underdevelopment in our country and continent', Mbeki assured a captivated San Francisco audience in May 2000, 'provided we can count on the kind of support you gave us as we fought together to end the system of apartheid.'[1] Thus the South African president invited leading representatives of US business, who in reality had for decades been diehard supporters of apartheid, nearly uniformly opposing ANC calls for comprehensive sanctions,[2] to help combat what Mbeki has already begun to term 'global apartheid' – a system nearly as profitable for US capital as was South African racism. Either Mbeki is lost, bewildered, capable of saying anything pleasing to any audience to curry favour, like any politician – or something else is going on.

Mbeki would argue strenuously against the former interpretation, as witnessed in August 2000 in his attack on the 'Caliban native petit bourgeoisie, with the native intelligentsia in its midst, that, in pursuit of well-being that has no object beyond itself, commits itself to be the foot-lickers of those that will secure the personal well-being of its members'.[3] It will become clear in excerpts from his speeches considered below that Mbeki's approach to the global ruling elite is *not* about personal self-advancement, or even advancement of a goal so narrow as merely increasing foreign investment in South Africa. Instead, let us take as a given that Mbeki's approach is to engage the global ruling elite so as to pave the way for a continuation of the South African 'revolution'.

For in the same speech as the one quoted above, Mbeki continued, 'Our own intelligentsia faces the challenge, perhaps to overcome the class limitations which [Walter] Rodney speaks of, and ensure that it does not become an obstacle to the further development of our own revolution.' Taking this position seriously, it is up to anyone engaging in analysis of global geo-politics and economics to determine not *whether* Mbeki is seeking to 'further develop' the South African revolution through ever-more strategic global insertions, but *how* he is managing such a challenge; what underlying analysis informs the approach; what strategies and tactics are appropriate; and whether alliances are properly considered – all of which are addressed in the pages that follow.

Chapters one and two established the premise that economic 'globalisation' – by which is generally meant free flows of trade, finance and direct investment, under conditions of overwhelming transnational corporate power, underpinned by a system of embryonic world-state institutions based mainly in Washington – *simply doesn't work for South Africa, or Africa*. For that reason, Mbeki and his closest colleagues – finance minister Trevor Manuel, trade and industry minister Alec Erwin, ANC secretary-general Kgalema Motlanthe and others – claim to be reforming the inter-state and embryonic world-state system.

The reform strategy will fail, though, not because of lack of will, integrity or positionality of those involved. After all, since 1994, extremely talented South African officials have presided over the board of governors of the IMF and World Bank, the Non-Aligned Movement, the United Nations Conference on Trade and Development, the Commonwealth, the Organisation of African Unity, the Southern African Development Community and a host of other important international and continental bodies.

Instead, the failure is already emanating from the very project itself, and its underlying philosophy, inappropriate practical strategies and ineffectual tactics (see Section 2). Instead of leading the world, Mbeki and his Pretoria colleagues run a different danger: treading a well-known, dusty path, a cul-de-sac of predictable direction and duration that, notwithstanding mixed rhetorical signals (see Section 3), for all effective purposes excludes or most often rejects, alliances with increasingly radical local and international social, labour and environmental movements who in reality *are the main agents of progressive global change* (see Section 4). Thus the South African post-apartheid official leadership will not achieve its own limited objectives, much less the further-reaching transformation required under the current extremely difficult global conditions. And in concluding that Thabo Mbeki *cannot* change the world, a more radical strategy necessarily arises as an alternative.

2. 'Globalisation made me do it'

According to economists Jonathan Michie and Vishnu Padayachee, 'In the South African context, globalization has become a synonym for inaction, even paralysis, in domestic economic policy formulation and implementation.'[4] Mbeki lectured the ANC's National General Council in July 2000 that globalisation 'impacts on the sovereignty of small states such as ours ... The globalization of the economy resulting among other things in rapid movements of huge volumes of capital across the globe, objectively also has the effect of limiting the possibility of states to take unilateral decisions.'[5]

Fin de siècle *strife*

For post-apartheid South Africa, the mood of liberation shifted quickly to despair during two moments of powerful international financial discipline, in early 1996 and mid-1998, when currency crashes and capital flight provoked dramatic interest rate increases and, in the first instance, the high-profile disposal of the Reconstruction and Development Programme.[6] The prime culprit in making South Africa so vulnerable was the government's decision in March 1995, under intense pressure from local and international financiers, to discard the 'financial rand' exchange control mechanism. This decision had the effect of attracting enormous speculative financial flows, which in turn fled rapidly as conditions changed and the investor-herd turned.

The country's allegedly 'sound' economic fundamentals were, of course, deteriorating markedly during the late 1990s. Growing foreign imports amplified local deindustrialisation and job losses, while trade with Africa became extremely biased, contributing to geopolitical tensions and the inflow of economic refugees from neighbouring lands (and the resulting xenophobia by South African workers). There was, moreover, a net outflow of international direct investment from South Africa during the first five years of democracy, while the uneven dribs and drabs of incoming foreign investment were largely of the merger/acquisition variety rather than new, fixed-investment (greenfield) projects.

Simultaneously, economic advice poured in from international financial centres, based upon persistent demands not only for macroeconomic policies conducive to South Africa's increased global vulnerability, but also for social policies and even political outcomes that weakened the state, the working-class, the poor and the environment. From 1996 to 1998, international financial turmoil offered Pretoria a learning curve to hell: among other outcomes, sinking the country's per-capita living standards while intensifying the world's worst inequality; sending real interest rates to their highest-ever levels; crashing the Johannesburg Stock Exchange more than ever before; generating unprecedented municipal bankruptcies; forcing cuts in water and electricity to the poorest citizens; exacerbating apartheid geographical segregation; and reducing the ratio of people formally employed to those desiring a job to levels unprecedented in a century.

Meanwhile, because Washington's grip on international economic power remained relatively undisturbed during the late 1990s, notwithstanding the arc of emerging market crises, other disappointments were still ahead. 'Debt relief' promised at the G-8 meeting in Cologne in 1999 turned out to be, as Jubilee 2000 South Africa critics had predicted, a 'cruel hoax'.[7] The guru of Post-Washington Consensus theory within the World Bank, chief economist Joseph Stiglitz, was fired in late 1999, and was followed by an angry Ravi Kanbur in June 2000 as the result of Summers' censorious interference in the drafting of a World Bank poverty report. A 'free trade' deal between Pretoria and the European Union was negotiated, and re-negotiated again and again when southern European countries protested at SA exporters' use of the names 'port', 'sherry', 'ouzo' and 'grappa'.[8] Another 'free trade' deal, like Europe's, catalysed and nurtured by lobby-ists of large corporations, between Africa and the United States likewise went through numerous palpitations, and eventually included ridiculous riders such as the requirement that clothing exports from Africa to the US would have to include vast amounts of US-sourced textiles.

Mbeki's self-mandate

The world was becoming an increasingly brutal place when Thabo Mbeki assumed the South African presidency in May 1999, as attested by rising levels of mass popular protest. Thus by mid-2000, just before his first anniversary in office, Mbeki emerged as an apparently far more aggressive critic of the global status quo. He made a series of trips to international political and economic centres, and debated global governance. His colleagues, as well as other compatriots, played active roles in key multi-lateral forums. Within Southern Africa, Mbeki burdened himself with increasingly hands-on diplomatic functions (particularly in relation to Zimbabwe and the DRC).

At first glance, this activity seemed to represent an impressive, forth-rightly progressive attempt to rejig the global economy in the interests of lower-income countries, to actualise the 'African Renaissance', and more generally to imprint the world with South Africa's successful political deal-making model and 'social democratic' approach to development.

But at second glance, with a more careful interpretation of Mbeki's agenda, cynics could justifiably object to his minor tinkering, confused and confusing rhetoric, reluctance to question received wisdom when applied to domestic macroeconomic and industrial policy, failure to work through the logic of the argument from broad generality to concrete settings, and questionable alliances. While key speeches containing insights into Mbeki's strategy are invariably eloquent and well received, they leave important intellectual questions hanging. This is obviously not because of a deficient intellect (nor the failure of extremely talented Government Communications and Information Services staff to stock the presidential website with his best work). It is because the approach taken is suffused with immense contradictions: on the one hand Mbeki argues that, to paraphrase, 'globalisation made me do it';[9] while on the other, he occasionally resorts to advancing what are among the richest, most profound critiques of international markets to be found in contemporary South Africa.

3. Mbeki v. 'the globalisation of apartheid'

South Africa exists within an extremely unfavourable balance of global forces; to point this out had, by the turn of the 21st century, become pedestrian. For Mbeki, though, this glaring power imbalance provoked moments of honest and impassioned confrontation, even in the presence of Bill Clinton at the outset of his (Mbeki's) vaunted US tour in May 2000: 'Mr President, during our discussion today we also observed that as the world globalizes, we continue to be confronted by unacceptable levels of poverty and deprivation, disease, war and conflict. Indeed the gulf between rich and poor has been widening.'[10]

Unethical development

With a distinctly distressed moral tone, Mbeki forthrightly complains about the unfairness of the international system. Amongst intellectuals gathering at a gala African Renaissance event in late 1999, for example, Mbeki's brilliant, wide-ranging speech tackled:

> the problem we are facing even as we stand here, of arriving at the point when we can conclude the bilateral agreement between our country and the European Union. Stripped of all pretence, what has raised the question whether the agreement can be signed today or not, is the reality that many among the developed countries of the North have lost all sense of the noble idea of human solidarity. What seems to predominate is the question, in its narrowest and most naked meaning – what is in it for me! What is in it for me! – and all this with absolutely no apology and no sense of shame.[11]

'What is in it for me!' The scorn with which Mbeki dismisses not only trade *realpolitik* but also the very foundation of Adam Smith's invisible hand as optimal allocator of resources is noteworthy. He invokes, periodically, deeply ethical contentions, as in this speech as head of the Non-Aligned Movement to the Group of 77's South Summit in Havana in April 2000: 'All of us present in this hall represent countries that can pride themselves on the continued existence of a strong spirit of communal, human solidarity among many of our people. The atomisation of the family and the individual, driven by the development and entrenchment of the capitalist system, has not reached the structural permanence it has attained in the developed countries of the North.'[12]

And again, in July 2000, just after Germany had won the 2006 soccer World Cup by one vote, he told his party's National General Council: 'As the ANC, we therefore understand very well what is meant by what one writer has described as the globalization of apartheid.'[13]

It is with such phraseology that Mbeki accomplishes a dual elision: on the one hand a displacement of the South's problems from the untouchable economic to the moral-political terrain, which in turn evokes calls for the reform – not dismantling – of existing economic systems and institutions; but on the other, as noted above, a relentless campaign to persuade his constituents that 'There Is No Alternative' to globalisation. For here, with Mbeki addressing the ANC National General Council meeting in Port Elizabeth in July 2000, we locate a striking difference in Mbeki's rhetoric regarding racial apartheid – which the ANC always insisted should be 'abolished' not reformed – and global apartheid:

> Let me now mention that big, and some think, ugly word – globalization. This is one of the contemporary phenomena we will have to ensure we understand. We will have to understand this because whether we like it or not, we are part of the world economy. It would neither be possible nor desirable that we cut ourselves off from that world economy so that the process of globalization becomes a matter irrelevant to our country and people.[14]

For Mbeki, the most important practical difference between racial and global apartheid seems to be the contemporary lack of a distinct 'enemy': '[T]here is nobody in the world that formed a secret committee to conspire to impose globalization on an unsuspecting humanity. The process of globalization is an objective outcome of the development of the productive forces that create wealth, including their continuous improvement and expansion through the impact on them of advances in science, technology and engineering.'[15]

Thus even though, *symptomatically* perhaps, power relations are skewed, the driving force of globalisation boils down, in Mbeki's neutral story, to little more than technological determinism. With this defeatist – and highly questionable – attitude, and considering that South African state elites were not managing their own developmental challenge particularly successfully, the next logical question is whether those elites should be entrusted with some of the world's most important development-management positions.

Ending global apartheid
Mbeki and his team would answer in the affirmative, combining self-confidence with a unique *noblesse oblige*. Alec Erwin, for instance, openly expressed Pretoria's grandest ambitions to his parliamentary colleagues, ironically just prior to the Seattle round of the World Trade Organisation: 'We will soon have to give leadership not just to the process of the development of our own economies [in the developing world] but to the equitable development of the world economy. The political capacity to do this and the will to do it in the G7 is weakening despite the power of the social democrats.'[16]

In the wake of defeating apartheid, the ANC in particular must dramatically expand its objectives, Mbeki told the Port Elizabeth gathering in

July 2000: 'When we decided to address the critical question of the ANC as an agent of change, the central subject of this National General Council, we sought to examine ourselves as an agent of change to end the apartheid legacy in our own country. We also sought to examine the question of what contribution we could make to the struggle to end apartheid globally.'[17]

The best answer – contradictory though it turns out to be – may come in the field of pharmaceutical products, especially access to anti-retrovirals to combat HIV/AIDS, as I will discuss below and in Part three. But the answer Mbeki has instead provided, e.g. in Havana, combines at least five basic challenges:

a) the alleviation of the debt burden carried by many ... countries, including its cancellation;
b) an effective mechanism to ensure a substantial increase in capital flows into the developing economies as this is a prerequisite for development;
c) the reversal of the trend resulting in a sharp drop in official development assistance;
d) the opening of the markets of the developed countries to our products, including agricultural products; and
e) the transfer of technology.[18]

Debt debacle
I will consider these challenges one by one, while saving technology transfer – in the case of drug patents – for Part three of the book. It is arguable that Mbeki's approach to the first challenge, debt relief, has done incalculable damage, mainly by virtue of his failure to endorse the Jubilee 2000 South Africa campaign against 'odious debt', including apartheid debt. Numerous vitriolic debates between civil society and government have occurred on this issue since 1996, and do not bear repeating in full here. Suffice to say, Jubilee 2000 critics argue, that had Mbeki and his predecessor Nelson Mandela been truly serious about the debt issue, they would not have:

a) agreed to repay the apartheid foreign debt to commercial banks when it was last rescheduled in October 1993;
b) claimed, repeatedly, that there *is no* foreign debt owed by the South African government (by ignoring roughly US$25 billion parastatal and private sector debt, for which the South African state inherited repayment and guarantor responsibilities);
c) negated the possibility of demanding reparations for previous foreign credits to the apartheid regime; and
d) endorsed, repeatedly, the Highly Indebted Poor Countries initiative of the G-8, IMF and World Bank, which proved such a distraction from the cause of debt cancellation.[19]

Reversing financial flows

Regarding the second of the five challenges mentioned above, inflows of capital, there are two kinds worth considering: financial and foreign direct investment. It hardly needs arguing that 'hot money' speculative inflow to emerging markets does not by any stretch of the imagination qualify as 'a prerequisite for development'. Nor do the vast majority of foreign loans granted to Third World governments over the past 30 years. Nevertheless, Manuel continues to argue – as in a speech in September 1999 to the US-South Africa Business and Finance Forum – that international finance should continue flowing freely to and from South Africa:

> South Africa remains committed to the gradual liberalisation of the capital account. These controls will continue to be reduced in a manner that does not destabilise the market, while ensuring that the financial system manages its risk exposure in a prudent manner ... In South Africa we have established certain principles: as financial flows are far larger than central bank reserves the rationale for defending the currency is questionable ... We are convinced that our banking system survived the difficulties of last year [1998] because the experience of currency movements in previous years had shown the Banks the value of having in place highly effective risk management systems and the need to be constantly conscious of the dangers of currency exposure.[20]

Yet to advance this Washington-friendly discourse, Manuel had to ignore all the evidence to the contrary: the exceptionally expensive effort by Reserve Bank governor Chris Stals to prop up the rand in mid-1998; the massive losses sustained by SA banks gambling in international financial markets, also in 1998; and the failure of a substantial chunk of the small-bank market, specifically because of ineffectual Reserve Bank supervision and regulation.[21]

Even if attracting financial flows is a questionable objective, the second type of potential capital inflow – plant, equipment and machinery – is typically understood as an essential ingredient in any Washington-approved development strategy. But after having done all in his power to attract foreign direct investment, Mbeki has not succeeded: South Africa has suffered a net *outflow* of such investment since the end of apartheid. Steve Morrison, the Africa expert at Washington's premier imperial think-tank, the Centre for Strategic and International Studies, confirmed that Mbeki 'has toed the line in a disciplined fashion, yet he has had very little return on that'.[22]

Is there, as Mbeki seeks, an 'effective mechanism' to reverse the problem of scarce capital inflows? The standard mechanism to date has been the 'seal of approval' of the World Bank and IMF, yet huge controversies surrounded the imposition in the late 1990s – and ongoing – of Washington

Consensus macroeconomic policy, dictated top-down, justified by Washington's need to rebuild the 'confidence' of international investors (using enormous bailouts paid for through huge cuts in living standards to do so). Would reforming the international financial institutions constitute a viable strategy for changing investment patterns?[23]

The chairperson of the IMF and World Bank during 2000, Trevor Manuel, describes his reform agenda mainly in terms of democratising the Bretton Woods institutions, by which is meant expanding developing country inputs to the board, rather than director-voting according to the present formula of ownership. As he explained in mid-1999,

> The power relations in these institutions need to change. This is a 'Catch 22' situation. Their Articles of Association go back to 1944, when the first shares were allocated. Voting is based on the amount of shares a country holds. The biggest problem that confronts us in relation to the Bretton Woods Institutions is that you need an 85% vote to effect any change. With the US holding about 17% of all shares, no reform can take place without its agreement. Therefore, the kinds of reforms we are hoping for are not going to happen unless the world takes a very different approach to these institutions.[24]

The 'kinds of reforms we are hoping for' in global financial markets have never been publicly spelled out in convincing detail. Chapter 12 considers some associated with financial taxation and capital controls, in favour of which Manuel has occasionally lobbied in public and private. But even when Manuel has talked of a globally co-ordinated 'Tobin Tax' against speculative financial capital flows (as in an interview in mid-1999), it has been conditioned by caution:

> As a small economy with low savings, however, we are dependent on foreign capital flows, and are likely to be punished if we took such a decision ... We are very mindful of the need to restructure the international financial system, and would want to be part of the first wave of constructing some 'speed bumps' to financial flows ... But now, as there doesn't appear to be a financial crisis anymore, too few of the appropriately placed people are asking what has happened to this idea.[25]

In contrast, early in the 21st century, at least a few people were asking what happened to Manuel when he became chairperson of the Bretton Woods institutions. From South Africa's standpoint, what would a reformed IMF and World Bank look like? One answer might be surmised by considering that, as Manuel put it, 'Our relationship with the World Bank is generally structured around the reservoir of knowledge in the Bank',[26] and that the World Bank itself considers its South African operations as the key pilot in its reinvention as a 'Knowledge Bank'.[27] Yet virtually without exception, development knowledge shared with post-apartheid South Africa – e.g. missions and policy support in fields such as water, land reform, housing, public works, healthcare and macroeconomics, as shown in Chapter three – was excessively neo-liberal in orientation, and failed to deliver the goods.

As a result, the ANC has had quite a schizophrenic relationship with the Bretton Woods institutions, and in the wake of the protests in Washington on 16 April 2000, this degenerated into defensiveness: 'It is very fashionable for people to say that the macroeconomic policy of the country was dictated by the International Monetary Fund or the World Bank', complained ANC secretary-general, Kgalema Motlanthe, in a *Mail and Guardian* newspaper interview shortly after the protests against the two institutions.[28] The verb 'dictated' insinuates unwillingness, and so may be a red herring. In reality, Pretoria and Washington have constructed a revolving door, as witnessed not only by Manuel's job as chairperson of the Bretton Woods institutions during 2000 (and persistent rumours he was going to take a permanent job there), but that of other bureaucrats who move seamlessly between the World Bank, the Department of Finance and the Johannesburg banks.

Residual suspicions of nefarious IMF and World Bank involvement in South Africa are worth noting in part because of their history. A National Reparations Conference opened by Archbishop Njongonkulu Ndungane in May 2000 resolved to demand that the IMF and World Bank repay black South Africans for apartheid loans. From 1951 to 1967, the World Bank lent Pretoria more than $200 million, about half of which went to support electricity generation in dirty coal-fired plants. Yet black townships and rural areas were denied electricity because of apartheid. As late as 1966, the World Bank granted $20 million in apartheid loans even after Albert Luthuli and the Rev. Martin Luther King, Jr. called for anti-apartheid financial sanctions, and the United Nations General Assembly explicitly requested it to stop (it replied to the UN, refusing to do so).[29]

In 1986, the World Bank again busted sanctions by indirectly lending to Pretoria through the Lesotho Highlands Water Project, using a special London trust-fund account to accomplish this. The IMF continued its apartheid lending into the early 1980s, including $2 billion in loans after the Soweto uprising began hurting Pretoria's credit rating. After the IMF was prohibited from lending by the US Congress in 1983, it continued to give the apartheid state economic advice, mainly to adopt neo-liberal policies during the late 1980s and early 1990s, including privatisation, extremely high interest rates, export-oriented strategies and the unpopular Value Added Tax.

But, claimed Motlanthe, 'We're not accountable to the IMF or World Bank, as we have not borrowed from them.'[30] This is incorrect, for in December 1993, an $850 million IMF loan was signed by the interim government, known as the Transitional Executive Council (TEC), purportedly for 'drought relief' (18 months after the drought ended). That loan bound Pretoria to cutting government deficit spending from 6.8% to 6% of GDP in 1994, and reducing wages. The conditions were kept secret until a *Business Day* leak in March 1994. That newspaper's top financial journalist concluded that 'The *Reconstruction and Development Programme* and the TEC statement of policies to the IMF are arguably the two most important clues on future economic policy ... The ANC, in signing the statement of policies to the IMF, committed itself to promoting wage restraint.'[31] The progressive sections of the RDP were subsequently ditched in practice.[32] Motlanthe was also not told, apparently, about a $46 million World Bank loan to promote exports in 1997, nor of tens of millions of dollars invested in South Africa by the World Bank's private-sector subsidiary, the International Finance Corporation.[33]

Aid fatigue
In relation to the third challenge mentioned above, regarding foreign aid, Mbeki calls for 'more and better managed aid so as to deal with the basic needs that will have to precede any form of development in certain areas'.[34] One problem is that Mbeki did very little in practice to dissuade Clinton and other international leaders from subscribing to the classically neo-liberal notion of 'trade, not aid' (the 1990s value of North-South aid in the 1990s fell by a third).[35]

But what lessons does South Africa itself have to offer? Were foreign donors encouraged, under post-apartheid rule, to turn aid pledges into real programmes; sustainably provide for basic needs; promote civil society; and support good aid-management (e.g. monitoring and evaluation, and regular collective consultations with government)? There is a strong case, made in Chapter four, that the Mandela and Mbeki governments were disastrous models in all these respects.

As one example, donor pledges of nearly $5 billion were made to Pretoria between 1994 and 1999. But just as government failed to disburse much of its own domestic-sourced development funding (80% annual RDP-related budget 'rollovers' were typical in the early years, but even during the late 1990s, inability to spend poverty relief funding became a national scandal), the record of South Africa's largest donor, the European Union, was also appalling. So, in making the case for more aid internationally, Mbeki has not yet provided a convincing case that such aid won't exacerbate well-known problems of bureaucratic capture and non-sustainability.

Trade rules
The fourth challenge deals with the opening of the markets of developed countries to Third World products. Mbeki wants to correct what he calls the 'rules and regulations that make the world trading system unbalanced

and biased against the very countries that need a fair trading system so that these countries, which represent the majority of humanity, benefit from international rules of trade'.[36] Even if the South African economy is on the margins of world trade, Pretoria has won a high profile in global circuits for at least three institutional reasons: Alec Erwin's 1996–2000 presidency of the UN Conference on Trade and Development; his controversial role in the WTO Summit in Seattle in 1999; and his subsequent attempt to bring together a new 'G-5' middle-income bloc to restart WTO negotiations. The latter two functions – particularly Erwin's distaste for the Seattle social-movement protesters and his near refusal to join the Africa bloc of trade ministers protesting against abominable treatment by US trade negotiator Charlene Barshefsky – must await treatment by other experts.[37]

Throughout, Erwin has argued for less Northern protectionism for 'dinosaur industries' like manufacturing and agriculture, but he has done so meekly and ineffectually: 'In addressing the challenge of trade and development in UNCTAD IX, we were attempting to break with a conception of contestation by stressing partnership.'[38]

'Partnership'. Yet it is worth asking how partnership has benefitted South Africa in the transfer of technology, e.g. in the case of patent surrender on vitally needed AIDS drugs? How has it generated mutual interest in trade – instead of the response 'What is in it for me!'? How has it transformed aid? How has it generated investment – with Mbeki bending over backwards to Washington's economic prescriptions? How has it accomplished even a modicum of debt relief?

Progress on any of these issues depends on who one is in partnership with, of course. At one point in his US trip, speaking to an African-American congregation at the venerable Ebenezer Church in Atlanta, Mbeki invoked the forces of social progress:

> In a world where no country can insulate itself from other parts of the same world, our success is highly dependent on your concrete support. This global solidarity between ourselves was part of the vocabulary of the civil rights movement, and some of us will remember that Dr King was one of the first world leaders to call for a boycott of South Africa as part of the struggle for democracy. This kind of solidarity amongst those who work for the same objectives, has been the hallmark of our own movement and struggle for democracy. We are therefore saying that we should continue with this struggle of working together and striving for social and economic justice for the poor, for countries of the South, and come with practical ways of assisting Africa to pull herself out of the quagmire of poverty. I can assure you that you will find many amongst Africans who are ready to work in honest partnership with yourselves.[39]

But with whom in the world does Mbeki really have an honest partner-ship, and with whom is he building genuine solidarity? Notwithstanding the eloquence of his Atlanta speech, the answers are not obvious.

Under Mbeki's influence, post-apartheid foreign policy examples of areas where solidarity was not extended to democrats include Western Sahara's Polisario Front, the Indonesian and East Timorese people suffer-ing under Suharto (recipient of a Cape of Good Hope medal in 1997), Nigerian opposition activists who in 1995 were denied a visa to meet in Johannesburg, the Burmese people (given the junta-controlled 'Myanmar's' unusual diplomatic relations with Pretoria), and victims of murderous central African regimes which were recipients of SA arms. The National Conventional Arms Control Committee reported that from 1996 to 1998, undemocratic regimes in countries like Colombia, Algeria and Peru purchased more than R300 million worth of arms from South Africa.[40]

4. Towards – or against – 'global solidarity'?

Is there, instead, scope for an honest partnership with the world's progres-sive social movements?

Allies in health?

Sadly, the answer is negative, as demonstrated by the single most evocative issue associated with globalisation and public policy in South Africa: HIV/AIDS treatment. Early signs were encouraging, as I will note in the next two chapters, for during a brief, extraordinary period, Mbeki and his then-health minister (now foreign minister) Nkosazana Dlamini-Zuma forthrightly attacked the prerogatives of transnational corporate capital in the pricing of pharmaceutical products, particularly anti-retroviral drugs used in the treatment of HIV/AIDS. Tragically, this was an exception that proved the rule, for the confrontation soon became Mbeki's most embar-rassing failure – not only to change the world, but to change the trajectory of mass death facing his desperately ill domestic constituency.

There was a chance for an alliance. A vibrant Treatment Action Campaign emerged in 1999, embarked on protests at US consulates in Johannesburg and Cape Town, and began networking with the Philadelphia, New York and Paris chapters of the advocacy group ACT UP. US vice-president Al Gore – a lobbyist on behalf of pharmaceutical firms – was confronted repeatedly and aggressively in Tennessee, New Hampshire, California and Pennsylvania at the very outset of his campaign. Numerous newspapers carried front-page stories on Gore's quandary.

Within weeks, the vice-president's own cost-benefit analysis began to reveal the danger of siding with the pharmaceutical firms, whose millions would not offset sustained damage to Gore's image. In a meeting with Mbeki in New York in September 1999, Gore conceded the validity of the

SA Medicines and Related Substances Control Amendment Act. With Thailand also making noises about exorbitant drug prices and with tens of thousands of protesters in the streets, President Clinton agreed at the Seattle WTO summit not to push for stronger TRIPS (trade in intellectual property rights) protection for US pharmaceutical companies.[41] The South African government then failed to take advantage of the space, as Mbeki searched for excuses *not* to implement aggressive anti-AIDS strategies, such as a controversial investigation into whether the HIV virus was indeed the cause of AIDS, instead of pursuing the parallel importation or generic options.

Whatever its final outcome, the joint struggle by the South African government and the activists against Gore and the pharmaceutical corporations was extremely important from the standpoint of my argument. In short, the David-versus-Goliath battle against pharmaceutical companies – and the White House – was effectively won, yet Mbeki quickly snatched defeat from the jaws of victory, and the broader war against AIDS took a sudden turn for the worse. As a result, Mbeki desperately needed to demonstrate that even though cheap drugs were available, his government would not make them available to the masses.

Voluntarism and activism

To understand how far the government must go to downgrade alliances with the Left, consider an ANC discussion document that appeared in 1996, which concluded with these lines:

> The democratic movement must resist the illusion that a democratic South Africa can be insulated from the processes that characterise world development. It must resist the thinking that this gives South Africa a possibility to elaborate solutions which are in discord with the rest of the world, but which can be sustained by virtue of a voluntarist South African experiment of a special type, a world of anti-Apartheid campaigners, who, out of loyalty to us, would support and sustain such voluntarism.[42]

But the Medicines Act of 1997 is, activists insist, precisely such a 'voluntarist … experiment'. It was, indeed, *only* sustained by virtue of an appeal by local activists to 'a world of anti-Apartheid campaigners' who, 'out of loyalty', militantly demonstrated in favour of the Act.

This is where, finally, the argument comes to a head. So far, we have taken seriously the extent to which Mbeki says he *wants* to change the world, even if the rhetoric has often confused listeners, the strategy is dubious and the tactics have not been effective. Central to this problem is the question of with whom Mbeki most comfortably allies himself. The social forces represented in the last example are emblematic of the challenge, for they evoke enormous potential for real solidarity, and *for changing the balance of forces.*

Mbeki must realise who the genuine allies of the South African people are, for he has invoked the Seattle phenomenon as a kind of threat, as a way of telling audiences that there is a more revolutionary option if they do not meet his demands. Speaking to Washington elites at Georgetown in May 2000, Mbeki quoted from Shelley's 'Ode to the West Wind': 'It may be that the protesters who besieged the negotiators at Seattle were, in their way, our own West Wind. What they said, if they spoke for the pestilence-stricken multitudes, yellow, and black, and pale, and hectic red, was indeed that since Winter was already upon these multitudes, Spring was not far behind.'[43]

To a different audience of social-democratic activists, Mbeki was resolute in his commitment to nurture challenges from the grassroots:

> All of us, but most certainly those of us who come from Africa, are very conscious of the importance that all tyrants attach to the demobilisation of the masses of the people. At all times, these tyrants seek to incite, bribe or intimidate the people into a state of quiescence and submissiveness. As the movement all of us present here represent, surely our task must be to encourage these masses, where they are oppressed, to rebellion, to assert the vision fundamental to all progressive movements that – the people shall govern![44]

The problem is that this kind of support – Mbeki generously praising demonstrators for raising consciousness – is not, in fact, mutual. For consciousness-raising is only a small fraction of the concrete challenge that many of the leading protest movement organisations have set for themselves, the essence of that challenge being to *shut down* the WTO, World Bank and IMF (see Chapter ten). Mbeki's approach is the precise opposite, i.e. to gain greater admittance.

Serious reform

The radical strategy is multifaceted, but at the end of the day is not merely destructive or protectionist, as Erwin and Manuel repeatedly posit. Recall the first great reformer of the IMF and World Bank, i.e. John Maynard Keynes, a key co-founder. When Keynes failed to persuade the dominant US negotiators of the need for a more politically neutral institution at the 1944 Bretton Woods and 1946 Savannah conferences, he was despondent. As one account has it, 'Keynes had argued so bitterly at Savannah with US Treasury Secretary Fred Vinson and was so distressed by the course on which the Bank seemed to be set that his friends blamed the meeting for the heart attack he suffered on the train back to Washington, and for a second, a month later, which killed him at the age of 63.'[45]

It may be useful to conclude with the kind of changes to the world economy for which Keynes once firmly argued. For, if one only added 'political solidarity' to the list of globalisation goods, the words that follow are perfectly consonant with the radical strategy noted above: 'I sympathise with those who would minimise, rather than with those who would maximise, economic entanglement among nations. Ideas, knowledge, science, hospitality, travel – these are the things which should of their nature be international. But let goods be homespun whenever it is reasonably and conveniently possible and, above all, let finance be primarily national.'[46]

This, to be sure, is the kind of either/or formulation that may well be objectionable to a both/and dialectitian of Mbeki's accomplishment. Keynes was perhaps not only a more active, successful and visionary shaper of global circumstances than Mbeki – albeit from a stronger power base in Britain, yet also ultimately a subservient and frustrating one – but in the words quoted above he also captured the essence of a bumper-sticker slogan that is often heard in the contemporary international social justice movement: *'The Globalisation of People, not of Capital!'* It is that slogan which says so much more about strategy, tactics and alliances than can Thabo Mbeki, and in turn hints more profoundly about why he probably won't – notwithstanding his ambitions, integrity and best efforts – change the world.

Notes

1 Mbeki, T. (2000), 'Address to the Commonwealth Club, World Affairs Council and US/SA Business Council Conference', San Francisco, 24 May.

2 Perhaps Desmond Tutu put it best: 'I would be more impressed with those [US companies] who made no bones about the reason they remain in South Africa and said honestly: "We are concerned for our profits" instead of the baloney that the businesses are there for our benefit. We don't want you there' (*New York Times*, 16 June 1986). For further reminders of the dissonance in Mbeki's remark, see also Innes, D. (1989), 'Multinational Companies and Disinvestment', in M. Orkin (ed.), *Sanctions Against Apartheid*, Cape Town, David Philip.

3 Mbeki, T. (2000), 'Ou Sont Ils, en ce Moment – Where are They Now?', second Oliver Tambo Lecture for the National Institute for Economic Policy, Johannesburg, 11 August.

4 Michie, J. and Padayachee, V. (1997), 'The South African Policy Debate Resumes', in J. Michie and V. Padayachee (eds), *The Political Economy of South Africa's Transition*, London, Dryden Press, p. 229.

5 Mbeki, T. (2000), 'Keynote Address to the ANC National General Council', Port Elizabeth, 12 July.

6 The post-apartheid government's uneven relationship to the RDP is documented in Bond, P. and Khosa, M. (eds) (1999), *An RDP Policy Audit*, Pretoria, Human Sciences Research Council Press.

7 Notwithstanding Mbeki's plea in Japan in July 2000, there was nothing further on offer to either the poorest countries or to those like Nigeria and South Africa that were victims of odious debt repayments. See the Jubilee 2000 South Africa and Jubilee South websites at http://www.aidc.org.

8 Though it was never pointed out publicly, the dispute mainly reflected the Orwellian power of the ad. man to brainwash European consumers, for while no

one challenged the right of South African producers to fill their bottles with port or sherry, they were prohibited from using what were formerly generic names on the outsides of the bottles.

9   As already noted in the Preface, I borrow John Saul's ironic phrase capturing at least one common justification for non-delivery; Saul expands on this theme in his latest book, *Millenial Africa: Capitalism, Socialism, Democracy*, Trenton, Africa World Press.

10 Mbeki, T. (2000), 'Remarks at the State Banquet, White House', Washington, DC, 22 May.

11 Mbeki, T. (1999), 'Speech at the Launch of the African Renaissance Institute', Pretoria, 11 October.

12 Mbeki, T. (2000), 'Address at the Opening of the South Summit', Havana, 12 April.

13 Mbeki, 'Keynote Address to the ANC National General Council'.

14 *Ibid.*

15 *Ibid.*

16 Erwin, A. (1999), 'Address to Parliament on the Challenges of Globalization at the "Millennium" Debate Occasion', Cape Town, 19 November.

17 Mbeki, 'Keynote Address to the ANC National General Council'.

18 Mbeki, 'Address at the Opening of the South Summit'.

19 See Bond, P. (2000), *Elite Transition*, London, Pluto Press and Pietermaritzburg, University of Natal Press, Chapters 5 and 6, and http://www.aidc.org.za.

20 Manuel, T. (1999), 'Address to the US-South Africa Business and Finance Forum', 24 September.

21 See Bond, P. (2000), 'A Case for Capital Controls', *South African Journal of Economics*, 68(4).

22 Cited in Plotz, D. (2000), 'How Others see the President: An American View', in *Slate* magazine, and reprinted in the *Mail and Guardian*, 21 July, p. 31.

23 A detailed description is in Bond, P. (2001), 'The World Bank, International Monetary Fund, Third World Debt and Foreign Finance: Southern African Debates', in J. Coetsee, J. Graaf, F. Hendricks and G. Wood (eds), *Development for the New Millennium*, Cape Town, Oxford University Press.

24 *Global Dialogue*, 4(2), p. 15.

25 *Ibid.*

26 *Ibid.*

27 This is confirmed in World Bank (1999), *South Africa – Country Assistance Strategy*, Washington, DC.

28 *Mail and Guardian*, 5 May 2000.

29 Caufield, C. (1997), *Masters of Illusion: The World Bank and the Poverty of Nations*, London, Macmillan, p. 206.

30 *Mail and Guardian*, 5 May 2000.

31 *Business Day*, 30 May 1994.

32 Bond, *Elite Transition*, Chapter 3.

33 These include stakes in Dominos Pizza (which subsequently went bankrupt), in for-profit healthcare, in housing securities to make the homes of high-income people more affordable, and in infrastructure privatisation, none of which fight poverty (and all of which add a US-dollar liability to South Africa's stressed current account). For details on the latter IFC strategy, see Bond, *Cities of Gold, Townships of Coal*, Chapter 4.

34 Mbeki, 'Address to the Commonwealth Club, World Affairs Council and US/SA Business Council Conference'.

35 *Financial Times*, 11 November 1998.

36 Mbeki, 'Address to the Commonwealth Club, World Affairs Council and US/SA Business Council Conference'.

37 See, for example, Keet, D. (2000), 'South Africa's Role in the WTO', Alternative Information and Development Centre occasional paper, Cape Town.

38 Erwin, A. (2000), 'Opening Address to the Tenth Session of UNCTAD', Bangkok, 12 February.

39 Mbeki, T. (2000), 'Address at the Ebenezer Baptist Church', Atlanta, 26 May.

40 Batchelor, P. (1999), 'South Africa: An Irresponsible Arms Trader?', in *Global Dialogue*, 4(2) p. 17.

41 The firms reacted with promises of cheaper, though not free, drugs, which in turn were spurned by activists as too little, too late. When faced with the prospect of local production, drug companies changed the subject by announcing offers of free medicine, which subsequently did not materialise.

42 ANC (1996), 'The State and Social Transformation', discussion document reprinted in *African Communist*, 4.

43 Mbeki, 'Lecture at Georgetown University', Washington, DC, 23 May.

44 Mbeki, 'Vox Populi – Is it Real?' speech at the International Union of Socialist Youth Festival, Stockholm, 28 July.

45 Caufield, *Masters of Illusion*, p. 47.

46 Keynes, J. M. (1933), 'National Self-Sufficiency', *Yale Review*, 22(4), p. 769.

PART THREE

Economic power and the case of HIV/AIDS treatment

ACT UP activists, Washington, September 2000.

CHAPTER EIGHT

Pharmaceutical corporations and US imperialism

1. Introduction

South Africa today records the world's fastest-growing HIV infection rates. At least 16% of the adult population, 20% of pregnant women and 45% of the armed forces test HIV-positive. In a context where many patients have little access to treatment until full-blown AIDS develops, the South African Department of Health has also tried to implement its transformation programme, including allocation of scarce financial resources away from First World curative facilities (which, among other things, boasted the world's first heart transplant) to new primary healthcare (PHC) clinics.

Paying for expensive pharmaceutical products licensed to extremely profitable international drug companies (one of which paid its chief executive officer a salary of $146 million in 1998) intensifies the problems South Africa faces in meeting its public-health policy objectives. Indeed, transformation to a system based on PHC has been retarded, primarily, by fiscal constraints, which have pitted the government against activist groups anxious to see more resources spent especially on preventing HIV transmission to young children. One means of relaxing the fiscal constraints is gaining savings of 50–90% on generic pharmaceutical products, including versions of anti-retrovirals to treat HIV. A law was passed by the South African parliament in 1997 and signed by President Nelson Mandela to this end, but was subsequently challenged in local courts as unconstitutional by the pharmaceutical industry.

The difficulties faced by the post-1994 ministers of health, Dr Nkosazana Dlamini-Zuma and Dr Manto Tshabala-Msimang, were and are tragic, particularly in view of Dlamini-Zuma's extremely active role in attacking inherited policies and practices.[1] Most other ministries fell far short of their transformation mandates, largely because policies favoured corporate interests or otherwise directly followed from neo-liberal, market-oriented precepts recommended, in a surprising number of cases, by World Bank advisors or their allies. In part because the inherited situation was so dire, in part because most wealthy white South Africans were covered by private-sector medical-aid services while most black people weren't, and in part because of personal conviction and courage, Zuma was far more radical in seeking social justice and redistribution than her colleagues. She challenged extremely powerful health-sector interests: tobacco companies, urban doctors, medical-aid companies and insurers. Her strongest campaign was against international pharmaceutical pricing, which she argued was discriminatory because it was based on extremely high levels of market concentration and which therefore prevented South Africa from having access to drugs at affordable prices, even those produced locally by subsidiaries of the major international firms.

Particularly in relation to HIV/AIDS treatment, this represented an area where Dlamini-Zuma could make amends with dissatisfied constituents. The minister was regularly criticised by AIDS activists during the ANC's first term for squandering millions of dollars on a questionable AIDS education drama, for mismanaging the alleged cure for AIDS known as 'virodene' (ultimately regarded as toxic and unusable), and for imposing mandatory notification for those determined to be HIV-positive, notwithstanding contrary advice from virtually all quarters. In addition, the closure of several major hospitals, the relatively slow pace at which clinics were being built, and ineffectual AIDS consciousness-raising meant that treatment and indeed education were severely hampered. Most importantly, however, in early 1999 Zuma claimed that budget shortfalls – in the context of South Africa's failed homegrown structural-adjustment programme (which cut the state budget deficit/GDP ratio from 9% in 1994 to just over 3% in 1999) – prevented her from providing HIV-positive pregnant women with zidovudine at several ante-natal pilot projects. (Thousands of lives would have been saved by treating such women with zidovudine, at a cost of about $13 million per year.) But, as I will discuss in the next chapter, the deterrent was funding. AZT, invented by the US government and made by Glaxo-Wellcome, costs $240 a month in South Africa, but just $48 a month using a generic Indian-made version. Glaxo-Wellcome offered to discount the price by 70% for the purposes of the pilot trials, which, controversially, Dlamini-Zuma refused because of the broader budgetary implications.

The high cost of AZT, zidovudine and other drugs was the basis for a major pharmaceutical-policy initiative to augment the Department of Health's more progressive policies. Consistent with the constitutional right to healthcare (within reasonable budgetary constraints), the Ministry of Health had committed itself to providing many health services free to all South African permanent residents. In 1994, free primary care was offered nationally to pregnant women and children under six, and in 1996 expanded (in policy if not in practice) to include 'all personal consultation services, and all non-personal services provided by the publicly-funded PHC system'.[2] Implementation at provincial level was uneven, with many provinces still limiting their free services to pregnant women and young children in 1999. But, according to the Department of Health, 'Independent evaluation of the implementation of the policy of free health care suggested that it has achieved its aims as most clinics report increased attendance; improved attendance at ante-natal and family planning clinics; and nearly three quarters of the health workers surveyed ... said that the policy was successful in preventing serious illness or death among pregnant women and children.'[3] In addition, four months unpaid maternity leave was legislated, and access to abortion became legal in 1996.

But with such increased healthcare entitlements, with increased coverage and with increased clinic construction (at the rate of four per week, costing roughly $50 million per year), access to pharmaceutical products became all the more important. Based on a 1994 campaign promise, government established an Essential Drugs List (EDL) in 1996, 'consisting of medicines critically required for use in the public sector for the prevention and management of 90–95% of the common and important conditions in the country ... EDL medicines will be available at all district hospitals, public providers and accredited private providers'.[4] To assure the availability of drugs on the EDL, Dlamini-Zuma won parliamentary passage of the Medicines and Related Substances Control Amendment Act ('Medicines Act') in 1997, which made provision for generic substitution by pharmacists of prescription medicine; scheduling of medicines; licensing of dispensers; establishment of a pricing committee; and prohibition of pharmaceutical bonuses and rebates for favoured bulk buyers. Its most controversial clause – clause 15 – includes the following provision:

> The registrar shall ensure that such an application in respect of medicine which appears on the latest Essential Drugs List or medicine which does not appear thereon but which, in the opinion of the Minister, is essential to national health is subject to such procedures as may be prescribed in order to expedite the registration ... The minister may prescribe conditions for the supply of more affordable medicines in certain circumstances so as to protect the health of the public, and in particular may ... prescribe the conditions on which any medicine which is identical in composition, meets the same quality of standard and is intended to have the same proprietary name as that of another medicine already registered in the Republic ... may be imported.[5]

The most important points in clause 15(c) are, first, that South Africa could seek the cheapest world price for a drug through 'parallel importing' (a practice common in European Union pharmaceutical retailing and, as noted below, proposed in a recent US congressional bill), and, secondly, could impose 'compulsory drugs licensing', i.e. the granting of rights to make copies of patented drugs without the approval of the patent holder (permissible in health emergencies under international law), if it follows safeguards and pays a royalty to the patent owner. According to James Love, director of the Consumer Project on Technology and an associate of consumer advocate Ralph Nader, 'For some drugs this reduces the price by 70 to 95%, depending upon manufacturing costs. Several of the drugs that are candidates for compulsory licensing, including AZT, ddI and ddC, were developed by the US National Institutes of Health.'[6] (In subsequent months, Love and his organisation became one of the central players in defending the Medicines Act, and his invaluable documentation is liberally utilised in the following pages.)

The Pharmaceutical Research and Manufacturers of America (PhRMA) typically accuses South Africa of theft: 'There are ways to make drugs available to the poor in a country like South Africa. We need to look for economic answers to economic questions ... and not say the answer to this economic question is we'll just steal [patents].'[7] (US firms are granted two-decade patent protection and hence monopoly pricing power, except in some circumstances in which 'fair pricing' is mandated, particularly where there has been extensive government support for a drug's research and development. Lower pricing is fairly rare, however.)

After failing in mid-1997 to lobby Dlamini-Zuma to change the clause, 40 South African and international pharmaceutical firms tied up the law (prior to promulgation) in South Africa's High Court, claiming violation of intellectual property rights on grounds that the Medicines Act would specifically override the Patents Act of 1978. In 1998–9, international pharmaceutical corporations – especially those based in the US – increased the pressure through a campaign backed by the White House. The South African Constitution guarantees property rights and other protection mechanisms from the Bill of Rights to 'juristic persons', i.e. corporations. These rights formed the basis of the pharmacorps' attack on the Medicines Act, which, as noted in the next chapter, was abandoned by them as the result of international pressure only in April 2001.

2. US government pressure points

As the leading neo-liberal health academic, Alain Enthoven, once famously remarked, 'The US political system is incapable of forcing changes in such powerful constituencies as the insurance industry, the hospital industry, organised medicine, the medical devices industry and the pharmaceutical industry.'[8] The converse appears more true: the major drug companies actively lobby politicians to change US foreign and trade policy to serve their narrow interests, notwithstanding potential damage to broader US interests (and America's image) and global health conditions. In South

Africa's case, this required US officials to ignore existing WTO rules governing TRIPS, which permit parallel imports and compulsory licensing, as well as identical provisions practised in various areas of US commerce, which South Africa wanted to impose on life-saving pharmaceutical products.

As James Love summarised the South African position:

- TRIPS requires 20-year patents on pharmaceutical, and South Africa has 20-year patents on pharmaceutical;
- parallel importing and compulsory licensing are part of the patent system, and both are legal under the WTO TRIPS agreement (for parallel imports the TRIPS provision is Article 6, Exhaustion of Rights, and for compulsory licensing it is Article 31) ... ;
- the South African government is simply trying to use the patent system in ways that the USA, Germany, England and other countries do, including the use of compulsory licensing, which is a common practice in the US for many areas ... ; and
- AZT and ddI, which are two of the prime candidates for compulsory licensing in South Africa, are US government-funded inventions.[9]

These arguments were consistently ignored or rejected by US officials. The US State Department and the US embassy in Pretoria, US commerce secretary Richard Daley, US trade representative Charlene Barshefsky and her assistant Rosa Whitaker, and Vice-President Al Gore together intensified pressure in 1998–9 to force Dlamini-Zuma to drop the 'offending passage' from the Medicines Act.

Imperialism, in their own words

For a flavour of the US 'full court press' (see below), it is revealing to consider an extensive citation from a State Department report in February 1999 by Barbara Larkin, assistant secretary for legislative affairs:

> Since the passage of the offending amendments in December 1997, US Government agencies have been engaged in a full court press with South African officials from the Departments of Trade and Industry, Foreign Affairs, and Health, to convince the South African Government to withdraw or amend the offending provisions of the law, or at the very least, to ensure that the law is implemented in a manner fully consistent with South Africa's TRIPS obligations.
>
> During early 1998, Embassy officials and the Assistant US Trade Representative for African Affairs made repeated requests to review the implementing regulations for Article 15(c) in order to ensure that application of the amendment would be consistent with South Africa's TRIPS obligations and commitments. However, the regulations for 15(c) have never been shared with the US Government, nor have they ever been formally

published and implemented. South African officials said a pending legal challenge of the amendments by pharmaceutical manufacturers precludes them from providing the USG with documents that could prejudice the case.

An international effort. In early 1998, the Embassy in Pretoria approached the Swiss and EU member embassies in South Africa to suggest a joint effort to protest the provisions of Article 15(c) since European pharmaceutical companies could be adversely affected by the amendments, and some are party to the pending litigation. Although European Governments preferred to let the US Government take the lead in demarching the South African Government on pharmaceutical patent protection, French President Chirac raised France's concerns during his July 1998 state visit to South Africa and the Swiss and German presidents also raised the issue privately with Deputy President Mbeki.

The United States government makes its case. Assistant US Trade Representative for Africa Rosa Whitaker traveled to South Africa in the Spring of 1998 and raised US Government concerns with both the Minister of Health and the Minister of Trade and Industry. She reiterated our request to review the draft implementing regulations. Her personal intervention reinforced the Embassy's clear message to the South African Government that the United States would not abide actions inconsistent with WTO obligations.

The ad hoc working group on intellectual property created at the July 1997 BNC held its first meeting in March 1998. The two hour conference call meeting did allow the US delegation – including representatives of the Departments of State, Commerce, the US Patent and Trademark Office and the Office of the US Trade Representative – to eliminate several lingering misunderstandings and clarify once more US Government views. However, since only officials of the South African Department of Trade and Industry attended the conference call, the South African delegation was not in a position to answer questions on the *Medicines Act* authoritatively nor were they empowered to negotiate on matters related to the amendments to the Act, since the *Medicines Act* is the bailiwick of the South African Department of Health.

Special 301 Watch List. On April 30, 1998, with the full endorsement and support of the Department of State, the United States Trade Representative designated South Africa a Special 301 'Watch List' country during USTR's annual worldwide review of intellectual property rights protection. This designation was based largely on the potential impact of Article 15(c), not only in the South African market but also due to its global precedent and the undermining of WTO principles. The State Department joined with other USG agencies with trade responsibility to insist on this designation in the hope that this special attention would spur South Africa to change or withdraw Article 15(c).

Withholding GSP. The Department of State, USTR, and the Department of Commerce developed an Administration decision to withhold preferential tariff treatment from certain South African exports in the early summer of 1998. On June 30, the White House announced that four items, for which South Africa had requested preferential tariff treatment under the Generalized System of Preferences (GSP) programme, would be held in abeyance pending adequate progress on intellectual property rights protection in South Africa. This action was widely reported in the South African press, but SAG reaction was muted.

Securing South African assurances. In March 1998, Secretary of Commerce Daley met with South African Health Minister Zuma to underline USG resolve to ensure South Africa would not use the provisions in 15(c) to undermine pharmaceutical patent rights or allow parallel imports. Dr. Ian Roberts, a senior official from the South African Department of Health, visited Washington in May 1998 and met with US Government patent experts and congressional staff, and attended a USTR-chaired US Government interagency meeting attended by State Department officials. At this meeting, US Government officials reiterated the US demand that South Africa comply with its international obligations to ensure adequate and effective protection to pharmaceutical patents. Dr. Roberts repeated South African Health Minister Zuma's pledge that it was not the SAG's intention to use Article 15(c) to abrogate patents or open the floodgates to parallel imports.

Repeated efforts to resolve the issue. An Embassy official traveled to Midrand, South Africa to speak at the June 1998 'Pharmecon SA 98' pharmaceutical industry conference. The official's remarks reinforced in a public forum the strong negative US views on Article 15(c) and made clear the possible ramifications of the Article's implementation, including trade sanctions.

In July 1998, Assistant US Trade Representative for African Affairs Rosa Whitaker met with the South African Charge d'Affaires in Washington to stress once again the US Government's concerns about pharmaceutical patent protection and parallel importation in South Africa. She also repeated the US Government's position that South Africa's requests for preferential tariff treatment on four key exports would be held in abeyance pending adequate progress on intellectual property rights protection.

During his September 1998 trip to South Africa, Commerce Secretary Daley made pharmaceutical patent protection a key item in his discussions with South African Trade and Industry Minister Alec Erwin. Daley re-emphasized the US Government position on Article 15(c) and reminded Minister Erwin of South Africa's obligations under the TRIPS agreement.

The Vice President's plan for a negotiated solution. During the August 1998 US-South Africa Binational Commission meetings in Washington, Vice

President Gore made the issue of intellectual property rights protection, and pharmaceutical patents in particular, a central focus of his discussions with Deputy President Mbeki. They agreed on a basis for a mutually satisfactory, Government-to-Government negotiated solution to the impasse. Suspended GSP benefits would be restored as progress was made in these negotiations. This basis was developed and unanimously supported by all interested US Government agencies. USTR was identified to lead the US Government's negotiation efforts. Initial discussion between the Assistant US Trade Representative for Services, Investment and Intellectual Property and the Deputy President's legal advisor took place in September 1998 and follow-on talks were conducted in November. During these discussions, the South African officials attempted to persuade the US Government to intervene with the US pharmaceutical industry to suspend or terminate its pending legal challenge to the offending provisions of the South African *Medicines Act*. The State Department, together with the Commerce Department and USTR, decided that such an action might undermine the leverage that US companies were exerting through their legal challenge. US officials told the South Africans that since the US Government is not a party to the litigation, the USG was unable to agree to this request. A subsequent round of face-to-face negotiations between USTR officials and Deputy President Mbeki's advisors is tentatively scheduled to be held in Cape Town just prior to the February 1999 Binational Commission meeting.

A 'new' medicines law. Meanwhile, during the fall of 1998, the South African parliament drafted and considered a new medicines law that would replace the existing *Medicines Act*, including the offending amendments. The State Department's Economic Minister Counselor in Pretoria met with a key Mbeki advisor in September 1998 to advocate the removal of Article 15(c) provisions from the new proposed law. In October 1998, at the State Department's suggestion, the Embassy dispatched an economic officer to Cape Town to monitor the committee and full chamber debates. He forcefully advocated the US position and advised parliamentarians that the new law should not include provisions that jeopardize patent rights. Despite these strenuous efforts, a new medicines bill was passed including provisions identical to Article 15(c), in November 1998. On December 4, 1998, the Assistant US Trade Representative for Services, Investment, and Intellectual Property sent a letter to Deputy President Mbeki's legal advisor Mojanku Gumbi noting the USG's interest that the discussions lead to a mutually agreeable settlement. As a way of spurring the discussions, he informed Gumbi that the US would be prepared to release a significant portion of the withheld GSP benefits should such a settlement be reached. Progress has been slow, but we understand talks are continuing.

In November 1998, the State Department's Economic Minister Counselor in Pretoria met with South African Department of Foreign Affairs officials to discuss resolution of the pharmaceutical patent controversy. The South Africans were eager to find a satisfactory solution to the ongoing dispute before the upcoming February 1999 Binational Commission meeting. Embassy officials reiterated the US position and noted that USTR officials talks with Mbeki advisors were the appropriate venue for seeking a negotiated settlement.

Secretary Daley paid a return visit to South Africa in December 1998. In his meetings with Deputy President Mbeki and Trade and Industry Minister Erwin during that visit, pharmaceutical patent protection was the most important bilateral issue under discussion. Deputy President Mbeki was hopeful that recent discussions between the pharmaceutical manufacturers and the South African Minister of Health would yield a solution. Secretary Daley noted the possibility of negative consequences should progress on resolving this most important issue stall.

The Embassy closely monitored the Zuma-pharmaceutical industry discussions, which continued through December 1998. Pharmaceutical industry officials have indicated that these talks have reached a sensitive stage and that further US Government efforts at this time could be counter-productive. The Embassy and Washington agencies have therefore deferred to the US pharmaceutical industry to take the lead. In mid January, the Assistant US Trade Representative for Services, Investment and Intellectual Property sent a letter to Legal Advisor Gumbi suggesting that specific discussion of pharmaceutical patents and Article 15(c) be put aside while Health Minister Zuma negotiates with the interested pharmaceutical manu-facturers. The pharmaceutical companies' discussions with Minister Zuma continue and their constitutional court challenge in South Africa remains pending. USTR officials and Mbeki's advisors plan to meet in February 1999.

Latest efforts. In January 1999, in the context of preparing for the February 1999 US-South Africa Binational Commission, the State Department's Economic Minister Counselor in Pretoria raised the pharma-ceutical patent protection issue with Deputy President Mbeki's economic advisor. Despite the Minister Counselor's reiteration of the US position, as well as a description of the ramifications of the suspension of aid to South Africa in the USG's FY 1999 appropriations law, Mbeki's advisor said the SAG was not considering repeal of the offending language in either the *Medicines Act* or the new bill. As indicated in previous sections, several adversely affected US pharmaceutical manufacturers have filed a constitu-tional court challenge to the amendments to the *Medicines Act* in South African courts. While the case remains pending, the South African Government is adamant that government-to-government discussions not prejudice the outcome. US Government attorneys share this view. Thus, our efforts are, in part, circumscribed by the ongoing litigation as well as a desire to be responsive to US industry's request to allow its current efforts time and opportunity to be effective. We hope the State Department's and other agencies' efforts to convince the South African Government to fulfill its international obligations and commitments on intellectual property rights together with a domestic legal challenge will provide sufficient incentive to achieve the suspension or removal of Article 15(c).

Next steps. The State Department, its Embassy in Pretoria, the Commerce Department and USTR will monitor closely the ongoing discussions between the pharmaceutical industry and the South African Minister of Health. We will continue our unflagging efforts to convince the South African Government to either repeal Article 15(c) or make it consistent with the TRIPS agreement, and thus eliminate the possibility of any abrogation of US pharmaceutical patent rights in South Africa. Should there be an actual violation of any US pharmaceutical patent right (e.g., patent abrogation) this Administration will respond forcefully in accordance with appropriate trade remedy legislation.[10]

The reason for such an unusually blunt official report is not only growing US arrogance during the 1990s. In addition, the Omnibus Consolidated and Emergency Supplemental Appropriations Act, 1999 provides

that none of the funds appropriated under this heading may be made available for assistance for the central Government of the Republic of South Africa, until the Secretary of State reports in writing to the appropriate committees of the Congress on the steps being taken by the United States Government to work with the Government of the Republic of South Africa to negotiate the repeal, suspension, or termination of section 15(c) of South Africa's *Medicines and Related Substances Control Amendment Act* No. 90 of 1997.[11]

This wording was proposed by Congressman Rodney P. Frelinghuysen (Republican, New Jersey), whose district's largest employer is the pharmaceutical industry. It followed his threat in July 1988 to cut off all US development aid to the South African central government. According to *Business Day* newspaper's Washington correspondent, Frelinghuysen 'believed that the trade representative was doing a sound job, but that the state department was waffling' – hence his attempt to force the issue through the threat to cut aid (see Chapter four, above).[12]

More restrictive than the WTO

The US government's position was clarified shortly after Larkin's report, at a meeting in March 1999 in Geneva sponsored by Health Action International, Médecins sans Frontières and the Consumer Project on Technology.[13] According to Lois Boland of the US Patent and Trademarks

Office, as quoted in Geneva, 'We acknowledge that our position is more restrictive than the TRIPS agreement but we see TRIPS as a minimum standard of protection.'[14] As a concession, the US government modified the phrasing of its objections to the Medicines Act, as shown below, to the 'appearance' of 'potential' abuse of 'ill-defined authority'.

Clearly, something else was now bothering US officials, presumably the international leadership South Africa was taking, in the wake of a similar battle in 1998 with an economically crippled Thailand, in which successful US pressure had led to the passage of a bill in Thailand that was more restrictive than TRIPS. According to the report from the Geneva Conference:

> Trade pressure against Thailand was most recently stimulated by the government's attempt to begin producing the anti-HIV drug ddI. The government was planning to offer people with AIDS at least one low-tech double therapy combination (AZT/ddI) at an affordable price. Currently, ddI is exclusively marketed by Bristol-Myers Squibb at a monthly cost of $166. Since July 1997, the daily minimum wage in Thailand has been frozen at $4.50. Thailand dropped its ddI plan when it was threatened with trade sanctions on some of its key exports. This threat came at a time when the Thai economy was reeling from the widespread South East Asian financial crisis. Thai physicians and patients were particularly outraged when they discovered that ddI was invented by the US government and is licensed on an exclusive basis to the US drug manufacturer Bristol-Myers Squibb. In addition, last summer the US stimulated a Thai legislative bill, expected to be signed into law soon, that severely restricts the use of compulsory licenses. Under the urging of US trade officials, Thailand will implement a law that is much more restrictive than the rules set out in the TRIPS agreement, the internationally accepted standard.[15]

As Professor Krisantha Weerasuriya of the University of Sri Lanka concluded, 'As a public health worker in the developing world, I feel like a child being told by the developed world, do as we say and not as we do.'[16]

The US twists tighter
Double standards set by the US and its allies were noted by the Geneva meeting, especially in the area of compulsory licensing:

> Although, according to a statement released before the meeting, the US government 'does not generally support the compulsory license of patents ... and regards compulsory licensing as unnecessary' it has liberally applied this tool in its own domestic market in hundreds of cases. Licenses on patents have been granted in diverse fields including biotechnology, pharmaceutical, aerospace, military technology, air pollution, computers, and nuclear energy.

The US has traditionally used compulsory licenses to counteract anti-competitive practices and a significant number have been granted royalty-free. In addition, many have been authorized for non-commercial government use.[17]

US pressure on South Africa intensified further in April, and for the first time explicitly cited the South African advocacy role. In late April, Barshefsky conducted an upgrade of the Special 301 Watchlist and formally instituted a more serious 'review':

> South Africa's *Medicines Act* appears to grant the Health Minister ill-defined authority to issue compulsory licenses, authorize parallel imports, and potentially otherwise abrogate patent rights ... During the past year, South African representatives have led a faction of nations in the World Health Organisation (WHO) in calling for a reduction in the level of protection provided for pharmaceutical in TRIPS ... We will continue to address these issues with the South African Government and will conduct an out-of-cycle review of South Africa's progress towards addressing these concerns in September 1999.[18]

Ralph Nader remarked: 'Among other things, the US government is officially punishing South Africa for permitting its public health officials to speak out on trade and intellectual property issues in the World Health Organisation ... In fact, everything South Africa is seeking to do is legal under the WTO/TRIPS agreement, so this and countless other statements by US government officials are bald lies. But regardless, the exercise of free speech in international forums is an astonishing basis for trade sanctions.'[19]

Vice-President Gore himself was now deeply involved in the arm-twisting, according to Love (based on a discussion with a Gore aide on the subject in April 1999):

> I was told that on every occasion that Gore has met with Mbeki, the issue of South Africa's intellectual property rules for pharmaceuticals has been raised, and that talking points on these issues are routinely prepared for the Vice President on this issue. I was also told that USTR is the policy making organisation on the issue of South Africa's use of compulsory licensing of HIV/AIDS drugs and other pharmaceutical IPR issues, and that within the Department of State, Stuart E. Eizenstat, the Under Secretary of State for Economic, Business and Agricultural Affairs [subsequently promoted to Deputy Treasury Secretary], has also been very active. Several persons have told me that Congress has also been active on this issue, and that USTR plays a role in determining if South Africa can obtain various aid programmes from the USA, based upon a USTR opinion that South Africa is adequately protecting intellectual property on pharmaceutical drugs. I expressed my opinion that USTR is not competent to make judgements in this area where

there are important public health issues. Apparently Vice President Gore's office, the Department of State and USTR are also using talking points to attack South Africa Health Minister Zuma on the grounds that she has rejected a Glaxo/US government offer to provide temporary AZT donations to some pregnant mothers, an offer that reportedly may contain other conditions on South Africa. I asked if anyone in the US government with a public health competence was involved in the decision to attack Dr. Zuma on this issue, and if this was part of a public relations ploy to undermine her positions on the broader International Property Rights issues. Apparently US trade officials are telling South Africa that any legislation that specifically provides for compulsory licensing of patents on public health grounds are a violation of the TRIPS, on the grounds that Article 27.1 of the TRIPS says that patent rights should be enjoyed 'without discrimination as to ... the field of technology,' and that any special programme for compulsory licensing on public health grounds is discriminatory. This is considered an absurd interpretation of the TRIPS by most trade experts, including the staff of the WTO, WIPO and the WHO, who point out the wide latitude of the TRIPS to provide for compulsory licensing in Article 31 on virtually any public interest grounds, subject of course to the Article 31 safeguards and requirements for remuneration. We intend to formally ask USTR for clarification on this point, and to seek outside opinions on what we consider a bad faith interpretation by the US (the same US that has several special statutory programmes for compulsory licensing under the *Bayh-Dole Act*, the *Clean Air Act* and for Nuclear energy). It goes without saying, but I was told that PhRMA and individual companies have a well functioning system of working with Congress and the heads of Administration agencies to advance their interests on this issue, and they have expressed concerns on several occasions about the compulsory licensing issue with South Africa.[20]

The most charitable interpretation possible of Gore's intervention was his desire to maintain drug-company research and development funds. According to a spokesperson, Gore and Mbeki were 'committed to working together to chart a course that will meet the medical needs of those infected with HIV or AIDS, without cutting off the commercial incentives that fuel medical research in the first place'.[21] Those commercial incentives are worth considering in more detail, for their uses extend far beyond research and development (R&D) costs, and into the corruption of the democratic political process.

3. Drug companies pressure the US government
Prodding the US government to force a repeal of South Africa's Medicines Act is a very active pharmaceutical industry with seemingly unlimited financial and public-relations resources, generous campaign contributions and

revolving doors with the US bureaucracy. Drugs companies have substantial motivation to kill the Medicines Act. According to the *Chicago Tribune*'s Washington correspondent, 'The law angered the US pharmaceutical industry, which fears that widespread licensing of its products will lead to a global "gray market" in low-priced drugs and undermine its profits and incentive to spend on costly research. It pressed its allies in the US government to swing into action against the South African law. They quickly complied.'[22]

On behalf of the PhRMA, 40 members of Congress wrote to President Clinton in 1997, warning him that the Medicines Act threatens the drug industry and demanding tougher action. A great deal was at stake, as *USA TODAY* pointed out: 'That the most powerful country in the world would spar with the most promising emerging democracy in Africa over access to AIDS drugs illuminates the daunting variety of challenges that the HIV pandemic presents worldwide. It also shows how fiercely drug companies will fight to protect profits from anti-HIV drugs, a rich market with sales totaling roughly $3 billion a year.'[23]

Debating the penalties

At the point the US withheld trade benefits to four South African exporters in July 1998, Tom Bombelles of the PhRMA welcomed the penalty as 'the type of thing we are looking for them to do'.[24] The organisation's president, Alan F. Holmer (formerly a USTR official), issued a press release in April 1999 applauding the USTR review of South Africa: 'South Africa could provide one of the first test cases for interpreting the scope of protection provided by TRIPs to all fields of technology, and thus has broad significance.'[25] Holmer continued, 'South Africa's intellectual property regime is deficient in many respects. It provides no protection for proprietary registration data. It allows for the parallel importation of pharmaceutical – i.e., for third parties to import drugs that are still under patent in South Africa. And it allows the Government to require a company to license its patented products to others in violation of the country's international commitments.'

Another PhRMA official, Jeff Truit, argued in *USA TODAY* in May 1999 that South Africa is mounting 'a brazen assault on patent protection, the lifeblood of our industry'. According to the newspaper, 'Truit says the South African government's stand threatens the development of medicines. The average drug costs $300 million to $500 million to develop. One company, which Truit declined to name, spent approximately $1 billion to create a single anti-HIV drug, he says.'[26]

The US corporate position was echoed internationally. As the director-general of the International Federation of Pharmaceutical Manufacturers Associations in Geneva, Harvey Bale (a US citizen and also a former USTR official) explained in April 1999:

If anyone wants to kill incentives for further research into a targeted disease area (e.g., AIDS) then one of the quickest ways to do this is to institute a compulsory licensing regime for drugs that treat that disease. Compulsory licensing benefits nobody except the fortunate commercial entity that is the beneficiary of the largesse offered by such licenses. In the medium and long-term, it is patients who will lack new treatments for serious diseases that suffer, as researchers will undoubtedly stay away from targeted disease groups subject to CL policies. Compulsory licensing seriously detracts from the purpose of the patent system, which as the 16th President of the US, Abraham Lincoln said, 'provides the fuel for the fire of genius'.[27]

Dubious incentives

But whether anti-retroviral drugs are the product of hundreds of millions of dollars worth of corporate R&D spending is hotly contested. To put the claim into perspective, Love cites studies that demonstrate the huge share of R&D covered by government:

> In 1997 prices, the average out-of-pocket costs of clinical trials needed for FDA approval were $25 million. Adjusted for risk, the 'per approval' cost of clinical trials was $56 million … [Higher estimates] adjust these costs some-what higher to include 'capital costs' for financing trials, but also and most importantly the cost of preclinical research, which accounts for 70 to 80 per cent of the total cost of drug development in some studies. Moreover, it is often governments rather than the drug companies that pay for clinical and preclinical research. For example, according to US tax returns, from 1983 to 1993 the pharmaceutical industry reported expenditure of only $213 million on clinical trials for orphan drug development. This was about $2.3 million for each of the FDA's 93 orphan drug approvals during the period.[28]

A debate over the R&D cost incidence of AZT arose in the *New York Times* nearly a decade earlier, in September 1989, following claims by a pharma-ceutical company that it was responsible for the original research. Five scientists from the National Institute of Health and Duke University rebutted this claim:

> The Sept. 16 letter from T. E. Haigler Jr., president of the Burroughs Wellcome Company, was astonishing in both substance and tone. Mr. Haigler asserts that azidothymidine, or AZT, was essentially discovered and developed entirely by Burroughs Wellcome with no substantive role from Government scientists and Government-supported research … Indeed, one of the key obstacles to the development of AZT was that Burroughs Wellcome did not work with live AIDS virus nor wish to receive samples from AIDS patients. In a number of specific ways, Government scientists made it possible to take a drug in the public domain with no medical use and

make it a practical reality as a new therapy for AIDS. It is unlikely that any drug company could have found a better partner than the Government in developing a new product. We believe that the development of this drug in a record two years, start to finish, would have been impossible without the substantive commitment of Government scientists and Government technology.[29]

Nevertheless, the pharmaceutical industry still uses a figure of hundreds of millions of R&D dollars per drug, as did Truit of the PhRMA.[30]

Spin-doctoring pharmaceutical imperialism

Ironically, if not for R&D, then enormous investments are readily found for matters of a public-relations nature when necessary. As media interest in the South Africa scandal intensified in 1999, Bristol-Myers Squibb (BMS) chairman and CEO Charles A. Heimbold, Jr. announced a gift of $100 million to, among others, Harvard, Morehouse and Baylor Universities, UNAIDS, and community treatment projects in South Africa, Botswana, Namibia, Lesotho and Swaziland. Love offered this critique:

> The Bristol-Myers Squibb announcement is a cynical public relations ploy by a company that is fighting to maintain its monopolies on government funded HIV drugs. The $100 million gift is about $3 or $4 for each infected HIV patient in Africa, and it is less than the $146 million that BMS paid its CEO last year. This press conference comes less than two weeks from the beginning of the World Health Assembly meetings in Geneva where nations will be debating proposals for compulsory licensing of essential medicines in poor countries. President Clinton, Vice President Gore and US government officials are pressuring South Africa, Thailand and many other countries, to prevent the use of compulsory licensing to expand access to US government funded HIV inventions like ddI, d4T – drugs currently sold at high prices on an exclusive basis by BMS.[31]

Challenging global drugs-apartheid

By now, a matter far more important than merely changing a law in South Africa – a country responsible, after all, for less than 1% of the global drug market – had emerged: Mandela's government was speaking on behalf of a variety of Non-Aligned Movement (NAM) countries on the pharmaceutical pricing issue (SA took the three-year leadership of the NAM in September 1998). In the PhRMA's submission to the US Trade Representative in February 1999, great affront was registered about a meeting of the Geneva World Health Assembly a month earlier:

> [The SA government representative] stressed that it is the intention of the South African Government and other Governments in the 'Non-Aligned

Countries' block to use every possible means and loophole in TRIPs to escape their obligations to provide patent protection for pharmaceutical, which reflects the Government's position in the South African litigation of refusing to answer affidavits on the question of whether any form of patent protection will be considered appropriate for pharmaceutical; and she emphasized her Government's 'unwavering' commitment against effective patent protection for pharmaceutical.[32]

Preparing to fight

Going into this battle, the pharmaceutical industry was well armed. The Center for Responsive Politics recorded the flow of funds to politicians and concluded: 'Long one of the most powerful lobbies on Capitol Hill, the pharmaceutical industry spent nearly $12 million in soft money, Political Action Committee, and individual donations during the 1997–8 elections – a 53% increase over donations during the last mid-term elections.'[33]

As just one positional reflection of the industry's power, the *New York Times* board of directors includes three pharmaceutical leaders: Richard Gelb, chairman emeritus of Bristol Myers Squibb; Raul Cesan, CEO of Schering-Plough; and Henry Schacht, a director of Johnson and Johnson. (Perhaps because insurance executives are also prominent on its board, the *Times* repeatedly editorialised during the mid-1990s in support of the alleged 'new consensus for healthcare reform', managed competition.)[34]

As a function of their networking within the US ruling class, pharmaceutical firms have become particularly close to Vice-President Gore. As Love points out,

> Gore is also closely linked to PhRMA and its lobbyists. Member companies contributed significantly to Gore's PAC. One of PhRMA's key lobbyists is Anthony Podesta, the brother of Clinton Chief of Staff John Podesta, a friend and advisor of Gore. Anthony Podesta also worked for Gore's David Beier when Beier – now Gore's chief Domestic Policy Advisor – was Genetech's lobbyist, and is the landlord of Simon Strategies, which shares office space and projects with Podesta's firm ... According to lobbying disclosure reports, Podesta.com ... have 11 persons working on the PhRMA account.[35]

4. Resistance

The pharmaceuticals industry requires excellent public relations – and spends lavishly on advertising (more than on drug R&D, typically) – for the ability to influence consumption. This is increasingly true in the Third World, where a typical country imports between 15 000 and 20 000 products, costing half their health budgets. In part as a result of rapidly growing

Third World consumption, even in the context of structural adjustment programmes which drastically reduced most residents' living standards, global pharmaceutical industry sales rose from $22 billion in 1980 to more than $260 billion by the mid-1990s, with profitability the third highest of any economic sector in the US.[36]

How the drug companies get away with this, while health conditions deteriorate around the world, has been partially demonstrated in the pages above. Unfortunately, though they distract attention from the more important structural features associated with what Werner and Sanders term the 'pharmaceuticalisation of health care', the sleazy links between US pharmaceutical companies and politicians remain essential to understanding the US government's outlandish argument that pressure on South African drug law serves the broader public-health interest.

Critique emerges

Hence, many critics have taken up the issue by publicising Gore's apparent hypocrisy. Writing in *American Prospect* (an influential political journal in the Clinton New Democrat tradition), an editor of the neo-liberal *New Republic*, John Judis, condemns the pharmaceutical lobby's White House clout:

> PhRMA, of course, is acting like a lobby – pressing the interests of its clients even when their case is weak and morally repugnant – but what is astonishing is that the Clinton administration has thrown its full weight behind their complaint … The Clinton administration has regularly put the export and investment concerns of American businesses above human rights and even security considerations. But in most of these cases, it could claim that it was acting in the national interest … Gore's willingness to do PhRMA's bidding in this case may indicate that on the issues that impinge upon his high-tech network of supporters, he is willing to do the wrong thing to keep them happy – and keep them in his corner.[37]

In May 1999, journalists began ridiculing Gore in liberal periodicals,[38] noting that a speech in Atlanta to prominent church-people that month included the line, 'Without values of conscience, our political life degenerates.'[39] Prominent activists attacked Gore publicly:

> According to Nader, 'Gore is representing the profit-glutted pharmaceutical industry, using the facilities of the US government, to browbeat the South African Ministry of Health' …
> Standing next to Mbeki at a February news conference in Cape Town, Gore, the favorite for the Democratic presidential nomination in 2000, called AIDS 'a crisis for South Africa' and said the problem 'must be faced with a new level of urgency'. AIDS activists, however, criticized Gore for

publicly promising to fight AIDS while working behind the scenes against South Africa's medicines law. 'It really is hypocritical for the administration to pretend to be concerned about AIDS when they're taking actions ... that are denying people access to very essential medicines,' said Eric Sawyer, executive director of the HIV/AIDS Human Rights Project ...

Gore was more worried about competing for campaign dollars from drug companies than in helping AIDS patients, Nader charged. Gore's only announced Democratic challenger, former Sen. Bill Bradley, hails from New Jersey, home of more than a dozen drug makers, Nader noted. 'He (Gore) wants to go up to New Jersey and curry favor with the pharmaceutical industry,' Nader said.[40]

The battleground shifts to the US

But for Gore, such a strategy had its contradictions, for a related struggle suddenly broke out in the US itself, where high drug prices also adversely affected consumers.[41] (For example, more than a third of senior citizens – 80% of whom use at least one prescription drug each day – lack prescription coverage.) The only pharmacist in the US Congress, Marion Berry (Democrat, Arkansas), regularly lambasted the industry and its government allies for overpricing. Berry, Bernie Sanders (Independent, Vermont) and Jo Ann Emerson (Republican, Montana) sponsored a bill in May 1999 to allow pharmacists to re-import drugs from Canada, Mexico, Europe and other countries at a cheaper price than that which pharmaceutical firms charge in the US.[42] The bill – HR 1885, the International Prescription Drug Parity Act, to amend the Food, Drug, and Cosmetic Act – was soon endorsed by several senators (Dorgan, Snowe, Johnson and Wellstone), who introduced the bill as S 1191 in June. US citizens' right to access to cheap drugs even became a campaign issue in the subsequent year's presidential campaign. Wellstone (Democratic, Minnesota) was lobbied intensively by Minnesota senior-citizen activists who regularly travelled to Canada to save hundreds of dollars on their drug purchases.[43] The Berry, Sanders and Emerson 'Dear Colleague' letter explained the need for reform:

> American consumers pay significantly higher prices for American-made prescription drugs than consumers in other countries. For example, the Government Accounting Office reported in 1991 that out of 121 prescription drugs surveyed, 99 had higher prices in the United States than in Canada (in 21 cases, the price differentials exceeded 100%). In a similar study conducted in 1994 looking at the price differentials in prescription drugs between the United States and the United Kingdom, GAO determined that 66 of the 77 drugs surveyed were priced higher in the United States. In fact, four of the five most commonly dispensed drugs in the United States cost anywhere from 58–278% more in the United States

than the United Kingdom, and 47 of the drugs evaluated had a mark-up of over 100%![44]

Moreover, early 1999 also witnessed an increase in resistance on the international level. At the 52nd World Health Assembly in Geneva in January, which had representation from 191 countries, a unanimous resolution was passed on the WHO's Revised Drug Strategy. According to Dlamini-Zuma's special advisor, Ian Roberts, 'The main importance of this resolution is that health now has a role in all international trade and finance agreements.'[45] Strategies to pin down pharmaceutical companies and untie their drug patents through clever wording in WTO/TRIPS and other international settings appeared set to continue.[46]

The contemporary balance of forces is not optimal for winning or implementing such agreements, as witnessed not only by the fact that the Medicines Act was tied up in South African courts from 1998 through April 2001, but more generally by how thoroughly Third World interests have been negated in most international trade and financial negotiating fora. In a letter to Gore in May 1999, Nader noted that the Vice-President's 'astonishing array of bullying tactics to prevent South Africa from implementing policies … designed to expand access to HIV/AIDS drugs … [amount to] an affront to the sovereignty of Third World nations'.[47]

Lessons from past struggle

This would not be the first such instance. In the early 1980s, a major challenge to the power of the pharmaceutical industry in Bangladesh – the prohibition of many non-essential drug imports – was rolled back not only by the US government's threat of foreign aid cuts. Drug companies themselves refused to sell Bangladesh essential medicines. Only Sweden's support for import substitution and the formation of the Gonoshsthaya People's Pharmaceutical Company (a non-profit-making factory producing low-cost generic substitutes) allowed some room to maneuver. The World Bank subsequently ordered Bangladesh to make 'detailed changes' in the National Drug Policy, consistent with the interests of pharmaceutical firms.[48]

Is it, therefore, realistic to expect sustained opposition from nation states (even leaders as bold as Dlamini-Zuma) to pharmaceutical pricing? The only way in which such resistance can be strengthened, Jacqueline Orr noted in 1987, was to strengthen civil-society understanding and campaigning: 'Currently, consumer critics, international public interest organisations, and grassroots activist offer the greatest hope for protection of people's health against the pharmaceutical industry's aggressive pursuit of healthy profits.'[49] Thai NGOs, for example, took this analysis seriously in 1998 when they embarked on sustained protest in favor of pharmaceutical law changes similar to South Africa's.[50]

The US domestic political situation is also revealing. Notwithstanding the apparent role of Congress as a nearly wholly owned subsidiary of corporate interests, there may occasionally emerge moments when progressives – for example, Southern Hemisphere Jubilee 2000 debt lobbies, the Nader groups and the '50 Years is Enough!' network – can engage the wider public through supporting oppositional legislation. As one reflection of the possibility of uniting US and international (especially African) struggles for lower pharmaceutical prices, Congressman Jesse Jackson, Jr. (Democratic, Illinois) sponsored a 'HOPE for Africa Bill' in 1999 which, among other provisions (especially debt cancellation without classic IMF-World Bank pro-corporate conditionality), would 'prohibit the US from spending funds to undermine African efforts to increase access to needed pharmaceuticals through intellectual property or competition policies'. Without even an outside chance of passage, the HOPE bill at least offered an alternative to the Clinton administration's neo-liberal US-Africa free-trade legislation (and in the process divided the black caucus in the US Congress), thus permitting progressive forces in civil society to mobilise without illusions.

For in all of this, conceptual clarity is critical. What was once considered 'imperialism' (i.e. US government actions on behalf of the desires of its major corporations to trade, finance and invest at will) was rebaptised 'globalisation' and declared by old and new ruling elites to be good for South Africa. The strategies and tactics of resisting the US-government and corporate squeeze on South Africa considered in this chapter should, if this analysis is correct, cohere in a sentiment against the very notion that essential drugs should be commodified by multinational corporations. That part of the story we turn to next.

Notes

1 For background, see, for example, Bond, P., Pillay, Y. and Sanders, D., 'The State of Neoliberalism in South Africa: Developments in Economic, Social and Health Policy', *International Journal of Health Services*, 27(1); and Bond, P. and Pillay, Y. (1995), 'Health and Social Policies in the New South Africa', *International Journal of Health Services*, 25(4).

2 Republic of South Africa Department of Health (1996), *Towards a National Health System*, Pretoria, p. 11.

3 Republic of South Africa Department of Health (1997), *Annual Report*, Pretoria, p. 6.

4 Republic of South Africa Department of Health, *Towards a National Health System*, p. 35.

5 Republic of South Africa (1997), Medicines and Related Substances Control Amendment Act, Cape Town, pp. 6–7.

6 Love, J. (1999), 'Info-Policy-Notes: US Law Requires US Department of State to Seek Repeal of South African Law on Essential Medicines', Consumer Project on Technology, Washington, DC, 7 April.

7 Richwine, L. (1999), 'US Blocking Distribution of AIDS Drugs, Critics Say', *San Francisco Examiner*, 12 April.

8 Cited in Navarro, V. (1994), *The Politics of Health Policy: The US Reforms, 1980–94*, Oxford, Basil Blackwell, p. 214.
9 Love, J. (1999), personal e-mail communication, Washington, DC, 16 April.
10 Larkin, B. (1999), 'US Government Efforts to Negotiate the Repeal, Termination or Withdrawal of Article 15(c) of the South African Medicines and Related Substances Act of 1997', US Department of State report, Washington, DC, 5 February.
11 United States Congress (1998), Omnibus Consolidated and Emergency Supplemental Appropriations Act, 1999 (HR 4328), Washington, DC, 21 October.
12 Barber, S. (1998), 'Plan Blunts Long-Term Threat to US Aid for SA', *Business Day*, 20 July.
13 Mitchell, D. (1999), 'Compulsory Licensing of Anti-HIV Drugs Stirs Debate in Geneva', *Journal of the American Medical Association*, HIV/AIDS Health Information (Internet version), 1 April.
14 Médécins sans Frontières Health Action International and Consumer Project on Technology (1999), 'AIDS and Essential Medicines and Compulsory Licensing: Summary of the 25–27 March, 1999 Geneva Meeting on Compulsory Licensing of Essential Medical Technologies', Geneva, 9 April.
15 *Ibid.*
16 *Ibid.*
17 *Ibid.*
18 United States Trade Representative (1999), 'Special 301 Review', Washington, DC, 30 April.
19 Nader, R. (1999), 'Medicine held Hostage by Profits', *San Francisco Bay Guardian*, 28 April.
20 Love, J. (1999), 'Gore/Mbeki Commission and Compulsory Licensing Disputes with South Africa', personal e-mail communication, Washington, DC, 2 April.
21 Richwine, L. (1999), 'Gore Worked to Soften South Africa Health Law', Reuters, Washington, DC, 16 April.
22 Goozner, M. (1999), 'Third World Battles for AIDS Drugs', *Chicago Tribune*, 28 April.
23 Sternberg, S. (1999), 'Victims lost in Battle over Drug Patents', *USA TODAY*, 24 May.
24 Barber, S. (1998), 'US Withholds Benefits over Zuma's Bill', *Business Day*, 15 July.
25 Pharmaceutical Research and Manufacturers of America (1999), 'PhRMA supports USTR on South Africa', Washington, DC, 30 April.
26 Sternberg, S. *op. cit.*
27 Bale, H. (1999), 'IFPMA Position on Compulsory Licensing', e-mail communication to Treatment-access Forum (treatment@critpath.org), Geneva, 15 April.
28 Love, J. (1999), 'Who pays What in Drug Development', *Nature*, 21 January.
29 Mitsuya, H., Weinhold, K., Yarchoan, R., Bolognesi, D. and Broder, S. (1989), 'Credit Government Scientists with Developing Anti-AIDS Drug', *New York Times*, 28 September.
30 Sternberg, S. *op. cit.*
31 Love, J. (1999), 'Statement on Bristol-Myers Squibb Announcement', Washington, DC, Consumer Project on Technology, 6 May.
32 Pharmaceutical Research and Manufacturers of America (1999), 'Submission for the "Special 301" Report on Intellectual Property Barriers', Washington, DC, 16 February.
33 Bailey, H. (1999), 'Bitter Pills: The Battle over Prescription Drug Prices', Center for Responsive Politics Money in Politics Alert, 5(17), 17 May.

34 Navarro, V. (1995), 'The Politics of Health Care Reform in the United States, 1992–94: A Historical Review', *International Journal of Health Services*, 25(2), p. 198.
35 Love, J. (1999), 'Washington DC as a Small Town', e-mail communication to IP-Health (ip-health@essential.org), Washington, DC, 13 April.
36 Werner, D. and Sanders, D. (1997), *Questioning the Solution: The Politics of Primary Health Care and Child Survival*, Palo Alto, HealthWrights, pp. 92–4.
37 Judis, J. (1999), 'K Street Gore', *The American Prospect*, 45, July–August.
38 Ridgeway, J. (1999), 'Gore AIDS Scandal Helps Drug Companies nix Cheap Medicines', *The Village Voice*, June 2; Caelers, D. (1999), 'Gore told to Ease up on Anti-South Africa Drugs War', Africa News Service, 18 May.
39 Corn, D. (1999), 'Gore to South Africans: Drop Dead', *New York Press*, 2 June.
40 Richwine, 'US Blocking Distribution of AIDS Drugs, Critics Say'.
41 Kelly, E. (1999), 'Cost of Prescription Drugs Drives Consumers to Canada', Gannett News Service, 21 May.
42 Quaid, L. (1999), 'Lawmakers push for Cheaper Prescriptions', Associated Press, 28 May .
43 Wolfe, W. (1999), 'FDA Head tells Seniors Agency can't Help cut Drug Costs', *Minneapolis Star Tribune*, 3 June.
44 Sanders, B., Berry, M. and Emerson, J. A. (1999), 'Dear Colleague Letter: Help Americans enjoy the Same Low Prescription Drug Prices as Other Countries', Washington, DC, US House of Representatives, 25 May.
45 Médécins sans Frontières Health Action International and Consumer Project on Technology, 'AIDS and Essential Medicines and Compulsory Licensing'.
46 Williams, F. (1999), 'Campaign over Drug Licensing to Grow', *Financial Times*, 29 March.
47 Russell, S. (1999), 'New Crusade to Lower AIDS Drug Costs', *San Francisco Chronicle*, 24 May.
48 Silverman, M., Lydecker, M. and Lee, P. (1992), *Bad Medicine*, Palo Alto, Stanford University Press; Werner and Sanders, *op. cit.*, p. 95.
49 Orr, J. (1997), 'Rexall for Profits', *Dollars and Sense*, 128, July–August, p. 21.
50 Assavanonda, A. (1998), 'NGOs Rally Against Patent Law Changes: Call on US to Stop Pressuring Thailand', *Bangkok Post*, 8 September.

CHAPTER NINE

Civil society conquest, state failure

1. Introduction

Contextualising the struggle for access to pharmaceutical treatment of HIV/AIDS requires that we immediately confront the bizarre twists and turns of South African policy in this regard. By illustration, consider the argument of Thabo Mbeki's key spokesperson on the issue (prior to his death in late 2000). In March 2000, Parks Mankahlana off-guardedly justified to *Science* magazine why the SA Department of Health refused to provide a relatively inexpensive (R100 million per year) anti-retroviral treatment to pregnant, HIV-positive women: 'That mother is going to die and that HIV-negative child will be an orphan. That child must be brought up. Who is going to bring the child up? It's the state, the state. That's resources, you see.'[1]

Yet as was subsequently pointed out – and confirmed by the Department of Health itself – the cost savings associated with treatment against mother-to-child transmission of HIV could potentially be enormous (R700 million per annum was one estimate).[2]

Thus at the Durban AIDS conference in July 2000, ANC parliamentarian Winnie Madikizela-Mandela accused her government of being 'an obedient servant of multinational companies that continue to put their profits above our people'. Acting SA Constitutional Court judge Edwin Cameron observed, 'The drug companies and African governments seem to have become involved in a kind of collusive paralysis. International agencies, national governments and especially those who have primary power to remedy the iniquity – the international drug companies – have failed us in the quest for accessible treatment.'[3]

This chapter makes the case that in spite of heroic efforts by radical civil society groups to gain access to anti-retroviral drugs through their formidable battle with multinational corporations and the White House, Pretoria failed miserably to follow up on these efforts, and is effectively losing the war against HIV/AIDS. To understand why it did so, at the expense of Mbeki's reputation, requires structural analysis of capitalism and health.

2. Pharmaceutical pricing and street politics

South African access to HIV/AIDS drugs suddenly emerged on the world stage when it became the first major issue in the US presidential-election campaign of 2000. Activists now joined debates that had, until June 1999, motivated mainly technical experts, academics, journalists, drug company spin-doctors and bureaucrats. In South Africa, an AIDS Treatment Action Campaign (TAC) mobilised a human chain at the US Johannesburg consulate in July, issuing an ultimatum that if the US did not reverse its position by October, the group would co-ordinate international protests outside US embassies on International Human Rights Day (10 December).

ACTing UP

In the US, Gore began to come under tough pressure, as ACT UP activists increased the profile of the issue up to the level of national media coverage through what the *Baltimore Sun* newspaper described as 'raucous demonstrations at campaign events' in June 1999.[4] Notwithstanding a meeting between activist leaders and top Gore officials (White House AIDS czar, Sandra Thurman, Al Gore's national security spokesman, Tom Rosshirt, and Tipper Gore's chief of staff, Clark Ray), ACT UP pledged to dog the presidential campaign with its banners: 'No Medical Apartheid!', 'Gore's Greed Kills!', 'AIDS Drugs for Africa Now!' Gore was confronted repeatedly and aggressively in New Hampshire, California and Pennsylvania at the very outset of his campaign, which he eventually lost by a few hundred (possibly miscounted) Florida votes in November 2000.

Reflecting the politicisation of the issue, columnist Arianna Huffington turned against former fellow Republican corporate allies:

> Allowing South Africa to license domestic production of the lifesaving drugs, known as 'compulsory licensing', is one of those rare issues – such as child abuse and drunk driving – on which there cannot possibly be two sides. After all, the country is suffering from an AIDS epidemic that our own surgeon general has compared 'to the plague that decimated the population of Europe in the 14th century'. The vice president's office says it is trying 'to help AIDS patients by making sure drug companies maintain profit levels to develop new AIDS medications.' But what good are AIDS medications if they can't get to the people with AIDS? And someone should remind the vice president that last year alone the three major AIDS-drug manufacturers – Glaxo Wellcome, Bristol-Myers Squibb and Pfizer – made respectively $4.43 billion, $3.64 billion and $3.35 billion.[5]

However, the *Washington Post* editorialised, 'Vice president Gore stands accused of defending pharmaceutical industry profits at the expense of South African AIDS patients. Welcome to campaign season. The AIDS activists who have heckled Mr. Gore at his early appearances, seeking to drown him out with chants of "Gore's Greed Kills," manipulate the facts in what is actually a much more complicated and interesting debate.'[6]

But the facts, as even the State Department acknowledged, boiled down to the US government's application of extraordinary pressure to a new African democracy so as to prevent it from engaging in parallel imports and compulsory licensing permitted by the WTO, as well as from making its case to the wider world through speeches to international organisations. While the context of US imperialism and multinational corporate power in an era of globalisation conditioned all aspects of the struggle, the most important motivating factor for Al Gore appeared to be pharmaceutical corporation campaign contributions.

Gore retreats

Perhaps, then, the activists could counter this immediate pressure point. For on 25 June Gore wrote a letter to black members of Congress stating that: 'I want you to know from the start that I support South Africa's efforts to enhance health care for its people – including efforts to engage in compulsory licensing and parallel importing of pharmaceuticals – so long as they are done in a way consistent with international agreements.'[7] This was the beginning of a climbdown on the issue, which culminated in Bill Clinton's concession in December 1999, at the Seattle World Trade Organisation meeting, that generic AIDS drug production or importation would not face US opposition.

But it soon became clear that intensified activism against and embarrassment of the pharmaceutical corporations and their Northern government backers was not sufficient to open space for more proactive Third World health and trade ministries to keep people alive. For those very Third World leaders – such as Mbeki – were confronted by their own perception of reality: the economic need *not* to treat HIV/AIDS.

3. A political economy of South African AIDS

The larger problem here transcends the cost of anti-retroviral drugs. At a structural level, the class/race/gender-biased character of South African social policy under conditions of a failing neo-liberal economic strategy is inhibiting prevention. It is this realisation that makes the dilemma for those like Zackie Achmat of the Treatment Action Campaign (see interview below) so terribly frustrating: the enemy is not only in the New Jersey headquarters of pharmaceutical corporations, but in the Pretoria economic ministries that dole out funds and attract multinational corporate investments.

Thus it becomes clearer why Mbeki spent several months in early 2000 trying (unsuccessfully) to shift attention from South Africa's ineffective HIV/AIDS policies: 'We cannot blame everything on a single virus. Poverty is the underlying cause of reduced life expectancy, handicap, disability, starvation, mental illness, suicide, family disintegration and substance abuse.'[8]

Denialism

This line of argument is also promoted by conservative 'AIDS dissidents', better termed 'denialists' – a small, marginalised bloc of researchers who deny a link between HIV and AIDS, instead attributing the disease to environmental factors. But no African public-health professional needs a lecture from University of California denialists on the relationship between poverty and health indicators. Mbeki dropped the denialist line from public statements late in 2000 after the confusion he was causing became untenable. But he didn't give up on it, and at a media dinner with World Economic Forum elites in Davos in January 2001 he repeatedly referred to the possible 'biological difference between Africans and whites' that affected the way the virus developed.[9]

Are there other explanations for Mbeki's shocking, tragic turn to HIV/AIDS denialism? Three come immediately to mind. The first is the presumption made by Al Gore that US pharmaceutical companies could get away with mauling SA's 1997 Medicines Act, reflecting the real power relations in global political economy, which persist even after Gore's humiliating retreats in 1999–2000. Secondly, ongoing neo-liberal pressure on South Africa's health and welfare budgets made it easier to deny than to treat HIV/AIDS. And thirdly, some top policy-makers in Pretoria seem ultimately indifferent to the health needs of masses of superfluous low-income people, who will never have a role as labourers in the formal capitalist sectors of the South African economy.

Let them eat placebos

The last is most interesting/horrifying, and is least explored in public policy discourses. Underlying the logic of denialism is a triple trumping of cost-benefit analysis. First, the cost savings associated with future treatment only hold true if the state healthcare system actually has capacity – and if its personnel even intend – to care for sick HIV-positive infants. Dr Costa Gazi, health secretary of the Pan Africanist Congress, argues that such an assumption is now in question, and not merely because the public-health service has collapsed in many impoverished communities. Worse, after HIV-positive infants get treatment for an initial ailment, care-givers (mainly grannies) are now sent home by local clinic staff in many areas, and simply told not to return.

Secondly, a false presumption, explicit in Mankahlana's comment given earlier, is that the state will be forced to look after orphans. In reality, the South African state has a practically non-existent social safety-net for black orphans. As a result, kinship networks are the only fallback when the HIV-positive mother dies. The orphan, whether HIV-positive or -negative, is usually looked after by desperately poor relatives. But it is very likely that the orphan will die by the age of five, even if she/he is HIV-negative, since the country has amongst the world's highest infant-mortality rates for black children. This practical reality lowers the likelihood of a future productive life for an AIDS orphan, even if the HIV-positive mother is treated with anti-retrovirals.

Thirdly, what if, against all the odds, the orphan does grow up to be a productive member of society? What jobs exist now, and will exist in the future, for her/him? If South Africa's 40% unemployed mass already provides an overstocked reserve pool of labor, why keep the 50 000 or so potentially HIV-negative children of HIV-positive mothers alive by preventing mother-to-child transmission? Why not, to invoke the mock-*Lugano Report* of brilliant social critic Susan George, allow AIDS to 'depopulate the vast underclass'?[10]

A related position is that AIDS is killing workers and low-income consumers at a time when South African elites in any case are adopting capital-intensive, export-oriented accumulation strategies. This political-economic condition was aired a whole decade before Mbeki's denialist turn, when a top bank economist, Edward Osborn, explained on US National Public Radio: 'As the numbers of sick and dying soar, the entire nature of the labor market will change drastically. There is likely to be even added incentive towards mechanisation and automation. The market could shift from a volume market to a quality market. The overall ceiling to the domestic market makes it imperative to promote South African exports and to widen and strengthen the range of exports.'[11]

AIDS and neo-liberalism are thus conjoined in cause and effect. But these are merely the most insane reasons for not treating HIV-positive pregnancies with anti-retrovirals, and for not taking AIDS seriously. Some critics, like Gazi and Thomas Coates (a professor at the University of California's AIDS Research Institute) conclude that the SA government is 'genocidal'.[12] Making the case for mother-child transmission treatment to the public in 1999, Gazi was suspended from a government hospital supervisory position for asserting that the SA minister of health should be charged with murder. Instead of shutting him up, the state made Gazi a martyr, and in his Eastern Cape public-health practice he spent his own money to give pregnant HIV-positive women the needed anti-retroviral treatment.

Setting a bad precedent

The second broad point above is a fear by the state that the floodgates might open if mother-child transmission becomes an initial wedge for providing more general treatment to low-income people. Giving anti-retrovirals to the country's 4.2 million HIV-positive residents would – under present pharma-ceutical-pricing constraints – cost roughly $12 billion per year, according to Zwile Mkhize, the KwaZulu-Natal provincial minister of health. The vast majority of treatment costs would have to be subsidised by a state whose entire annual budget is less than $40 billion and whose budget for HIV prevention is less than $25 million.

But while the cost of treatment access to all who need it did initially appear insurmountable, two rebuttals quickly emerged. First, determina-tions of fiscal priorities still reflect durable apartheid-era political-economic power. The society's transformation was closely monitored by financial interests, who demanded drastic cuts in the state budget deficit (from 9% of GDP in 1993 to less than 3% today), in the context of a 'homegrown' structural-adjustment programme and dramatic corporate tax cuts (from 48% in 1994 to 30% today). Moreover, activist campaigns like Jubilee South Africa's call to repudiate tens of billions of dollars in inherited apartheid-era local and foreign debt were dismissed as dangerous by financiers and their comprador friends in the new government's Department of Finance.

Yet debt repayment is the second-largest budget expense, accounting for more than $6 billion a year. A controversial new high-tech military spend-ing package adds nearly another billion dollars a year. Dramatic shifts in spending priorities, including a dramatic kick-start to the economy through widespread public-works projects – which have been rejected by the neo-liberal Department of Finance as inflationary – would change the basic parameters.

The even more decisive rebuttal to the argument that treatment for all HIV-positive South Africans is cost-prohibitive comes, ironically, from the government itself. For the Medicines Act provides for the Department of Health to override the trade-related intellectual property provisions of the World Trade Organisation, which South Africa joined in apartheid's dying months. Those provisions are malleable, allowing violation of patents in cases of extreme emergencies, such as AIDS. It should therefore have been uncontroversial for the SA government to import cheap drugs, at less than 5% of the price they are sold at locally, from markets like India and Brazil, or to permit local generic production of such drugs. This should have negated the cost-prohibitive argument entirely.

But given the lucrative upper-income (mainly white) market for medi-cines in South Africa, the major transnational pharmaceutical companies quickly objected to the Medicines Act. The country lost many thousands of people to curable opportunistic infections while the legality of the patent-violation clause was contested in court. The often explicit threat was that if the Medicines Act prevailed, the companies would disinvest from SA. This was the third political-economic rationale for allowing the continuation of mass death.

Pharma-corporate power

Hence after activists won the space for Pretoria to go through with compulsory licensing and parallel imports of cheap anti-retrovirals, Pretoria failed to take advantage of it. Mbeki snatched defeat from the jaws of victory by beginning his bizarre questioning of the link between the HIV virus and AIDS. The broader war against AIDS took a quick turn for the worse. But the fiasco unfolded not just because of Mbeki's mercurial personality, and won't be resolved by a change of mind – or even by ex-President Nelson Mandela's closing exhortation to the Durban conference that preventing mother-to-child transmission should be of highest priority. Necessary as these personal interventions are, they are not sufficient.

The political-economic facts of AIDS point out the need for a yet more profound struggle against the underlying assumptions and characteristics of South African – and international – capitalism. Part of the problem remains the awesome profits that private firms can achieve – and seem to feel they have the right to achieve – through monopoly pricing power backed by patent protection (see Table 4).

Table 4: Comparison shopping for life-giving drugs in October 2000[13]

Product[14]	SA Pub. Sector	SA Priv. Sector	Thailand
Fluconazole (200 mg)	R28.57	R80.24	R 1.78
AZT (100 mg)	R 2.38[15]	R 5.54	R 2.38
ddI (150 mg)	NA	R10.90	R 6.00
d4T (40 mg)	NA	R26.00	R 2.75
3TC (150 mg)	NA	R22.80	R16.30
Nevirapine (200 mg)	NA	R31.75	R12.00

But this power is only as strong as the ability of pharmaceutical corporations to intimidate Pretoria. This became clear in an interview with Zackie Achmat I conducted for *Multinational Monitor* in January 2001. His analysis is worth citing at length:

Multinational Monitor: You've led intense struggles to get better drug access for South Africa's 4.2 million HIV-positive people, yourself included. This has pitted you against both multinational corporations and the South African government, especially president Thabo Mbeki. Late last year, Mbeki reportedly called the Treatment Action Campaign a 'front for the drug companies' during an internal caucus with his African National Congress members of parliament, because of your campaign's emphasis on treatment.

Zackie Achmat: Let's deal with this forthrightly. Mbeki also said that TAC had infiltrated the trade unions, and that we wanted to embarrass him because of his statements from a year ago questioning the link between the HIV virus and AIDS. In reality, Mbeki embarrassed himself.

As for the trade unions, they had just demanded, at their September congress in front of Mbeki himself, that government reject this bizarre theory of AIDS and government policy. Are we a front? We get no donations from drug companies, and we were the first and loudest organisation to tackle them. So after Mbeki's outburst, we went to the South African government Public Protector to demand that he retract the statement, but that office hasn't responded yet.

Meanwhile, the union leaders like Zwelinzima Vavi were furious about this insult to their integrity. The South African Democratic Teachers Union, for example, headlined their newspaper the next month in huge letters, 'Sorry Mr President, we can't infiltrate ourselves.'

MM: Mbeki soon backed down and said he wouldn't make further statements on AIDS.

ZA: Yes, but he had already done a tremendous disservice to the country, particularly to the ANC. There is no doubt in my mind that a lot of people didn't vote ANC in the recent municipal election because of the AIDS issue. The ANC vote went from 67% in the 1999 general election to 60% in December. Thankfully, the trade unions pushed Mbeki into silence, saying very explicitly, 'You're wrong on HIV and we want treatment!'

But the other point that most critics are making now is that while Mbeki claimed that poverty was the key cause of AIDS deaths, in fact if you look at the SA government's position on poverty reduction, it is also a disaster. The country's worst-ever outbreak of cholera, which affected 12 000 people in low-income rural areas with more than 50 fatalities during the last five months of 2000, was catalysed by the inhuman cut-offs of clean water by government bureaucrats because people couldn't pay a R51 ($6.80) connection fee.

TAC hopes that the ANC's municipal election promise of free water and free electricity is implemented, but we desperately need the leading advocacy groups in South Africa, like Jubilee 2000 and Cease Fire, to work closely with trade unions to redirect the budget to that end, and to increase the health budget. We need a 33% increase to develop infrastructure, to train, and to employ more staff, up from R24 billion ($3.2 billion) to R32 billion ($4.3 billion). Recently, per-capita health spending has been declining, which can only be considered politically irresponsible, in the midst of the AIDS disaster.

MM: This would be aimed, mainly, at assuring all who are HIV+ ultimately get treatment.

ZA: Yes, but for us, a move away from the multinational corporate producers to local generic production is the only way. We actually need not only state production of drugs, but also private generic competition here in SA.

MM: What, realistically, can you expect government to do on treatment?

ZA: We would like to see, by mid-year, the implementation of what the government said it would do last August on prevention/treatment of opportunistic HIV-related diseases. For example, the tuberculosis budget is just R500 million per year, which just scratches the surface of what's needed. We have a TB case rate in South Africa of more than 350 per 100 000 people, which is the world's worst. In the mining industry, it's as high as 3 000 per 100 000. The main problem in the lowest-income provinces is that between a quarter and three-quarters of rural clinics don't have TB drugs. This is partly because of limited managerial capacity in rural areas, combined with budget cuts, especially to hospitals, which always drop consumables like medicines first. So the TB budget needs a massive increase.

We are also demanding introduction of cotrimoxazole to prevent PCP-pneumonia, which kills mainly HIV+ infants. A monthly supply would cost R4 ($0.53) for children and R8–24 ($1.06–3.18) per adult, which is a great savings over hospitalisation costs, which are up to R150 000 per patient ($20 000). But right now, there's not sufficient political commitment from the government to get access to drugs even for these extremely obvious areas of treatment.

MM: What do you say to critics who claim that expanding treatment through cheap parallel imports, as you advocate, risks introducing drugs of questionable quality, is infeasible due to lack of health-system capacity to administer drugs properly, and consequently will expand drug-resistant strains of HIV?

ZA: First, on the quality of imports, we now have official clearance to import Fluconazole, at 2.2% of the price charged by private-sector clinics, and we've shown that the drug is high quality. Even the Medicine Control Council, which charged me with illegal importation of medicine when I brought in 10 000 Fluconazole capsules from Thailand last year just to make the point, also concedes that the quality is fine.

By the way, TAC is still being investigated by the SA Revenue Services for that civil disobedience, and they'll probably charge me for tax evasion. They won't get more than R2 800 from Value Added Tax on the symbolic shipment I brought in, so it's clearly petty harassment by the ANC loyalist who runs the tax system.

Second, we should not underestimate the difficulties of providing anti-retrovirals, and we don't. If it's done on the basis of a clear, well-defined plan, it shouldn't be beyond our capacity in South Africa to establish an effective system for administering treatment.

Third, we agree that if you have weak implementation, drug-resistant strains will emerge. Certainly, our health professionals need more training in prescription techniques.

Still, 12% of new infections in the US are found to be based on drug-resistant strains. Is anyone saying that the US must stop providing treatment? Moreover, it is well known that rich countries have witnessed a dramatic overprescription of antibiotics, leading to many kinds of drug-resistant diseases. So this isn't just a problem of HIV/AIDS treatment, and we shouldn't be the class of patients denied access as a result.

The problem of drug resistance can be addressed through other means as well. Our private medical-aid insurance system puts an excessive limitation on payment for therapy, which leads doctors to prescribe a dual-therapy treatment instead of triple therapy, or even to prescribe AZT as monotherapy, which gives rise to much quicker drug-resistance. In addition, South Africa is the most frequent site for clinical trials in the developing world, due to good infrastructure. After treatment is halted when trials are finished, there is a problem of drug resistance. But none of these problems should be grounds for saying, no more treatment, especially since it is mainly low-income black women who are the beneficiaries of treatment.

MM: Is the South African government moving towards establishing a clear, well-defined plan?

ZA: Right now, the minister simply does not have a plan for anti-retrovirals. But there are two other ministries who are also blocking progress. The finance ministry does not provide enough money, and the ministry of trade and industry has not taken a clear position on local production. This is important, because the minister, Alec Erwin, is scared to offend the WTO and the investment community by allowing local generic production. He knows that this will send negative signals to other corporate investors.

But what these South African ministers are dead wrong about is that every other well-informed business leader in the world now realises that unless there is generic production, then too many people will die, and overall health-system costs will be much higher than the cost of alienating the pharmaceutical firms by violating their patents.

MM: It looked like you won the first major battle in the war with pharmaceutical companies in September 1999, when then-vice president Al Gore agreed to back off the pressure he put on Mbeki and Erwin to withdraw a South African law which made it possible to import drugs and license generics for local production. Then came Mbeki's turnaround. What did you learn from that struggle?

ZA: As I said, the bigger problem is the government's unfounded fear of alienating investors in general. But on the positive side, we had the most exciting experience in rallying international solidarity since the anti-apartheid struggle. The most helpful research organisation was the Consumer Project on Technology. The most important voice to help generate a global consensus that drug companies were committing genocide against the poor was Médécins sans Frontières. The most serious activists fighting against profiteering on AIDS and other diseases were ACT UP in New York, Philadelphia and Paris.

But what ultimately also is critical for us is the conscientisation now under way in broader civil society, here and elsewhere. Last year, the Congress of SA Trade Unions and their Southern African allies pushed through a resolution supportive of generics at the Durban conference of the International Confederation of Free Trade Unions. This issue is resonating with trade unions across the South, including Korea and indeed throughout Africa.

MM: The drug companies are claiming that with their donations, they are now doing as much as can be expected. UNAIDS is under pressure because they aren't monitoring the donations in Africa, but was the UNAIDS/Industry initiative fatally flawed from the outset?

ZA: Well, first, the various donations have come only because of protest. These are, in any case, just holding operations for the drug companies, which hope they can delay the import or local production of generics in Africa. And the very large South African private sector is still not covered in one of the largest deals, between Pretoria and Pfizer, for Fluconazole.

Whatever the nature of a particular donation, we can't afford to let up pressure on the drug companies, otherwise prices will go way up again after they capture the market. In any event, some of these programmes are also financially self-interested. In Botswana, for every dollar Merck gives, the Gates Foundation gives a dollar, which comes back to the company when they buy Merck drugs at wholesale prices, which can be added to Merck's tax deduction on the donation. The big question about the drug companies' donations is how long they can be sustained, and how many people will be reached. Evidence so far is not encouraging.

What is, however, most disturbing about the drug companies' philanthropy, is their ability to buy off potential protest from the established AIDS organisations and researchers. Bristol-Myers-Squibb, for instance, has given $120 million to a 'Secure the Future' programme over three years, directed at women, children and NGOs. That gives them the clout to go into established AIDS organisations and literally purchase loyalty by researchers and NGO leaders. Some NGOs have become much less critical than they should be. And BMS' two drugs are ddI and D4T, which in any case were developed by the US National Institute of Health and Yale University. Yet both are still priced prohibitively in South Africa.

MM: Finally, from your perspective, is progress being made on a vaccine, and how are drug companies doing in R&D more generally?

ZA: Of course we would support a vaccine, but in reality, there's no chance of getting even a 50% effective vaccine within 7–10 years, according to the main scientific researchers. The World Bank, Gates and other funders, including our government, all hope for a magic bullet.

In the meantime, millions are due to perish, and millions more will contract HIV. We wish they would spend a lot more of the resources now going into vaccine work into something more practical, namely a microbicide gell or spray which can prevent HIV transmission during vaginal and anal sexual intercourse, because it kills off lots of sexually-transmitted disease bugs. It's much more promising, but it's massively underfunded. I think that so few companies are doing serious work on microbicides because people who will use them most are poor women. If the perception within the drug companies is that the rich, white, heterosexual market doesn't need it, you can expect it to become a fatally low priority.[16]

State failure, social struggle.

The obstinacy of the Mbeki government knew no bounds. As the class struggle associated with AIDS raged, he misjudged friends and enemies, and hence chose disastrous strategies and tactics. Mbeki and top officials had promoted the scam Virodene industrial solvent while questioning the toxicity of vitally-needed (well-tested) drugs. Notorious oddball dissidents were invited onto a presidential panel to help explain that HIV doesn't cause AIDS, hence drugs would not help fight the battle. In another bid to avoid increasing access to emergency anti-retroviral treatment, senior leaders derided the accuracy of rape statistics and the extent of HIV transmission by rape. Mbeki ignored Mandela's July 2000 AIDS Conference advice to proceed immediately with mother-to-child-transmission treatment, and his health officials terminated an Mpumalanga NGO's access to health facilities because they were offering antiretrovirals to rape victims. The health department's AIDS directorate didn't spend 40% of its budget in 1999/2000 just as the South African treatment crisis was becoming an international scandal, and while Mbeki and health officials repeatedly claimed that the country was too poor to provide adequate medicines. Caught out again and again, Mbeki turned to conspiracy theory, alleging TAC relations with drug companies and infiltration of trade unions. He played the race card on the courageous campaigning-journalist Charlene Smith. (At one point, the CIA also reportedly entered into Mbeki's paranoia.) Through such obfuscation, the South African government found a myriad of ways to protect the very international corporations which made it most difficult to treat AIDS.

An alternative strategy was available. Appropriate allies were all around, including those courageous health and trade officials in other Southern governments prepared to do battle with what blockbuster novelist John LeCarré came to call Big Pharma. By April 2001, the court challenge by drug companies to the Medicines Act had generated such an extraordinary backlash—forcing the 39 companies to withdraw their case after waves of international protest in dozens of cities, coordinated by TAC, ACT UP, Medicins sans Frontiers and Oxfam – that Mbeki could easily have changed direction to widespread applause. He didn't, and his lawyers were instructed to plead in court that the implications of the *Medicines Act* would not extend to producing generic drugs in South Africa, but only to importing drugs from Big Pharma where they were sold cheaper abroad. Dropping its momentary alliance with Mbeki, TAC was compelled to file case in the Constitutional Court in mid-2001, alleging that the government's ongoing failure to autho-rise anti-retroviral distribution was killing Mbeki's most loyal constituents.

Trapped like bucks in the spotlights of a speeding vehicle, Mbeki and his colleagues stumbled ever more quickly towards the oncoming collision, making themselves ever more vulnerable both in medical terms and in the court of public opinion. But in doing so, the government repeatedly mistook the economic threats associated with the AIDS wreck – Big Pharma's monopoly pricing power and patent protection, Trevor Manuel's extremist fiscal austerity, and pressure against adding to the ranks of the unemployed, orphaned and welfare-dependent (by allowing more people to live) – as aspects of globalisation *that had to be nurtured*. The fealty to neoliberalism which Manuel had earlier termed 'impotence' would soon haunt South Africa, as the president began to be termed Chief Undertaker Mbeki.

Recall the ANC discussion document cited at the end of Chapter 7, which concluded by repudiating potential government actions that are 'in discord with the rest of the world, but which can be sustained by virtue of a volun-tarist South African experiment of a special type, a world of anti-Apartheid campaigners, who, out of loyalty to us, would support and sustain such voluntarism.' In reality, the world of anti-Apartheid campaigners grew and grew. Just over a year after the discussion document's circulation, the *Medicines Act* had become the experiment that millions of desperate people were awaiting, poised on the line dividing life and death. And within three years, the ANC document's last lines had become so profoundly fallacious that tens of thousands were dying unnecessarily, because of Pretoria's stub-born refusal to break the chains of global pharma-apartheid. Still, radical groups in civil society soldiered on, and the TAC's alliances – with trade unions locally, and many other activists internationally – offered hope for saving lives at home, and, abroad, for sustaining a full-fledged attack on the international financial pillars of global apartheid. As we review in the final Part of this book, debates over fixing or nixing the major institutions at the nerve centre of finance would first be necessary – while incorporating the aspirations and sensibilities of African and Third World activism – followed by the elaboration of a concrete alternative: an experiment 'of a special type' in locking capital down, driven by coalitions of grassroots activists who would take their inspiration from the fight for life, against the fatal combi-nation of AIDS and economic power.

Notes

1 Cited in *The Citizen*, 14 July 2000 and the *Mail and Guardian*, 21 July 2000. Mankahlana – who a week earlier said he would toss the Durban Declaration on AIDS signed by 5 000 people into Mbeki's 'dustbin' because it strongly refuted the AIDS-dissident camp – immediately denied making the statement: 'Their story is a complete fabrication.' *Science*'s editor replied that his reporter had recorded Mankahlana in his Pretoria office on 24 March, and offered to play the tape. I include this tragic incident because, notwithstanding Mankahlana's subsequent denial that the statement reflected policy, there was a general sense amongst health professionals in South Africa that the *Science* quote was indeed official thinking. (Mankahlana had personal experience that is perhaps worth citing for further context. He was, at the time of making these quotes, the target of two paternity suits based on failure to pay child maintenance.)

2 Both the Madikizela-Mandela and Cameron quotes are from the *Mail and Guardian*, 21 July 2000.

3 Both quotes in the *Mail and Guardian*, 14 July 2000.

4 Weisman, J. (1999), 'Activists doubt Gore tries to Reduce Cost of AIDS Drugs: ACT-UP, Candidate's Staff Talk on Medicine in Africa', *Baltimore Sun*, 23 June.

5 Huffington, A. (1999), 'Pharmacologic Al', http://www.ariannaonline.com/columns/files/062899.html, 28 June.

6 *Washington Post*, 24 June 1999.

7 Gore, A. (1999), 'Letter to James E. Clyburn, Black Congressional Caucus', 25 June, partially published in the *Multinational Monitor*, January 2001.

8 Mbeki, T. (2000), 'Welcome Address', opening speech to the 13th Annual International AIDS Convention, Durban, 9 July.

9 As reported to the author by a journalist at the dinner.

10 George, S. (1999), *The Lugano Report*, London, Pluto Press.

11 I was the reporter, and cited the comment in Bond, P. (1991), *Commanding Heights and Community Control: New Economics for a New South Africa*, Johannesburg, Ravan Press.

12 *Mail and Guardian*, 21 July 2000.

13 Sources: Thai GPO and Biolab; India CIPLA; South Africa Department of Health; Private Discount Pharmacy. Prices valid as of 16 October 2000. (Drugs and dosages are used to compare prices rather than to indicate proposed treatment regimens.)

14 The following are the holders of the patents on the above drugs, responsible for the extremely high prices paid by South Africans: Bristol-Myers-Squibb (ddI – didanosine); Bristol-Myers-Squibb (d4T – stavudine); Glaxo-Wellcome (AZT – zidovudine); Glaxo-Wellcome (3TC – lamivudine); Glaxo-Wellcome (AZT/3TC); Pfizer (Fluconazole); Boehringer Ingelheim (Nevirapine).

15 Lower-cost AZT is the result of activism. The AZT price was reduced from R5.54 in the public sector following TAC demonstrations and protests. The same applies to the lower cost of Nevirapine for mother-to-child transmission.

16 Edited version published in *Multinational Monitor*, January–February 2001.

PART FOUR

Globalisation?
Or internationalism plus the
nation state?

'Defund the Bank, Break the Bank, and Dump the Debt' – activists in
Prague, September 2000.

Top: The World Bank under siege, April 2000.
Bottom: Policing for capital, Prague, September 2000.

CHAPTER TEN

The 'Fix-it-or-nix-it' debate

1. Introduction

We have established, so far, that global apartheid is no accident, but is a logical outcome of the operations of international capitalism at the turn of the 21st century. We have correlated the rise of financial and commercial dynamism and power to the underlying economic slowdown during the last quarter of the 20th century. We have seen how that power intimidated the nationalist leadership of even a newly liberated society like South Africa. We have considered the ideology that supports and reflects financial and commercial power, namely neo-liberalism. We observed how neo-liberalism – particularly the freeing of barriers to financial, trade and investment flows – serves the interests of multinational corporations and banks, and explicitly threatens the lives of those whose need for even essential goods and services is frustrated by financial turbulence, property rights and other manifestations of irrational market power. And we have located the 'brain' and 'nerve centre' of neo-liberalism in two Washington-based institutions – the International Monetary Fund and World Bank – as well as in the Geneva-based World Trade Organisation. This chapter considers the strategic implications of these findings, from the standpoint of the progressive 'global justice movements' described in Chapter five.

The two once-impenetrable international public-financial institutions came into focus for a critical mass of activists at the turn of the century, in a way that in turn sharpened what were previously quite fuzzy discussions surrounding globalisation and popular resistance. The point of departure for that focus was mid-April 2000, when an estimated 30 000 protesters joined the 'Mobilization for Global Justice' in Washington, capping a week that began ominously with a poorly attended Jubilee 2000 USA debt-relief rally on 9 April (controversially addressed by neo-liberal Clinton economist Gene Sperling). In the middle of all this was a 'No Blank Check for China' demonstration of 15 000 workers – from the right wing of the American Federation of Labour-Congress of Industrial Organizations (AFL-CIO) – at the Capitol building on 12 April, which raised the spectre of a new 'yellow peril' campaign. The international economic debate in the

US was bedeviled, it appeared up until 16–17 April, by the standard twin evils of reformism and narrow, xenophobic protectionism.

Auspiciously, in contrast, the bulk of the protesters on 16–17 April rallied around a call for the IMF and World Bank to be closed down (not reformed), taking further the street slogan that had divided the two main blocs of demonstrators in Seattle at the World Trade Organisation meeting 18 weeks earlier. On that occasion, younger, militant activists engaging in a 'lockdown' in the streets to prevent WTO delegates from meeting were on one side, and on the other were those tens of thousands of ordinary workers channelled by the US labour and environmental movement leaderships away from the Seattle Convention Centre into a holding area, where they were prevented by marshals from supporting the demonstrators.[1] The AFL-CIO leaders and moderate environmentalists merely wanted access to the negotiating table, where their agenda was to reform the multinational-corporate trading system by adding clauses providing for labour and ecological protections.

In Washington, however, the 16 April protest was endorsed by organised labour, the programme was internationalist in character and Third World activists were prominent guests. Momentum was thus captured by the far more radical Mobilization, and enormous ideological progress and political maturity were claimed and consolidated. 16–17 April was built upon a militant platform and slogan – 'Break the Bank, Defund the Fund, Dump the Debt!' – promoted by a strong, diverse coalition of forces. Skilfully, the Mobilization's official core of left-leaning Washington think-tank and NGO staff[2] helped to at least temporarily merge the very different agendas of reformist bureaucrats and grassroots activists. Labour/NGO/green officials historically wobbled when faced with global political-economic issues, as a result of factors that included the disadvantageous balance of forces prior to Seattle, their often debilitating ties to the Democratic Party (and fears of being seen in alliance with Republican IMF/World Bank bashers), and an apparent professionalism heightened by dependence upon bourgeois funders. The AFL-CIO had even supported the $18 billion recapitalisation of the IMF in late 1998, after making some kind of obscure deal with Bill Clinton.

The activists, in contrast, were anxious to conduct a joyous symphony of Seattle-like lockdowns and street parties to blockade the IMF/World Bank spring meetings. To do so, they introduced a cultural-liberation ambience virtually unknown to Washington, utilising radical participatory democracy and affinity-group cell-structuring in strategy sessions and trainings, facilitated by striking young talents from the Direct Action Network. In this milieu, Z's Michael Albert reported:

> The various tactical wings of the movement – whether seeking to get arrested, to militantly protest, to make a public but peaceful statement, or

just to learn or teach – worked together marvelously. Diverse tactics did not trump one another. Tension was minimal. Intercommunication was considerable. Coalitions were strengthened rather than dissolving into tactical disputes. There was in-the-street mutual aid, careful planning of venues and events, and pre-demonstration communication of aims.[3]

Results included abundant forms of civil disobedience and 1 300 arrests (although the first 600 were unwilling, as police used dramatic force during an 15 April Free Mumia protest march and also closed the activists' Convergence Centre on absurd fire-code charges). Encouragingly, unlike Seattle, the 1 000-strong Revolutionary Anti-Capitalist Bloc of black-clad anarchists worked in harmony with those carrying out civil disobedience, and had the honour of attracting a police helicopter devoted solely to trailing their movements across Washington on 16 April.

But most importantly for my purposes in this chapter, the Mobilization drew the eco-socio-economic concerns of the Global South far deeper into the fabric of the US movement than ever before. Granted, the protest failed to obstruct the IMF/World Bank meetings (the Washington police spread protest-boundary perimeters widely, paralysing over 90 city blocks in the centre of town, but also gaining the physical space required to sneak several hundred delegates into the meeting at 5 a.m. on the two mornings, while groups of 100–500 protesters subsequently clogged 18 intersections and turned away numerous late-rising delegates). No matter, the combination of thorough preparation and the large size of the turnout in Washington:

- helped raise public consciousness about the IMF and World Bank to unprecedented levels;
- brought sympathetic activists from different constituencies into successful coalition;
- taught organisers a great deal about Washington logistics (and how they can be gummed up next time);
- showed South allies the extent of solidarity possibilities, encouraging them to intensify their own local critiques of the IMF/World Bank; and also
- facilitated a long-overdue split amongst development NGOs (a group of 22 conservative organisations sent a bizarre, self-discrediting endorsement note to the IMF and World Bank).

The Washington protests set an excellent stage for several years of intense grassroots campaigning aimed at closing down the Bretton Woods twins, thus fundamentally reorienting our understanding of development finance, and in the process realigning power relations in ways that could benefit democratic political movements across the South. This chapter makes the case that just such an aim should be amongst the highest priorities of those (especially Northerners) who are supportive of global justice.

There remains, of course, a standard concern on the Left, namely, whether the activist focus on the *institutional forms* of global-capitalist (mis)management – the IMF, World Bank and WTO – risks detracting from understanding both the capital-accumulation process and class-based resistance, hence leading to partial and imperfect strategic insights about power and social transformation.[4] There are also mixed views emerging amongst progressive scholars and activists about the optimal scale (national, regional and global) at which politics and policy should be resisted and perhaps even reconstructed.

Such debates resonate throughout this chapter, which first attempts to summarise why so many activists are now intent on 'nixing' – not fixing – the IMF and World Bank (Section 2). We then interrogate divergent lines of thinking about the IMF, World Bank and international capitalism, both between reformers and radicals (Section 3) and within the radical camp (Section 4). Finally, we brainstorm about the different tactical ways forward for the global justice movements, particularly in relation to the debate over whether a World Bank is even needed in the Third World (Section 5). The next chapter locates these dynamics more explicitly in Third World social, labour and environmental activism.

What, then, are the central intellectual and practical dilemmas surrounding the emergence of an embryonic world 'state' based in Washington, and how do these debates relate to street-level consciousness, and to strategies and tactics adopted by leading campaigners for global justice? Once these questions have been answered, we can conclude that, as an inspired tactic, 'bond-boycotting' the World Bank should be supported as an integral, unifying component – and excellent local approach – within the broader mobilisation for class, gender, ethnic and environmental justice.

2. The World Bank under siege

The year 2000 was by no means the first time that activists united in mass numbers at an IMF/World Bank office. Each time since around 1979 that Washington increased the pressure on Africa and the Third World generally, social pain generated resistance. For most of the first two decades, this mainly took the form of 'IMF riots' that were unsustained, chaotic and often self-destructive. The next chapter considers the maturing of Third World protest into more formidable, sustained protest.

Surprisingly, during the late 1990s, an equivalent degree of anger emerged in the North (beyond sites such as South-Central Los Angeles, often considered part of the 'global South'). After numerous discreet, fragmented attacks on particular global-elite initiatives and corporations, it was astonishing how cogently 'anti-globalisation' protests were suddenly directed towards nerve centres of the international financial and trading system, in cities like Seattle, Washington and Prague. The idea that tens of thousands of people would converge with the aim of disrupting the IMF, World Bank and WTO gatherings of elite rulers and corporate chiefs *as a movement*, would have been dismissed as a leftist fantasy during the late 1990s, but after Seattle, anything seemed possible.

April in Washington

Consider the circumstances of April 2000 at the IMF/World Bank head-quarters in Washington, at the obscure spring meeting attended by only a few hundred officials. Although in Berlin (1988) and Madrid (1994), previous IMF/World Bank annual meetings attracted tens of thousands of demonstrators, the mass of the US population had never cared much about the Bretton Woods institutions. Likewise, US leftists long suffered an inward-looking history, broken only occasionally by solidarity struggles against Spanish fascism, the Vietnam War, apartheid and Central American terror. Conditions for activism against global-scale institutions were notoriously lacking in Washington during the Cold War, until trade unions, environmentalists and the Ralph Nader organisation Public Citizen put the Seattle WTO meeting on the protest map on 30 November 1999.

A closer examination of Washington's opponents is in order.[5] The 'N30' and 'A16' protests (so-called because of the dates of their occurrences) broadened and deepened the existing left-wing but technicist critiques of the WTO, IMF and Bank. The WTO attracted domestic dissent partly on the basis of its explicit threat to US environmental and labour standards. Mass consciousness against globalisation was already increasing dramatically, in the wake of specific campaigns against, amongst others, oil companies, textile/clothing sweatshops, fast-food outlets, shoe firms, chemical and biotech companies, advertising agencies and even coffeehouse chains.[6] Key events that brought large numbers together in coalition included the North American Free Trade Agreement debate in 1993, the Vancouver protest against the Asia Pacific Economic Cooperation meetings in 1997, successful attacks on Clinton's proposed Fast-Track Trade Negotiating Authority in 1997 and on the OECD's Multilateral Agreement on Investment in 1998.

Yet these precursors were relatively sporadic and disconnected from the base. And as was often remarked, the ideological diversity of the protesters still proved a major stumbling block. However, while there was no obvious grounds for protest co-ordination, and while the particular demonstrations are mainly defensive – 'against' some or other attack upon basic socio-economic and democratic rights – the exuberance must, eventually, cohere in programmatic terms. At some point soon, the movement could throw up not only that which it is 'for' – as have the Zapatistas, who served as a catalyst for rebellious spirit, with their Intergalactic Encounters For Humanity, Against Neoliberalism – but also a rough outline of the strategy and alliances needed to realise more universal ambitions, transcendent of communitarianism.

For and against

Until then, semantics should not confuse the movement's fairly clear orientation. Protests have come down explicitly *against* large corporations, the commodification of daily life, the commercialisation of culture, the destruction of indigenous livelihoods, the intensification of patriarchy, the fouling of the environment and the construction of undemocratic, world-state institutions in Washington and Geneva. The movement is, quite simply, against uneven capitalist development, in this its purest, most international neo-liberal stage.

What the movement is *for* can only be sensed through exploring the organic demands that arise from a myriad of concrete struggles, e.g. affordable drinking water in Bolivian cities and historic, sustainable systems of irrigation in the Thai countryside, jobs in a pseudo-liberated Johannesburg and energy in oil-rich Lagos, a softer economic landing in Seoul, transparency in Washington, community in London, national economic sovereignty in New Delhi, and so forth. Although it is too early to say this with certainty, it would appear that the 'decommodification' and 'destratification' of basic goods/services, respect for ethnic identity and indigenous culture, deracialised and degendered access to resources, and recognition of ecological integrity will all have to be intertwined threads in whatever programmatic fabric is ultimately woven. As I will argue in the next chapter, African social struggles are already defining these objectives with a surprising degree of detail.

All things considered, it is evident that from an existing patchwork quilt of diverse struggles, a formidable movement for social justice is emerging to engage simultaneously in international relationship-building, 'policy advocacy' (i.e. concrete socio-economic demands), local empowerment, and militant campaigning for national democratic processes that surmount the barriers erected by both domestic state bureaucrats and Washington's international financial bureaucrats. To these ends, *shutting down* the WTO, IMF and World Bank is a logical strategy that brings the movement together at the international level, so that its particular components are more free and powerful to carry through their local projects.

Not constrained, at this stage, by a typical party-political aim of taking state power, the movement's leading cadres will probably have to await more opportune conditions before making either an electoral or insurgent run at their own states (whether at national, provincial or municipal levels). Once having done so, they will also have to remember that top-down radical reforms must always be conjoined with constant pressure from mass-democratic labour, community and related organisations emanating from below.[7] A hopeful sign is the movement away from NGO jaw-jaw sessions over potential reforms of the IMF and World Bank to radical activism.

Eluding the co-option trap

Indeed, to sense the new dynamic, it is worth recalling that until 2000, the merits of abolishing the IMF and World Bank were outside the bounds of acceptable discussion in NGO circuits. *The Economist* captured at least something of World Bank president James Wolfensohn's charm, shortly after Seattle:

> The 50 Years is Enough campaign of 1994 was a prototype of Seattle (complete with activists invading the meeting halls). Now the NGOs are surprisingly quiet about the World Bank. The reason is that the Bank has made a huge effort to co-opt them. James Wolfensohn, the Bank's boss, has made 'dialogue' with NGOs a central component of the institution's work. More than 70 NGO specialists work in the Bank's field offices. More than half of World Bank projects last year involved NGOs. Mr Wolfensohn has built alliances with everyone, from religious groups to environmentalists. His efforts have diluted the strength of 'mobilisation networks' and increased the relative power of technical NGOs (for it is mostly these that the Bank has co-opted).[8]

Yet in the wake of Seattle and a meeting in Johannesburg of the radical Jubilee South movement,[9] slumbering Washington NGO-technocrats awoke with a start. The 50 Years is Enough coalition took ever-tougher positions and injected excellent content into the imagery and slogans of the A16 actions, i.e. 'Defund the Fund, Bankrupt the Bank and Dump the Debt!' Just as importantly, the mass-popular outpourings in Seattle, Washington and Prague turned the broader relationship between NGO strategists and grassroots campaigners on its head.

The more radical activists from the base increasingly served not just as hands and feet, but also as the movement's eyes, ears and brains. The Direct Action Network brought an unprecedented dose of participatory democracy to Washington, as hundreds of spokes-council representatives strategised long into the nights during the week preceding 16 April. From San Francisco, Global Exchange continued its key ideological role, Ruckus Society did excellent training, the Rainforest Action Network helped with direct action, and the International Forum on Globalization sponsored a well-attended teach-in. A new generation of Washington-based radicals emerged quickly from obscure networks, NGOs and think-tanks, i.e. 50 Years is Enough, Alliance for Global Justice, Center for Economic and Policy Research, Center for Economic Justice, the Nader group Essential Action, and Jobs with Justice. Key activists from these groups managed to pull along many of their somewhat frightened Washington colleagues to welcome the influx of radicals and guide the protesters.

The police won elite praise for 'saving Washington' (see above). However, the cops' amateurishly repressive streak was disclosed by the clumsy way they shut the protesters' Convergence Centre on the morning of 15 April and the brutal means by which they rounded up an initial 600 protesters (plus bystanders) – not to mention 50 giant papier-mâché puppets – at a Mumia Abu-Jamal support rally that afternoon.

Likewise, actions against the IMF and World Bank annual meeting in Prague on 26 September 2000 had similar dynamics. Thousands of protesters were denied entry to the Czech Republic, yet 15 000 did manage to gather in protest streams leading up to a key bridge in the vicinity of the meetings. Small groups of militant anarchists – joined by documented provocateurs from the Prague police – tossed rocks and even molotov cocktails from sites very close to the hall. The bankers' meeting had to be closed a day early, as a direct result of the mayhem.[10]

As a result, logistical struggles against the Washington centres of international financial power will transpire again, with even more intense confrontations likely. It may even be possible at the IMF/World Bank annual meeting in September 2001 for tens of thousands of activists to cause sufficient chaos to prevent business-as-usual by the 5 000 delegates. Wolfensohn has already begun to publicly ask whether it is possible – and safe – to hold these meetings in future, given the persistence of the demonstrators.

A radical movement mainstream?

But the movement's strategies are not based solely upon convening large numbers of people outside gatherings of important bureaucrats. Its maturing political analysis leaves the biggest impression. Thus in April, in Washington, it could not have escaped the notice of mainstream organisations – trade unions, big environmental groups and the development NGOs – that the demonstrations that most angrily attacked the IMF and the World Bank attracted by far the most people of any events during the week of protest, even though 16 April had the least institutional backing.

The direct action and parallel rally of the Mobilization for Global Justice represented the core sentiments of the growing movement. In contrast to conventional wisdom, the call to 'Defund the Fund, Break the Bank and Dump the Debt' outdid the weaker call of Jubilee 2000 USA for limited debt relief with strings attached. The same radical sentiments were evident in Prague, where at the famous debate within Prague Castle on 23 September, Wolfensohn, IMF managing director Horst Kohler and the institutions' South African chairperson, finance minister Trevor Manuel, were unable to dissuade key progressive spokespeople from maintaining the call for abolition. Abolition as a strategy pursued through the 'World Bank Bonds Boycott' tactic, which I will explain below, has already generated impressive momentum, with three major US West Coast cities (Berkeley, Oakland and San Francisco) and major socially responsible investment funds committing themselves not to buy the bonds within their first six months.

Such militancy, however, must now not only be amplified in coming demonstrations, but it has also to be captured back within a programmatic vision of 'development' beyond what is now on offer, i.e. to seek out de-commodified, destratified, degendered and environmentally responsible development strategies. 'Fixers', however, still pose a threat to such visions.

3. Reformers run into trouble
It is worth dwelling on the fact that a large body of more conservative Washington NGOs, labour groups, environmental lobbies and develop-ment think-tanks will probably continue to slow this progress down. A few sites of debate can be briefly surveyed.

Co-opted NGOs
Perhaps most notable as a symbol of what is wrong with the mentality that wants to work within the system, an 'Interaction 22' grouping of US-based NGOs, all funded by the neo-liberal US Agency for International Development, wrote a letter to World Bank president James Wolfensohn on 14 April 2000, two days before the main protest at the spring meetings. They expressed 'deep concern at the impression created by some of our NGO colleagues in the streets this week that the World Bank and the IMF are at serious loggerheads with the entire not-for-profit community ... We have a very different perspective on recent positive directions taken by the Bank'.[11]

Inside the World Bank, chief NGO liaison official John Clark – formerly a leading World Bank critic based at Oxfam UK – issued an e-mail memo to colleagues a few days later, ridiculing the Interaction 22 for being 'much less skeptical about these reforms than most of us inside the Bank!'. However, pursuing triage, he also identified what he termed a 'dilemma' for a middle-ground group of NGOs, namely, 'how to respond to the demo organisers' request to all NGOs to boycott all meetings with the Bank and Fund ... For some the compromise was to take part in meetings with Bank staff off the premises (some said this was because they didn't want to be seen and identified by demonstrators and be accused of co-option); but others – notably Jubilee 2000 [US] – were quite open that they intended to ignore the request.'[12]

Such divisions and even ruptures are probably inevitable, not only amongst *petit-bourgeois* NGO cadres, but across the political spectrum, as the world economy continues on its volatile, apparently self-destructive course. The global establishment also writhes with conflict, including squabbles in 1999–2000 over US vetoes of proposed new WTO and IMF managers; over the US congressional 'Meltzer Commission' in February 2000, which advocates substantial downsizing of the IMF and World Bank; and over the breakdown between US, European and allied Southern negotiating partners at the World Trade Organisation ministerial summit in Seattle.

Washington's left-wing opposition is just as likely to reproduce long-standing, self-defeating tendencies – sectarianism, nationalist-revivalism and reformism/demobilisation – in the period just ahead, as it is to gravitate towards more radical syntheses within the diverse component parts of the movement, in the varied settings around the world, through the uneven impulses that can be found within it. Still, the oppositional processes are definitely under way, and worthy of celebration at this juncture. It is no insult to what has been achieved this far to note that strategic interventions are continually required to maintain, nurture and align a radical internationalism within the movement.

In this, it must be conceded, the *petit-bourgeois* strategists are still defining much of the terrain, the slogans and the 'alternative' ideas. Feuds within the ranks are important, obvious and deserving of debate. NGO Stalinism made open and frank disagreement terribly difficult at times. But of the various strategic currents in the movement, only one – campaigning to abolish the IMF, World Bank and WTO – will take us to the mass base of the movement's leading edge. Unfortunately, a residual bloc of big-labour officials and moderate debt-campaign bureaucrats remain ambivalent or even opposed to this agenda, in a conflict that should first be reviewed.

Labour lurches
By early 2000, two controversial Clinton-administration trade deals (the US-China agreement and the Africa Growth and Opportunity Act) faced stiff opposition from domestic constituencies, and the corporatist Advisory Committee for Trade Policy and Negotiations broke apart thanks to a walk-out by justifiably frustrated AFL-CIO leaders. At about the same time, *Business Week* reported that nine out of ten US residents polled labelled themselves either 'fair traders' or 'protectionist', with just one in ten identifying her/himself as a 'free trader'. Clinton's trade policy was generally understood, according to the main survey on the topic, to serve the interests of multinational corporations 'too much' (according to 54% of respondents) and working Americans 'too little' (according to 72%).[13]

In this unusual US context, the movement against globalisation was radicalised. The logistics of the Seattle protest had distinguished stodgy, suited leaders from front-line labour, social and environmental movement activists. Whether the WTO should be a site of 'reform' – usually through introducing social, labour and environmental conditions, known as 'Social Clauses', to trade agreements – came under fierce debate. For although some Southern trade unions backed the Social Clause strategy through their (often subordinate) role in the International Confederation of Free Trade Unions, many influential Southern social-movement leftists condemned it for leaving in place the existing anti-democratic structure of the international trading system. To improve the WTO, they argued, simply amplifies imperialist power relations.[14] The point, instead, should be to attack the power that the WTO has to overrule and undermine international agreements and national laws that protect human rights and the environment (e.g. a selective-procurement law in Massachusetts, directed against Burma and ruled illegal by the WTO), and to find effective means to defend these rights.

Because his administration's efforts to politically rehabilitate the 'free trade' agenda were to some extent blocked by organised labour and environmentalists, Bill Clinton announced apparent support for the Social Clause in the wake of the Seattle protests (his officials immediately announced that he 'misspoke' on the issue, however). Some groups, including conservative leadership factions within Northern trade unions, would no doubt have been happy to settle for lip service to an unenforceable Social Clause in exchange for allowing a new WTO Millennium Round to go forward. But these forces were successfully marginalised, and found themselves neither strong enough to sell the strategy to the broader movement nor to inject Social Clauses into the Clinton administration's Africa and China trade pacts.

But a serious danger of backsliding emerged in the wake of Seattle, namely the xenophobia encapsulated in the slogan of the Naderite organiser Mike Dolan: 'China, we're coming atcha!' If trying to keep China out of the WTO in early 2000 was the 'proxy for all our concerns about globalisation', as the AFL-CIO's Denise Mitchell had it, then the global labour movement would suffer. US-based journalist and social critic Alexander Cockburn rightly concluded that the responsibility of labour and social movements lay elsewhere:

> There's no win-win situation for workers of the world, in the current era at least. American steelworkers here do better, ergo Russian and South Korean steelworkers overseas do worse. A garment worker here loses a job, a Central American makes a dime. Capitalism dictates the choices. So what can we do here? I don't think we should be trying to fix up the WTO or keep China out. That's not the sort of currency radicals should have truck with. Our currency is solidarity.[15]

As I will discuss in more detail in Chapter eleven, the Congress of South African Trade Unions followed a slippery logic and strategy with Southern African trade unions similar to that of the AFL-CIO, generating conflict in the process.[16] (For US labour, there is a preferable strategy to tinkering with trade deals and the WTO, i.e. one of either attacking particular corporations (consistent with solidarity campaigning principles), or passing restraining legislation against transnational corporations, similar in scope to the 1977 US Foreign Corrupt Practices Act, which penalises specific firms – not the countries they victimise – for explicitly anti-social behaviour.)[17]

Debt debate

Similarly, the international movement against Third World debt was divided through the late 1990s between, on the one hand, reformers in Jubilee 2000's US, British, German and Japanese networks, who largely accepted the framework imposed by the IMF, World Bank and G-8 countries, and on the other, radicals in Jubilee South and allied Northern groups (especially Jubilee Canada), who attempted to break open that framework. The latter camp included critics who viewed campaigns against debt as inextricably linked to fighting structural adjustment in general – at national policy level or in very direct forms such as the privatisation of municipal utilities – and the power of the IMF and World Bank in particular. Fortunately, in early 2001, Jubilee US began moving to this position.

As I will discuss in the next chapter, leading African Jubilee proponents tended to be more structuralist and also more militant, especially chapters in South Africa, Zimbabwe, Nigeria and Malawi. When the Jubilee 2000 South Summit convened in Johannesburg in November 1999 and Dakar, Senegal in December 2000, the best social movement leaders and activists from Africa met partners from around the Third World, and resolved to pressure their respective national leaders to collectively repudiate the debt.[18] The Jubilee Summit also called for the closure of the IMF and World Bank.

In contrast, some Jubilee chapters in the North were directed by NGO and mainstream-church staff who preferred keeping economic policies out of the discussion, and who consciously acceded to the frames of reference of the IMF, World Bank and G-8 finance ministers. They persistently compromised on partial debt-forgiveness/relief – the 'unrepayable' debt of the poorest countries – not cancellation or reparations. They conceded that even meagre portions of relief (e.g. in Mozambique, as discussed in Chapter three) must be linked to structural-adjustment policies that left the IMF and World Bank in control of Southern economies, and barely blinked at the IMF's renaming of these policies as 'poverty reduction'. Worst of all, they embraced the false claim that the IMF and the World Bank needed more funding from taxpayers in the G-8 countries in order to compensate for the fraudulent, highly conditional debt relief. And if this strategy was a disaster, so too was the conservative Jubilee faction's sense of tactics, as they insisted on no threat of any kind, particularly on the funding front.

The limits of reformism

What would reformers claim to have achieved with their mild-mannered approach to the IMF and World Bank, and what are the limits of the gains won to date? In areas including environment, gender, transparency, participation and post-Washington Consensus economics, it is important to evaluate the balance sheet.

Some reforms, like transparency and participation with civil society, were easily ignored or manipulated. After a critical mass of problems in projects were exposed, the World Bank set up the 'World Bank Inspection Panel' within the institution. Its skimpy oversight power was soon whittled back after it made a few telling criticisms of South governments, and in any case the panel failed to critically examine key projects in which World Bank malfeasance was obvious. (I considered the attempt by South Africans to contest the Lesotho Highlands Water Project in Chapter three, above.)

Other apparent gains in the environmental and gender-and-development spheres were corrupted immediately by neo-liberalism, whether in pushing women's microcredit as a safety net for defunded social policy, or in commodifying natural ecological processes. Environmental-impact assessments might be added to projects at the last minute, but rarely halted the approval of new hydrocarbon power plants that soon made the World Bank the world's leading contributor to global warming. Lawrence Summers, chief economist at the World Bank, was ironic, perhaps, but spot-on when remarking in the infamous internal memo leaked to *The Economist* prior to the 1992 Earth Summit in Rio, 'I think the economic logic of dumping a load of toxic waste on the lowest-wage country is impeccable and we should face up that.'[19]

Another telling experience was that of Herman Daly, the creative environmental economist who left the World Bank's employ greatly disgruntled.[20] Still, empowered by the World Bank's plagiarism of NGO rhetoric, some inside-the-Beltway policy-makers (e.g. in the often-admirable international-advocacy office of Friends of the Earth) even suggested a dramatic switch in World Bank lending towards sectors like basic education. The slogan this invoked – 'Public funds for public good' – was fundamentally misguided, as we will observe below.

Indeed, the hardest area to reform would be the deeply rooted fealty to neo-liberalism of IMF/World Bank economists. Dishonesty in economic analysis finally caught up with the Bretton Woods twins during the late 1990s emerging-markets crises. The ideology of the Washington Consensus was thoroughly discredited, and for a brief while it appeared that the World Bank's obvious interpretation of the *East Asian Miracle*, as debunked by Robert Wade,[21] would be reversed by the arrival in 1997 of an honest and open-minded chief economist, Joseph Stiglitz, from service as frustrated chief of Bill Clinton's Council of Economic Advisors.

But even though Stiglitz offered very little substantive policy change in his 'information-theoretic' critique of market imperfections, and even though his Post-Washington Consensus did not break from most neo-liberal shibboleths,[22] he was roundly despised by IMF and US Treasury staff. Within 30 months, after robust debates over IMF competence, he was pushed overboard. Stiglitz diplomatically claimed to have jumped ship, in order to have more freedom to launch his critiques – such as a scathing attack in *New Republic* in April in which he slated 'third-rank economists from first-rate universities'.[23] But according to a reliable World Bank insider quoted in the February 2000 issue of *Left Business Observer*, US treasury secretary Summers 'made it clear that if Wolfensohn wanted a second term as World Bank president – to start on 1 June 2000 – Stiglitz had to go'.

In sum, IMF/World Bank reforms haven't worked, and serious reform-ers have been pushed out or have quit in disgust. The latest gambit, the announcement in October 1999 of the 'Poverty Reduction Strategy Paper' (PRSP) as central to future IMF/World Bank activity in any developing country, was revealed as a scam in May 2000, in the institution's own main pilot case, Bolivia. According to an NGO reportback, 'The IMF resident representative in Bolivia remarked that although the PRSP would take civil society's recommendations into account, the macroeconomic targets previously agreed to by the Bolivian government were by no means open to negotiation ... The presenters of this macroeconomic model did not adequately respond to questions from the audience on how their approach differs at all from the past.'[24]

A month earlier, at the height of the Bolivian water privatisation crisis (generated by explicit World Bank advice which sent water prices soaring to more than a quarter of a typical household's wage packet), Wolfensohn himself unveiled his own lack of comprehension: 'The biggest problem with water is the wastage of water through lack of charging,' he pronounced on 12 April at a press conference, when asked about the World Bank's role in the Cochabamba crisis. 'In the riots that you had in Bolivia – which, I'm happy to say, are now quieting down – it was about a new dam, a new power, in (*sic*) which the Bank on this occasion had nothing to do.'[25] His entire answer was fallacious, and the leader of the Cochabamba protests, trade unionist Oscar Olivera, took the opportunity in October 2000, in the wake of a new round of protest, to join several South Africans in a North American tour to support the World Bank Bonds Boycott initiative.

At precisely the same time, as I will discuss in the next chapter, Wolfensohn's Africa department was insisting on full-cost-recovery strategies for even basic water supplies. The one reform that appeared appropriate at this point was an October 2000 Congressional prohibition on the World Bank invoking user fees on Third World education and health services, which was mainly an ideological victory over neo-liberalism.

Turning to the right?

A final point is that the US Right also mulls over abolition/reform. Aside from predictable hard-right rabble-rousers, even high-profile establishment conservatives (including incoming undersecretary of the Treasury, John Taylor, when he was a Stanford professor) began calling for the closure of the Bretton Woods institutions in the wake of their hapless management of the East Asian crisis, as noted in Chapter 5. Subsequently, the Republican-dominated Meltzer Commission reported to Congress that the IMF and World Bank were so badly warped that they must shrivel, quite dramatically, before being straightened out.

On such a terrain, it is not unusual to find tactical intersections where Right meets Left. These are worth worrying about, although a key Left navigator – Nader advisor Rob Weissman of *Multinational Monitor* magazine – insisted recently, 'For now, we're so relatively powerless compared to [the IMF and World Bank], our primary mission is to restrain their power. So it's less important to focus on the day when we run global institutions than on limiting the harm that they do.'[26]

4. Strategic divergences on the left

In contrast to the political strategy of national, and potentially regional, democratic reconstruction from a militant local base, the case for an alternative conception of feasible global politics must also be aired. This approach envisages generating seeds in the present of a future democratic world state cast in the image of the global working class. The point here is to contend with both capital's internationalism as well as 'global governance' challenges, e.g. environmental protection, wealth redistribution, peace-keeping, human rights policing, etc. But how realistic and appropriate is this strategic approach? We begin by reviewing some of the key intellectual arguments.

A world state ahead?

Quite a hot debate rages within the World Systems branch of sociology about the character of strategic engagement with the globalisation process. It is helpful to draw out the arguments to illustrate the strategic options. Perhaps the strongest possible case in favour of a 'world state' was a book published in 1992 by Warren Wagar,[27] positing a global social-democratic political party taking control of world government midway through the 21st century. This general theme has circulated for some time, and *The Spiral of Capitalism and Socialism*, a forthcoming book by Terry Boswell and Chris Chase-Dunn,[28] makes the argument forthrightly:

a world polity of global institutions, for the first time ever in world history, is becoming capable of directing the processes of the modern world-system

... 'Global governance' has increased geometrically in the period following World War II as the strength of a globally-oriented world bourgeoisie has increased *vis-a-vis* the nationally-oriented fractions of capital. These processes, like market integration, are driven by the falling costs of communications and transportation and the increasing size of business enterprises. They are also driven by the interaction between the logic of capitalist accumulation and the organisational efforts by people to control and to protect themselves from market forces.

The formation of a global polity opens the possibility of alternate paths to hegemony and even of a transformation of the system to include a world government. Of course, it is also possible, and perhaps, probable, that these changes are temporary, and that the cycle of hegemonic rivalry and war will again repeat in devastating fashion. But the possibilities for fundamentally changing the system are greater now than in the previous century.

Boswell and Chase-Dunn immediately confront potential criticism that the dominant institutions today will be terribly difficult to influence:

While the idea of a world state may be a frightening specter to some, we are optimistic about it for several reasons. First a world state is probably the most direct and stable way to prevent world war, which must be at the top of everyone's list. Secondly, the creation of a global state that can peacefully adjudicate disputes among nations will transform the existing interstate system. The interstate system is the political structure that stands behind the maneuverability of capital and its ability to escape organized workers and other social constraints on profitable accumulation. While a world state may at first be largely controlled by capitalists, the very existence of such a state will provide a *single focus* for struggles to socially regulate investment decisions and to create a more balanced, egalitarian, and ecologically sound form of production and distribution.

The importance of this argument for many of us in the developing world is that the semi-industrialised 'semi-periphery' (which in Africa includes Egypt, Nigeria and South Africa, and possibly Zimbabwe, Kenya, Botswana, Ghana and Mauritius) is the site from which campaigns to radicalise governance of the world state would come. For Boswell and Chase-Dunn, 'Semiperipheral locations are especially conducive to institutional innovations that have the potential to transform systemic logic. The most powerful movements toward the creation of a socialist mode of accumulation have emerged in the modern semiperiphery.'

The UN and global regulation?
In a similar spirit, but with a more nuanced approach, political philosopher Iris Marion Young recommends closure of the IMF and World Bank

(which 'do not even pretend to be inclusive and democratic') so as to pursue a 'reasonable goal': reform of the United Nations, 'the best existing starting point for building global democratic institutions ... As members of the General Assembly, nearly all the world's peoples today are represented at the UN.' Moreover, the UN is a site where imperial powers 'seek legitimacy for some of their international actions' and where states 'at least appear to be cooperative and interested in justice'. Likewise, civil society organisations have mobilised around UN events and issues.[29]

The primary problem here is that given the existing and foreseeable balance of international power, hopes for eco-social progress through world-state building are utopian (maybe dangerously so). Far more likely if this course is pursued is an expansion of neo-liberalism, the universal rule of property and the commodification of all aspects of daily life everywhere, with the consequent destruction of non-capitalist eco-socio-economic processes, amplified through far more devastating punishments meted out in the 'international community' when oppositional states or popular movements transgress the rules.

Fix it or nix it?

If running part of a world state remains out of the question, Left strategists are faced with the crude choice captured in the slogan 'Fix it or nix it'. (A more complex 'Fix it or [else we'll] nix it' lay in between, and when adopted in mid-2000, allowed Public Citizen and the AFL-CIO an opportunity to work fruitlessly for a year on WTO reform before perhaps then advocating abolition, and more recently a left-leaning 'shrink or sink' line to accommodate Public Citizen's newly radicalised constituents.) Fixers argue that the IMF and World Bank were pressured to adopt reforms over the past 15 or so years. Nixers rebut this by saying that these reforms must be measured against the worsening scale of eco-socio-economic damage over the same period of crisis displacement.

Indeed, thanks to the combination of deeply unsatisfying reforms won to date, the sour-grapes Stiglitz departure and the Interaction letter distancing co-opted NGOs from the A16/17 protests, organisers in the Mobilization for Global Justice could seek and achieve a rare clarity of radical strategic purpose.

Likewise, one of the leading Third World advocates of radical international economics, Walden Bello, director of Focus on the Global South in Bangkok, made a crucial intervention in early 2000 in favour of abolition:

> Seventy per cent of the Bank's non-aid lending is concentrated in 11 countries, while the Bank's 145 other member countries are left to divide the remaining 30 per cent. Moreover, 80 per cent of World Bank resources have

gone, not to poor countries with poor credit ratings and investment ratings, but to countries that could have raised the money in international private capital markets owing to their having investment grade or high yield ratings.

In terms of achieving a positive development impact, the Bank's own evaluation of its projects shows an outstanding 55–60 per cent failure rate. The failure rate is particularly high in the poorest countries, where it ranges from 65 per cent to 70 per cent. And these are the very countries that are supposed to be the main targets of the Bank's anti-poverty approach …

Rather than expect the highly paid World Bank technocrats who live in the affluent suburbs of Northern Virginia to do the impossible – designing anti-poverty programs for folks from another planet: poor people in the Sahel – it would be more effective to abolish an institution that has made a big business out of 'ending poverty,' and completely devolve the work to local, national and regional institutions better equipped to attack the causes of poverty.[30]

5. After the IMF/World Bank have gone: Local/national/regional development finance?

Marx once asserted that prior to constructing world socialism, each working class must first deal with its own national bourgeoisie, a position that still incorporated a fairly advanced critique of early colonial globalisation. Global deconstruction and national reconstruction may be a useful formula with which to begin a conclusion to the struggle. For implicit in the argument sketched out above is that the nation state requires relief from the pressures of global financial capitalism, especially those pressures represented by IMF/World Bank missions that so decisively squeeze and shift power relations at the domestic level.

And there is no shortage of class and political struggles on the national level. During the late 1990s, mass strikes by national workers' movements shook Nigeria, Indonesia, Paraguay and Taiwan (1994); Bolivia, Canada and France (1995); Argentina, Brazil, Canada, Greece, Italy, South Korea, Spain and Venezuela (1996); Belgium, Colombia, Ecuador, Haiti and South Korea (1997); and many other important sites of East Asian, East European, African and Latin American proletarian suffering when neoliberal economic disaster intensified in 1998–9.

A political warning is clearly in order, from David Harvey: 'Withdrawing to the nation-state as the exclusive strategic site of class organisation and struggle is to court failure (as well as to flirt with nationalism and all that that entails). This does not mean the nation-state has become irrelevant – indeed it has become more relevant than ever. But the choice of spatial scale is not "either/or" but "both/and" even though the latter entails confronting serious contradictions'.[31]

Yet identifying and confronting such contradictions can probably best be advanced by building international solidarity to delegitimise, defund and decommission the IMF and World Bank – which will, in the process, raise questions about the politics of scale associated with a more liberatory form of development finance than could ever conceivably be on offer from these two institutions. To consider this argument even briefly entails a review of the experience of post-apartheid South Africa. Three universal reasons have emerged in South Africa for nixing the IMF/World Bank (other reasons drawn from specific project and policy experiences were considered in Chapter 3):

- Virtually all possible core-value reforms in key areas of IMF/World Bank eco-socio-economic advocacy have been explored, and their profound limitations unveiled.
- There is a greater urgency to restore nation-state sovereignty (and hence mere bourgeois democracy, which has also ebbed), mainly through lifting IMF/World Bank pressure, than there is time to convince several tens of thousands of hardened Washington economists to reverse the policy advice that has defined their world view since grad. school.
- The hard-currency component of IMF and World Bank lending should not be required once appropriate conditions are achieved.

This latter argument deserves justification, for, if local, national and regional development finance is appropriate, then the technical (not political, moral or environmental) reasons to have an IMF and World Bank evaporate. Such was the viewpoint of the African National Congress in its Reconstruction and Development Programme of 1994, in a principle won only after much left-wing lobbying: 'The *RDP* must use foreign debt financing only for those elements of the programme that can potentially increase our capacity for earning foreign exchange.'[32] (The ANC broke many such promises, but the principle here is worth careful reflection.)

The motivation for rejecting hard-currency loans for 'development' was the ANC left's fear of the rising cost of repayment on foreign debt, once the currency declines, and the use of hard currency to pay not for initiating a basic education project but instead for repaying illegitimate apartheid debt, importing luxury goods for the rich and replacing local workers with inappropriate job-destroying, dependency-inducing technology from abroad. In sum, why take a US-dollar loan for building and staffing a small rural school that has virtually no foreign input costs?

If real development comes from local resources, since only a tiny fraction of basic-need inputs in most developing countries require foreign loans, and if the hard currency needed to import petroleum or other vital inputs can usually be readily supplied by export credit agencies (competing against each other, in contrast to centralised financial power and co-ordination in

Washington), the basic rationales for the World Bank fall away. And instead of relying upon the IMF to maintain a positive balance of payments when fickle international financial inflows dry up or run away frightened, Third World countries that in the future climb out from under the heel of the IMF and World Bank could realistically impose Malaysian-style exchange controls and tax unnecessary imports. (They would also have more freedom to default on illegitimate debt.)

In short, the South ultimately shouldn't need a dollar-denominated IMF and World Bank for development. Indeed it is probable that only when Washington's institutional power fades that local-, national- and perhaps regional-development finance officials can reacquire the ability they once enjoyed, a few decades ago, to tame their own financial markets. (Such 'financial repression' entailed state interest-rate subsidies, directed credit, prescribed asset requirements on institutional investors, community re-investment mandates and other means of socialising financial capital.)

The one remaining point to make is the easiest, most practical concern: is defunding actually feasible? The same question was asked of advocates of anti-apartheid financial sanctions, and answered in the affirmative in 1985, just a few years after campaigning became serious. In addition to defunding the IMF through popular pressure on Congress – and indeed all parliaments – to deny further resources, activists returning from A16 began taking advantage of the World Bank's extreme reliance upon international bond markets. Nearly 80% of its funds for onlending come from bonds, making this the most compelling pressure point and local handle for the medium-term struggle. Hence, the World Bank Bonds Boycott was initiated by Haitian, South African, Brazilian and many other activists and debt campaigners across the world in late 1999, and launched in April 2000.[33]

Berkeley City Council offered the initial commitment that its municipal fund managers won't buy World Bank bonds (they were also the first municipality to record anti-apartheid divestment). All investors of conscience – pension funds, churches, university endowments, individuals – are being asked not to profit from poverty and ecological destruction through increasing the World Bank bond holdings of their portfolios. In particular, the Rainforest Action Network combined with the World Bank Bonds Boycott campaign to target Citibank for its marketing of World Bank Bonds. A frightened *Washington Post* lead editorial called the World Bank Bonds Boycott 'crazy'.[34] In coming months and years, activists will prove establishment concerns entirely justified, as they did using the financial sanctions that demonstrably helped sink the Botha and De Klerk regimes in Pretoria.

For progressive internationalists, breaking the Bank and defunding the Fund can dramatically improve global and local power balances, open up radical development-finance alternatives, and contribute to a solidarity unfettered by controversy over reform of imperialist institutions. A16 gave thousands of activists an initial opportunity to make the Bank and Fund run. The followup challenge is to keep the institutions running, until they drop of exhaustion.

But this has to happen globally and locally. Is there similar sentiment and activism under way in the Third World?

Notes

1 St Clair, J. (1999), 'Seattle Diary: It's a Gas, Gas, Gas', *New Left Review*; see also Charlton, J. (2000), 'Talking Seattle', *International Socialism*, 86.

2 Core groups included 50 Years is Enough, Alliance for Global Justice, Jobs with Justice, Essential Information, Center for Economic and Policy Research, Center for Economic Justice and several others. From their bases outside Washington, Global Exchange continued its leading ideological role, Ruckus Society did excellent training, the Rainforest Action Network helped with direct action, and the International Forum on Globalization sponsored a well-attended teach-in.

3 Albert, M. (2000), 'Assessing A16', *Z Magazine*, 19 April.

4 The most eloquent critique of these tendencies is to be found in Hart-Landsberg, M. and Burkett, P. (2000), *Development, Crisis and Class Struggle: Learning from Japan and East Asia*, New York, St. Martin's Press.

5 The main published account to date, focusing on West Coast movement infrastructure, is by Dan LaBotz in *Against the Current*, September 2000.

6 The lead up to the current moment of anti-corporate protest is brilliantly analysed by Klein, N. (2000), *No Logo*, London, Flamingo.

7 A recent discussion of the necessary tension between party and mass grassroots organisation is Kagarlitsky, B. (2000), *The Return of Radicalism: Reshaping the Left Institutions*, London, Pluto Press.

8 *Economist*, 11–17 December 1999.

9 http://www.aidc.org.za and http://www.jubileesouth.net/.

10 Kagarlitsky, B. (2000), 'Prague: The People's Battle', unpublished manuscript, October.

11 Among the 22 thriving charities and agencies were the National Peace Corps Association, Overseas Development Council, Pathfinder International, Refugees International, Save the Children and World Vision.

12 Clark, J. (2000), 'Not all NGOs hate the Bank: memo to Katherine Marshall,' World Bank e-mail, 18 April.

13 *Business Week*, 24 April 2000; Program on International Policy Attitudes (2000), *Americans on Globalization: A Study of US Public Attitudes*, College Park, Maryland, p. 13.

14 One leading South advocacy group, Third World Network of Penang, Malaysia, offered powerful opposition to Social Clauses from the outset, and their Africa affiliate, Isodec, Ghana's premier NGO, co-ordinated an Africa Trade Network which included the main left-wing organisations across the continent. See, for example, Danaher, K. and Burbach, R. (eds) (2000), *Globalize This!: The Battle Against the World Trade Organization and Corporate Rule*, Monroe, Common Courage Press, especially the chapter by Walden Bello, 'Why Reforming the WTO is the Wrong Agenda'.

15 The quotations from Mitchell and Cockburn both appear in *The Nation*, 3 January 2000. Cockburn continued, 'We should be making war on the IMF and World Bank, helping poor countries fight to develop internal markets, hence better-paid workers

and stronger agriculture. We have plenty to denounce right here. The Jubilee 2000 campaign against World Bank bonds is a great thing.'

16 Bond, P. (2000), 'Workers of the World, Transcend the Wedge!', *Z-Net Commentary*, 24 February; for more on the Social Clause debate, see http://www.aidc.org.za.

17 See, for example, the writings of William Greider in *The Nation*.

18 It was Rosemary Nyerere Mwamakula who made this statement to the press in Johannesburg, in honour of her late father's unheeded call in 1983 for a debtor's cartel.

19 *The Economist*, 7 February 1992.

20 Daly, H. (1996), *Beyond Growth*, Boston, Beacon Press.

21 Wade, R. (2000), *The Gift of Capital*, London, Verso.

22 Stiglitz, J. (1998), 'More Instruments and Broader Goals: Moving Toward a Post-Washington Consensus', WIDER Annual Lecture, Helsinki, 7 January. The limits are addressed in Fine, B. (1998), 'Industrial Policy Revisited', *Indicator SA*, 15(4).

23 Stiglitz, J. (2000), 'What I Learned at the World Economic Crisis', *New Republic*, 17 April.

24 Selvaggio, K. and Deng, D. (2000), 'Impressions of WB/IMF PRSP Training', e-mail, Catholic Relief Services, 11 May.

25 Transcript of 12 April 2000 press conference held by James Wolfensohn, Washington, DC.

26 http://www.intellectualcapital.com/issues/issue364/item9048.asp.

27 Wagar, W. (1992), *A Short History of the Future*, Chicago, University of Chicago Press. See reactions in *Journal of World Systems Research*, 2, 1996 (including Bond, P. and Mayekiso, M., 'Towards the Integration of Urban Social Movements at the World Scale').

28 Boswell, T. and Chase-Dunn, C. (2000), *The Spiral of Capitalism and Socialism*, Boulder, Lynn Reiner. Both the quotations that follow are taken from the Conclusion.

29 Young, I. M. (2000), *Inclusion and Democracy*, Oxford, Oxford University Press, pp. 272–4. Young grounds the UN argument in the work of Erskine Childers, Brian Urquhart and Chadwick Alger, and in David Held's theory of cosmopolitan democracy.

30 Bello, W. (2000), 'Meltzer Report on Bretton Woods Twins Builds Case for Abolition but Hesitates', *Focus on Trade*, 48, April.

31 African National Congress (1994), *Reconstruction and Development Programme*, Johannesburg, Umanyano Publications, sec. 6.5.16. See the discussion in Chapter three, above.

32 Harvey, D. (1998), 'The Geography of Class Power', in L. Panitch and C. Leys, *The Communist Manifesto Now: Socialist Register 1998*, New York, Monthly Review Press, p. 72. Similar points have been made to me in very useful personal correspondence with Ellen Wood, Susan George and Jeremy Brecher, amongst others. Wood may be correct that 'the opposite of fix-it may be something else – not nix-it, but getting behind various kinds of local and national anti-capitalist and anti-imperialist struggles, which isn't quite the same thing'.

33 http://www.worldbankboycott.org/.

34 *Washington Post*, 11 April 2000.

CHAPTER ELEVEN

The Third World in the movement for global justice

1. Introduction

Consider a couple of thoughts from leading South Africans:

> I know what the protesters are against, but I don't know what they are for!

That was Trevor Manuel, South African finance minister and chairperson of the IMF/World Bank board of governors, quoted after closing the Prague IMF/World Bank annual meetings a day early, in September 2000.

> The protesters don't know what they're talking about.

That was by Alec Erwin, South African minister of trade and industry and the then-president of the UN Conference on Trade and Development, in remarks at the World Trade Organisation's Seattle summit, in December 1999.

To find South African ministers of state so confident as to the rightness of their views about the wrongness of their opponents at Prague and Seattle suggests that someone has got something wrong somewhere. But who? The ministers inside the halls of power or the protesters out on the streets? Were the events in Prague and Seattle merely incomprehensible flukes – or instead, can we say that at the outset of the 21st century, there exists a movement for global social justice? And if so, are African and other Third World progressive activists necessarily left behind, 'marginalised' from globalisation, or are they instead near or at the cutting edge of this movement?

If the period since Seattle provides reliable evidence, it is possible to confidently answer these questions with optimism. Diverse social forces, north and south, east and west, are feeding into international and local demonstrations with increasing militancy, and with comparable values, norms and discourses. Parallel strategies and tactics are even emerging.

And as for the Third World? In contrast to the mainstream media belief firstly, that Africa and other Southern sites of poverty and oppression are increasingly marginalised from global processes, and secondly that the international movement for social justice mainly consists of white, middle-class youth of the North, this chapter focuses on Third World activists and intellectuals who are on board the movement and exerting important influences. I begin by listing two dozen of the most recent protests against neo-liberalism around the world (Section 2). Then I move to one of the most important influences in the international movement, the Zapatista struggle for justice in south-eastern Mexico (Section 3), followed by a discussion of parallel rhetorics and activist initiatives in African social movements (Section 4). This evidence allows me to conclude by considering prospects for alliances within civil society on a 'South-South-North' basis (Section 5).

2. The world against Washington

Beginning with the protest against the World Trade Organisation in Seattle in November 1999, the global movement has indeed gained the right to call itself such, not only because masses have turned out at Northern events, but because these now interrelate so well with even larger, if often unreported, organic struggles under way across the rest of the world, including Africa. So while the movement commenced its activities by breaking up the WTO opening ceremonies and helping prevent the launch of a Millennial Round, its spirit was subsequently echoed in many places and in many ways over the subsequent 12 months:

- An indigenous people's uprising against neo-liberal policies in Ecuador in January 2000 generated a momentarily successful alliance with military coup-makers.

- A few days later, half way across the world, high up in the Alps, hundreds of young left-wing protesters from across Europe crashed barriers at the World Economic Forum in Davos – and the world's richest men inside the conference centre furnished high-profile radical commentators with respectful platforms.

- The movement's energy shifted to Bangkok in February, where a formidable Thai network of unemployed rural and urban activists protested daily at the semi-decennial meeting of the United Nations Conference on Trade and Development.

- In early April, grassroots anti-globalisation protest intensified in the main square of Cochabamba, Bolivia, where thousands of residents forced water-privatiser Bechtel out of the country – and precipitated a national state of emergency in the process.

- Washington, DC then came under unprecedented attack from 30 000 militants who paralysed a large area surrounding the IMF and World Bank headquarters for two days. At the same time, solidarity protests and public events took place in Johannesburg, Cape Town, San Francisco, Seattle, Paris, Jerusalem, Vancouver and Winnipeg. Especially notable, under harsh circumstances, were anti-IMF demonstrations mainly by women in Lusaka and Nairobi, which were broken up by police.

■ Millions of people turned out in global anti-capitalist demonstrations on 1 May, perhaps most visibly (even if unsuccessfully in logistical and PR terms) in the City of London.

■ A few days later, the small Thai city of Chiang Mai was awoken by 5 000 angry students, unemployed workers, environmentalists and displaced rural people, who overwhelmed police lines protecting an Asian Development Bank meeting.

■ On 10 May, South Africa was the site of a national general strike by half the country's workforce, furious over job-killing neo-liberal policies adopted at the behest of the World Bank, and protest marches brought 200 000 out into the streets in several cities.

■ The next day, 20 million Indian workers went on strike explicitly to protest against the surrender of national sovereignty to the IMF and World Bank.

■ Smaller but still very sharp anti-IMF demonstrations quickly led to police crackdowns in Argentina in mid-May, followed by a mass protest of 80 000 people.

■ Turkish police also repressed anti-austerity demonstrations in May.

■ In Port-au-Prince, Haiti, thousands turned out in June for anti-debt activities.

■ In Paraguay, a two-day general strike was called against IMF-mandated privatisation.

■ Also in June, Nigeria's trade unions allied with Lagos residents in a mass strike aimed at reversing an IMF-mandated oil-price increase, which also had the effect of cutting short US treasury secretary Laurence Summers' visit.

■ Meanwhile, in Washington, protesters unsuccessfully tried to halt the infamous World Bank Chad-Cameroon pipeline loan, but their vigils at the headquarters of the World Bank did force China to withdraw a proposal for a World Bank loan that would have increased Beijing's grip on Tibet.

■ In July, South Korean workers repeatedly demonstrated against IMF-mandated austerity policies.

■ Protests continued against international elite gatherings, including the Organisation of American States summit in Windsor and the Okinawa G-8 meeting in July. The latter further radicalised Jubilee 2000 chapters (who realised the mistake made a year earlier in Cologne when British, US and German chapters endorsed the meagre debt relief on offer from Summers and his colleagues, only to discover it was a sham).

■ In the US, the political party conventions in Philadelphia and Los Angeles were sites of confrontation in August.

- The Brazilian left hosted a plebiscite in August on whether Brazilian society should accept an IMF austerity programme, and more than six million people voted, nearly all against it.
- In September, large crowds gathered in New York, many in protest, to mark the United Nations Millennium Summit; more thousands protested at the Melbourne meeting of the World Economic Forum; and later in the month, an estimated 15 000 mainly European demonstrators converged on the IMF/World Bank annual meetings in Prague, generating a small, violent confrontation and forcing closure a day early. Across the world, many other protesters staged solidarity events.
- Shortly afterwards, Bolivia exploded with varied urban and rural protests against neo-liberal policies.
- Tens of thousands of Korean workers, students and social-movement protesters prepared for a day of confrontation in late October, at a gathering of European and Asian leaders in Seoul.
- Many dozens of other protests occurred over the period, from Argentina to Zimbabwe.[1] And dozens more occurred in subsequent months.

Common opponents

Whether located in obscure Third World cities or the centres of global commerce, the struggles increasingly intersect, because they focus on virtually identical opponents, i.e. the agencies and representatives of neo-liberal capitalism – global, regional, national and local.

If there is, therefore, a genuine movement afoot, and *if that movement aims not to further exacerbate uneven global development*, it is reasonable to posit the need for a greater recognition of and influence by varied Third World grassroots organisations – community-based groups, trade unions, co-operatives and mutual aid systems, traditional and ethnic-based organisations, church networks, women's and youth clubs, environmental groups and many others.

What, then, can be said about the current role of these organisations, their potential for participating in local and global alliances, and their relations with their own states and ruling parties? What opportunities are emerging for the parallel heightening of consciousness, politicisation and democratisation that will flow, South-North and North-South, through the greater involvement of grassroots African activists and strategists?

Most importantly, many of the key Third World grassroots organisations have a common *experience*, facing not only an anonymous force field of international capital flows and policies shaped by persistent 'advice' from Washington, but also concrete institutions responsible for the most direct source of austerity, i.e. the IMF, World Bank and World Trade Organisation.

Water and micro-neo-liberalism

It is, however, a mistake to limit our analysis to well-known macroeconomic concerns like structural biases in international trade and debt flows (see Chapter one). For it is at the microlevel, in Brazil's favela households and Africa's rural kraals, for example, that we can observe the most direct damage done by Washington's edicts. Consider, as just one instance, a reasonably fresh (March 2000) self-mandate from the World Bank's *Sourcebook on Community Driven Development in the Africa Region: Community Action Programs*:

> Water Supply in Villages, Towns and Urban Centers:
> ... We need to ensure that all countries have clearly defined policies ... work is still needed with political leaders in some national governments to move away from the concept of free water for all ...
>
> Promote increased capital cost recovery from users. An upfront cash contribution based on their willingness-to-pay is required from users to demonstrate demand and develop community capacity to administer funds and tariffs. Ensure 100% recovery of operation and maintenance costs ...[2]

The more sophisticated grassroots, environmental and labour movements across the Third World are truly repelled by such language, especially when (as in this and many cases) it is dressed in 'community-driven' and 'demand-responsive' jargon. For example, South Africa has recently witnessed an exceptionally interesting social struggle for free water – specifically, 0% recovery of operation/maintenance costs for at least the first 50 litres consumed per person per day – led by the Johannesburg Anti-Privatisation Forum of community, worker and student groups; by the Rural Development Services Network (with its dozen affiliate organisations delivering water/sanitation to impoverished communities across the country); by the SA Non-Governmental Organisation Coalition and its 3 000 member groups; and by the 120 000 strong SA Municipal Workers Union. In addition, most major South African cities, as well as smaller towns, have witnessed periodic rioting and protest by communities against water cut-offs since the mid-1990s.

These organisations claimed a partial victory when, in September 2000, President Thabo Mbeki addressed a major conference of the Congress of South African Trade Unions, promising that all households would get 6 000 litres of water per month free (slightly over half the amount the advocacy groups demanded). Mbeki's reversal followed a period during which 100% recovery of operation, maintenance and replacement costs was official policy in water systems.[3] The damage associated with such a policy is incalculable, but as one example, cut-offs of what had been a 17-year-long free water supply in August 2000 forced thousands of residents in rural KwaZulu-Natal to fetch water from impure sources. Within a month, a cholera outbreak occurred, which, by the end of the year, had affected more than 12 000 people, of whom more than four dozen died.

Cross-subsidisation of water and provision of a free lifeline supply would, by all accounts, have prevented the tragedy. But in the urge to privatise water, bureaucrats in both rural district councils and large-scale municipalities felt compelled to commercialise, turn their water supplies into arms-length utilities (instead of being integrated with municipal health offices), and avoid 'non-economic' pricing. Indeed, precisely such provision of cross-subsidies and lifeline tariffs was opposed by World Bank staff in South Africa, when they explicitly warned the minister of water affairs, Kader Asmal, in 1995 that sliding-scale tariffs favouring low-volume users 'may limit options with respect to tertiary providers … in particular private concessions [would be] much harder to establish'.[4]

At both national and local levels in Africa, even in South Africa (which is both the world's most unequal country in terms of the gap between rich and poor, and the wealthiest country in Africa), such 'market-oriented' policies – whose effects are to exacerbate poverty and decrease access to state services – are pervasive.[5] That the World Bank remains extremely dogmatic on cost-recovery, as witnessed in its recent *Sourcebook*, is one reflection of the weakness of the 1980–99 movement to reform the World Bank and IMF, and of the need to go further and shut both down.

A parallel from Latin American grassroots experiences of fighting neo-liberalism is found in the Zapatista struggles of the late 1990s, which did much to inspire the independent Left in South Africa and across the world. But are the Zapatistas just a case of Northern *petit-bourgeois* radical chic, or does the plight of impoverished people in rural Mexico have any relation to impoverished South Africans' own traditions of political mobilisation?

3. Lessons of Zapatismo[6]

During the second half of the 1990s, a vision of radical social change emerged from the mountains of south-east Mexico. Looking carefully, we will find that South Africa's own heightened, multi-faceted rural crisis and half-hearted, sporadic reforms compare objectively to the oppression faced by indigenous people in Chiapas, Mexico. This is particularly true of the World Bank-designed 'willing-seller/willing-buyer' land redistribution deals that, together with mass evictions of farmworkers and labour tenants and exceedingly slow land restitution, have angered and sometimes demobilised rural social-change activists since 1994.

In Mexico, the Zapatista National Liberation Army, named after charismatic early-20th-century folk hero Emiliano Zapata, who united indigenous and 'mestizo' (mixed-race) peasants against plantation owners, is only the best-known wing of a robust social movement that offers us much inspiration. Theirs is not a new fight, even if the rhetoric, strategies and tactics are innovative. More than 450 years ago, it was in the Lacandan jungle – in the mountainous south-east corner of Mexico (near what is now the Guatemalan border) – that Spanish colonisers met their match and were forced to withdraw. The dense bush, difficult peaks and proud Mayan people were never conclusively tamed by 'civilised' invaders, who looted and raped and spread holocaust-scale diseases elsewhere in the surrounding lowlands. Likewise, since the late 1980s, Chiapas has hosted a remarkable guerrilla force renowned not only for determination, but also for a profound sense of humanity and humour.

The Zapatista army first made headlines by forcibly (though mainly non-violently) occupying the municipal headquarters of several provincial towns on 1 January 1994. The date chosen was the day a free-trade agreement with the United States came into effect. Although more than 100 of roughly 2 000 Zapatista troops were killed by army bombing during their retreat back into the mountain villages over the subsequent days, their dramatic debut served to awaken Mexico, and indeed the whole world, to racial discrimination, poverty and outright physical repression.

Pent-up rural fury

Land is central to the Zapatista struggle. Some 3.6 million people live in Chiapas, of whom a million are of Mayan descent. But ownership of arable soil, in a province nearly devoid of industry and a modern service sector, is nearly as skewed as in South Africa. Large-scale cattle ranchers, backed by the Mexican government and also, from the 1960s, by the World Bank, engaged in displacement tactics that would be envied by old-timers from the SA Agriculture Union or British colonial settlers.

The landed bourgeoisie were joined, more recently, by multinational logging firms – also funded in part by the World Bank – and oil companies anxious to pillage yet more natural Chiapas wealth. To enforce their piracy after the Zapatistas surfaced, an alliance of ranchers, local police and government officials organised six vicious paramilitary gangs, which, like the Third Force in South Africa in the early 1990s, have systematically terrorised the guerrillas' supporters.

So, as was the case in South Africa during the last years of apartheid, the main above-ground liberation forces – among them, the Organisation of Campesinos of Emiliano Zapata, the Organisation of Proletarians of Emiliano Zapata and thousands of Catholic liberation theology activists ('catechists') – spent the late 1990s trying to fend off a lethal combination of military occupation, paramilitary massacres and day-to-day economic violence generated by the neo-liberal (free-market) model of development. In December 1997, for example, 45 women and children were slaughtered in the town of Acteal, an incident so vile that the Mexican government felt sufficiently pressured to arrest a local mayor and army general for facilitating that particular paramilitary force's deed. Subsequent massacres and the occupation of Chiapas by 70 000 Mexican security personnel – half the army's entire national force – cast a pall of tension over the mountains. Under these difficult conditions, the Zapatista army's indigenous leadership and its wily spokesperson, Subcomandante Marcos (a poetic ex-academic from Mexico City), played cat-and-mouse with the authorities, capturing the democratic imagination, though not a great deal of maneuvering room, during the on-off process of negotiations, which have been almost entirely fruitless so far.

Unlike South Africa in the early 1990s, though, the Zapatista strategy is fully in harmony with intensified direct action across the countryside. Formal negotiations broke down repeatedly when the government violated several pledges regarding freedom of Zapatista movement in the occupied territory, and the guerrilla leadership went into hiding deep in the Lacandan jungle.

Byzantine Mexico

But while the state's grip on the throat of Chiapas appears firm, the Zapatistas are intent on prying it loose and, one day, singing their songs of liberation freely. The Mexican ruling regime during nearly all of the 20th century, the Party of Institutional Revolution (PRI), was the world's longest-serving government, before its defeat by Vicente Fox in 2000. Though stitched together from a series of progressive battles against dictatorship during the 1910s, the PRI degenerated and survived through a mixture of conservative economics, vote theft, self-serving patronage and straightforward brutality. Its leaders consistently pledged far-reaching 'economic reform' as part of a campaign to bring Mexico from the Third to the First World. But to do so – in the process pleasing foreign investors and lining their own pockets – PRI elites shrunk a once-proud Mexican state-owned industry to nothing through giveaways, free-trade zones and crony capitalism as corrupt as any on the global scene.

Things went from bad to worse, in various ways. Superficially, one recent Mexican president – Carlos Salinas, once touted by the Clinton administration to head the World Trade Organisation – was so badly shamed by the exposure of his family's milking of public monies in 1995 that he went on a farcical hunger strike to clear his name and then fled to self-imposed exile. Another predecessor retreated to Italy with an alleged billion dollars in stolen slush money.

The last PRI president, Ernesto Zedillo, inherited from Salinas an economic *Titanic* barely afloat on a tumultuous sea of credit and, in terms of the coherence of national industry, simply tearing apart at the seams. In the space of a few weeks in early 1995, not long after Zedillo's inauguration, international speculators proceeded to submerge most of the economy's passengers. Two million workers lost their jobs and much of Mexico's middle class sank directly into poverty. The currency fell by 65%, the stock market crashed, and interest rates soared from 14% to more than 100%. As 200 000 small businesses were declared bankrupt, a million Mexicans joined a debtors' cartel of consumers and the *petit bourgeoisie* who – calling themselves 'El Barzon' (the cattle yoke) – collectively refused to honour loans that had become unrepayable. Their slogan was 'I don't deny I owe – but I'll pay what is just!', and their solidarity with the Zapatistas included a pledge that 'if one of us is attacked, we will act, and vice versa.'

One tempting recourse for Zedillo and his allies was to blame the Zapatistas for the overall crash of the neo-liberal model. In February 1995, an infamous Chase Manhattan Bank memo (authored by Johns Hopkins academic Riordan Roett) publicly advised the Mexican state to 'eliminate' the guerrillas. But by then, Chiapas protests had turned from the Zapatista army's mainly symbolic military action – replete with ski masks, red bandannas and a romantic renaissance of Che Guevarraism – to mass democratic mobilisation. After a formal peace accord and truce were finally agreed by a humiliated Zedillo, two huge Zapatista conferences of progressive activists (one a national democratic Mexican gathering and the other an 'International Encounter Against Neoliberalism and For Humanity') were staged in distant jungle villages. Most Zapatista troops soon melted back into their communities, to continue their struggle in an increasingly militant civil society.

Later, as social divisions reopened across Mexico and as opposition political parties won gains in still-tainted elections (including more than half the Mexican parliament and some large cities, including the capital), Zedillo appeared more determined, even desperate, to rid national politics of the Zapatistas, and to send an uncompromising signal to other indigenous insurgents who have since begun to surface elsewhere in Mexico.

Development for whom?

What the Zapatistas termed their 'Bad Government' not only cracked the military whip. PRI authorities also adopted a divide-and-rule strategy against the opposition, and turned to neo-liberal economic techniques at both national and local levels. But from being the 'golden-haired boy' of the World Bank and International Monetary Fund prior to 1995, Mexico was suddenly their most spectacular structural-adjustment flop.

Locally in Chiapas, state and private-sector resources aimed to exploit hydro-electric power and commercial agriculture, but after the Third World debt crisis broke out in 1982, the momentum of accumulation slowed markedly. Mayan villages languished in poverty through the 1980s and early 1990s, but after the Zapatista's uprising in 1994, state finances suddenly flowed back through closely-guarded channels into those towns where a critical mass of government supporters could be bought.

But this was an unsustainable approach. The power of mass-popular protest – expressed, for example, in a Chiapas-wide mass electricity-payment boycott, or in periodic sit-ins by indigenous women activists on the Pan-American Highway (which cuts through the Zapatista heartland) – has been sufficient to force serious concessions from the regime. The state power company acknowledges it cannot force Zapatista households to pay the $7 billed each month for, typically, powering a couple of light-bulbs.

Leading Zapatistas in both the guerrilla force and civil society groups adopted a long-term strategy: political (even constitutional) autonomy from the centre. But at the same time, they demand financial resources from the state, recognising that it will never be possible to develop Chiapas without reclaiming the surplus drained away by the state and big capital. However, during the 1990s, they did not seek to defeat the PRI in tainted electoral battles. A widespread sentiment expressed by most hard-core activists was distrust of not only the state machinery, but also of orthodox political parties, including even the social-democratic Party of Revolutionary Democracy (PRD), which only just lost – due to notorious fraud – the presidential elections to Salinas in 1988.

One Zapatista stepping stone to a more thorough-going, radical democracy is consolidation of popular participation in nearly three dozen 'autonomous municipalities', each consisting of thousands of rural residents in loosely connected villages. During the late 1990s, these became effectively 'ungovernable' sites of dual power. Zedillo demanded that the autonomous municipalities disband. The Mexican army has occupied several of them. But most remained vibrant and functioning reminders of the Zapatista spirit, and were rewarded at the time Fox took over the Mexican presidency with a pledge by the Chiapas state government to review their status with the prospect of formalisation and recognition.

The courageous public identification of these villages with the rebel cause was not the only visible evidence of space contested and won. Organised land invasions of the plantations of absentee landlords were regular occurrences, and by determinedly facing down the paramilitary eviction teams, several communities won formal acknowledgment that they control and effectively own the invaded land of their forebears.

Such organic strategies and tactics were part of an emerging, systematic approach to local development aimed to reflect the image – and serve the interests – of the indigenous and mestizo peoples. No doubt, missions comprised of World Bank loan-pushers and jet-set development experts will reinvade Chiapas when the military tensions finally cool, aiming to modernise the peasants, break their hard-won land into atomistic individually-titled units, addict people to credit and pesticides, price water according to 'economic resource cost', cost-recover on electricity and all other government services not already privatised, erode economically inefficient forms of traditional expression and cultural survival, threaten stable natural ecologies, and in the process uproot socio-political solidarity – in the very manner that many rural (and urban) South Africans have suffered in the past, continue to suffer in the present, and will suffer in the future, unless something is done to prevent it.

However, through their world-class resistance to military domination and economic neo-liberalism, the Zapatistas may have dug roots so deep and durable that South Africans – and others across the Third World – will have opportunities well into the 21st century to admire, offer solidarity and draw out crucial lessons about rural social struggle.

In sum, the Zapatistas have helped catalyse the international movement for justice. A core component of that movement is the disempowerment of the World Bank and IMF, as the major representatives of international injustice. So the responsibility now shifts back to Africa, especially South Africa, to think through the implications of this strategic orientation.

4. Does Africa need Washington?

'Without the international financial institutions, things would be even worse for poor countries,' insisted Trevor Manuel at the Prague debate in late September 2000. This is, indeed, the core argument Manuel and other defenders of Bretton Woods resort to, i.e. access to capital markets is impossible for poor African countries, and hence the IMF and World Bank are crucial sources of hard-currency financing.[7]

New architecture, not old buildings

There are many technical responses to such an assertion, which should be mentioned at least in passing (Chapter twelve provides a lengthier rebuttal). The main argument is that by restructuring international financial architecture in the interests of the world's majority, there would be no need for IMF/World Bank loans (which for impoverished countries are extremely expensive when currencies crash, and when hard currency is required to repay the lender, even if the loans are provided at a 'soft' interest rate of less than 1%). Instead of hard-currency loans (for soft-currency purchases such as rural schools and teacher salaries, or microcredit programmes), an ideal type of alternative development-finance strategy at global and national levels would have the following elements:

- Third World debt should be completely canceled once and for all.
- Capital controls should be permitted, to allow states to adopt pro-poor policies without fear of a run by the rich.
- Local basic developmental needs with no foreign inputs should only be paid for with local currency, not on the basis of loans denominated in dollars, yen or euros.

- Development loans should carry subsidised interest rates where needed (even if that 'distorts' local and global financial markets).
- To the extent that redistributive North-South funding flows can be established – drawn, for example, from taxes on financial speculation or strings-free overseas development assistance – they should occur on a grant (not loan) basis.
- Finance-agency economists should not be allowed to whimsically impose neo-liberal conditionality.
- For vital imports, trade finance should be freely available from export credit agencies for progressive input requirements (instead of just for inappropriate megaprojects and the import of luxury goods).

Active struggles
But far more important than technical utopianism, what case are grassroots organisations actively involved in these issues arguing? Much can be gleaned from specific social struggles associated with local campaigns. For example, in mid-2000, when the US EximBank offered $1 billion in loans for African countries to import anti-retroviral drugs to combat HIV/AIDS, Africans involved in grassroots advocacy (especially South Africa's Treatment Action Campaign) recommended that their nation states reject the advice, and instead import parallel, generic drugs at as little as 5% of the US corporate price from countries like Thailand, India and Brazil.

Another African example is the grassroots campaign for the return of the billions of dollars looted by Nigerian dictator Sani Abacha and hoarded in Swiss and London banks. Early success has helped to break open Swiss secrecy (following similar campaigns waged over 15 years by citizens' groups and governments in the Philippines and Haiti in relation to the Marcos and Duvalier hoards). The British government was particularly embarrassed by the failure of its regulators to prevent the largest London banks from laundering Abacha's – and no doubt many other tyrants' – dirty money without qualms.

In addition, progressive local African groups and international allies have also attacked specific World Bank projects, including the Chad-Cameroon pipeline and the Lesotho Highlands Water Project. Aside from events such as 26 September 2000 solidarity activism against the Bank/IMF, other growing campaigns that link African and international civil society organisations include the environmental debt that the industrial North owes the South, and the campaign to ban trade in so-called 'conflict diamonds' that contributes to civil war in Sierra Leone and Angola.

Converging rhetorics of resistance
African networks that build these campaigns are evolving continually, and several are worth citing at this juncture.

- The 'Lusaka Declaration' was signed in May 1999 by the leading African social movement and church organisations working on debt.[8] Dozens of participants in the Lusaka meeting launched a process for drafting a mass-popular 'Africa People's Consensus' to transcend the development orthodoxy of the Washington Consensus and the slightly reformed Post-Washington Consensus, and to do so by building upon similar regional meetings in Accra, Lome and Gauteng in 1998–9.
- The Africa People's Consensus went to West Africa in December 2000, via the Dakar 2000 Co-ordinating Committee.[9] This initiative took on momentum in a conference in Yaounde in January 2000, and by May the Organising Committee released a major statement condemning the status-quo debt-reduction strategy: 'The new slavery in Africa, which results from the burden of the debt and the enforcement of structural adjustment policies, is an unprecedented shame at the beginning of the 21st century ... Like all previous gestures, the initiatives taken in Cologne (June 1999) and in Cairo (April 2000) do not offer any actual solution.'
- In Dakar, a variety of organisations united behind a tough analysis, i.e. that 'Third World debt to the North is at once fraudulent, odious, illegal, immoral, illegitimate, obscene and genocidal' and that instead, '[c]ountries of the North owe Third World countries, particularly Africa, a manifold debt: blood debt with slavery; economic debt with colonization, and the looting of human and mineral resources and unequal exchange; ecological debt with the destruction and the looting of its natural resources; social debt (unemployment; mass poverty) and cultural debt (debasing of African civilizations to justify colonization) ...'[10]
- The Accra-based Africa Trade and Development Network[11] was similarly active in opposing the United States free-trade legislation known as the Africa Growth and Opportunity Act. Its member organisations pledged in October 2000 to lobby their governments to refuse to join the deal, which provides a slight amount of market access to those countries that Washington (this time, the US State and Commerce Departments) deems economically responsible. This follows similar work by the network to promote Africa-Caribbean-Pacific unity in relation to Lome and European Union trade negotiations more generally, and early critiques of the Poverty Reduction Strategy Paper initiative of the IMF and World Bank.
- Free trade within a given region is also problematic, particularly under the influence of Washington, the Southern African Peoples Solidarity Network argues.[12] Meeting in Windhoek in August 2000, it resolved

'that the governments of our countries
  • have for long mainly engaged in rhetorical declarations about national

development, and development cooperation and regional integration, with few effective achievements;
- are mainly concerned with preserving and promoting their own individual and group status, power and privileges, and their personal and aspirant-class appropriation of our nations' resources; and, for these reasons, are frequently engaged in divisive competition and even dangerous conflicts amongst themselves at the expense of the interests of the people at national and regional levels;
- are, at the same time, committed to supporting and defending each other whenever the interests and power of the ruling elites come into conflict with the human rights, and the democratic and development aspirations of their own populations; and are using SADC as a self-serving "old boys' club" for such mutual support;
- are increasingly responsive and subordinate to external inducements and pressures from governmental agencies in the richest industrialised countries, and their global corporations, banks and other financial organisations, and the "multilateral" institutions dominated and used by them.'

After a series of demands – in favour of inward-oriented, basic-needs development strategies that promote regional integration rather than disintegration (as is happening through free trade under South Africa's domination) – the Network warned that: 'Whether or not our governments accept and act on the above vitally important demands, we as members of peoples organisations from the whole of Southern Africa will continue to pursue these aims and deepen our work in and with existing and emerging mass movements to challenge and change our governments' policies and strategies; and – if that fails – to change our governments.'[13]

The main point to make here is not that these and other important networks (e.g. labour-related networks, health-equity specialists, numerous types of environmentalists, and so on) are advancing strong, mature, explicitly 'post-nationalist' ideological statements about the debt, trade and related economic oppression they face. What is perhaps of greater interest is that instead of working merely through NGO-type circuits, they are increasingly tying their work to militant street action.

Beyond 'civil society' co-option
In the past, in contrast, instead of working through mass protest, some local activities undertaken by grassroots groups too easily fell into the trap of neo-liberal economic policies. This was a logical corollary to the rise of so-called 'civil-society' discourses, and was not unique to Africa by any means. Since the 1980s, Claude Ake warned in a book completed just prior to his death in 1996, that:

there has been an explosion of associational life in rural Africa. By all indications, this is a by-product of a general acceptance of the necessity of self-reliance, yielding a proliferation of institutions such as craft centres, rural credit unions, farmers' associations, community-run skill development centres, community banks, cooperatives, community-financed schools and hospitals and civic centres, local credit unions, even community vigilante groups for security. Some have welcomed this development as a sign of a vibrant civil society in Africa. It may well be that. However, before we begin to idealise this phenomenon, it is well to remind ourselves that whatever else it is, it is first and foremost a child of necessity, of desperation even.[14]

The rise of community-based organisations (CBOs) and associated development NGOs closely corresponds with the desire of the international agencies to shrink Third World states as part of the overall effort to lower the social wage. The result is an ongoing conflict between technicist, apolitical development interventions on the one hand, and the people-centred strategies and militant tactics of mass-oriented social movements of the oppressed on the other.

So by the early 1990s, two out of five World Bank projects involved NGOs (well over half in Africa), and in projects involving population, nutrition, primary healthcare and small enterprise, the ratio rose to more than four out of five. In his seminal study in 1995, Paul Nelson found that NGOs were 'primarily implementors of project components designed by World Bank and government officials'. Moreover, especially since an upsurge in such participation began in 1988, NGOs have often been used to 'deliver compensatory services to soften the effects of an adjustment plan'. In some cases, the NGOs were not even pre-existing but were 'custom-built for projects' and hence could 'neither sustain themselves nor represent poor people's interests effectively'.[15]

But from a recent era in which 'Co-opted NGOs' – CoNGOs, as they are termed – happily picked up crumbs from the neo-liberal table, we may be on the verge of a return to dominance by radical, people's-movement NGOs. In South Africa, the SA Non-Governmental Organisation Coalition deserves this recognition, as do its allied think-tanks and campaigning groups currently fighting for free access to anti-retroviral drugs, water, electricity and the like.

Conditions for converging struggles

The greatest potential in all of this, however, is the increasing correlation of issue-development by social, environmental and labour organisations with mass, lumpen-proletarian protest. The main scholars of the IMF riot, Walton and Seddon, argue that the shrinkage of the state under conditions of structural adjustment generates a 'broader trend toward the decline of clientism and, conversely, the growing autonomy of urban low-income groups'.[16] As states lose their patronage capacity to channel social surpluses to supporters, social movements can cast off influences of corporatism and corruption associated with urban and rural civil society under populist regimes.

Such autonomy contributes to more generalised political processes of self-enlightenment, with the potential for transcending spontaneous and unsustainable reactions to economic crisis, such as the IMF riot. It is here that rural/urban, worker/lumpen, male/female and other vital alliances can be built, perhaps using a 'rights-based discourse' that at present in South Africa is responsible, as I noted at the outset of this chapter, for a great upsurge of protest and social-policy concessions.

Before taking these matters back to the global level in search of South-South-North alliances, let us return to the terrain explored in Chapter two, i.e. the Southern African region. Chapter two demonstrated that a sub-imperialist project emanates from Pretoria, drawing in neo-liberally-minded regional elites. The question then is whether regional resistance can emanate from the grassroots, led by the working class, in response?

At the turn of the 21st century, Southern African workers and their allies could not claim to have found a unified or unifying approach to what by all accounts should be a universal challenge, namely the multifaceted struggle against neo-liberalism.

Trade disputes

Can internationalist strategies and tactics reconfigure regional class struggle in a more favourable way? In the case of trade agreements, the interests of the world's workers *appear* to lie in a concerted programme to raise the standard of living (including gender and environmental protections) of those at the bottom of the global hierarchy, by attaching clauses to trade agreements enforced by the WTO. Yet as we saw in Chapter ten, the debate on the inclusion of social, labour, governance and environmental clauses in trade agreements to this end became extremely thorny during the 1990s, serving as a divisive 'wedge issue' within the international movement.

Divisions were clear in Southern Africa. From Johannesburg, Zwelinzima Vavi and other Cosatu leaders pushed for such clauses to be applied against regional trading partners. In contrast, many progressive African social movements, NGOs, churches and women's groups, development agencies, technical think-tanks and intellectuals – some of them gathered in the Ghana-based Africa Trade Network – condemned the imposition of conditions on what they argue is already a terribly unequal trade, investment and financing relationship with the South.

A workshop of SATUCC and regional social-movement activists in November 1999 issued a 'Statement on the Seattle Ministerial' rejecting 'the widening of the ambit of issues under the WTO through the inclusion of the Social Clause'.[17] The potential value of such clauses was outweighed, in the activists' view, by the damage done to power relations through amplifying the legitimacy and power of the WTO. But Cosatu's Vavi – who did not attend – immediately disassociated SATUCC (over which he presided) from the workshop statement. Instead, in Seattle a few days later, Vavi joined forces with the South African government and local big business, to demand less protectionist trade rules, but nevertheless including the Social Clause. The delegation gained prized access to Green Room deliberations, though it returned empty-handed (and Erwin soon dropped his support for the Social Clause). The Social Clause strategy thus appeared discredited, but that was no loss.

Just how visionary, then, could regional and international labour and social solidarity be in the early 21st century? The examples considered above suggest strategic orientations that can promote unity and avoid divisive tactics, even if key divisions continued in debt and trade struggles. It is time, then, to consider the key targets, strategies, tactics and alliances, in the spirit that Southern African and other Third World grassroots inputs can help the international movement develop a more progressive, forward-looking consciousness.

5. South-South-North alliances against global finance/commerce

To begin with targets, as the institutional expressions of international financial and commercial capital (led by Wall Street), the IMF, World Bank and WTO provide the movement with an opportunity to both confront power in a concentrated form, and to unmask the deeper institutional meanings of these organisations within world capitalism. Africa demonstrates this in many ways, from macroeconomics, to conditionality associated with debt relief, to local issues such as cost-recovery on basic services. In addition to providing a large, highly visible focus for protesters working from a myriad of locations and situations, the IMF and World Bank also generate feedback mechanisms that can amplify the local struggles through their connectivity to the rest of the movement.

The need for solidarity around local IMF/World Bank/WTO campaigns will grow, the more that South struggles evolve into full-fledged attacks on the international institutions. Already, calls for the IMF/World Bank to quit Seoul, New Delhi, Pretoria, Brasilia, Mexico City and the like are made regularly by local activists, and are rebuffed by the comprador elites who hold local power. In somewhat more marginalised capitals, like Kuala Lumpur, Harare and Caracas, government leaders echo the activists' distaste for Northern bankers and Washington economists – although often for reasons that have to be carefully and critically considered.

Therefore, there are two potential lines of solidarity to tighten, i.e. North-South and South-South, deepening international popular-movement unity, and exploring – but with extreme care – alliances with South states that need the movement's support so as to achieve their own limited objectives.

Allying with nationalists?

To consider this last matter first, the question arises of how to ally with states that are resisting neo-liberalism. Here the answer can only be case-specific, and can only be firmly established once local progressive struggles are clearly understood and terrains of solidarity mapped out. Cuba and Venezuela represent instances where two leaders, Castro and Chavez, attack the IMF and World Bank from a position of far greater integrity and popularity than, say, Malaysia and Zimbabwe, where an entirely different logic is in play, namely the invocation of opportunistic populism by Mahathir and Mugabe so as to shore up local support.[18]

And there are other cases – China, Hong Kong, India and Taiwan, for example – in which the retention of national sovereignty and rejection of Washington Consensus financial- and trade-liberalisation advice during the East Asian crisis in 1997–9 created a cushion against external shocks. Here, obviously pursuing national sovereignty should not lead to nationalism and xenophobia, which are the agendas of Buchanan, Le Pen and Haider. To this end, pre-existing nation-state economic tools can serve as a basis for restoration of more thorough-going demo-cratic processes, including a 'development' strategy appropriate to local needs and conditions, rather than one predetermined by Washington financiers.

Even if insensitive to the profound environmental problems provoked by industry, Keynes was correct that in the economic realm, financial regulation – especially capital controls – and inward-oriented industrial modernisation are crucial to those processes, at a time that the balance of global forces precludes a serious effort at building a progressive world state with substantive financial, trade and other regulatory responsibilities and powers. Instead of aspiring to utopian, democratic global government through reform of the WTO, IMF and World Bank, the movement more logically aims to smash the embryonic neo-liberal world state.

Internationalist nationalism[19]

Within the struggle to expand national democratic sovereignty, the progres-sive position is therefore to fight for national concerns that fit best into a framework of international solidarity. This entails rejecting a threatening external Other, and redirecting attention against elites at home whose inter-national financial allies and neo-liberal export-oriented rhetoric represent the more fundamental erosion of democracy, as well as of ecological balance and balanced economic development.

As Marx wrote, 'Everywhere the bourgeoisie are traitors to their own country.'[20] Thus a key ingredient – namely political solidarity with radical movements – must be added to Keynes' menu of international goals, from which can be derived a bumper-sticker slogan with which the contemporary movement would be quite comfortable, i.e. 'Globalisation of people, not of capital'. This is not an 'anti-globalisation' movement, then; instead, the movement demands both anti-corporate globalisation and anti-nation statism in cases where compradors in finance ministries and central banks use globalisation as the excuse for imposition of the neo-liberal agenda, claiming that 'There is no alternative'.

Internationalist solidarity

If this is a correct description of the forces in play, it may be time for a greater redirection of movement resources into both intensified base-building and international alliances. One example is the case of alliances around access to pharmaceutical products to combat HIV/AIDS, as I discussed at length in Chapters eight and nine. Another telling case looms where social resistance is emerging and such alliances could again, one day, be called into play to ensure exclusion from world trading/investment pressures, that of access to clean water.

French and British water and essential-services firms have led the commodification, corporatisation and privatisation of municipal water for many years, in part to cross-subsidise other high-risk ventures.[21] The codification of this process at the Hague World Water Forum in March 2000 was all the more important because of the high-profile role of World Bank vice-president Ismail Serageldin and the endorsement by the United Nations Development Programme. But resistance has been bubbling up in the water sector for many years, long before the Cochabamba riots. On the Narmada River, India's social movements have become expert at periodically disrupting the Sardar Sarovar dam project, even to the extent of kicking the World Bank out. But dam protesters are concerned not only with supply-side environmental and displacement problems.

The World Bank is evidently not open to pro-poor reform in this area. This was demonstrated when, in Johannesburg's impoverished Alexandra Township, a leap forward was taken in 1998 with protest against the Lesotho Highlands Water Project, a series of dams that comprise Africa's largest-ever public-works project. The demand-side implications of piping Lesotho water across a mountain range to Johannesburg include further hedonistic consumption by rich, mainly white, suburban users and a disproportionate increase in water tariffs for low-income users. Though the Alexandra protest – a formal complaint to the World Bank's Inspection

Panel – was not immediately successful in its dual goal of curtailing further dam construction and changing Johannesburg water consumption habits (so that cross-subsidies will pay for a free 'lifeline' supply of 50 litres per day per person and also encourage water conservation), it injected class struggle into public environment and development debates in an unprecedented manner.

In doing so, the technicist Alexandra complaint to the World Bank joined an increasing series of mass-popular, anti-privatisation, anti-commodification uprisings in South Africa, where neo-liberal World Bank policy advice on infrastructure has encouraged African National Congress municipal governments to cut off the water supplies of low-income residents in a manner that even the apartheid regime did not dare. As in the case of essential drugs, the cost of supplying basic needs to those who need them was eminently affordable, and could easily be achieved by raising fees on hedonistic consumers by an average of 5%. But the problem, as I noted at the outset of this chapter, was the policy to price water increasingly at marginal cost.[22]

Strategies and alliances

In these cases, the alliances have been far stronger between local activists and international allies (including *petit-bourgeois* technocrats from inside-the-Beltway NGOs) than they have with local officials. It is because class conflict in national settings suffering neo-liberalism is far more likely than a momentary convergence of interests between radical grassroots organisations and local elites, that the growing global movement has to reach out even further, and maintain an air of scepticism about statements in Havana by G-77 elites.

As opposition to the neo-liberal mantra 'Get the prices right!' is not only a morally essential strategy in order to assure universal access to water and other basic goods, it also often works in vulgar economic terms if applied intelligently. This was as true in high-growth, authoritarian sites as diverse as Korea (1955–63) and Rhodesia (1965–74), as in the industrialisation era of the East Bloc. Any such development strategy that conflicts with the Washington Consensus will, as Keynes advised, rely far more on resources drawn from domestic sources, including halting capital flight through tough exchange controls, directed credit and perhaps even nationalised banks, interest rate subsidies to promote key branches of production and consumption, and various other forms of financial repression. Beyond such nationally grounded projects, as I noted above, lies the idea of progressive regionalisation.[23]

How to get from here to there through genuine shopfloor/grassroots empowerment rather than through standard modes of populist regime-building is subject to enormous debate, and there remains reasonable doubt as to whether such 'people's-movement', NGO-influenced strategies will ever substitute for traditional revolutionary class-oriented approaches to socialism-from-below.[24] Nevertheless, the syntheses of so many anti-neo-liberal outbursts across the world suggests that the movement is achieving sufficient maturity to no longer become confused or co-opted by reformism at the global, national or local levels.

The political strategy advocated here – namely, global attacks by the working class and allies from social and environmental movements against financial/commercial capital's nerve centres in Washington and Geneva, combined with local, national (and then regional) class struggles to re-establish radical 'development' visions – skirts the intellectuals' vertical/horizontal debate. It does so by invoking the need for critique of the neo-liberal Washington Consensus as a pure form of capitalist economic doctrine with all that this entails, and for the global targeting of the multi-lateral institutions that are the most direct sites of the command and control functions that subordinate so much of the world to neo-liberalism.

If this strategy does indeed have merit, then the Seattle, Washington and Prague demonstrations – and many other moments in the movement's recent growth – helped break the grip of the greatest tool of repression, i.e. the belief that nothing can be done. In future, not only will every major meeting and gathering of the major powers become a site of torment for global elites. Co-ordination will also intensify across the globe in support of 'abolitionist reforms' that reduce the power and resources of the global institutions, such as blocking the World Bank's role in the privatisation of education, shutting down egregious projects such as the Chad-Cameroon pipeline, delinking 'debt relief' from IMF/World Bank policies and separating international aid and credit from compliance with the same policies.

Defunding the World Bank

Indeed, decommissioning the Bretton Woods institutions through a mass-popular defunding strategy is the culmination of this line of attack. As I discussed in Chapter ten, such a struggle is already under way, not only by pressing parliaments to reject periodic recapitalisation (i.e. bailout) requests from Washington, but more importantly through the World Bank Bonds Boycott, which aims to take away the World Bank's AAA bond rating through anti-apartheid-style 'divestment' campaigns. Municipalities, churches, union pension funds, university endowments and individuals with investments that include an international-portfolio component are now, at no cost to themselves, informing their fund managers to avoid buying World Bank bonds, whose decline in value once the strategy unfolds will in any case persuade managers to boycott the World Bank simply because of their own fiduciary responsibility.[25]

Susan George's mock *Lugano Report* sums up nicely the necessity of the Bretton Woods institutions for elite crisis management: 'They continue to serve as the guarantors of liberalisation, privatisation and structural adjustment in large parts of the world; a task which no individual Northern government or group of governments should consider undertaking directly. They also remain useful, particularly to the G-7 countries, because they preclude the need for the latter to intervene overtly in the affairs of other 'sovereign nations' undergoing financial crisis'.[26]

For these reasons, in the context of sustained structural crisis and displacement (not resolution), the necessity – and feasibility – of closing the institutions as a *first relatively simultaneous step* towards a deeper, global anti-capitalist project is convincing. For here, what David Harvey terms the 'local and universal taken together' is being daily devised and controlled by large-scale financial and commercial capitals and their multilateral institutional instruments in Washington and Geneva (albeit mediated by the US treasury secretary and US trade representative).

Local and universal together
Harvey argues that the challenge also lies in transcending two typical dead-end responses by anti-globalisation activists, i.e. 'to regret the passing of the old order and to call for the restoration of past values (religious, cultural, national solidarities, or whatever)', and similarly 'to pursue the utopian vision of some kind of communitarianism (including movements of national redemption as an answer to the alienations and abstractions of a globalising political economy and culture) ... sometimes appealing to some sort of political mythology laced with nostalgia for a golden age of organic community'. These won't do: 'The third path is to take globalization seriously and make universal claims of precisely the sort that the Zapatistas have advanced from their mountainous retreats in Southern Mexico. These claims rest firmly on local experience but operate more dialectically in relation to globalization.'[35]

The Zapatistas' alliances with international social movements are a model along these lines. But so too, the Zapatistas are distinctly radical-democratic in making short-term demands upon their nation state to deliver the goods – and tellingly, when this is not forthcoming due to neo-liberalism, Zapatista self-activity takes forms such as liberating electricity from the pylons that cross Chiapas, invading under-utilised ranches and plantations, and declaring municipal autonomy in dozens of sites of community struggle.

For the rest of us, working in solidarity with such Southern rebellions – and in self-interest, too – the next common target, which at the moment functions locally, globally and universally, is, taken together, the IMF, World Bank and WTO. A prerequisite of global social justice is to fell the agencies

which most directly negate our claims of universal access to decommodified, destratified, degendered and environmentally responsible 'rights' such
as essential drugs and clean water. It is here that the strategy and
self-activity of the movement appear most coherent, reasonable and feasible. Despite Alec Erwin's pronouncement, the international protesters do
know what they're talking about. And contrary to Trevor Manuel, both the
international and African contributions increasingly represent an encouraging basis for answering his question: 'What are the protesters *for*?'

Notes

1 See documentation by the World Development Movement:
  http://www.wdm.org.uk/cambriefs/DEBT/unrest.htm.
2 World Bank (2000), *Sourcebook on Community Driven Development in the Africa
  Region: Community Action Programs*, Africa Region, Washington, DC, 17 March
  (signatories: Calisto Madavo and Jean-Louis Sarbib, vice-presidents for Africa),
  Annex 2.
3 The first democratic government's *Water/Sanitation White Paper* (1994) and *Urban
  Infrastructure Investment Framework* (1995), both influenced by World Bank
  personnel, together established principles of communal – not individual household
  – standpipes, ventilated and improved pit latrines instead of water-borne sanitation
  for those households earning $110 per month or below, full marginal-cost recovery,
  and cut-offs of water supplies to those who can't pay. A minor subsidy was permitted through an 'equitable-share' grant, which subsequently declined dramatically
  (by 85% in real terms) through the 1990s. For details, see Bond, P. (2000), *Cities of
  Gold, Townships of Coal: Essays on South Africa's New Urban Crisis*, Trenton, Africa
  World Press.
4 Roome, J. (1995), 'Water Pricing and Management: World Bank Presentation to the
  SA Water Conservation Conference', power-point presentation, South Africa,
  2 October.
5 Bond, P. (2000), *Elite Transition: From Apartheid to Neoliberalism in South Africa*,
  London, Pluto Press and Pietermaritzburg, University of Natal Press.
6 The information in this section was gathered during a visit to Chiapas in July 1998,
  shortly after the official expulsion of similar human-rights observer delegations from
  Italy, as part of a Mexico Solidarity Network visit facilitated by Global Exchange
  and two pro-Zapatista NGOs based in San Cristobal de las Casas.
7 See also Manuel's arguments in the documentary film 'Two Trevors go to
  Washington' (http://go.to/two.trevors).
8 Present were the main Jubilee chapters, other faith/justice organisations, NGOs,
  progressive think-tanks and human-rights bodies from Burkina Faso, Lesotho,
  Kenya, Malawi, Mozambique, Nigeria, Cameroon, Swaziland, Tanzania, Togo,
  Uganda, South Africa, Zambia and Zimbabwe.
9 Dakar 2000 Organising Committee (2000), 'Declaration', Dakar. The Dakar summit
  was supported by groups like the Association des Femmes Africaines pour la
  Recherche et le Développement as well as numerous West and Central African social
  movements and NGOs. Dakar 2000 is networked across the Third World through
  the International South Group Network's well-respected Harare branch, and internationally through the Paris-based Association pour la Taxation des Transactions
  financières pour l'Aide aux Cityens, and the Comité pour l'Annulation de la Dette
  du Tiers Monde in Brussels.

10 'The Dakar Declaration for the Total and Unconditional Cancellation of African and Third World Debt', Dakar, December 2000.

11 The Trade and Development Network secretariat NGO, Isodec, is also affiliated to the Penang-based Third World Network, and has consistently been the most powerful African critic of the WTO. Along with the Harare NGO Southern and Eastern African Trade Information Initiative (Seatini), these were the major players behind the collapse of the WTO Seattle Round, working both in the streets and inside the official African delegation. South Africa attempted to cut a side deal in the Green Room deliberations of key countries, but minister Erwin was eventually shamed into accepting the Organisation of African Unity resolution that prevented consensus on establishing a Seattle Round.

12 Participants included the following organisations: African Organisation on Debt and Development, Africa Trade Network (Southern Africa), Alternative Information and Development Center (South Africa), Associacao para Desenvolvimento Rural de Angola, Council of Churches/Ecumenical Institute (Namibia), Centre for Southern African Studies (South Africa), Ecumenical Support Services (Zimbabwe), Food and Allied Workers Union (South Africa), Gender and Trade Network (Southern Africa), Jubilee 2000 Angola, Jubilee 2000 Malawi and CCJP (Malawi), Jubilee 2000 South Africa, Jubilee 2000 Zambia and CSUZ (Zambia), Jubilee South (Southern Africa), Labour Resource and Research Institute (Namibia), Ledikasyon pu Travayer (Mauritius), Mineworkers Development Agency (Lesotho), Mwelekeo wa NGO (Southern Africa), Namibian Food and Allied Workers Union (Namibia), Open Society in Southern Africa, South African NGO Coalition, Swaziland Youth Congress, and Zimbabwe Coalition on Debt and Development.

13 Southern African Peoples Solidarity Network (2000), 'Making Southern African Development Cooperation and Integration a People-Centered and People-Driven Regional Challenge to Globalization: Declaration to the Governmental Summit of the Southern African Development Community', Windhoek, Namibia, 1–7 August, available at http://aidc.org.za.

14 Ake, C. (2000), *The Feasibility of Democracy in Africa*, Dakar, Codesria, p. 47.

15 Nelson, P. (1995), *The World Bank and Non-Governmental Organisations: The Limits of Apolitical Development*, London, Macmillan.

16 Walton, J. and Seddon, D. (1994), *Free Markets and Food Riots*, Oxford, Basil Blackwell, p. 336.

17 Workshop on Trade and Investment in Southern Africa (1999), 'Statement on the Seattle Ministerial', Johannesburg, 11–13 October; SATUCC, 'Communique', Johannesburg, 5 November; for more on the debate, see http://www.aidc.org.za.

18 For Malaysia, see Jomo, K. S. (1999) 'Capital Controls: Jury Still Out', paper presented to the conference on 'Economic Sovereignty in a Globalizing World', Bangkok, 24 March; for Zimbabwe, see Bond, P. (1999), 'Zimbabwe's Political Reawakening', *Monthly Review*, 50(11) and (1998) *Uneven Zimbabwe*; for Cuba, see Castro, F. (2000), 'Address to the South Summit', *Monthly Review*, 52(3).

19 I am indebted to Robert Naiman for the argument below.

20 Marx, K. and Engels, F. (1978 edn), *The Communist Manifesto*, New York, Norton, p. 488.

21 For the South Africa municipal privatisation case, see Bond, P. (2000) *Cities of Gold, Townships of Coal*.

22 Bond, P. (2000) 'Economic Growth, Ecological Modernisation or Environmental Justice?: Conflicting Discourses in Post-Apartheid South Africa', *Capitalism Nature Socialism*, 11(1).

23 Amin, S. (1999) 'Regionalisation in Response to Polarising Globalization', in B. Hettne, A. Inotai and O. Sunkel (eds), *Globalism and the New Regionalism*, London, Macmillan, 1999, p. 77. See also work by Walden Bello along similar lines.
24 For Asian debates, see Burkett, P. and Hart-Landsberg, M. (2000), *Development, Crisis, and Class Struggle: Learning from Japan and East Asia*, New York, St. Martin's Press, Chapter 14; and Ungpakorn, J. G. (1999), *Thailand: Class Struggle in an Era of Economic Crisis*, Hong Kong, Asia Monitor Resource Centre. More generally, see the warnings in Kagarlitsky, B. (2000), *The Return of Radicalism: Reshaping the Left Institutions*, London, Pluto Press, pp. 89–92.
25 Aside from its uncompromising radicalism, one of the impressive characteristics of the campaign's website is the diversity of international endorsement and South catalysts: http://www.worldbankboycott.org.
26 George, S. (1999), *The Lugano Report: On Preserving Capitalism in the Twenty-First Century*, London, Pluto Press, p. 20.
27 Harvey, D. (2000), *Spaces of Hope*, Edinburgh, Edinburgh University Press, p. 85.

CHAPTER TWELVE

The case for locking capital down

1. Introduction

It is time to make some concluding arguments, and to offer an alternative strategic course of action. First, five theses follow logically from Part 1, above.

1) To break – *not shine* – the chains of global apartheid, requires ending the tyranny of neoliberalism, and reversing the power relations that underlie that ideology.

2) The neoliberal ideology and the power relations are themselves amplified by the desperation measures – characterised by shifting and stalling the spreading economic crisis – adopted by capital in general since the mid-1970s.

3) The most important manifestation of economic crisis since the 1980s has been the rise of financial power, and the most important nerve centre (really, brain and muscles combined) is the Washington/Wall Street axis combining the World Bank, IMF, US government economic agencies and private-sector financial institutions.

4) However, this kind of economic power, based not upon a durable model of development but instead upon unsustainable flows of funds into financial assets, is also fraught with vulnerability, volatility, and self-destructive tendencies, and is susceptible to 'hard landings'.

5) The self-destructive tendencies will continue to worsen, given an existing balance of forces in the world economy in which there is not much reasonable hope that matters can be reformed from within; instead, international finance will continue to heighten world poverty and inequality, unless it is conclusively disciplined.

If this analysis holds, several political implications emerge. This chapter turns to what I think is an optimal 'way forward', in South Africa and other settings, for previously misguided government policy-makers who unrealistically promote reform (Part two) and for the social movements and political parties which pressure them to do far more (Part four). In short, my argument is that in the short-medium term, *there are enormous unexplored opportunities for nation-states, working with progressive activists and invoking international solidarity, to withstand international capitalist tyranny.* The case of pharmacorporate pricing of HIV/AIDS drugs suggests both the possibilities and limitations of the existing government of South Africa, in this regard, so deserves a brief recap (Part three).

In 1997, a well-meaning health minister with tough advisors and an international technical support network promoted and passed legislation that gives South Africa the chance to import or even manufacture generic versions of the branded HIV/AIDS drugs that are denied to millions of ill people, by virtue of discriminatory pricing by drug companies in search of monopolistic profit. When the leadership of the US government, acting on behalf of those companies, opposed the law in 1998–9, activists punished the vice-president, through public protest, to the point that he surrendered. When drug companies continued to pursue the matter through a court challenge in 2000, protests were amplified, culminating in a day of action in early 2001 with demonstrations in dozens of cities across the world. Although at this writing there is no resolution, the blockages – including the South African trade and industry minister, scared of offending international corporations by permitting violations of drug-patent rights – are being identified and addressed. After widespread protest during 2000, the South African president even retreated from an untenable position, through which he refused to consider implementing the drugs legislation on spurious grounds.

In sum, in this case study we discover an appropriate formula for broader action: the combination of inspired, sustained, internationalist activist protest against global apartheid, on the one hand, and on the other, the dormant but viable technical capability of nation-states to act against a powerful bloc of global capital, in favour of the interests of their citizenries, once social struggle has achieved a critical mass of attention and pressure.

Can we learn from this example, so as to more generally 'lock capital down'? If financiers are simultaneously the most powerful but also most vulnerable fraction of capital, and if the damage they are doing is increasingly obvious, it may be that this arena deserves more attention. Indeed in South Africa, there are a variety of leading-edge activists who have come to this conclusion: Jubilee South Africa, SA Communist Party leaders, township community groups, and many others. If there is a single arena of practical action within nation-states that would reduce the power of financiers, it is probably *the reimposition of capital controls*, in combination with *the redirection of financial investment into socially productive activities*, unhindered by the many anti-social financial-sector practices common in South Africa and in many similar settings.

By way of an initial definition, capital (or 'exchange') controls regulate the way the local currency relates to international currency markets.

Numerous rules prevent full 'convertibility' (direct exchange) of the rand and many other currencies. Capital controls refer mainly to prohibitions against the export of capital by either residents or non-residents, but also to a variety of controls on financial and investment processes applied to residents and non-residents.

In South Africa, in the wake of the lifting of the finrand in 1995, there are no capital export controls on non-residents, while residents have ceilings of several hundred thousand rands on export of their capital. Until March 2001, institutional investors were limited to investing 15% of their portfolio abroad, under the condition that they arrange an asset-swap with foreign investors, but the 2001 budget tightened restrictions by abolishing the swap mechanism because of abuse. Certain other regulations (such as in relation to deposit accounts, and against foreign sales of locally-owned shares) were retained on currency exchange and capital investments for residents and non-residents.

Pretoria's loosening of capital controls in March 1995 was, in retrospect, disastrous. As explained earlier, the bouts of global financial turbulence in the late 1990s had devastating effects on the South African economy. Over the course of a few weeks in mid-1998, for instance, more than R30 billion was effectively wasted by the Reserve Bank in unsuccessful attempts to defend the rand; interest rates were raised by 7 percentage points (with a subsequent slowdown of the economy); and the value of the currency dropped by nearly 30%. A previous currency crash was set off by a Union Bank of Switzerland report in February 1996, in turn inspired by a false rumour that then-president Nelson Mandela was ill.

But South Africa was not uniquely affected, nor was this experience unprecedented in local economic history. During prior bouts of instability in the 1990s, policy-makers had implemented a variety of restrictions on finance, dual exchange rate. Other countries (including Malaysia and even Zimbabwe) have had even more ambitious capital controls, financial transaction taxes, and other regulatory interventions. Ultimately, locking capital down through controls that limit the inflows and outflows of finance is crucial for South Africa's future. This is especially true given the sudden surge in international financial volatility since the Mexican 'meltdown' of 1994–5, and the extraordinary range of both public and private international bankruptcies.

There are now, indeed, three essential changes in global financial management with which South Africa must come to grips:
1) Although there is an urgent, universally recognised need for stronger international financial regulation – and indeed for a new 'global financial architecture' – the G-8 countries and multilateral financial institutions have done virtually nothing to this end, and appear ideologically opposed to taking the steps necessary for averting further meltdowns;

any further efforts by Pretoria to promote international reforms from within the centres of power are misguided and even dangerous to South Africa's interests.

2) Any individual country's overreliance upon (and likewise vulnerability to the reversal of) hot-money inflows is not good public policy; *individual countries do indeed have options for exercising national sovereignty in the face of international finance.*

3) In relation to a country's own investable resources, it is vital to redirect domestic financial assets away from speculative activity into productive outlets so as to maximise the broader economic good, even if that interferes with narrow, short-term financial self-interest, *requiring extremely firm regulation of the financial sector.*

To make this interrelated case, the following pages review international evidence of capital controls, historical and contemporary (Section 2). The point is to expand the current international room for manoeuvre for the nation-state, by considering recent capital-control experiences in other developing countries. We then consider local conditions, by tracing historical evidence that shows how both foreign and domestic financial flows have been central to patterns of economic development and underdevelopment (Section 3), and by assessing Pretoria's control options (Section 4). The conclusion (Section 5) emphasises the overall point of this book: to show that the struggle against global apartheid can be won, even on the terrain – international finance – where capital is strongest, because here too it is potentially most vulnerable.

2. Comparative capital controls

Historical precedents

There have been capital and exchange controls as long as there have been forms of money and states. These have included controls on foreign and local expatriation of investment income, controls on domestic ownership of foreign assets and vice versa, controls on currency convertibility, and restrictions on financial flows related to local branches of foreign banks.[1]

Virtually all countries have used capital controls, and even since the 1980s, studies have shown that these controls effectively prevented capital flight during financial crises,[2] in the process dampening local financial volatility and allowing interest rates to be kept at relatively lower levels.[3]

A list of post-war capital controls in developing countries includes the various measures listed, together with the number of countries that had utilised each type of control:[4]

Table 5: Post-war capital controls in developing countries

Category	No. of countries
Any form of capital control	119
Controls on foreign direct investments	107
Controls on non-residents	84
Controls on residents	35
Profit repatriation and capital liquidation	34
Taxes on capital transactions	9
Controls on deposit accounts	83
Of non-residents in local currency	52
Of non-residents in foreign exchange	37
Of residents abroad	29
Of residents in foreign currency (local banks)	23
Other capital transfers	70
Personal capital transfers	34
Blocked accounts	24
Controls on financial transactions	78
Of non-residents	41
Of residents	66
Trade-related financial transactions	7
Comprehensive controls	67
Controls on outflows	67
Controls on inflows	17
Controls on portfolio investments	61
Of non-residents	30
Of residents	33
Security issuance by non-residents	15
Security issuance abroad by residents	6

Beginning in the 1970s, as international banking expanded and as the Washington Consensus gradually achieved hegemony, many controls were rolled back by policy-makers, often under pressure from international financial institutions. By the 1990s, the key forces insisting on the deregulation of capital and exchange controls were the International Monetary Fund and US Treasury Department. Following the Mexican peso crisis of 1994–5, the IMF admitted that controls on incoming hot money would have been appropriate, but by 1997, US policy-makers had stepped up pressure on all countries, through the IMF, to liberalise their capital accounts.

The Asian revelation

However, in August 1998, Massachusetts Institute of Technology economist Paul Krugman stunned the economics profession and policy-makers more generally when he told a seminar in Singapore of his switch from advocating classical Washington Consensus crisis-management techniques of high interest rates and austerity ('Plan A'), to the 'radical' notion of exchange and capital controls. 'We tried Plan A', he told CNBC television, 'but it didn't work. Then what do you do? It's hard for the IMF and the US Treasury to admit it was wrong and to do something different. But the time has come … We cannot cut interest rates because the currency may fall and we can't get more IMF funds because the IMF didn't have enough. The only possibility I see is imposing capital controls … It's a dirty word, capital controls, but we need them to get out of the bind.'[5]

In a subsequent article in *Fortune* magazine, Krugman elaborated: 'In short, Plan B involves giving up for a time the business of trying to regain the confidence of international investors and forcibly breaking the link between domestic interest rates and the exchange rate. The policy freedom Asia needs to rebuild its economies would clearly come at a price, but as the slump gets ever deeper, that price is starting to look more and more worth paying.'[6]

What Krugman was expressing was the dilemma of the so-called 'impossible trinity' of macroeconomics.[7] Of three free-market ('open macro-economic') objectives – a fixed exchange rate pegged to a strong currency, potentially through a Currency Board,[8] full capital mobility and monetary policy independence – only two, i.e. any combination of pairs, can ever be sustained. Amongst East Asian countries, the conditions of free capital mobility meant that when the crisis began to unfold, either or both monetary policy independence, especially relatively low interest rates, and currency values were sacrificed.

Krugman argued that in order to restore economic growth to a region suffering its worst depression in living memory, domestic interest rates would have to come down. To gain the 'policy freedom' to recover, imposing exchange controls would be necessary. Without exchange controls, wrote Krugman, 'the region's economic policy has become hostage to skittish investors ... "Plan B" is a solution so unfashionable, so stigmatised, that hardly anyone has dared to suggest it. The unsayable words are exchange controls.' As practised throughout modern economic history by many countries, Krugman went on, their implementation assured both currency-price certainty and affordable interest rates:

> Exporters were required to sell their foreign-currency earnings to the government at a fixed exchange rate; that currency would in turn be sold at the same rate for approved payments to foreigners, basically for imports and debt service. Whilst some countries tried to make other foreign-exchange transactions illegal, other countries allowed a parallel market. Either way, once the system was in place, a country didn't have to worry that cutting interest rates would cause the currency to plunge. Maybe the parallel exchange rate would sink, but that wouldn't affect the prices of imports or the balance sheets of companies and banks.[9]

Hence the relevance of Keynes' remark, cited earlier, that 'the whole management of the domestic economy depends upon being free to have the appropriate interest rate without reference to the rates prevailing in the rest of the world'. Unfortunately, as I will discuss below, South Africa has suffered a distinct loss of macroeconomic managerial control because of the need to maintain an emerging-markets premium on interest rates, and even with such a premium and dramatic increases in already unprecedented real interest rates from time to time so as to attract foreign finance, speculators regularly make bear raids on the rand. Preventing this kind of loss of macroeconomic control was one reason behind Malaysia's imposition of direct exchange controls in September 1998, but as I will discuss next, other characteristics – especially corruption and 'cronyism' – also provide lessons for South Africa.

Malaysia's ambiguous capital controls
On 1 September 1998, Malaysian prime minister Mahathir bin Mohamad applied strong restrictions to the trading of the Malaysian currency, the ringgit. The measures followed a decline in GDP growth in 1997 of 7.7% to a depressionary –6.7% in 1998, and a 77% crash of the stock market from its peak in February 1997 through August 1998. The controls imposed in September 1998 included the following components:[10]

- *Measures to reduce and eliminate international trade in the ringgit*, by bringing back to the country ringgit-denominated financial assets such as cash and savings deposits through the non-recognition or non-acceptance of such assets in the country after a one-month deadline. (Permission was, however, given under certain conditions.)

- *The official fixing of the ringgit at 3.80 to the US dollar*, thus removing or greatly reducing the role of market forces in determining the day-to-day level of the local currency (the ringgit's value in relation to currencies other than the dollar would still fluctuate according to their own rates against the dollar). This measure largely removed uncertainties regarding the future level of the ringgit.

- *Measures relating to the local stock market*, including the closure of secondary markets so that trade could be done only through the Kuala Lumpur Stock Exchange (this was to prevent speculation or manipulation from outside the country); and the measure that non-residents purchasing local shares had to retain the shares or the proceeds from sale for a year from the purchase date (this was to reduce foreign speculative short-term trade in local shares).

- *Several other foreign exchange restrictions related to trade, investment, domestic credit and travel/education.*[11]

- *Continuing convertibility to foreign currencies for purposes of trade, e.g. export receipts and import payments, inward foreign direct investment and repatriation of profit by non-residents.*

Even before the controls in September 1998, Malaysia had wisely prohibited its local firms from borrowing abroad unless they could demonstrate that they could earn sufficient foreign exchange to service the foreign loans. This provided partial insulation, and avoided the buildup of large foreign liabilities or hidden state subsidies through mechanisms such as a central bank forward cover book. (A similar provision in relation to government development-related debt exists in Chapter 6 of the South African Reconstruction and Development Programme. It was endorsed by *Business Day* and *Finance Week* in 1994, but was not implemented in practice.)

Notwithstanding initial hostility from the IMF and speculative financial funds, Mahathir's capital controls were widely praised,[12] at least for having accomplished a more effective stabilisation of Malaysia's economy than witnessed elsewhere in the region. As the *Asian Wall Street Journal* commented, 'the failure of IMF orthodoxy to arrest the contagion sweeping through Asia has made ideas like capital controls intellectually respectable again. Policy makers can't help but notice that China and Taiwan both have capital controls and neither has succumbed to the region's contagion.'[13]

The UNCTAD *1998 Trade and Development Report* (which was drafted in July but published in September 1998) described capital controls as 'an indispensable part of [a country's] armoury of measures for the purpose of protection against international financial instability'. In mid-1999, Joseph Stiglitz pointed out in a World Bank report that it was evident Malaysia's restrictions had not harmed growth or investment prospects: 'There was no adverse effect on direct foreign investment ... there may even have been a slight upsurge at some point.'[14] When introducing the *World Development Report* for 1999 in September of that year, Stiglitz added, 'There has been a fundamental change in mindset on the issue of short-term capital flows and these kind of interventions – a change in the mindset that began two years ago … in the context of Malaysia and the quick recovery in Malaysia, the fact that the adverse effects that were predicted – some might say that some people wished upon Malaysia – did not occur is also an important lesson.'[15]

But to fully understand the background to and application of the controls requires a nuanced view. During the mid- and late 1980s, Malaysian officials believed they could break the impossible trinity. The Mahathir regime liberalised Malaysian financial markets and pegged the ringgit to the US dollar. With currency inflows increasing, the central bank began engaging in foreign currency speculation, until $8 billion in national assets were lost during the crash of the British pound in September 1992. The system deteriorated further from 1995, when the dollar rose in value against the yen, rendering Malaysian exports less competitive. The full brunt of the crisis hit in 1998, when the debt of many corporations could not be serviced. Non-performing bank loans soared, but in crucial cases such as the Renong conglomerate and the Bank Bumiputera, both closely linked to the ruling party, clear government favouritism allowed enterprises to continue operating which elsewhere in the region would have been shut down under IMF pressure.

In short, insists Jomo, KS, a University of Malaya economist, 'For the Malaysian authorities, capital controls have been part of a package focussed on saving their friends, usually at the public expense.'[16] Likewise, as I will discuss below, South Africa witnessed a great deal of cronyism and outright corruption during the 1985–95 period of dual currency controls. A lesson is that exchange controls without corruption controls will not resolve the underlying economic development challenge of achieving growth and equity.[17]

Therefore, although it is clear that capital controls did no damage per se, the more important questions are, according to Jomo:

Will capital controls be used in the interests of workers, consumers or the national public interest? Or are they mainly being used to save the politically well connected? It is also important to know whether controls are meant to avert crisis or to assist recovery. In its *1998 Trade and Development Report*, the United Nations Conference on Trade and Development recommended capital controls as means to *avoid financial crises*. Almost as if endorsing the Malaysian measures, MIT Professor Paul Krugman recommended such measures in early September 1998 to create a window of opportunity to *facilitate economic recovery* – which is another purpose, though the considerations are not altogether different.[18]

The ability of some East Asian countries – notably China and Taiwan – to avoid the recent crisis is worth considering, as are measures adopted by Chile to slow movement of hot money. But so too is the experience from neighbouring pre-independence Zimbabwe (i.e. during the Rhodesian era), in which exchange controls facilitated a spectacular recovery from an economic crisis in the early 1960s. I will consider these examples in turn.

Exchange controls to avoid financial crisis

The case of Malaysia suggests that certain technical interventions to lock in capital are feasible and have had the desired effect. But there are a variety of other measures that may also prove worth South African consideration.[19] For example, responding to excessive financial inflows during the 1960s, Germany, the Netherlands and Switzerland imposed limits on the purchase by non-residents of local debt securities and on their bank deposits. Most countries maintained exchange controls during the 1970s, and as late as 1990, 35 countries still had controls.

More recently, Chile attracted excessive capital inflows and responded during the early 1990s with reserve requirements of 30% for a one-year period, which represented both an interest-free source of funds for the government and a penalty tax in the event of early departure; Chile hence coined the phrase 'speed bump' as applied to inflows of hot money. But notwithstanding the speed bump, excessive short-term capital flowed in during 1995–6. Robert Blecker, analyst at the Economic Policy Institute, concluded: 'Small countries like Chile may find it simply impossible to control the huge tides of funds that may wash onto their shores or back out to sea. The Chilean experience thus points out the need to consider other, tougher restrictions on capital flows and foreign exchange ... Speed bumps are *part* of the solution.'[20] (In 1998, Chile revoked its controls on capital inflows, as a result of excessive financial liberalisation that resulted in its domestic institutions placing large investments in the financial markets of neighbouring countries in search of higher returns, hence forcing the now-vulnerable Chilean authorities to attempt to attract greater inflows.)

Brazil adopted a similar tax-based strategy against foreign capital in 1994, in the form of levies on Brazilian-based foreign-currency bonds issued abroad, on non-resident investment in the stock market, and on non-resident purchases of domestic fixed-income investments. Regrettably, once liberalised, Brazil's financial markets became particularly vulnerable to foreign speculation, and its enormous $75 billion foreign reserve pool came under severe attack in 1998–9. A year later, the Czech Republic imposed a tax of 0.25% on foreign exchange transactions with banks, and limited the ability of its banks and companies to borrow from foreign sources.

A variety of other exchange and capital controls exist in China, Hong Kong, Taiwan and India, which were remarkably effective in preventing contagion of the East Asian crisis. For example, fears that China would follow other countries in devaluing its currency, hence raising the spectre of massive overtrading and ultimate deflation, only receded because of China's strong currency controls. And Hong Kong and Taiwan took particularly active measures against speculators in September 1998, according to Malaysian economist Martin Khor:

> Hong Kong authorities reportedly spent over US$14 billion to buy shares in the local stock market to prop up the Hang Seng index in an attempt to defeat speculators that had placed heavy bets on a fall in the index. It also introduced measures to curb the short selling of Hong Kong shares. The new rules are aimed against speculators who have been short-selling shares whilst at the same time speculating that the currency will drop. Firstly the stock exchange reinstated a rule that shares in a company can be sold short only when they are rising. Secondly, the exchange also announced it had temporarily banned short sales on the shares of three of Hong Kong's biggest companies, HSBC Holdings, HK Telecommunications and China Telecom (Hong Kong). Thirdly, the Hong Kong Securities Clearing Co. increased regulations on settlement of stock trades, giving brokers two days after a deal is executed to deliver the shares. Previously more time was allowed. According to the *Asian Wall Street Journal*, this change of rules will hurt speculators who had entered contracts to sell shares short without even having those shares on hand. There have been protests from dealers, investors, analysts, and commentators about how the series of interventions by the Hong Kong authorities would cause tremendous damage to Hong Kong's free market reputation. The authorities have, however, countered that manipulation of the financial markets itself has distorted the market and has to be curbed ...
>
> Also in September, Taiwan authorities took measures to prevent illegal trading of funds managed by George Soros, which have been blamed for causing the local stock market to fall. A task force was formed to investigate sales and trading by Soros-managed hedge funds via proxy accounts in Taiwanese markets. Although local sales by Soros' funds are banned, at least six local securities firms were selling those funds on proxy accounts, according to officials. The Securities and Futures Commission announced that securities firms would have their licenses revoked and dealers could face two years jail for selling the unauthorised funds.[21]

UNCTAD's *1998 Report on Trade and Development* endorsed a variety of similar capital inflow restrictions: licensing; ceilings on foreign equity participation in local firms; official permission for international equity issues; differential regulations applying to local and foreign firms regarding establishment and permissible operations and various kinds of two-tier markets; a special reserve requirement for liabilities to non-residents;

forbidding banks to pay interest on deposits of non-residents or even requiring a commission on such deposits; taxing foreign borrowing to eliminate the margin between local and foreign interest rates; and requiring firms to deposit cash at the central bank amounting to a proportion of their external borrowing.

But just as important are controls on capital outflows, which can include limits on outward transactions for direct and portfolio equity investment by residents as well as foreigners. Technically, such controls amount to specifying when repatriation is allowed, and phasing the outflow according to a country's hard-currency requirements. Restrictions can be placed on resident ownership of foreign financial assets, such as bank accounts and stock-market shares. Dual currency systems, such as the finrand, can make foreign investment by residents more expensive by compelling expatriation through a second-tier currency. A central bank and finance ministry can restrict currency convertibility.

In addition to Malaysia, countries that have successfully adopted controls on outward flows include Colombia, India, Malaysia, Sri Lanka, Taiwan, Thailand and Zimbabwe. But in many cases, these amounted to crisis prevention. What must still be considered is the use of exchange and capital controls as a means of contributing to economic growth.

Exchange controls to generate economic growth

A final example of the use of exchange and capital controls not merely as a response to conditions of financial volatility or as a disincentive to speculators, but as a strategy for insulating an economy so as to achieve inward-oriented capital accumulation comes from Zimbabwe during the Rhodesian settler-colonial period prior to independence in 1976, i.e. the period of the Unilateral Declaration of Independence (UDI). UDI was declared by Ian Smith in November 1965, and, for the purposes of our argument, represented more than just a political rebellion against British decolonisation policy by a small (200 000-strong) white community, fearful of democracy and anxious to maintain a hold over privileges defined by race. Such a lesson would be irrelevant for contemporary South Africa.

But UDI also represented an attempt by central-bank and finance-ministry personnel to deal with capital outflow in the context of sustained economic stagnation. The local economy had slumped from the beginning of the early 1960s, partly due to overinvestment and partly to uncertainty associated with the demise of the Central African Federation after Zambia and Malawi won their independence. Although Rhodesian capital controls were already fairly tight, they had to be strengthened in 1961 and 1963 to prevent the transfer of resident funds through the London-headquartered banks. But it was only in November 1965 that full exchange and capital controls were applied (including prohibitions on profit repatriations and blocks on non-resident funds deposited in Rhodesia), along with a standstill on repayment of Rhodesian foreign debt to Britain, the World Bank and other creditors. These actions generated what economist Ann Seidman has termed a 'hothouse effect', leading to dramatic economic restructuring and growth for nearly a decade.[22]

Disaggregating the causes of Rhodesia's dramatic growth, which averaged 9.5% from 1966 to 1974, Roger Riddell, former chief economist of the Confederation of Zimbabwe Industries, concluded that 61% of the manufacturing sector's UDI expansion could be attributed to domestic demand (as against 30% to sanctions-related import-substitution, and 9% to export growth).[23] As John Handford confirmed, 'The directors of the national economy were already using their main weapon: bottling up capital by severe exchange control restrictions.'[24] The capital was then directed into areas of the economy where linkages could still be fruitfully developed, leading to Rhodesia's increasing self-sufficiency. This virtuous cycle eventually ran out, particularly when overinvestment in heavy industry combined with unique 1970s factors like the liberation war, imported inflation, oil shortages, etc. But until that time, Duncan Clarke concluded in an UNCTAD study:

> The controls worked, especially when combined with buoyant growth conditions in the economy associated to high net white immigration (and rising mortgage demand), rapid industrial development through diversification (and demand for hire purchase and leasing facilities), and expanded primary sector output (with demands for short and medium-term financing). All these developments widened the base of the institutions, led to diversification within them, increased inter-sectoral linkages and flows, and strengthened the financial sector's structure.[25]

The South African financial system in the early 21st century also requires diversification and developmental linkages so as to generate more balanced economic growth, and to finally transcend skews in resources and international vulnerabilities associated with two centuries of uneven development, amplified by the domestic financial system.

3. A brief history of South Africa's domestic finance and uneven development
The economic history of South Africa is strewn with extraordinary instances that demonstrate the need to lock financial capital down. Enormous destruction occurred in this country because of the failure of successive colonial and apartheid regimes to regulate flows of finance in the broader public interest. Periodically, patterns of convergence involved excessive debt and financial speculation, geopolitical machinations and crises of overaccumulation of capital (see Chapter one for an explanation of

these). A synthetic, qualitative sketch of this history provides enough evidence to suggest that crucial mistakes are being made as a result of the relatively orthodox approach to finance and development upon which the South African government embarked during the initial post-apartheid era.

Finance, development and space

Extending formal monetary relations through provision of organised credit to nascent (or malfunctioning) markets is a central tenet of the orthodox, modernisation strategy of development. If this strategy works – and there is much evidence to question the efficacy (as well as the distributional effects) of finance as the motor force behind economic activity[26] – it has the effect of generating an expansion of the spatial economy *through time*. This has, for many years, been observed as the 'annihilation of space by time', in order to reflect the temporal (time-related) characteristic of credit. From the bill of exchange (the primary breakthrough in trade centuries ago) to contemporary innovations in financial securitisation, finance allows spending to take place today but to be paid for tomorrow, the effect of which can be devastating when boom-bust cycles reach the point of downturn.

This can be documented by examining the great bursts of financial and economic transformation that occurred during a dozen distinct periods in South Africa's history:
- the early crises of the 1810s–60s;
- the turbulent emergence of the financial-mining nexus during the 1870s–80s;
- the massive centralisation of financial-mining capital during the 1880s;
- the relation between financial speculation and politics during the 1890s–1900s;
- the reassertion of local control during the 1910s;
- the financial restructuring of local economic geography during the 1910s–20s;
- international financial collapse during the 1930s;
- the gold-based recovery of the 1930s–40s;
- the rise of Afrikaner finance during the 1930s–50s;
- the financing of post-war development; and
- the contemporary rise of finance.

Such a breakdown into periods may be most useful in linking 'uneven development' – i.e. the polarisation of resource distribution and investment across sectors, spaces and levels (local, regional and global) – to financial processes that seem to recur in patterns closely related to cycles of capital accumulation. The central issue in uneven development is the differentiated return on investment associated with the creation and/or destruction of built environments (and the social structures that accompany them), particularly given the fact that different kinds of investors have different time horizons.[27]

With the exception of the work of Alan Mabin,[28] previous studies of South Africa's uneven geographical development have not typically given much emphasis to switches in funding flows between production and finance.[29] Therefore, according to Mabin, 'the debate on uneven development has assumed such generalised form' in South Africa in part because it has avoided 'the more intricate and difficult questions posed by the rise of new foci of investment and power'.[30] Nor have economic studies helped matters, for even if banking and monetary matters are well researched and even if the historico-geographical facets of finance have been acknowledged by economists, nevertheless space as the receptacle of financial capital's ebb and flow has not been systematically documented or theorised.[31]

All of this is not to argue that financial capital is *always* the driving force behind either systematic political-economic inequalities or geographical expansion and contraction; but it is to note that at particular moments the rise of finance becomes a dominant factor in the space-economy of investment, and that this amplifies unevenness.

Early financial crises, 1810s–60s

Formal, government-run banking in the Cape Colony began during the 1790s, 140 years after the first white settlers arrived. Before long this set in motion an important shift in the local circuit of capital, i.e. from an economy structured along purely commercial and agricultural lines to one dangerously geared, at times, to the logic of finance. For example, during the 1810s, following the British occupation of the Cape as a spoil of the Napoleonic Wars and concomitant with a similar process under way in Britain, the colonial government printed excessive amounts of money. Succumbing to international financial power in this manner quickly led to currency devaluation and vicious inflation, which severely damaged local and international trade.[32]

Ironically, such imported financial negligence created enough uncertainty in local markets to limit the subsequent penetration of foreign merchant and financial capital, and so permitted the growth of some small, indigenous Cape banks, especially during the 1830s and 1840s. But in their ascendance, they in turn imitated the colonial government's lax monetary style, printing money freely against risky investments. In his study of South African business cycles, economic historian C. G. W. Schumann concludes that the most spectacular early boom and collapse in the Cape – the 1854 'copper-mining mania' (which was also an early indication of the power of finance to affect the region's spatial evolution, in this case the previously undeveloped Karoo of the western Cape) – was:

evidently of a purely financial and speculative character. It reminds us strongly of the speculative manias during the 18th century in Europe and England, especially the South Sea Bubble of 1720. They might with some justification be called the growing diseases of a rising Capitalism, for since the Company form and the 'Effektenkapitalismus' (stock-market capitalism), in its initial stages, gave rise to the many speculative excesses, this short but intense speculative mania at the Cape points to the rise of a more modern capitalistic and credit economy in the older parts of the Colony.[33]

During the 1860s, far more mature financial capital from London – especially the Standard Bank of British South Africa, Ltd. whose initial capitalisation was seven times that of the single largest locally funded bank – entered the Cape Colony and was overwhelming in its application of similar principles. Following the 'intense boom in banking expansion' of the 1860s, as Schumann describes it, there came the 'inevitable reaction'. Another severe banking crash started in Port Elizabeth in 1865, borne of 'overintensified speculation which had reached breaking point'. In turn, this kicked off one of the century's worst depressions.[34]

Crises in mining and finance, 1870s–80s

Diamonds were found at Kimberley two years later, and so flows of capital in the Cape colony gradually switched circuits again, moving from agriculture into mining. Yet prosperity largely depended on expanding the geography of regional trade, reflecting the power and vision of finance, according to Mabin: 'The banks, and particularly the imperial banks, had been instrumental in creating the urban system by 1880.'[35] Again the spatial and sectoral switch in accumulation was a function of financial capital's capacity to respond to – and in turn to influence – the market, and of its concurrence with that era's geopolitics, the deepening of colonialism.

With the diamond finds, Britain rediscovered South Africa, and carried out both the full-fledged subjugation of African kingdoms during the 1870s and the invasion of the Afrikaner Transvaal Republic in 1877. Foreign investor confidence, spurred by Rothschilds in particular, was high at the time, thanks largely to the millions of pounds the British pumped into the local economy to ensure victory in the various wars. The Transvaal fighting can itself be traced, in part, to a financial foreclosure, for the powerful Cape Commercial Bank was facing problems in getting Transvaal government loans repaid. Once the British had annexed the province, Standard immediately moved in to set up branches. The ill-will this created catalysed the Afrikaner nationalist movement that subsequently fought the Anglo-Boer War so vigorously.[36]

However, geographic expansion pushed by and flowing from the power of finance was incapable of solving the underlying problems in the productive sector, i.e. the lack of sustainable, balanced routes for accumulation. Actions of the London-based banks exacerbated the structural dilemma. As Schumann concludes about speculation in diamond mining shares:

> Unsound banking practices, over and above the natural credit expansion inherent in an elastic monetary system, had greatly contributed to the over-intensity of the boom, while the rapid curtailment of credit after 1881 must be considered as the main cause of the extreme severity of the depression. There can be little doubt that the banks had acted indiscreetly. They were severely criticised at the time, and the criticism was largely justified. The undesirability of having bank directors overseas, who did not know local conditions well enough and who were apt to apply the banking principles of an established industrialised country, especially during the period of depression, to a young developing country ... became very clear during this time.[37]

Schumann here identifies what seems to be a universal dynamic, one which characterises the combined power and vulnerability of finance equally well a full century later (witness the Third World debt crisis, which he could easily be describing). Yet even if the conditions for crisis were deep-rooted, the 1881 crash could be blamed (as J. A. Henry, Standard's biographer did) on an individual, the general manager of Standard at the time (a frugal Scottish immigrant), who 'decided that the time had come to call a halt' to the diamond share speculation:

> It cannot have escaped him that in doing so he would expose his bank, and South African banks in general, to an intense degree of embittered opprobrium, corresponding to the inflated hopes of the bubble which he was about to prick. Fortunately he was a brave man. What Robert Stewart could not have foreseen without an unhuman degree of second sight was that his pricking of the bubble would coincide with the onset of an almost un-exampled depression in other fields of the South African economy.[38]

Such interference was not taken lightly by its victims, especially innocent farmers driven to ruin. In what was to become a repeating pattern, the Afrikaner Bond gained political mileage from bank-bashing, claiming in the early 1880s that the imperial bankers were 'draining the country'. In an early call to ethnic nationalism, the Afrikaner Bond went so far as to start its own banks in Stellenbosch and Hopetown. Standard, labelled a 'gigantic devil fish' by leading Afrikaners, responded to the populist anger by officially dropping 'British' from its name in 1883.[39]

The centralisation of financial-mining capital, 1880s
Notwithstanding Standard's own self-inflicted troubles during the periodic banking crashes, the rise of finance at key moments of capital accumulation would reoccur intermittently in the future. Initially this was somewhat

more muted, as circuits of capital began to include manufactured commodities – not just mining, which was subject to speculation, and agriculture, which faced uneven development of markets and weather-related interruptions. During the 1880s, as gold began to play a role in the economy, capitalism as an economic system was still underdeveloped and dependent. The articulation of capitalist wage relations with pre-capitalist traditions, through racial oppression, was only just becoming a challenge, along with more traditional forms of labour control. Industrialisation was limited to the manufacture of primitive mining equipment and a few rudimentary goods.

But from the start, mining companies displayed the classic organisational tendencies of capitalism, i.e. increased concentration and centralisation of capital, under the direction of Rhodes and Barnato. Again, the accumulation process was inordinately influenced by the banks, which, notes Mabin, 'facilitated both the enrichment of the magnates and their purchase of still more shares. The involvement of bankers in attempts to merge companies at Kimberley in the mid-1880s was largely due to their desire to recover losses incurred through speculation in poorer companies.'[40] In the process, the financiers transferred a great deal of the region's wealth from investors in the coastal areas to the emerging diamond magnates, and hence subsequently to the mining houses that would so profoundly shape the development of the entire sub-continent. This was accompanied by concentration of the financial sector itself, as the big imperial banks shook out smaller competitors.

However, as the influx of overseas capital and the concentration of the banking system proceeded, the supply of credit ballooned and then burst again in 1889. Again the crash followed intense financial speculation, and again the catalyst for speculation was the discovery of minerals – this time gold – and the excessive issue of mining company shares (some fraudulent). Bank branch officers on the Rand were hopelessly out of touch with their head offices, according to accounts of the time, and overfed the stock market beyond what company balance sheets could bear. The subsequent collapse of the productive economy in 1890 was heightened by the simultaneous depression in England arising from another financial crash, the Barings crisis. The downturn allowed further centralisation of capital, through the support given by the banks to the emerging corporate form known as mining-finance houses.

During the late 19th century, therefore, as a result of the weakness of the agricultural elite and the lack of industrialists, widespread financial catastrophe often resulted in an even more powerful centralisation of capital, which in turn prepared the ground for an even deeper round of speculation and economic manipulation. Even more telling, suggests Schumann, 'The crises of 1881 and 1889–90 marked the culmination points of business cycles in a more modern sense. They had become organic in character and had affected the whole of the South African economic system.'[41]

South Africa was not alone in facing these turbulent, finance-driven economic processes. It was a period, Phimister contends, of the political realignment of an entire continent, Africa, emanating from 'capitalism's uneven development during the last third of the nineteenth century, particularly the City of London's crucial role in mediating the development of a world economic system'.[42] As Britain faced industrial decline during the 1870s in both absolute and relative terms, manufacturers unable to compete in European markets joined ascendant London financial and commercial interests in promoting the philosophy of Free Trade (in contrast to the protectionism of other Europeans and the United States). Cain and Hopkins report that as London financial power increased and as the prospects for domestic tariff-protection waned, 'industrial interests in Britain shifted, around 1880, into decisive support for the acquisition of new markets in Asia and Africa'.[43] Indeed, it is here, and in a parallel crisis of French merchant capital in West Africa, that Phimister locates the well-spring of the 'Scramble for Africa', which played such an important role in the continent's subsequent development.

Financial speculation and politics, 1890s–1900s

As deep-level mining of gold began on the Reef, the most speculative tendencies of the ascendant financial and mining circuits were heightened. By 1895, the five largest networks of banks included 182 branches (Standard, 81; Bank of Africa, 29; National Bank of the SA Republic, 27; African Banking Corporation, 19; National Bank of the Orange Free State, 14; and Natal Bank, 12).[44] At this point, speculation again reached fever-pitch, according to Henry:

> The market value of South African shares quoted on the London Stock Exchange, which had stood at less than £20 million at the beginning of 1894, had risen to over £55 million by the end of that year. The movement continued without interruption for nine months more, so that the figure of £55 million was itself trebled ... Nor was speculation entirely confined to shares. Land and property in Johannesburg were also changing hands at fantastic prices and the whole town was in a fever of excitement.

With English-Afrikaner tensions heavy in the air and the Jameson Raid imminent, confidence suddenly faltered:

> The crash came at the end of September, and was started by heavy selling in Paris which may have been at least partly due to politics. Increased continental interest in the mines had introduced new influences and susceptibilities, while the rift between the mining interests and the Transvaal

Government had been widening ominously. In November 1895 the President of the Chamber of Mines publicly declared that the industry and the Uitlanders could not for ever remain politically powerless in a country which they had made rich. Attributing the crisis mainly to the 'scarcity' of native labour, which was limiting output and restricting profits, the companies suspected the Kruger Government of deliberately checking development, for fear that the industry was becoming too formidable for such a small country to assimilate easily.[45]

The key components of South Africa's historical geographical development – the power of mining houses, limits to the availability of super-exploitable labour, and tensions between imperial capital and Afrikaner nationalism – are all present here, and were reflected in the machinations of financial markets. While the 1895 crash of speculative mining investments was not as serious as others preceding it, violent rebellions against gold prospecting in Zimbabwe also made investors more nervous.[46] In South Africa, the impact of financial chaos was contained, partly because of the Standard Bank's ability to protect itself by channelling surpluses back to its London headquarters rather than investing them wildly in Johannesburg. So the 19th century ended with increasing evidence of the all-pervasive influence of geographic financial flows.

As the 20th century began and the Anglo-Boer War came to a close, the banks continued to shape development through an overly conservative lending policy for commerce and industry, but enthusiasm for the speculative land market. As seen from the offices of the Standard Bank in 1907, reports Henry, 'The country's superstructure of capital and credit was still too heavy for the volume of trade, and although the four colonies were beginning to work more freely together, the salutary process of reducing the number of commercial units by stress of competition would have to be carried further.'[47] Such convictions may have crucially dampened prospects for economic recovery, but the final straw was the 1907 financial crash in the US, which led to the collapse of South Africa's exports of diamonds for luxury consumption. It was only after 1910 that accumulation began again.

Local control of finance, 1910s

During the late 1910s, the geography of finance and local capital accumulation again came into profound conflict. Alongside the growing mining houses, the imperial banks were still at the centre of the economy, and smaller district banks foundered badly. Following another round of takeovers from 1910 to 1926, South Africa's banking system was reduced from seven banks to just two big London banks – Standard and Barclays – and the smaller Netherlands Bank of South Africa, with its headquarters in Amsterdam. Collusion wasn't difficult, and even before Union in 1910 the main banks were able to set artificial interest rates and banking charges to the disadvantage of savers. Lending, however, remained influenced by speculative tendencies, according to Henry:

> Certainly until 1920 a spirit of reckless competition had tended to reduce progressively the quality and security of bank advances, as well as to endanger the cash position of the banking system as a whole. Profits had in some quarters been expanded at the expense of reserves, and the provision against bad debts and contingencies was sometimes so neglected that in times of stress the position became critical far too easily. This, in a country as much exposed to natural hazards as South Africa, was to play with fire.[48]

Although technically the banks were still controlled from abroad, pressures on the international gold standard – the system which rendered local and British currency directly convertible to gold – were, by the end of World War I, weakening the power that the City of London exerted over South Africa's financial system.[49] London banks were under extreme war-time and post-war stress as a result of inflation, the devaluation of the British pound and the rise of New York as a competitor. Their South African branches were able, for the first time, to more fully turn their attention to local manufacturing, e.g. the National Bank, later to be taken over by Barclays, helped set up the state-owned National Industrial Corporation in 1919 to support manufacturers.

The banks' easy credit policies had plenty to do with the inflationary boom of 1918–20, and there was great fear of a repeat of the financial chaos of the previous century. Some of the tension also arose from nationalist concerns that England was still playing too dominant a role in the South African economy, while some revolved around the uncertain role of gold as a base for the currency. In 1918 a gap between the value of gold and the declining South African currency – which was technically still tied to gold – led to enormous gold smuggling. To halt this, gold was formally delinked from the currency in 1920. When conditions improved in 1925, South Africa, like Britain, returned to the gold standard.

Ultimately, Union of South Africa authorities decided, the only solution to the financial uncertainty was to create a local Reserve Bank to act as a guarantor for the banks and for the South African currency. In the ensuing struggle over the character of banking regulation, the Reserve Bank was essentially put under the direct ownership and control of bankers, unlike in other countries where the state owned the central bank. For London financial capital, the compromise 'was an attempt to adapt, so as to defend its own interests', Steven Gelb concludes. 'It necessarily meant a diminution of The City's earlier influence and control, to ensure that its profits, supplies and influence were not completely destroyed.'[50] Meanwhile, J. P. Morgan's

New York-based financial empire gained a toehold in South Africa through its role in the founding of Ernest Oppenheimer's Anglo American Corporation.

The weakening of London's links to South Africa opened space for local capitalists to influence financial and monetary policy. The Reserve Bank's first big challenge was a bailout of the National Bank, a victim of the financial chaos of the early 1920s. The rescue was facilitated by the Bank of England and by the conclusive rescue of the National Bank in a 1926 takeover by the Anglo-Egyptian Bank and the Colonial Bank, the result of which was the formation of Barclays Bank.[51]

Financial restructuring of economic geography, 1910s–20s

While changes in the international financial system were having a dramatic impact on the South African economy's capacity for self-reliance, similar processes were unfolding at the local level in many rural areas. They involved the indebtedness of both Afrikaner farmers and black share-croppers. As historian Timothy Keegan reports, this was a phenomenon with deep historical roots, such that 'a chain of debt leading to the whole-salers was at the basis of agrarian exchange relationships'. When formal property loans began determining land-ownership patterns, matters became serious:

> From the 1840s onward in the sheep districts, increasing land values, the penetration of the interior by mortgage and speculative capital and the wide-spread contractions of debt that these entailed, combined to render landownership a precarious status for many, particularly during commercial depressions ... As a result of the unrelenting pressures on landowners with heavy mortgage debts to meet, there was a strong resistance amongst many Boer farmers to bonding their property. The grip of mortgage capital was an irksome burden, and farmers were deeply conscious of the greatly unequal exchange relations that their own dependence on the credit of others imposed ... It was hardly surprising, given the vicissitudes of agriculture, drought, stock disease, pests and war, that wherever loan capital penetrated it could potentially reduce the landowner to a state of dependence.[52]

Bankers had been especially active in foreclosing on Afrikaner land during the early 1880s, the late 1890s and during the depression of the 1910s. Intensification of production on indebted land was one logical structural result of such pressures. Another was the strength of populist protest politics, according to Herman Giliomee: 'To an important extent Malan's more exclusivist nationalist movement which gathered momentum from 1915 built on an Afrikaner consciousness that had been forged by the material concerns of commercial farmers and the efforts of financial and legal middlemen to mobilise Afrikaner savings.'[53]

In 1912, such demands led to the formation of a state Land Bank whose operations, nevertheless, still reflected the power of bankers and large landowners (i.e. it allowed them to use state funds to liquidate land taken by foreclosure, even where speculation had pushed land values to new heights). Disaster struck when the next severe economic downturn arrived in 1920. The banks were, perhaps now by habit, easy to blame. Prime Minister Smuts castigated them for having 'granted credit too easily and then curtailed it too drastically', and after surveying the evidence, Schumann concludes, 'The indictment against the banks at the time that they became somewhat hysterical in their contraction of credit seems to be not unfounded.'[54] White farmers demanded a moratorium on loan fore-closures and a state bank to compete with the commercial banks. According to Henry: 'Government was even considering the appointment of district committees to intervene when debtors were unduly pressed, and to publicise the facts.'[55]

By 1923, South Africa had 11 times as many insolvencies as England and 34 times as many as Scotland. In 1924 the Agricultural Credits Bill promoted the introduction of rural Credit Societies, a stronger Land Bank, and a favoured position for farmers in their dealings with lenders. Nevertheless, credit again began to spin out of control, and was not limited to over-indebtedness on the farms: 'The larger centres in South Africa were overburdened with members of a trading and speculative class whose act-ivities had a disproportionate influence on prices and prospects, but contributed very little to output and production,' reported Henry about the mid-1920s. 'This was beginning to look too much like an endemic weakness in the commercial community and in the social structure of the country.'[56]

International financial collapse, 1930s

The year 1929 brought many of the tensions into sharp relief. Local bankers were extremely bullish, as their ratio of loans to deposits soared from 63% in 1926 to 85% in 1930, with half of the increase coming in 1929. Land speculation meant that 'in some districts the value attributed to farm prop-erty looked to be 50% too high', according to Henry. 'Standards had changed, and these were the days of the motor-car, bought for 30% of its cost in cash, and the rest on credit.'[57] As often happens just before a fall, overproduction of agricultural goods became rife, and the government intervened with increasingly protectionist policies. Imports of wheat, flour and sugar were discouraged, and a Marketing Board was established to support South African exports.

Speculative activity in overseas stock markets also became quite acute during the late 1920s, reflecting the global rise of overaccumulation crisis. Even prior to the 1929 crash, foreign investment in South Africa essentially dried up (although this was also related to occasional official hostility to the mines). Government borrowing brought in some new money from overseas, especially in 1930, but South African financing on the London Stock Exchange in 1929 fell to less than half that raised in 1928, and less than a quarter of the 1927 total. As one example of the strain between local and international financial forces, Standard Bank was under a great deal of pressure to export funds to its London office. The Reserve Bank intervened, imposing a levy for bank remittances and increasing the interest rate it charged local banks.[58]

The 1929 crash was initially felt mainly by the diamond merchants, since rich New Yorkers' panic liquidation of their personal assets flattened diamond prices. As the broader depression set in and the general price level of most goods fell over the next few years, agricultural products bore the brunt of the devaluation. Further state intervention was required on behalf of rural whites, especially in the form of laws supporting debtors' rights. White workers and displaced farmers made a series of proposals for rural credit co-operatives and for municipal banks in Johannesburg and Durban during the mid-1930s.

South African exports – with the exception of gold – were also affected. When exports decline, one antidote is to devalue the currency. But when a country is on the gold standard, the currency is valued according to how much gold the county has in reserve stockpiles. When such countries go deeply into debt and import more than they export, their gold stocks naturally decline in order to make payments. Most major countries had already adopted the gold standard in the last quarter of the 19th century, mainly because of pressure from commercial capitalists to have convertible currency so as to lubricate international trade. It was in this process that the national monetary systems of most industrial countries emerged or stabilised, which led Clarke to conclude that the rise of the modern nation state was actually a function of the power of international finance.[59]

The South African situation after the 1929 crash was heavily influenced by this logic. As the full force of what would be a decade-long depression came to bear upon the global economy, and as country after country fell into debt, the gold standard became an anachronism. It had been re-surrected by Britain in 1925, following a six-year lapse, in order to stimulate international trade. But during the 1930s, too many countries simply couldn't afford to back their currencies with gold, and in 1932, after Britain – still at the centre of international finance – abandoned the gold standard, 32 countries followed, with only France, Belgium, Switzerland and the Netherlands holding out until 1936.

Without a way to root the value of currencies, international trade stagnated and protectionist currency blocs developed. South Africa was part of the British colonial Sterling Area, while North and South America traded with dollars, central and south-east Europe were ruled by German finance, the Japanese yen was the East's currency, and a small gold bloc was maintained in western Europe. As the world's leading gold producer, South Africa had no technical difficulties remaining on the standard. But because the value of the South African currency remained high relative to other currencies, exports suffered. At the same time, investors were shifting enormous amounts of money out of South Africa (£20 million in 1932). By the end of 1932, the tensions were overwhelming and the country's social fabric was tearing, so mining houses led the charge to abandon the gold standard and devalue the currency.

This was one route out of the local depression, but not the only one. Another might have been a major public-works and employment programme, some components of which did indeed occur for the benefits of whites later on during the 1930s. Because popular organisations like the Industrial and Commercial Workers Union, Communist Party and African National Congress were weak following five years of intense repression, and because white workers continued to place priority on their struggle for racial supremacy, the mining houses were able to determine the path out of depression. In a vacuum of international economic leadership, they bene-fitted from the pressure brought to bear on South Africa by speculators run amok in the global economy. 'The purely speculative flight of capital made the maintenance of the gold standard temporarily difficult in South Africa', Schumann concedes, but adds: 'Theoretically as well as practically, and from a purely technical or economic point of view, the country could have remained on gold through suspension of the convertibility of notes into gold, so as to prevent an internal drain, mainly through a policy of imme-diate and drastic foreign exchange control.'[60]

Instead, the *laisser faire* route of currency devaluation was chosen. As the tie to the South African currency was broken, more and more gold could be mined without weighing down the rest of the economy. Gold now allowed the country 'the prosperity of the undertaker in a plague', thanks to residual international fears of paper financial assets.

Recovery, 1930s–40s
The first result of going off the gold standard was that vestiges of specula-tive financing again appeared from abroad, pushed away from Europe and the United States by the deepest depression in capitalist history. South Africa's banks still weren't increasing their loan portfolios, as the produc-tive economy had not begun to recover. Given fresh sources of funding and few projects, the banks restructured interest rates. For several decades before 1932, banks lent to companies at around 6% (for three-month commercial bills) while paying savers 3.5% (for six-month deposits). Bank lending was controlled less by price, i.e. the interest rate, and more by restrictive conditions. (These conditions even applied to the Oppenheimer

empire. Before the gold standard was abandoned, Anglo American was unable to raise just £50 000 from either Standard or Barclays for mining expansion.) By early 1933, the rates changed dramatically, becoming 5% for loans and 0.5% for savers. Where demand for loans existed, enormous financial profits were gained from this interest-rate spread.

Within months of going off the gold standard, gold and agricultural exports picked up again (though diamonds remained weak because of their status as a luxury good), and the rest of the economy followed. According to Schumann:

The immediate effects of the depreciation of the currency were

- a rapid change-over from an extreme scarcity of money to an almost unprecedented plentifulness, as evidenced in the increase in bankers' deposits and the fall in short-term interest rates;
- an exceptional boom in gold-mining shares and in promotion and building activity on the Rand and elsewhere;
- a proportionate increase in the export prices of farm products, and a consequent improvement in the relative position of the heavily depressed agriculture;
- an expansion of industrial production, in transport, in imports; and
- an exceptional improvement in Government revenue.[61]

Foreign interests profited, as interest and dividends paid to investors (down from £17 million in 1926 to £13 million in 1932) rose dramatically to £18 million in 1933. Yet during the subsequent 15 years, the South African economy was relatively isolated from international manufacturing trade, and so financing was increasingly directed towards the nascent local manufacturing industry. In a manner Andre Gunder Frank observed occurring elsewhere on the global economic periphery and which helped generate many of the insights of the 'dependency school', manufacturing grew in inverse relation to the strength of trade in the international economy.[62] Positively affected by Northern depression and war, South Africa spent the period from 1933 through the 1940s growing faster (8% average GDP increase per annum), more evenly across sectors, and with larger relative wage increases for blacks (from 11% to 17% of the total wage bill) than at any other time in the 20th century.[63] (Later, as South Africa reintegrated into the world economy, racial biases were amplified, e.g. the black wage share stagnated, reaching just 21% by 1970.)

In general, at particular moments of turbulence in world economic history, gold plays a crucial role as the ultimate store of value. South Africa was able to take advantage of this role, but in this instance did so by following the particular path chosen by the mining houses. This was a less direct way of kick-starting post-depression growth than through state intervention, but prevailed due to the balance of forces at the time (1933), during the waning months of what was nominally a popular ruling alliance of white workers and farmers.

Afrikaner finance, 1930s–50s

Even though the mid-1930s through 1940s were years of growing prosperity, a sore point remained, i.e. age-old conflicts between English-speaking financial elites and Afrikaner farmers. During the 1940s, financiers continued to resist the farmers' state subsidies and took advantage of their overproduction and land-speculation problems. In 1944, when the Bretton Woods agreement regulating international finance through a semi-gold standard was announced, the mining houses and English-speaking businesses benefitted. The Johannesburg stock-market boom of 1946 doubled the number of companies listed, but was far more beneficial to English-speakers than Afrikaners.

Once in power in 1948, the National Party focused not only on institutionalising existing racial practices through apartheid, but also on overcoming ethnic imbalances in the financial system. Ground had been prepared a decade earlier. According to Dan O'Meara, through a 'process of the centralisation and segmentation of latent money-capital generated in agriculture, a new class of Afrikaner financial industrial and commercial capitalists would be brought into existence ... M. S. Louw was indeed correct when he declared to the second Ekonomiese Volkskongres that the greatest achievement of "the Afrikaner" as an entrepreneur during the 1940s was as the "founder and controller of credit institutions"'.

Still, 'only slightly more than 20% of potential Afrikaner capital had been placed in Afrikaner financial institutions', so after 1948, 'a number of government and NP-controlled authority accounts were switched to Afrikaner institutions'.[64] O'Meara documents the diversification of financial flows into commerce and industry through Cape-based Sanlam and Rembrandt, just as the apartheid state was established: 'This weaning of Afrikaner financial capital from its dependence on accumulation in agriculture, and its increasing cooperation after Sharpeville with non-Afrikaner finance capital, led to important shifts and struggles in nationalist politics ... The *verligte* phenomenon was a response to the emergence of a class of aggressive, self-confident Afrikaner capitalists whose interests now went beyond those of the narrow class alliance out of which they had emerged.'

There was, however, a natural backlash: 'The *verkramptes* attempted to use the traditional organisation of the Afrikaner petty bourgeoisie, the Bond, against what they labelled the "finance power of the South". A strong move was mounted to portray the factional struggle as a simple conflict between the Bond as the guardian and soul of Afrikaner values on one hand, and the *nouveau riche* "money capitalists" of the south on the other hand.'[65]

The conflict played itself out in various ways, but ultimately led to such severe splits in Afrikanerdom during the 1970s and 1980s that ideological commitments to apartheid could be broken.

Financing post-war development, 1950s–60s

The two decades after World War II witnessed the intensification of production, i.e. higher capital intensity in mining, agriculture and the production of middle-class consumer goods.[66] Access to international capital, organised by the local mining houses and stock market immediately after the war, was checked only briefly by Afrikaner nationalist threats of nationalisation. There were a variety of new financial innovations, including accommodation of corporate investment needs by emerging money markets and of housing needs via building society expansion.

Duncan Innes argues that creative financing arrangements in the years following World War II reflected a broader process of concentration and monopoly control unfolding at the international level: 'By adapting and reorganising their methods of fund-raising to meet the requirements of the new system the [South African mining-based] groups participated directly in the process of restructuring the financial relations of international monopoly capitalism.'[67] A quarter of mining-industry funds were raised from mining trust funds in the US and Switzerland, while 7% came from new local financing sources such as the government's National Finance Corporation, founded in 1949 to gather and deploy corporate savings. The brunt of the money was sourced from British financial institutions, mainly banks, insurance companies, pension funds, investment and trust units, and various other institutional investors. Such funding capacity and reach reflected the rise of the British economy to commanding heights, which began during the 1920s, and, in spite of the global financial crisis of the early 1930s, culminated in its holdings of more than half of the stock-exchange shares by the mid-1950s.

The financial links forged during the 1950s drew South African capitalism into the global economy. In turn, this led to such financial dependence that by the 1970s the international anti-apartheid movement discovered that this represented the country's Achilles heel, and hence began to focus sanctions pressure on international banks.

Substantially similar processes of financial expansion were under way within the English-speaking sectors of the South African economy during the 1940s and 1950s, paralleling the Afrikaner route to broader economic control through finance. Consumer-credit markets blossomed, and urban areas sprawled thanks to new institutional sources of finance. Construction grew by a factor of more than six between 1943 and 1952, twice the growth rate of industry. As a result, the apartheid state found major private sector allies, including banks and building societies, for the construction of

Soweto, Guguletu, Kwa-Mashu and many other townships whose match-box houses multiplied during the 1950s. Peter Wilkinson reports: 'Johannesburg property speculators, estate agents, building societies and construction firms had mobilised and were lobbying for a policy of home ownership and massive state financed building programmes.'[68] That they were unsuccessful on the home-ownership front for a period of some three decades – falling victim to the larger apartheid vision of blacks as temporary sojourners – did not ultimately prevent a new generation of creative financiers from returning to the issue with renewed vigour during the 1980s.[69]

As industry became more capital-intensive and internationally oriented during the 1950s, a much more sophisticated financial system was required. The channelling of funds from mining companies to manufacturers was achieved in large part through the expansion of mining houses into industry. But it also occurred through the development of money markets, which centralised finance and then disbursed it to where it could realise the highest rate of return. These markets were serviced by brand new financial institutions, which were largely set up by the big mining houses. According to Innes: '[this] was the clearest form yet of the merging together of bank capital and productive capital – that is, of the emergence of the phase of finance capital. It was thus during the late 1950s that South African capitalism *as a whole* – and not just specific sectors of the economy – displayed the first clear signs of having entered the monopoly phase of its evolution.'[70]

Regulation of the national financial structure would also need to adapt to keep pace with developments. A banking law passed in 1964 allowed banks and building societies greater depth and reach. Funds available to the banking sector soared, and financing on the Johannesburg Stock Exchange was boosted dramatically until a crash in 1969, following a huge increase in inventories in the consumer-goods sectors, the first signs of overaccumulation of capital.

Geography and financial ascendance, 1970s–90s[71]
From the 1960s, high levels of capital-intensive investment led to chronic overproduction, relative to the size of the local market. The results were a leveling off of new fixed-capital investment by private corporations, both local and TNC, from 1973; a substantial decline in the economy's growth rate from late 1974; a steady drop in manufacturing employment from 1975; and a substantial fall in private-sector investment in plant and equipment from 1976. Liquid capital flowed out from productive sectors and into the money and capital markets. Fuelled by the dramatic rise in the international price of gold once the US ended its Bretton Woods-era linkage to the dollar, an inordinate amount of capital was subsequently attracted into geographical expansion over the subsequent decade.

Vehicles included the internationalisation of the mining finance houses and the enormous boom in construction. There was unprecedented parastatal expansion (iron and steel, electricity, oil-from-coal, transport); outward-oriented investments such as Richards Bay, Sishen-Saldanha and the unprecedented upgrade of SA Airways; a renewed commitment to world-class transport more generally; improvements to infrastructure for business and residential development; and the extending of urban sprawl. From 1970 to 1977, state spending in transport, storage and communications increased by 65% each year in real terms beyond similar investments during the 1960s; and during the same period new infrastructure for electricity grids and water lines attracted 28% more funds each year than during the 1960s.

The major projects also involved a great deal of foreign borrowing: nearly a quarter of government parastatal investment from 1972 to 1978 was funded through international capital markets. After the Soweto uprising in 1976, Pretoria gained access to several International Monetary Fund loans amounting to nearly $2 billion (until borrowing rights were cut in 1983). However, given the durability of the overaccumulation problem and the fact that the 1979–81 gold boom had to run its course, foreign banks finally lost confidence in apartheid and agreed to cut credit lines for all but short-term trade finance.

Unable to roll over the vast loans contracted by private-sector borrowers, especially the large banks, Pretoria was ultimately forced to call a 'debt standstill' in 1985 and refused to make repayments on more than $13 billion in foreign debt, out of a total of $20 billion then outstanding. This came at a moment when the country's townships were in flames and its factories besieged by militant workers. Relations between Pretoria and international finance were, as a result, hotly contested by the liberation movement, reflecting not only the increased power wielded by international financiers over South Africa's future, but also the increased vulnerability of the apartheid regime to popular pressure.

This in turn compelled Pretoria to follow 'loose-money' policies locally that included encouraging the allocation of credit into geographical areas it had not penetrated in the recent past, namely black townships. Financial liquidity was growing, with the private-sector-debt/GDP ratio rising from a stable level of 30% during the post-war era, to 50% during the 1980s, and reaching more than 65% by the late 1990s.

Housing finance grew especially rapidly during the last half of the 1980s, as banks and building societies invested R10 billion in township bonds. Politically, this addressed an often-articulated need to identify a new outlet for surplus funds, i.e. black townships, which would both enhance the potential for piling on even more consumer credit once collateral, i.e. the house, had been established, and introduce an inherently conservatising form of social control, i.e. repayment of a 20-year bond. But the R10 billion was enough to saturate only the top tenth of the market, those who could afford new houses costing in excess of R35 000 (smaller loans were administratively too costly), and cemented rather than undermined apartheid urban planning. Moreover, the variable-rate bonds were largely granted at an initial 12.5% interest rate (–7% in real terms).

With an official return to monetarist ideology, as well as anti-apartheid financial sanctions and fear of capital flight, nominal interest rates on housing loans soared to 21% (then 6% in real terms) in 1989, leading to the country's longest-ever depression (1989–93) and, in the process, a 40% default rate on the 200 000 bonds granted to black borrowers. Moreover, the financial explosion also infected commercial real estate and the stock market with untenable speculation. For notwithstanding the overall economic stagnation, from 1982 to 1990, the JSE produced an eight-fold nominal increase in share values, and was the fastest-growing stock exchange in the world from 1989 to mid-1992. In 1991, JSE industrial shares increased in price by 56%, while the industrial economy suffered negative growth. This 'financial explosion', as it was termed across the world during the late 1980s,[72] was profitable to South African banks, which increased their margins between what they charged borrowers and what they rewarded savers (from 2.25% during the late 1980s, the spread doubled by the end of the depression, with a consequent growth in profits to record levels and a huge rise in share values of banking stocks). In short, financial activity borne of economic crisis had helped reshape South African geography, in the process intensifying uneven development.

Learning from history

Relying upon finance as the driver of economic development, we have observed in a brief historical sweep, typically intensified local-level uneven development. Simon Clarke has assessed historical processes in Britain that, as in South Africa, point to contradictory roles of geography and finance:

> In the initial phase of development of the credit system accumulation was frequently disrupted at an early stage by the failure of local banks. Although this was often put down to unsound banking practices, it was primarily a result of the geographical unevenness of accumulation which led to imbalances in the inter-regional flows of commodities and of capital, which resulted in an inflow of money into some regions and an outflow from others. Banks in some regions accumulated ample reserves of the money commodity, while banks elsewhere found themselves under increasing pressure.[73]

In sum, across a variety of levels, uneven development is generally *accentuated* during those periods, such as at present, when financial institutions increase their range of movement, the velocity and intensity of their operations, and simultaneously, their power over debtors (whether companies, consumers or governments). It is at such points that David Harvey asserts the 'hegemonic role' of finance:

> The power of money capital is continuously exerted over all facets of production and realisation at the same time as spatial allocations are brought within its orbit. The credit system affects land and property markets and the circulation of state debt. Pressure is thereby brought to bear on landowners, developers, buildings, the state and users. The formation of fictitious capital, furthermore, permits interest-bearing money capital to flow on a continuous basis in relation to the daily use of fixed, long-lived and immobile use values. The titles to such revenues can even circulate on the world market though the assets themselves are immobile.[74]

But with power comes vulnerability, as is evident enough at the turn of the 21st century, after two decades of spectacular financial crises across the world. Yet there are policy options available to contemporary South Africa, including exchange controls, to help lock capital down.

4. Exchange control options for South Africa [75]

The previous pages in this book have documented how international financial markets continue to spin out of control and how global economic management has failed to cope with the situation (see especially Chapters one and five); how some countries have invoked a combination of capital and exchange controls – some directly, some through taxation – both to avoid contagion of financial crisis and to promote economic growth; and how South Africa's own history records instances of financial volatility and extreme unevenness of capital accumulation as a result. What are the implications of all this for contemporary South Africa?

The vicious cycle of financial liberalisation

In particular, does South Africa need to worry about further international financial turbulence? Are there ways in which South Africa can protect its foreign currency reserves against speculator bear raids? Are there opportunities for strengthening South Africa's capacity to deal with a currency crisis even before it hits?

In this section, I will consider the economic characteristics of international financial vulnerability. But a strong case could be made, on moral grounds, that since the main holders of South African wealth – who are overwhelmingly white men – derived that wealth through morally odious and economically irrational apartheid advantage, there is no ethical basis for their now departing South Africa with such wealth now that their apartheid advantage is eroding. While some (such as Stellenbosch economics professor Sampie Terreblanche) have argued that a wealth tax is the only convincing way to redistribute apartheid-era wealth, it is obvious that until such a wealth tax is imposed, there is a strong moral case for capital controls to at the very least retain the wealth within South Africa, for the beneficial investment of all its citizens.

But whatever moral stance is adopted, contemporary South African economic vulnerability is also a problem worthy of note. Although South Africa has had its own complex history of dramatic financial bubbles and bursts dating from the early 19th century, stability and domestic financial security was largely achieved during the long post-war era of highly regulated global financial markets. Recall that even during the late 1980s and early 1990s, Pretoria achieved a surprising degree of domestic financial security, in spite of extremely effective anti-apartheid financial sanctions imposed by most western governments and banks at the request of the liberation movement.

Beginning in September 1985, in the context of a hot-money withdrawal (most western banks cancelled short-term credit lines), the Reserve Bank and Finance Ministry asserted sovereignty over financial flows through a combination of a foreign-debt repayment 'standstill' (followed by re-negotiations every three or so years) and the introduction of a dual exchange-rate system. Once the $13 billion in short-term debt due in 1985 had been renegotiated, the financial rand ('finrand') became Pretoria's primary tool to control capital outflows.

The finrand was aimed not at foreign companies that wanted to repatriate either profits or capital investment, but rather at owners of financial assets. The controls substantially slowed the flight of financial capital, by serving as a form of tax on outflows. The premium ranged from 10% to 40%, depending upon exchange rates and political circumstances.

However, it must be acknowledged that, as in the case of Malaysia's capital controls in 1998–9, an element of cronyism and corruption was evident. The Reserve Bank was investigated periodically for involvement in illegal currency 'round-tripping' (by which finrands were purchased at a discount by local financiers and converted into higher-value commercial rands). Amongst its many questionably close relations with Afrikaans banks, the Witwatersrand attorney-general discovered that virtually all major forex transactions of R300 million and above approved by the Reserve Bank during the late 1980s were tainted. Its Durban branch manager, for example, was taken to court for $1 billion in irregular forex transactions.

Nevertheless, the finrand made the rampant capital flight and foreign exchange dealing that characterised South Africa's mid-1998 crash impossible. Although the emerging-markets crisis played a role, particularly in view of Russian-caused global turbulence in mid-1998, South Africa's own banks were notably very active in betting against the rand, and recorded large foreign-exchange account profits as a result. The role played by South

African banks requires further investigation, and much greater supervisory oversight by the Reserve Bank, particularly given spectacular growth in foreign-exchange trading particularly by Standard Bank and First National Bank (FNB). In comparative international terms, Standard Bank's forex-trading rank rose from 96th most-active bank in the world in 1998 to 65th in 1999, while FNB's rose from 111th to 78th. In addition, the two most active banks, each with more than 7% market share, are Citibank/Salomon Smith Barney and Deutsche Bank, and each has an active Johannesburg office.[76]

During the first half of 1999, the prime rate fell in real terms back to around 12%, but this remained an enormous premium compared to the main capital-exporting countries in May 1999: the United States (5.7%), Britain (5%), the Euro-11 (3.3%) and Japan (1.9%). With South African inflation down to its lowest levels since the early 1970s, thanks mainly to a drastic fall in consumer demand in 1998, the real effective exchange rate firmed (it was down slightly against the dollar and yen), giving foreign investors an extremely high rate of return during the first half of 1999. Against the euro, the rand appreciated 9.4%, and against the pound, the rand was up 1.1%.

Yet while in mid-1999, economic relief appeared momentarily (aside from dramatic job-cuts in mining and parastatal companies), the vicious cycle associated with financial liberalisation threatened to return. Either the rand's value would have to be allowed to fall, interest rates would have to be kept at extraordinarily high levels (i.e. monetary independence would have to be surrendered, for example, through a Currency Board arrangement), or some change would have to be made to capital convertibility. During 2000, further runs on the rand – which drove the value down by 20% over two months, and by a further 5% by the end of the year – resolved the tensions somewhat. But there were no safeguards, either at the nation-state or global levels, to assure that financial speculation would not, once again in future years, destroy 20–30% of the value of the currency in a single swoop.

Revisiting rationales for financial liberalisation
The power of the Washington Consensus has to date prevented the third option (changes to capital convertibility). Yet the continuing cycle of economic turbulence associated with financial liberalisation suggests that a rethink is in order. The rationale for South Africa's financial liberalisation has, after all, been two-fold, i.e. to attract short-term portfolio capital so as to maintain support to the balance of payments, and to demonstrate to potential longer-term foreign direct investors that the South African government has sufficient self-confidence in its prospects to allow capital to move freely. Both rationales deserve reconsideration at this stage.

First, there are other ways of assuring balance-of-payments stability, including Malaysian-style capital controls; an indirect finrand-type dual exchange system; other modes of taxation to prevent capital outflows; more direct controls on imports (especially luxury goods, which until 1996 were taxed fairly heavily); and the renegotiation of payments on apartheid-era foreign debt (mainly taken on by private borrowers, but guaranteed by the government).[77]

Secondly, the effect of financial liberalisation on foreign direct investment has not been impressive. As a psychological tactic, it may in theory have had merit. But the practice of FDI has not met expectations. Virtually all FDI into South Africa has been of the merger/acquisition variety, instead of into greenfields projects entailing the import and establishment of new plant, equipment and job opportunities. Moreover, since the finrand was lifted in 1995, over R10 billion more has been exported through the direct investment of South African firms out of the country than new FDI has brought into South Africa.

In addition, portfolio investment by South African financial institutions since 1990 has included the growing operations of the major banks in offshore financial centres (the Cayman Islands, the Bahamas, Panama, Jersey, Guernsey, the Isle of Man, the Isle of Wight, etc.) and questionable South African bank loans to Russia and Brazil. The listing of several large companies on foreign stock markets was meant to bolster the foreign reserves through remittances to local shareholders. But they also represent a future flow of capital appreciation and dividends to non-residents, and the recipients of the sales receipts of local shares are amongst those South Africans most likely to emigrate, demanding expatriation of their funds.

In short, the strategy of attracting foreign investment through financial liberalisation has not worked well where it is most needed, i.e. in long-term, greenfields FDI in productive sectors of the economy; and it has worked perversely to undermine South Africa's domestic financial security by subjecting local markets to global turbulence.

The failure of South Africa's financial liberalisation could have been anticipated as a function of one other relatively unique factor. Unlike most countries, which guard against hidden subsidies to corporate borrowers seeking foreign loans, the South African Reserve Bank has developed since the late 1980s an ill-advised 'forward-cover book'. This technique of risk-sharing effectively guarantees South African corporate borrowers against any exchange-rate premium on their foreign loans. Over time the forward-cover book has ebbed and flowed, but still represents a well-recognised invitation for speculators to sell South African assets short, on the grounds that the enormous liability ensures the country's vulnerability – in the absence of exchange controls.

Towards domestic financial security

To sum up, after several years of financial turbulence, there are no defensible rationales for South Africa's experiment in financial liberalisation. There is only one problem involved in not just reversing recent liberalisation but going further and establishing proactive development-capital and foreign-exchange controls. That is the question of whether South Africa would be able to get away with interventionist measures aimed at restoring domestic financial security – or whether a cartel of international financial institutions would intervene to impose sanctions (credit boycotts, etc.).[78]

In any attempt to answer this question, the case of Russia's default in August 1998 is instructive, for the anticipated negative impact on access to trade financing was not affected, and Russia was given repeated new international loans so as to roll over some (though not all) of the debt still coming due in 1999. Neither was Malaysia cut off from international finance required to facilitate trade and investment after its imposition of exchange controls in September 1998, and indeed, after a short-term decline in its international credit rating, it quickly re-established itself with ratings comparable to similar South-east Asian countries. Similarly, apartheid-era South Africa was not denied short-term trade finance following its 1985 debt standstill.

The variety of measures utilised by developing countries to control capital and exchange movements have already been noted; and the need to reimpose these has been widely acknowledged, with UNCTAD specifically mandating several types of controls. With the historically successful experiences – in contrast to the failures of liberalisation in recent years – and the growing acceptance even within the IMF of certain kinds of controls, the danger of retribution from international financial markets has waned. To reiterate, previous capital controls employed by developing countries have included:

- comprehensive controls on outflows and inflows;
- controls on portfolio investments of non-residents and residents, particularly so as to prevent inflow of speculative hot money (including not only share and bond transactions, but also security issuance);
- controls directed at foreign direct investments (inward by non-residents and outward by residents), including profit repatriation and capital-liquidation rules, as well as taxes on capital transactions;
- controls on deposit accounts of non-residents and residents in local currency and foreign exchange held in such countries, and on other capital transfers, personal capital transfers and blocked accounts; and
- controls on other financial transactions of non-residents and residents, as well as trade-related financial transactions.

UNCTAD-authorised capital controls include:
- licensing;

- ceilings on foreign equity participation in local firms;
- official permission for international equity issues;
- differential regulations applying to local and foreign firms regarding their establishment and permissible operations, and various kinds of two-tier markets;
- a special reserve requirement for liabilities to non-residents;
- forbidding banks to pay interest on deposits of non-residents or even requiring a commission on such deposits;
- taxing foreign borrowing to eliminate the margin between local and foreign interest rates; and
- requiring firms to deposit cash at the central bank amounting to a proportion of their external borrowing.

The key means of capital and exchange controls applied by numerous countries in the past have included controls on foreign and local expatriation of investment income, controls on domestic ownership of foreign assets and vice versa, controls on currency convertibility, and restrictions on financial flows related to foreign banking offices. The most important such controls for South Africa include seven elements of a revised strategy for domestic financial security.

A strategy and plan for locking capital down
The seven areas of state regulatory/taxing capacity that can and should be expanded in the near future, assuming a change in the balance of forces, can be implemented through ten specific programmatic decisions. The seven strategic areas (A–G) are given below, interspersed with suggestions about ten concrete steps required for implementation.

A. Halting further financial liberalisation and revoking aspects of recent liberalisation which are economically and morally questionable
1. Halt any further moves to liberalise international financial flows to or from South Africa (or, as has been proposed by the governor of the Reserve Bank, to dollarise the South African economy through a Currency Board arrangement).
2. Conduct a full, transparent, participatory study of the direct and indirect effects of previous rounds of liberalisation (dating at least to the finrand liberalisation in March 1995).

B. Imposing feasible, Malaysia-style capital and exchange controls at the earliest opportunity, and certainly prior to a renewed state of financial turmoil and crisis when they might become vitally necessary
3. Rapidly impose capital controls for the purposes of deterring foreign speculative activity, preventing capital flight and providing a necessary

(though insufficient) condition for bringing down interest rates within South Africa and hence restoring growth.

4. Force South African firms and individuals with externalised assets (including the proceeds of overseas listings) to return them to South African resident control through regulated foreign-currency accounts in SA-based financial institutions, using enhanced disclosure and surveillance mechanisms traditionally employed by the Reserve Bank, Ministry of Finance and SA Revenue Service and associated with resident tax status. In the process, prohibit further international listings, revisit asset-swap arrangements between major institutional investors and immediately end the present right of residents to invest locally sourced funds abroad.

5. Discourage, or even prohibit, local firms from borrowing abroad, whether in search of lower interest rates or as a means of externalising their assets, through measures that include:

   – cessation of the costly Reserve Bank forward-cover-book guarantee;
   – forced repatriation to the Reserve Bank of foreign currency associated with foreign borrowings, for translation into local currency;
   – forced interest-earning foreign-exchange-reserve requirements under Reserve Bank control, as a major proportion of any foreign borrowing; and/or
   – requirements that local firms convincingly demonstrate their ability to service any present and future foreign loans through foreign-exchange-based revenue streams, under existing conditions and potential conditions of exchange rate volatility.

C. Restoring confidence in the Reserve Bank, as a crucial logistical vehicle for exchange controls, at a time when it is introducing new leadership and systems

6. Promote professionalism and patriotism within the Reserve Bank, in part through extensive audits of past conduct and prosecution of those officials, whether currently employed or not, found guilty of aiding and abetting illegal capital flight.

D. Distinguishing between inflows of hot money (which should be actively discouraged) and production-oriented FDI (which, in contrast to existing merger/acquisition FDI, should be encouraged)

7. Impose disincentives to inflows of hot money, such as temporary taxation or application of a finrand-type penalty on all profits not made through fixed investment. In particular, Tobin-style taxes should be applied to all international transactions emanating from or coming to South Africa, beginning, at the very least, with the imposition of a reserve requirement and premature exit tax of the type that worked effectively in Chile. A general increase in taxation associated with

financial profits should also be immediately imposed, given the financial sector's windfall profits over the past decade as a result of high real interest rates, an historically high savings/lending spread and rising fee income. The objective would be to reverse existing market incentives that reward disinvestment from productive activity and reinvestment in financial assets. In order to shift the balance from merger/acquisition-type FDI (such as has occurred through parastatal privatisations) towards productive FDI, far greater differential treatment in relation to taxation and profit-repatriation should be adopted, with high penalties on transactions of a mainly speculative nature.

E. **Revisiting South Africa's current and capital accounts, including imports and the inherited apartheid-era foreign-liability structure**
8. South African finance, tax, trade, customs, currency and related authorities should urgently convene and adopt intersectoral strategies aimed at reducing the country's current- and capital-account vulner-abilities. This would probably entail the imposition of a tax on luxury imports, more strategic approvals on imports of capital-intensive equipment, and an examination of import-substitution possibilities.

F. **Lowering interest rates**
9. Once many of the short-term controls on capital flight have been tight-ened and other measures I have suggested above have been imposed, it is vital that the Reserve Bank immediately begin substantially reducing the bank rate to achieve real interest-rate levels close to the rate of real GDP growth or lower, and in turn compel the commercial banks and other lenders to maintain historic norms of interest-rate spread, instead of present norms often double the historic average, so as to pass such savings directly on to savers and borrowers.

G. **Redirecting financial resources into productive purposes, including meeting human needs, away from largely speculative and unproductive outlets**
10. Finally, a variety of changes should be made in domestic monetary and financial regulation to both enhance the security of investment port-folios and to direct funds to economic activities oriented much more towards production and basic consumption. These would include the reorientation of monetary policy towards balancing growth and devel-opment objectives with the imperatives of financial stability; the targeting of subsidised credit towards key industries and enterprises; the implementation of community reinvestment legislation that induces commercial banks to provide financial services to the poor; the revitali-sation of the postal bank and the redirection of postal-bank resources

towards poor communities; other legal prohibitions against financial discrimination on the basis of race, gender, class and geography; prescribed assets for major institutional investors; variable asset-based reserve requirements to promote production; dual interest rates for social purposes (including cross-subsidised credits for small businesses, emergent farmers, housing and tertiary education); and the establishment of other state-supported special-purpose financial agencies that serve the majority.

The search for capital to finance 'even' development

If a coherent case is made for exchange and capital controls, as has been done for South Africa by many leading economists and UNCTAD, and if the moral weight of South Africa's democratic leadership and the support of numerous international allies are added, there is no reason that South Africa could not take a bold position, and perhaps truly assume an international leadership role, on restoring domestic financial security.

This chapter has assumed that the present international economic system is mired in crisis; that there are no real prospects for global regulation on the immediate or medium-term horizon; that crisis-response mechanisms are ineffectual in restoring the conditions for long-term stability and prosperity; that the threat of US economic imbalances remains severe; and that the vast volume of private hot-money flows is not receding, notwithstanding a temporary 1997–8 decline (see Part One for argumentation).

Following from these assumptions, it can be argued that such conditions have had a substantial adverse impact on South Africa's own prospects. The two major post-1994 currency crises have been handled poorly by the prior Reserve Bank management; vulnerability to future crises has increased; interest rates have been demonstrably higher, in turn catalysing recessionary conditions; costs of imported inflation and foreign-debt repayment have increased; vast amounts of scarce reserves have been wasted; and the government has lost an opportunity to question the moral implications of allowing those who benefitted from apartheid to take their wealth offshore. This is no short-term fluke, but represents a recurrent condition that, as has been documented historically, causes financial turbulence to amplify uneven development in South Africa.

Based on the evidence I have presented, there are a variety of currency- and exchange-control options that could readily be implemented by the South African government, not only to resolve the growing vulnerability South Africa faces in international financial markets, but to restore domestic growth, equity and security. But it is highly significant that these options are not being seriously considered by the government (much less parliament or the press), and that they have only been posed in a consistent way by the more radical social forces in South Africa.

5. From global apartheid to democratised investment

The 'price' of 'satisfying the international bankers'

Detailed alternative policy proposals such as those in the pages above are invariably unsatisfying, if they are not rooted in traditions of politics that generate such programmes through organic, mass-based demands, and sustain them through intensely democratic advocacy. Without the latter, the 1994 Reconstruction and Development Programme mandates for reform of both South Africa's international financial relations and internal financial investment processes were ignored by the neoliberal clique in the ANC, which took over key sections of the Treasury, Department of Trade and Industry, and Reserve Bank.

But that clique's failures are today widely recognised, and not only by the Left within and without the ANC-Cosatu-SACP Alliance. Even the main voice of business in South Africa's quality Sunday newspaper, David Gleason, contended that Trevor Manuel and Maria Ramos

> have clung with an almost religious fervour to the mantra of fiscal orthodoxy; discipline has been their war cry, and they've succeeded. But it's now time to consider the price that has been paid to achieve this. If it was done to satisfy international bankers and foreign investors, all in the name of encouraging inward investment, it hasn't paid off. Foreigners continue to stay away from Africa. Our reputation for fiscal and monetary conservatism has earned us brownie points and not much else. Meanwhile, part of the price we've paid to achieve fiscal discipline has been self-induced starvation ...
>
> I am bound to ask whether this rigid adherence to policies designed to placate mealy-mouthed Western investors has been worth it? A meaningful national debate must now begin.[79]

But how meaningful can a debate be, when there is an international financial gun persistently cocked at South Africa's head? The risks associated with any of the public-policy measures – especially imposition of exchange controls and default on the apartheid debt – discussed in the previous pages are real, if ultimately indeterminate. Yet they are certainly worthy of intelligent probing.[80]

Such probing typically happens behind closed doors or over drinks at quiet times during international conferences, although occasionally written transcripts are kept. At such meetings, the dilemma of the quality of the 'relationship' between borrowers and lenders arises, especially 'when you are about to default on your debt', as Maria Ramos remarked at a 1999 workshop attended by top IMF officials. At that stage, 'Does it help to have a pre-defined set of rules?' The question emerged at a recent strategy session of major developing countries where 'there was a strong feeling that we needed some rules of the game'.

However, Ramos continued, 'I think Brazil was the first to change its mind when it had to go into negotiations. I was very sympathetic to this because it becomes a very different environment when you have to negotiate a debt standstill or a change in your debt structure with your creditors.' Indeed, Ramos conceded,

> in an extreme crisis situation, default will have to be part of the equation. In that case, the only way in which you are going to prevent a short-term outflow of capital is through some pretty tough exchange control measures. I don't know if there are too many options available. In 1985, during the Apartheid era, South Africa unilaterally declared a debt standstill and re-imposed very draconian exchange control measures. However, it's not something one would like to advocate.[81]

But rather than await for the next crisis to emerge, as it surely will, the seeds of a new way of thinking about democratised investment are today being sown by many critics who understand how undemocratic, out-of-control financial markets, international bankers and World Bank/IMF missions together amplify global apartheid – and also ensure the rise of class-apartheid within South Africa. Such an understanding either escapes those in Pretoria with clout, or doesn't bother them sufficiently to do anything meaningful to correct matters.

The alternative: nurturing 'socialism from below'

Would a 'national debate' over the problem of Pretoria's surrender to international financiers be limited to technocratic suggestions for reform, rather than the kinds of radical changes that are obviously necessary? Would there, in short, be space for advocates of a revitalised socialism-from-below?[82]

It is to this tradition that I turn in conclusion, in part because I began this book by citing the diagnosis of organic left-wing intellectuals, and in part because writers of the independent, non-sectarian left (for example, in the annual *Socialist Register*) have also made the conquest of finance, mainly by the nation-state, one of their main challenges, as a necessary (if insufficient) step on the long march to a more profound transformation of society.

Recall the concise summary of finance-driven, crisis-ridden globalisation-from-above posed by the ANC Alliance leftists at the outset, in their 1998 discussion document:

> The present crisis is, in fact, a global capitalist crisis, rooted in a classical crisis of overaccumulation and declining profitability. Declining profitability has been a general feature of the most developed economies over the last 25 years. It is precisely declining profitability in the most advanced economies

that has spurred the last quarter of a century of intensified globalization. These trends have resulted in the greatly increased dominance (and exponential growth in the sheer quantity) of speculative finance capital, ranging uncontrolled over the globe in pursuit of higher returns.[83]

If so, then what? A critical prerequisite for socialism-from-below, is cited by one of the world's most far-sighted political scientists, York University professor Leo Panitch:

> The key long-term condition for an alternative to globalisation is democratic investment control within each state – the opposite goal to that of today's multilateral international negotiations. This must mean going beyond the type of quantitative controls on the inflow and outflow of capital allowed under Bretton Woods, let alone beyond the Tobin Tax on capital flows now being advanced by many on the left. A campaign for qualitative democratic capital controls is required.[84]

In general, not merely in South Africa, a feasible menu of developmentalist-state interventions along these lines would include imposition of watertight exchange controls; careful reflation of the economy through strategic state spending; imposition of prescribed assets on financial institutions so as to redirect finance to social uses; increasing nationalisation of strategic sites of the economy; creative juggling of import/export requirements so as to avoid foreign debt and wastage of resources on luxury consumption; default on illegitimate foreign debt; and a more general commitment to 'get the prices *wrong*' in financial markets through interest rate subsidies and directed credit to socially-useful producers, if need be, to assure the maximum developmental return on democratic investment.

These kinds of interventions in financial markets – well tried and tested in numerous settings around the world, including even South Korea when during the 1960s the banks were nationalised – are obviously no use merely by themselves. A full-fledged democratisation of political-economic processes is also crucial. Indeed, the lack of democracy associated with top-down international and local economic reforms is one key reason for their persistent failure.

And indeed that is why nothing can really be expected from the 'Millennial Africa Recovery Plan' that Mbeki developed in various closed-door seminars during 2000–1. Rather than seek self-reliance from the most damaging international financial and trade circuits, Mbeki seeks yet further integration, and worse, to expand the role of international financial and trade institutions, and orthodox aid, in Africa.[85]

Instead, the dynamic of progressive change will emerge from the alienation of those who suffer most from neoliberalism, in South Africa and across the world, and from the creativity of those who demand and imagine a better world.[86] Those social forces include: labour under threat of privatisation and plummeting real wages; communities facing water and electricity cut-offs or simply more years of non-delivery; students facing exclusion due to inability to pay soaring tuition fees; disabled people and the elderly whose pensions are denied by uncaring financial bureaucrats; and those millions of South Africans facing early death due to the failure of governments to challenge the private-profit character of the health system, especially in relation to anti-retroviral drugs, the dispensing of which should have begun years ago through state-owned generic production facilities.

These are amongst the main social forces arguing for the *decommodification* of basic-needs goods and services. They argue for the *destratification* of society so that access becomes an *entitlement* that all citizens must enjoy. They insist on *degendered* provision of goods and services so that, it is no longer women who pick up the pieces when the state fails. And, as demonstrated by the Alexandra and Soweto protesters against the World Bank's Lesotho megadams, they have an often stunning awareness of the *harmony between society and nature* that is required to make all the above happen 'sustainably'.[87] Alongside genuine workplace democracy and increasing citizen planning of production, these are the vital elements in socialism-from-below.

Naturally, this cannot come from above. It is only from the activism on shopfloors and in communities that a durable economic democracy can emerge, although a nurturing state can make all the difference between defeat – a few small pilot projects fizzling out – and sustained victory. Thus another editor of *Socialist Register*, Greg Albo, sets out ten 'transitional' principles highlighting the role of workplace transformation, of which the first three are more broadly political in nature:

1) inward-oriented economic strategies will be necessary to allow diversity of development paths and employment stability;
2) financial capital must be subjected to democratic controls on debt payment and capital mobility; and
3) macroeconomic balance requires not only aggregate demand management, but also new forms of investment planning and collective bargaining norms.[88]

Democracy now
Such radical reforms would necessarily be located at the scale of the nation-state. Achieving these probably requires a revolution in power relations, which is precisely why the state – the traditional site of politicised class struggle, as argued in Chapter ten – remains the unit of analysis amongst even those who (like myself) consider themselves vigorous internationalists.[89]

Another leading international political scientist, Boris Kagarlitsky of the Russian Academy of Sciences, confirms that since 1998, the global capitalist crisis has

> forced even the neoliberal mainstream to change its attitude towards the role of the state. Experts of the IMF suddenly declared that 'certain types of capital controls may be justified in some circumstances.' American businessmen agreed: 'Maybe some sort of protectionism makes sense for Russia.' The state must use its strength to overcome the crisis of the market. 'If that means instituting wage and price controls, or renationalising basic industries to ensure supplies and employment, so be it.

To be sure, Kagarlitsky also advocates international regulation but correctly concludes that

> no international regulation will work unless it is based on national and regional bodies. If it is not, the rules and decisions made by international bodies simply will not be implemented. And no democratisation of international relations is possible without democracy at the level of a nation state.[90]

That, indeed, is the bottom line. In so many respects, thorough-going democracy is what has been most surprisingly absent in a society which won its formal 'bourgeois' democracy after so much bloodshed, so recently. In setting the macro-economic rules, virtually no meaningful inputs from mass organisations like Cosatu have been allowed. The case of the Treatment Action Campaign proves that sometimes international solidarity against the source of oppression – whether pharmacorps or the Bretton Woods institutions – will be required, simply so as to ensure that nation-states can gain the space to implement measures in the interests of their constituencies, where these conflict with transnational corporate and banking interests.

The formula of 'internationalism plus the nation-state' becomes vital under such circumstances, and as a result, is anathema to neoliberals who would avoid any such 'voluntarist experiments' as the 1997 Medicines Act. Indeed where the trade union movement has begun veering leftwards and into internationalist terrain, the neoliberal clique in Pretoria has squirmed most uncomfortably. To illustrate, according to front-page *Business Day* coverage in late August 2001, just before Cosatu's two-day strike against privatisation, as conflicts within the Alliance reached a boil,

> Cabinet ministers were subsequently dispatched to influential radio and television programmes first to 'clarify' government positions, but also to 'show Cosatu members they are being urged to committing suicide', according to an official involved in the spin-doctoring offensive. Also part of the strategy – championed by Trade and Industry Minister Alec Erwin, Transport Minister Dullah Omar and Public Enterprises Minister Jeff Radebe – was to

seek to caution Cosatu members against the possible hijacking of their strike by outside elements such as those protesting at World Bank and International Monetary Fund meetings.[91]

Bizarre as it sounded at first blush, Johannesburg's *Business Day* demonstrated the underlying rationale for hijack-phobia on the following day:

> SA needs to cut import tariffs aggressively, privatise faster and more extensively, promote small business effectively and change labour laws to achieve far faster growth and job creation. This is according to a World Bank report that will soon be released publicly and has been circulating in government. It stresses 'the overarching need to improve the investment climate' in SA for faster growth and job creation.[92]

Like the reported claim by Thabo Mbeki that the Treatment Action Campaign had 'infiltrated' Cosatu, it would be up to the trade union movement to rebut the state's delusional paranoia about those allegedly 'outside elements' opposed to the World Bank and IMF, through their actions over subsequent months and years.[93] Although danger always exists of reversion to the bureaucratic trade-unionism characteristic of a sub-imperial 'labour aristocracy', the opposite is more likely: the actions of the organised South African working-class, and its allies, can only become more radical and internationalist, the more that global inequality and financial turbulence together intensify, and the more that Mbeki, Manuel, Erwin, Ramos, Mamphele and other South African elites shine – rather than break – the chains associated with the most oppressive international institutions.

A crucial preliminary ingredient in the campaign to establish the broadest and deepest possible form of economic democracy, is a growing sense in society 'as a whole' that things have swung perilously far towards undemocratic rule by corporations, financiers and their Washington helpers. The swing of the pendulum back requires not only the activism which this book has celebrated. It also requires the contemporary rulers, including elite opinion-makers outside government, to realise that their own course is self-destructive.

As a result, it is only appropriate to end a book with as controversial and provocative tone as I have sought to implant here, by resorting to impeccable establishmentarian logic. So I borrow a quote in closing, from another *Socialist Register* contributor who also recently posited the need to end international financial tyranny:

> Once a nation parts with its currency and credit, it matters not who makes the nation's laws. Usury, once in control, will wreck any nation. Until the control of currency and credit is restored to government and recognised as

286 GLOBALISATION? OR INTERNATIONALISM PLUS THE NATION STATE?

its most conspicuous and sacred responsibility, all talk of the sovereignty of parliament and of democracy is idle and futile.[94]

The quote is from William Lyon McKenzie King, a long-serving Canadian prime minister, and was uttered at the time (1935) of the last great come-uppance for global apartheid. *Genuine* establishment critics of the excesses of capitalist globalisation, as King or Keynes might be were they to have seen the 21st century, or as George Soros and Joseph Stiglitz have some-times been in recent days, do recognise that nothing less than democracy is at stake.

For South Africa to finally establish sovereignty and democracy, in place of the unsatisfying, continuity-based transition from apartheid to neoliberalism, requires precisely such insights, as well as corresponding actions that, finally, speak louder than words. I have no doubt that a movement for genuine democracy is on the immediate horizon, and that it will be victorious, so long as those protesting in the streets and shopfloors maintain their vigilance and recruit more and more to their cause – and so long as social progress is not delayed much longer by those in Pretoria, Washington and other sites of power, who remain intent on polishing, not abolishing, global apartheid.

Notes

1 For more information, see Blecker, R. (1999), *Taming Global Finance: A Better Architecture for Growth and Equity*, Washington, DC, Economic Policy Institute.
2 Pastor, M. (1989), *Capital Flight and the Latin American Debt Crisis*, Washington, DC, Economic Policy Institute.
3 Rodrik, D. (1998), 'Who Needs Capital-account Convertibility?' in P. Kenen (ed.), *Princeton Essays in International Finance*, Princeton, Princeton University Press; Grilli, V. and Milesi-Ferrati, G. M. (1995), 'Economic Effects and Structural Deter-minants of Capital Flows', *IMF Staff Papers*, 42(3).
4 Quirk, P. and Owens, D. (1995), 'Capital Account Convertibility: Review of Exper-ience and Implications for IMF Policies', IMF occasional paper 131, Washington, DC, International Monetary Fund.
5 CNBC report, 'Asia in Crisis', 29 August 1998.
6 Krugman, P. (1998), 'Saving Asia: It's Time to Get RADICAL', *Fortune*, 7 September.
7 The impossible trinity is explained in the Mundell-Flemming Model. See Flemming, J. M. (1962), 'Domestic Financial Policies under Fixed and under Flexible Ex-change Rates', *International Monetary Fund Staff Papers*, 9; and Mundell, R. (1963), 'Capital Mobility and Stabilisation Policy under Fixed and Flexible Exchange Rates', *Canadian Journal of Economics and Political Science*, 29.
8 A Currency Board system rigidly correlates money supply and domestic interest rates in regard to a country's foreign reserves.
9 Krugman, *op. cit.*
10 Recounted in Martin Khor (1999), 'Why Capital Controls and International Debt Restructuring Mechanisms are Necessary to Prevent and Manage Financial Crises', paper presented to the conference on Economic Sovereignty in a Globalizing World, Bangkok, 24 March.

11 Resident travelers were allowed to import ringgit notes up to RM1 000 only and any amount of foreign currencies, and to export only up to RM1 000 and up to the equivalent of RM10 000 in foreign currencies only. Except for payments for imports of goods and services, residents were freely allowed to make payments to non-residents only up to RM10 000 or its equivalent in foreign currency (previously the limit was set at RM100 000). Investments in any form abroad by residents and payments under a guarantee for non-trade purposes required approval. The prescribed manner of payment for exports was in foreign currency only (previously it was allowed to be in foreign currency or ringgits from an external account). Domestic credit facilities to non-resident correspondent banks and non-resident stockbroking companies were no longer allowed (previously domestic credit up to RM5 million was allowed). Residents required prior approval to make payments to non-residents for purposes of investing abroad for amounts exceeding the equivalent of RM10 000 in foreign exchange. Residents were not allowed to obtain ringgit credit facilities from non-residents. There were measures imposing conditions on the operations and transfers of funds in external accounts. Transfers between external accounts required prior approval for any amount (previously they were freely allowed); transfers from external accounts to resident accounts required approval after 30 September; sources of funding of external accounts were limited to proceeds from the sale of ringgit instruments and other assets in Malaysia, salaries, interest and dividends, and the sale of foreign currency.

12 As Khor, *op. cit.*, notes:

Business groups, consumer groups and trade unions in the country supported the measures and the local stock market went up. Foreign investors in the country, through the International Chamber of Commerce, also expressed support. The *Financial Times*, which represents an independent and conservative opinion within the financial establishment, gave guarded support, stating that there was an argument for temporary capital controls in a time of crisis. An editorial noted that some economists argued that controls on short-term capital should be a standard part of policy for emerging markets to avoid destabilising capital inflows and outflows that were at the heart of the Asian crisis.

13 *Asian Wall Street Journal* (1998), 'Acceptance of Capital Curbs is Spreading', 2 September.

14 Agence France-Presse, 23 June 1999.

15 Associated Press, 16 September 1999.

16 Jomo, K. S. (1999), 'Capital Controls: Jury Still Out', paper presented to the conference on Economic Sovereignty in a Globalizing World, Bangkok, 24 March.

17 Mahathir promised that Malaysia would withdraw the currency controls in September 1999. Given the ongoing problems of cronyism, fear of a dramatic exit from the country persuaded Mahathir to sanction early (February 1999) withdrawals of stock-exchange investments, but only if a tax was paid.

18 Jomo, K. S., *op. cit.*

19 Filomeno S.Sta.III (1999), 'Why Tax Portfolio Investments?', paper presented to the conference on Economic Sovereignty in a Globalizing World, Bangkok, 24 March.

20 Blecker, *op. cit.*, p. 101.

21 Khor, *op. cit.*

22 Seidman, A. (1986), *Money, Banking and Public Finance in Africa*, London, Zed Press, pp. 64–7.

23 Riddell, R. (1989), 'Zimbabwe', in R. Riddell (ed.), *Manufacturing Africa*, London, Overseas Development Institute, pp. 340, 344.

24 Handford, J. (1976), *Portrait of an Economy under Sanctions, 1965–75*, Salisbury, Mercury Press, p. 16.

25 Clarke, D. (1981), 'The Monetary, Banking and Financial System in Zimbabwe', in UNCTAD, *Zimbabwe: Towards a New Order*, vol. 1, Geneva, p. 325.
26 Corbridge, S., Martin, R. and Thrift, N. (eds) (1994), *Money, Power and Space*, Oxford, Basil Blackwell.
27 Smith, N. (1990), *Uneven Development*, Oxford, Basil Blackwell; Bond, P. (1999), 'Uneven Development', in P. O'Hara (ed.), *The Encyclopaedia of Political Economy*, London, Routledge.
28 Mabin, A. (1984), 'The making of colonial capitalism: Intensification of the economy of the Cape Colony, South Africa, 1854–1899', unpublished PhD thesis, Simon Fraser University, Vancouver; (1985), 'Concentration and Dispersion in the Banking System of the Cape Colony, 1837–1900', *South African Geographical Journal*, 67(2); (1986), 'The Rise and Decline of Port Elizabeth, 1850–1900', *International Journal of African Historical Studies*, 19(2).
29 Browett, J. G. (1976), 'The Application of a Spatial Model to South Africa's Development Regions', *South African Geographical Journal*, 58; Crush, J. (1982), 'The South African Regional Formation: A Geographical Perspective', *Tijdschrift voor Economische en Sociale Geografie*, 73; Christopher, A. J. (1984), *South Africa: The Impact of Past Geographies*, Johannesburg, Juta.
30 Mabin, A. (1989), 'Waiting for Something to Turn Up? The Cape Colony in the Eighteen Eighties', in A. Mabin (ed.), *Organisation and Economic Change*, Johannesburg, Ravan Press, p. 82.
31 Arndt, E. H. (1928), *Banking and Currency Development in South Africa, 1652–1927*, Cape Town, Oxford University Press; Houghton, H. (1978), *The South African Economy*, Cape Town, Oxford University Press; Solomon, V. E. (1983), 'Money and Banking', in F. L. Coleman (ed.), *Economic History of South Africa*, Pretoria, HAUM Educational.
32 Schumann, C. G. W. (1938), *Structural Changes and Business Cycles in South Africa, 1806–1936*, London, Staples, pp. 63–9.
33 *Ibid.*, pp. 63–74.
34 *Ibid.*, pp. 75–80.
35 Mabin, 'Concentration and Dispersion in the Banking System of the Cape Colony, 1837–1900', p. 150.
36 Giliomee, H. (1989), 'Aspects of the Rise of Afrikaner Capital and Afrikaner Nationalism in the Western Cape, 1870–1915', in W. G. James and M. Simons (eds), *The Angry Divide: Social and Economic History of the Western Cape*, Cape Town, David Philip.
37 Schumann, *op. cit.*, pp. 85–6.
38 Henry, J. A. (1963), *The First Hundred Years of the Standard Bank*, London, Oxford University Press, p. 32.
39 Giliomee, *op. cit.*, p. 76; Henry, *op. cit.*, p. 85; Standard Bank (1988), *An Historical Overview*, Johannesburg, p. 8.
40 Mabin, 'Concentration and Dispersion in the Banking System of the Cape Colony, 1837–1900', p. 150.
41 Schumann, *op. cit.*, p. 128.
42 Phimister, I. (1992), 'Unscrambling the Scramble: Africa's Partition Reconsidered', paper presented to the African Studies Institute, University of the Witwatersrand, Johannesburg, 17 August, p. 7.
43 Cain, P.J. and Hopkins, A.G. (1980), 'The Political Economy of British Expansion Overseas', *Economic History Review*, 33(4), pp. 484–5.
44 Mabin, A. and Conradie, B. (eds) (1987), *The Confidence of the Whole Country, Standard Bank Reports on Economic Conditions in Southern Africa, 1865–1902*,

Johannesburg, Standard Bank, p. 387.
45 Henry, *op. cit.*, p. 101.
46 Bond, P. (1998), *Uneven Zimbabwe: A Study of Finance, Development and Underdevelopment*, Trenton, Africa World Press, Chapter 2; Arrighi, G. (1973), 'The Political Economy of Rhodesia', in G. Arrighi and J. Saul, *Essays on the Political Economy of Africa*, New York, Monthly Review Press.
47 Henry, *op. cit.*, p. 150.
48 *Ibid.*, p. 222.
49 Ally, R. (1994), *Gold and Empire*, Johannesburg, University of the Witwatersrand Press.
50 Gelb, S. (1989), 'The Origins of the South African Reserve Bank, 1914–1920', in A. Mabin (ed.), *Organisation and Economic Change*, Johannesburg, Ravan Press, p. 65.
51 Barclays Bank (1938), *A Banking Centenary*, London.
52 Keegan, T. (1986), *Rural Transformations in Industrialising South Africa: The Southern Highveld to 1914*, Johannesburg, Ravan Press, pp. 44, 97.
53 Giliomee, *op. cit.*, p. 79.
54 Schumann, *op. cit.*, p. 263.
55 Henry, *op. cit.*, p. 222.
56 *Ibid.* p. 227.
57 *Ibid.*, p. 230.
58 *Ibid.*, pp. 235–48.
59 Clarke, S. (1988), *Keynesianism, Monetarism and the Crisis of the State*, Aldershot, Edward Elgar.
60 Schumann, *op. cit.*, p. 263.
61 *Ibid.*, p. 295.
62 Frank, A. G. (1967), *Capitalism and Underdevelopment in Latin America*, New York, Monthly Review Press.
63 Nattrass, J. (1981), *The South African Economy*, Cape Town, Oxford University Press, Appendix.
64 O'Meara, D. (1983), *Volkskapitalism*, Cambridge, Cambridge University Press, p. 114.
65 *Ibid.*, p. 251.
66 Fine, B. and Z. Rustomjee (1996), *The Political Economy of South Africa*, Johannesburg, University of the Witwatersrand Press.
67 Innes, D. (1984), *Anglo American and the Rise of Modern South Africa*, New York, Monthly Review Press, p. 150.
68 Wilkinson, P. (1981), 'A Place to Live: The Resolution of the African Housing Crisis in Johannesburg, 1944–55', Johannesburg, African Studies seminar, University of the Witwatersrand.
69 Bond, P. (2000), *Cities of Gold, Townships of Coal*, Trenton, Africa World Press, Chapter 6.
70 Innes, *op. cit.*, p. 150.
71 Bond, P. (1991), *Commanding Heights and Community Control: New Economics for a New South Africa*, Johannesburg, Ravan Press, Chapter 2; and (2000), *Elite Transition: From Apartheid to Neoliberalism in South Africa*, London, Pluto Press and Pietermaritzburg, University of Natal Press, Chapter 1.
72 Sweezy, P. and Magdoff, H. (1987), *Stagnation and the Financial Explosion*, New York, Monthly Review Press.
73 Clarke, *op. cit.*, p. 110.
74 Harvey, D. (1982), *The Limits to Capital*, Chicago, University of Chicago Press, p. 396.

75 All the data below are from the Industrial Development Corporation (1999), *Core Economic Indicators,* Sandton, third quarter.
76 Hayward, H. (1999), *The Global Gamblers: British Banks and the Foreign Exchange Game,* London, War on Want, pp. 15–16.
77 For more information on this latter point, see the various documents produced by the Jubilee 2000 South Africa campaign and the Alternative Information and Development Centre at http://aidc.org.za.
78 An example of this kind of pressure, as reported by the *Singapore Business Times* (14 June 1999), involved a visit to Indonesia by IMF official Stanley Fischer:
    A policy stand-off is developing between the International Monetary Fund and the Indonesian Democratic Party of Struggle (PDI-P) which has emerged as a strong political force following its strong early lead in the just-concluded general election. The issue is the PDI-P's plan to introduce Malaysian-style currency and foreign exchange controls, which was a key campaign platform for the party led by Megawati Sukarnoputri. Unless the PDI-P backs down and swings more firmly towards a pro-market policy which the IMF is comfortable with, the stand-off will sharpen … But even before preliminary results of the polls came in, the IMF, through its Jakarta-based representative, Kadhim al-Eyd, has expressed concern over the PDI-P's plan for currency controls … The sentiment emerged during private talks last Friday between Mr Kadhim and a noted local economist, Hartoyo Wignyowiyoto … Dr Hartoyo believes the IMF wants to avoid being blamed again should the IMF programme fail under a new government. Following the fall of Mr Suharto, the Fund has come under fire from many local as well as foreign economists for contributing to the economic mess in Indonesia with its strict conditions for loans.
79 *Sunday Business Report,* 26 August 2001.
80 Critics are often frustrated at the lack of seriousness from government's side. For example, all late 1990s efforts to establish a meaningful dialogue between Jubilee South Africa and the Treasury were foiled when Manuel, Ramos and Gill Marcus persistently denied that there was an apartheid foreign debt (see documentation at http://aidc.org.za). The officials insisted on not counting apartheid-era borrowing by Eskom, Telkom and other parastatals, or the private sector debt that the apartheid state had guaranteed at the time of, and after, the 1985 debt standstill. Of course while in exile, the ANC had insisted that there be no such foreign loans to apartheid state agencies and proxy fundraisers. When one parastatal – the Independent Development Trust – tried to raise credit from Germany during the early 1990s, the then secretary general of the ANC, Cyril Ramaphosa threatened to default after the first democratic election, a successful tactic that put off the Frankfurt banks.
    To fail to agree upon even the simple factual basis for a discussion about apartheid debt, as just one example, suggests the difficulty of reasonable debate with the neoliberal clique about South Africa's international financial relations. Likewise Parliament has been useless as a venue, as a result of the main opposition party's advocacy of neoliberalism on the one hand, and on the other, the unwillingness of finance committee chairperson Barbara Hogan to even consider a proposed R1.6 billion World Bank hospital loan worthy of a hearing, in mid-2001. It appears that it is only in the media and on the streets that concerns over the international financial strangulation of South Africa can occur, but this occurs – with the rare exception – without meaningful engagement from Pretoria.
81 For Ramos, the main issue here was whether the cost of foreign borrowing would rise, in the event that 'rules' were imposed on banks aimed at pricing financial-panic

risk beforehand – versus a 'catalytic' approach which buys in the private lenders only at the point of crisis so as to 'try to prevent the banks from rushing for the exit.' (In either case, needless to say, Ramos accepted the broader rules of the game without questioning the legitimacy of the inherited foreign debt.) 'If South Africa went into default mode, which one would I prefer?', Ramos asked. 'I guess my gut reaction would be that I would take my chances trying to negotiate this out with the creditors by using the catalytic approach.'

Ramos, M. (2000), 'Comment on A New Framework for Private Sector Involvement in Crisis Prevention and Crisis Management by Jack Boorman and Mark Allen', in J. Teunissen (ed.), *Reforming the International Financial System: Crisis Prevention and Response*, The Hague, Forum on Debt and Development, pp. 125–7.

Actually, the central question at that moment would not revolve around the negotiating prowess of Manuel and Ramos, but instead whether the balance of forces in the world economy would permit a 'voluntarist experiment' – to recall the 1996 slur in an ANC discussion document, mentioned in Chapter seven – such as a South African default. The only way to establish such a favourable power balance would be to systematically disempower the creditor cartels ahead of time. Those cartels' most important assets are, of course, the IMF and World Bank. But that conclusion Ramos would not broach, much less arrive at herself. It is up to the movements for global justice to do so, notwithstanding the self-defeating attempt to empower the IMF and Bank being made from Pretoria.

82 The most convincing recent 'how-to' guide for establishing democracy during a socialist transition, transforming the inherited state, and consolidating power through empowered popular and workplace councils, is by James Petras and Henry Veltmayer (2001), *Globalization Unmasked: Imperialism in the 21st Century*, Halifax, Fernwood and London, Zed, pp. 166–74.

83 ANC Alliance (1998), 'The Global Economic Crisis and its Implications for South Africa,' ANC Alliance Discussion Document, Johannesburg, reprinted in *The African Communist*, Fourth Quarter 1998.

84 Panitch, L. (2000), 'Reflections on Strategy for Labour,' in L. Panitch and C. Leys (eds), *Working Classes, Global Realities: Socialist Register 2001*, London, Merlin and New York, Monthly Review, p. 381.

85 This was to be expected, what with men who enjoy such questionable political reputations, and who oversee such corruptly-run economies, as do Mbeki's MAP co-sponsors Olesegun Obasanjo of Nigeria and Abdelaziz Bouteflika of Algeria, and with the MAP's debut in settings such as a secret meeting 'at an undisclosed Gauteng location' – as reported in *Business Day* – in November 2000 with James Wolfensohn, at the Davos World Economic Forum in January 2001, and for Wolfensohn and Horst Kohler in Mali in February 2001, *prior to discussion in Mbeki's own political party, in South African or other African parliaments, or with African civil societies*. For a critical perspective on the MAP process, see Taylor, I. (2001), 'Getting the Rhetoric Right, Getting the Strategy Wrong: New Africa, Globalisation and the Confines of Elite Reformism,' Unpublished paper, University of Botswana Department of Political Science, Gaborone.

86 The most important analysis of this movement is Amory Starr (2000), *Naming the Enemy*, London, Zed Press. See also http://www.zmag.org and various linked websites. For particularly anarchist perspectives, see http://www.infoshop.org

87 My forthcoming (2002) book on this movement from below, and what it objects to in the country hosting the September 2002 Rio+10 World Summit on Sustainable Development, is provisionally entitled *Sustainable South Africa? Environment, Development and the Post-Apartheid State*.

88 The other seven, spelled out in detail, are:
   4) reducing unemployment will entail both less work and a redistribution of work;
   5) a 'politics of time' should extend beyond setting standard hours to consider the allocation of work-time and free-time;
   6) productivity gains in the labour process should be negotiated against the re-qualification of work;
   7) the requalification of work should be linked to quality production within a quality-intensive growth model;
   8) the decline in work-time allows the administrative time for workplace democracy;
   9) local planning capacities will be central to sustaining diverse development and full employment; and
   10) socialist economic policy should encompass new forms of democratic administration.
   Albo, G. (1997), 'A World Market of Opportunities? Capitalist Obstacles and Left Economic Policy,' in L.Panitch (ed.), *Ruthless Criticism of all that Exists: Socialist Register 1997*, London, Merlin.

89 For alternative radical points of view which reject the nation-state as the preferred site of socialist struggle, see (in addition to those discussed earlier) Hardt, M. and A. Negri (2000), *Empire*, Cambridge, Harvard University Press; and Brecher, J., T. Costello and B. Smith (2000), *Globalization from Below: The Power of Solidarity*, Boston, South End Press.

90 Kagarlitsky, B. (2000), *The Twilight of Globalization: Property, State and Capitalism*, London, Pluto, p. 39.

91 *Business Day*, 27 August 2001.

92 *Business Day*, 28 August 2001.

93 Likewise, the case of the April 2001 announcement of a plot to overthrow Mbeki by three members of the aspirant black bourgeoisie, suggests that Pretoria spin-doctors have been taking lessons from Harare.

94 Cited in Tickell, A. (1999), 'Unstable Futures: Controlling and Creating Risks in International Money,' in L. Panitch and C. Leys (eds), *Socialist Register*, London, Merlin, p. 267.

International finance defeats South Africa

1. Introduction

When Thabo Mbeki welcomed dignitaries to the World Summit on Sustainable Development in August 2002, he spoke of the need to 'confront the social behaviour that has pity neither for beautiful nature nor for living human beings. This social behaviour has produced and entrenches a global system of apartheid.'[1]

Since the first edition of *Against Global Apartheid* went to press in September 2001, Mbeki and his closest cabinet colleagues – finance minister Trevor Manuel and trade minister Alec Erwin, as well as Reserve Bank governor Tito Mboweni – had many chances to confront the economic behaviour associated with global apartheid. Over the subsequent two years, these included:

- the Durban World Conference Against Racism (September 2001);
- the launch of the New Partnership for Africa's Development at Abuja (October 2001);
- the World Trade Organisation's Doha ministerial summit (November 2001);
- the New York World Economic Forum (February 2002);
- the UN's Financing for Development conference in Monterrey, Mexico (March 2002);
- the G8 summit in Kananaskis, Canada (June 2002);
- the launch of the African Union in Durban (July 2002);
- the Johannesburg World Summit on Sustainable Development (September 2002);
- the Davos World Economic Forum (January 2003);
- the US/UK war against Iraq (early 2003);
- the G8 summit in Evian, France (June 2003); and
- the Cancun WTO ministerial summit (September 2003).

A sufficient review of Pretoria's failed reform efforts at all of these venues requires full book-length treatment.[2] At the conclusion to this Afterword, the scanty results of those frustrated efforts are summarised. However, the main focus of the pages that follow is on what the South African citizenry understands as the most obvious aspect of international financial relations: the roller-coaster currency.

In looking at this problem, I retain the critical spirit evident in Chapter Twelve, which insisted on the need to 'lock capital down'. Indeed, to genuinely achieve nation-state sovereignty in the field of finance will ulti-mately require internationalist policies by countries in a similar situation to South Africa. Since 1995, those have included the many countries and regions identified in Chapter One. However, local democratic, progressive forces have not been sufficient in any single setting to conclusively reverse neoliberalism's momentum. The ascension of Brazilian Workers Party leader 'Lula' Ignacio da Silva to the presidency in January 2003 should have helped, but power relations there were so skewed that the former metal-worker only acquired power via a coalition with the moderate bourgeoisie, which entailed a pledge to follow International Monetary Fund dictates and repay the inherited foreign debt – the Third World's largest at over $300 billion.

Likewise in South Africa, Pretoria's existing policies remain a far cry from the feasible strategies advocated in Chapter Twelve. Quite simply, the liberalisation drum-beat from financial markets and the business media has been deafening. Had Pretoria not listened, and maintained existing controls in 1995 and perhaps even further tightened them, it is fair to predict that the currency would not have crashed, from R3.5/US$ in 1994 to R6/US$ in January 2000 to R13.85/US$ in December 2001. The rand's subsequent rise to the R7/US$ level in May 2003 also generated all manner of economic distortions and dislocations. Looking longer-term, the outflow of capital which will leave South Africa a terminally ill economy could still be arrested.

Sadly, given the ongoing failure of neoliberalism and Pretoria's insistence on sticking the course, there remain too many reasons to doubt South Africa's economic future. To illustrate, one of the main tools for distracting society from the reality of the global economy was a commission appointed by Mbeki in January 2002 to examine why the rand crashed so far so fast. It is there that we begin this update on how international financial apartheid is eroding the victory against domestic racial apartheid.

2. Amidst the rand wreckage, a confused commission

The rand's crash followed a period of disastrous financial deregulation, which included the lifting of the 'financial rand' (the dual-rate exchange control system) in March 1995. Then at the end of the decade, Manuel gave permission to South Africa's largest firms to escape abroad. Hundreds of billions of rands slid away.

Why, then, did the rand fall so inordinately in 2000-01? Many reasons were cited: Zimbabwe, Argentina, Turkey, a current account deficit, persistent Reserve Bank dollar liabilities, failure to privatise, the resignation of a senior Reserve Bank official, the global economic slowdown, etc. But most of these factors remained intact in 2002-03e.g. Zimbabwe deteriorated much farther and faster, while the rand rebounded remarkably, suggesting that investor psychology about geopolitics (or any of the other factors above) could be discounted as a durable factor. As another example, the Reserve Bank's net open forward position (its primary liability) had been reduced from nearly $24 billion in 1998 to $4.8 billion at year-end 2001: meanwhile, the rand fell at its fastest-ever rate.

For statistical context, in April 2001, the daily turnover of the rand in currency trades within South Africa was around $8 billion, and another $3.5 billion in trades occurred offshore, mainly London and New York. In contrast, in 1995, there was insignificant offshore trade, and internal trade was only $2.7 billion. The bond exchange had annual turnover in 2001 of R12.4 trillion, up from just R2.0 trillion in 1995. Most spectacularly, the total value of shares traded on the stock exchange rose from R63 billion in 1995 to R606 billion in 2001. Non-residents were a large part of the turmoil, for their net purchases of JSE shares rose from R5.3 billion in 1995 to R26.2 billion in 1996, to R40.6 billion in 1999, but fell back to R17.4 billion in 2000 and rose again to R29.8 in 2001 as the rand became progressively cheaper. These net purchases were offset in 2000-01 by net sales of bonds by foreigners, of R20.2 billion in 2000 and R25.9 billion in 2001 (up from a net positive inflow into the local bond market of R3.4 billion in 1996).[3] Put bluntly, for international financial punters, South Africa had become a casino economy.

Questioning the mandate
Even under conditions of overwhelming local/global financial turmoil, it is telling that the bigger questions were not on government's agenda. There was no better illustration than a thoroughly inconsequential official enquiry into the rand crash by judge John Myburgh and Development Bank of Southern Africa manager Mandla Gantsho (formerly of the World Bank), along with a slightly more creative minority report by commissioner Christine Qunta in 2002. (According to a *Business Day* interpretation, 'On the basis of her report, Qunta might plausibly be classified as an economic nationalist, who views big corporations with suspicion and probably sees greater regulation and not less as the solution to the country's vulnerability.')[4]

One serious methodological problem was that Myburgh/Gantsho did not investigate the substantial decline of the rand during 2000 (from R6/US$ in January to R7.6/US$ in December). To their great discredit, Myburgh/Gantsho said they didn't actually want to know: 'The Commission does not consider it necessary to extend the inquiry to any period before or after 1 January 2001 to 31 December 2001 as the benefits derived therefrom will not justify the additional costs and efforts required.'[5] Nor, methodologically, did the Commission consider non-resident transactions between offshore investors, in spite of the fact that it was these sorts of transactions that Malaysian authorities were so intent on stopping so as to stabilise their currency in 1998. Nor did Myburgh/Gantsho table any of the most serious ethical issues associated with outflows of apartheid-era wealth, which are of such great importance for a genuine reparations process.[6]

Myburgh/Gantsho's offhanded conclusion to the milquetoast final report – namely, 'One must understand that South Africa has an open economy and it is inevitable that from time to time there will be turbulence'[7] – followed logically from the self-delimiting mandate, which prevented the Commission from even bothering to ask the three most obvious questions:

- to what extent did persistent capital flight by residents and corporations affect the underlying value of the rand?;[8]
- wouldn't stronger controls (to guard against both dividend/profit outflows and speculation) have insulated South Africa from the most destructive currency volatility of 2000-01?;[9] and
- shouldn't Pretoria now consider stronger exchange controls?[10]

For Pretoria's neoliberal managers and their allies, the stakes in keeping these specific questions below the Commission's radar screen were high indeed. This was not only because of the huge devaluation of South African assets that occurred during the run, but because the logical policy conclusion – stop the rot by imposing stronger exchange controls, including on profit/dividend outflows to the London stock market – would have to be systematically excluded from public discourse.[11] Ironically, at the very time the Myburgh Commission began it's work, the then Zambian president Frederick Chiluba very publicly announced that he was, reluctantly, considering applying exchange controls because of corporate abuse (although ultimately he didn't).[12]

Merely blaming speculators and currency-trading profiteers – instead of systemic outflow – was, therefore, an easy out.[13] Just at the point the rand fell hardest and furthest, in late December 2001, Reserve Bank governor Tito Mboweni and finance minister Manuel together insisted, 'It is important to point out that much of the volatility is driven by sentiment and opportunism.'[14] This was not untrue by that stage of the currency slaughter. However, as discussed below, the two failed to cover up Mboweni's own extraordinary decision to pour petrol on the fire, by allowing another R2 billion to flow offshore the previous few days through exchange control *liberalisation*.

Financial 'opportunism'

Within days, four specific targets appeared in view, courtesy of an insider source – probably from the Reserve Bank, but possibly a hypercompetitive commercial banker – who informed SA Chamber of Business chief executive Kevin Wakeford. He, in turn, quickly wrote a grammatically-challenged letter to Mbeki to tell him the street gossip in early 2002. The word was that shady forex deals between Deutsche Bank and local corporations Sasol, Nampak and M-Cell in early 2001 catalysed the crash. Wakeford's letter, responsible for the Commission's very existence, accused Deutsche Bank and its three customers of unpatriotic manipulation of exchange controls which had the effect of driving down the currency. Critics replied that Wakeford was merely relying upon gossip, not good information, and that once the information about the Deutsche Bank deals was indeed confirmed, the chronology of the rand's crash (mainly in late 2001) did not correspond to the dates of the deals (mainly in early 2001). Myburgh/Gantsho dismissively called Wakeford's testimony 'hearsay based on hearsay', suggesting it came from a Deutsche Bank competitor.[15]

However, the Commission's report did also record a much more sceptical finding by the Exchange Control investigators: Deutsche Bank Johannesburg's (DBJ's) 'applications for share placements did not disclose all the related or subsequent transactions which were implemented or were to be implemented, i.e. the hedging, funding and related transactions; and some or all of the hedging, funding and other transactions prejudiced the obligation placed on DBJ to ensure reserves neutrality.' Germany's largest bank, managed from Sandton by former early 1990s ANC economic desk official Neil Morrison, ultimately paid the equivalent of a small penalty – estimated at R500000, namely the interest foregone on R10 million deposited at the Reserve Bank – in a formal settlement with the Exchange Control authorities. As a *Business Day* writer noted, 'Compare the paltry fine with speculation not denied that Deutsche made R80 million on the Sasol deal alone.'[16]

Yet even if Deutsche had skirted the exchange control system, as certainly seemed the case, the Myburgh Commission (to its credit) pointed out that this problem was at least partially home grown on Church Street in Pretoria, thanks to Mboweni's deregulatory orientation: 'Speculative positions against the rand were by and large risk free. In essence, most, if not all, market players believed that even the SA Reserve Bank was neither inclined nor in a position to do anything that would strengthen the currency.'[17] Knowing there would be no penalty, aside from market risk, speculators stepped up the attack on the currency as it headed downward in December 2001, in a classical example of the herd instinct.

South Africans 'rush to get their money offshore'

In fact, however, speculative wilding wasn't the underlying problem. Why was there continual downward pressure on the rand *prior* to the fourth quarter of 2001? More honest analysis did poke through now and then, even if the obvious conclusions were never stated. Noticing the populist tendency by October 2001, a *Business Day* writer warned of the

> danger that the rand's weakness will be blamed solely on speculative activity, which would be wrong. Granted, it suits us to think that brash yuppies in London trash the rand all in a day's work before going off for a Red Bull and vodka.
>
> Yet it is not quite that simple. One of the reasons for the rand's weakness is the large outflow of capital from SA companies that have moved offshore. Dividend payments and profit repatriation to head offices in London are taking their toll. At the same time, there is little new foreign capital flowing in. Hardly surprising, if South Africans are in such a rush to get their money out of the country.[18]

Indeed, though it was not even mentioned by Mboweni and Manuel at their year-end 2001 press conference, this interpretation became the common-sense capitalist point of view, as articulated in technical articles and editorials published in *Business Day* repeatedly at the time: 'It has been clear that government opened a can of worms in allowing a number of SA companies to emigrate. Profit repatriation and dividend payments offshore are taking their toll on the rand. Perhaps the best example is De Beers, which is no longer listed, but is now owned by foreign shareholders. It is common cause that part of the rand's recent weakness can be ascribed to De Beers sending cash to its owners.'[19] As the rand kept 'plummeting like a skydiver whose parachute won't open', the paper's editorialists admitted to 'counting the cost of the corporate exodus from SA. In the absence of significant inflows, big outflows in the form of profit repatriation offshore and foreign dividend payments knock the rand, especially when the market is thin.'[20]

As the extent of dividend outflow became public knowledge, partly thanks to *Business Day* front-page headlines, a critical mass of currency dealers and ordinary investors came to understand that smart capital had moved from Johannesburg to London, *forever*.[21] It was widely understood by December that a R4.7 billion net financial inflow during the third quarter 2001 would give way to an outflow of capital in the fourth quarter (the amount, R1.5 billion, was not significant but the direction was crucial).[22] By deconstructing the main components of capital outflow over a longer period, however, it is obvious that South Africa's problems are much broader and deeper than one bad quarter.

Crucially, a vast net outflow of R67.6 billion in portfolio capital was experienced throughout 2001, on top of a lost R13.8 billion in 2000. In addition, R29.3 billion in other net outflows of capital – trade credits, short-term and long-term loans and cross-border bank deposits – occurred throughout 2001. South Africans were themselves responsible for R24 billion of net outflow from March-December 2001: R7 billion lost to the investment allowances of individuals; R13.5 billion via foreign direct investment of SA corporations; and another R3.8 billion in the form of foreign portfolio investments by SA fund managers.[23]

To what extent were the large corporate profit/dividend outflows - especially to London shareholders of Anglo American, DeBeers, South African Breweries, Old Mutual, Liberty and Didata - responsible for the capital flight? Insufficient information was gathered by Myburgh/Gantsho and their KPMG assistants, who didn't even ask the question properly. Because of accounting tricks that create 'fungibility' in a corporate headquarter's balance sheets – e.g., transfer-pricing, exploitation of differential tax requirements, and profit/dividend deferrals – the final returns to shareholders can be manipulated, and hence it is extremely is difficult to pin down a number.

Still, the available statistics – South Africa's overall deficit on the services and income account[24] v offer some indication of the vast scope of the problem. During 2001, the services and income deficit reached R51 billion.[25] As this massive outflow came to the notice of the investor community and the business press, the bet on the rand was 'one-way', i.e., you couldn't lose by predicting its short-term downfall.[26]

3. Recovery?

Of course, at some point this had to change. No one could have reasonably predicted that a crash from R6 to R13.85 to the dollar might transpire within a 24-month period. Once it did, a very sharp rebound was inevitable, and indeed the rand was the world's top currency gainer in 2002. As speculators punted on the recovery, beginning the day after the low point, the rand subsequently rose to as high as R7/US$ in May 2003 (although in June, as this book went to press, another small crash took it back below R8/US$).

The main reason for the rand's spectacular recovery in 2002 was the extreme strategy adopted by Pretoria, specifically the Reserve Bank, but with no discernable opposition by Mbeki or Manuel. Mboweni wanted to both attract portfolio flows of capital back to South Africa and cool the economy so as to limit the resulting spike in inflation caused by the currency crash. He ratcheted interest rates up 4% over a short period, to the point that most business commentators accused Mboweni of killing the patient with monetarist medicine.

Rates remained at the new levels until June 2003, when a 1.5% decline was finally conceded. Commentator Paul Malherbe, complained that Mboweni's 2002 strategy was 'usurious and extortionate'. Malherbe's main gripe, interestingly, was that the high rate regime 'entrenches the disparity between rich and poor.' He continued: 'As expected, foreign speculators bought billions of rands, getting ten for each dollar as they cashed in on our high interest rates. Messrs Erwin and Manuel joined Mr Mboweni in self-praise at the [January 2003] World Economic Forum meeting in Davos over how well our currency had strengthened as a result of hot money flowing into the country. They happily ignored the fact that they had made home ownership impossible for most and that joblessness was as bad as ever.'[27] Indeed, at this point, the fact that only 5% of the recipients of individual housing subsidies (still a paltry R16 000) could acquire 'top-up' credit from banks, due to unaffordability that catalysed bank redlining (geographical discrimination), led to a national outcry.

Elusive stability

Did the partial currency recovery between January 2002 and May 2003 mean that the 2000-01 panic should simply be forgotten? Or did the fall and subsequent rise of the rand again amplify the need for much stronger exchange controls? It was not an academic question. After reaching the higher range in mid-2003, exporters – especially mines – were uncompetitive again, leading to tens of thousands of retrenchments. However, instead of tightening, Manuel relaxed controls further in his 2003 budget statement, unblocking the accounts of emigrants who wanted to liberate their apartheid-era loot, and offering amnesty to those who had previously engaged in illegal financial capital flight.

Still, notwithstanding a 79% annualised rise in the South African rand relative to the US dollar in the first quarter of 2003 compared with the previous quarter, Mboweni argued the rand was still 'undervalued... Although there are disagreements as to the appropriate level of the exchange rate, there is general consensus that the more important issue is the volatility of the exchange rate.'[28] The main tool which Mboweni chose to control volatility, interest rate manipulation, was obviously now utterly ineffective. Further controversy emerged in May 2003 when it emerged that the inflation rate upon which Mboweni based monetary policy decisions was incorrectly calculated, because a cost-conscious government agency (Statistics SA) discontinued a real estate rental price series survey three years earlier.

Under the circumstances, financial journalist David Gleason described the early 21st century environment well, in a 2003 *Business Day* article ominously entitled 'SA may be nearing slippery slope towards recession'. He complained of Mboweni's 'huge policy error, [namely] subservience to

the old Stals doctrine... What we need is a permanently stable and competitive exchange rate.'
What prevents currency stability? Gleason answered;

With equity markets either in poor state or going nowhere fast, speculators have turned increasingly to the currency markets in which to play. The result is that currency speculation has become a vast industry and a major source of making money for those bold and brave enough to participate. The trouble for them is that, even here, there are not many alternative products. The obviously big bets are on the euro (now at record highs against the dollar) and the pound. There are some side bets around, such as the Norwegian krone. On the other hand, and though the rand is minuscule in the scheme of things, the 'carry' is potentially large – which explains why it is easily subject to raids.[29]

The ongoing danger to South Africa and other emerging markets was captured by the *Financial Times* in mid-2003: 'A three-year bear market has left many money managers lucky to have a single-digit return – so, suddenly, a 10% currency move meant a lot.' Bank of America's lead speculator, Beau Cummins, admitted that 'Trading houses are like surfers. They are catching a good wave and liking it.'[30]

Given the failure of Mboweni's interest rate ratcheting to intimidate the surfers, it should have been obvious that the only way to achieve the stability and balance required in a particular country is through exchange controls. The only strategy to conclusively stop the currency raiders, internationally, is through a sufficiently punitive Tobin Tax (see Chapters Five and Twelve). But to even begin discussion on the matter will require a more open mind than the South African elite possess.

Censoring capital controls

The degeneration of state sovereignty under conditions of globalisation is not so much *necessary*, as it is an *ideological* decision. This is easily illustrated by considering the possibility of renewed exchange controls in South Africa. The man responsible for the existing controls, Mboweni, admitted in October 2001 that he had not been enforcing those controls which still discourage pure currency speculation. *Business Day* advised that this Reserve Bank oversight presented a huge potential problem: 'Turnover in the rand/dollar market runs into billions of dollars every day. The value of the forex traded on the SA forex market exceeds an entire month's imports and exports added together every day. That means a massive amount of forex trade occurs which is not trade-related and over which there could be potential questions.'[31]

Rather than addressing the potential for chaos thus created, Mboweni appeared intent on exacerbating it. On the one hand, he issued a statement proclaiming that existing controls would now be enforced. This was a major surprise to the financial markets, leading to a short-term intensification of the run, as some international players became nervous and withdrew. On the other hand, Mboweni also simultaneously confirmed that Pretoria remained 'committed to the orderly and gradual process of relaxation of exchange controls' – a recipe for perpetual currency volatility.[32]

Mboweni was prepared to persevere no matter the costs. To prove it, on 13 November, his Exchange Control unit issued a new rule allowing not only institutional investors like pension funds, long-term insurers and unit trusts to invest abroad. From November 2001, fund managers were allowed to join the group benefiting from liberalisation. The managers immediately applied for permission to buy nearly R2 billion worth of foreign currency, which Mboweni approved in December. The approval expired on 31 December, compelling rapid rand sales. 'As a consequence,' Myburgh/Gantsho reported, 'the foreign currency equivalent of R1.7 billion was bought by institutional investors in an illiquid and volatile market.'[33] The rand fell from R10.25 on 1 December to R13.85 twenty days later as the fund managers – and everyone else – divested as much as possible from South Africa.

Looking back on the currency crash, Mboweni was uncharacteristically bashful in his testimony to the Myburgh Commission: 'It is virtually impossible to estimate the exact extent to which exchange control liberalisation has contributed to rand weakness but there can be no doubt, as the figures above show, that it could at times have been an important structural factor.'[34] Yet no matter how stark this evidence and chronology, Myburgh/Gantsho repeatedly refused to apply their minds, on this and indeed on any other difficult matter. Instead of discussing the 'important structural factor' that created such volatility, Myburgh/Gantsho took the self-interested advice of bank economists and market analysts on capital controls. The Commission's final report uncritically parrots their contradictory psycho-babble, namely that

> exchange controls which are still in force potentially deter foreign investment because foreigners believe that the gradual or sudden removal of such controls would lead to a gradual or sudden further depreciation of the rand; the partial lifting of exchange controls over the years has probably made the enforcement of the remaining measures much more difficult; and remaining exchange controls are rendering the rand a weak currency because of the fear that comprehensive exchange controls may again be implemented at any time.[35]

Myburgh/Gantsho concluded, illogically, that once financial liberalisation 'is implemented, and controls removed, the negative perception of foreign investors towards exchange controls, should change to the benefit of the rand. As was experienced in October 2001, the change in behaviour of market participants based on a perception that in enforcing existing exchange controls a reversal of the policy of liberalisation had occurred, may be negative for the rand.'[36]

Actually, there was an experiment along precisely those lines in March 1995 which Myburgh/Gantsho could have investigated had they been so inclined: the dropping of the financial rand (finrand), South Africa's long-standing dual exchange rate system. After that point, foreign investors had no psychological, material or metaphysical barriers to retrieving their funds from South Africa. Of course, they still refused to invest. *Business Day* editor Peter Bruce quite frankly interpreted 'the feeling we call uncertainty. Foreigners show it by a lack of confidence. We are, we are told, a political risk. Why? The ANC will be in power for at least another 10, probably 20, years. The risk arises because everyone knows you cannot survive as a democracy when the poor outnumber the rich 20 to one. And people, ourselves included, count our poor and wonder, even with all the tools at our disposal, how so many millions of people can ever be rescued from the trap they are in.'[37]

A very good question, that. By answering it in two ways – firstly by liberalising financial controls, more hundreds of billions of rands left South Africa during the late 1990s, and secondly by raising interest rates to sado-monetarist levels (mainly double-digit from 1995 onwards) – the Reserve Bank made the dilemma both more urgent and intractable than ever in history. Yet I know of only one other attempt to start a discussion about the finrand, other capital controls or a Tobin Tax: the impassioned writings of a progressive Keynesian economist, Margaret Legum, who for a few years had a column in the *Mail and Guardian*.[38] Instead of discussing the merits of capital controls, the Treasury and Reserve Bank repeated the mantra, 'there will be no big bang for the few remaining controls – just a phased liberalisation.'

Shock absorber?

With the scope for public debate so severely limited, Myburgh/Gantsho could perhaps be forgiven for their innocence of how exchange controls work. For example, they endorsed an extraordinary perversion by Manuel: 'The Government has chosen to follow a flexible exchange rate to act as a shock absorber against global developments.'[39] In the context of periodic currency crashes and dramatic interest rate increases every two years following the finrand's extinction, it was peculiar to describe financial liberalisation and the floating exchange rate as a 'shock absorber'.

Myburgh/Gantsho not only repeated the metaphor four times in the Commission Report, they embroidered it with an equally dubious proposition attributed to Treasury director-general Maria Ramos: 'Exchange rate adjustments help cushion the economy from external trade and capital flow shocks and mitigate the impact of economic contraction, *especially in respect of the poor*' (emphasis added).[40] The poor, in fact, were hardest hit because the 2000-01 currency crash translated directly into much higher consumer prices, not just of imports. Even maize witnessed a 100%+ price increase because of shortages and a dollar-denominated market that resulted from South African exporters' extremely competitive dollar price, which in turn attracted most large commercial farmers away from the domestic market.

The direct opposite of Myburgh/Gantsho's conclusion was, ironically, located within the main section of the Commission's final report dealing with 'The performance of the rand.' According to the author of this section, 'Most of the rand's history incorporated a dual exchange rate system. The financial rand acted as a shock absorber for the commercial rand traded at a significant discount of between 15% and 55% to the commercial rand over the thirty years that this mechanism was in place.'[41] *This* statement, at least, was true. Regrettably, given the cacophonous chorus of bank and media voices against exchange controls,[42] Myburgh/Gantsho could not conceive of returning to the finrand (or tougher controls). They even became advocates of further deregulation.

4. South Africa's frustrated international reforms

The farce associated with the rand's roller-coaster ride isn't merely quantitative in nature. It also reflected a deep-seated failure of governance, at a time when it would have been reasonable and logical for Pretoria to intervene with currency controls so as to mitigate market failure. Even setting aside the moral issue of white South Africans escaping with hundreds of billions of rands worth of apartheid loot, the incident tells us a great deal more about the incapacity and deficit of passion apparent in the inaction by Mbeki, Manuel, Erwin, Mboweni and their colleagues.

For if global apartheid is, in a sense, the failure of the world market to reproduce itself in a sustainable manner – whether socially, geopolitically, economically or environmentally – then the main Third World government opponents, namely Pretoria's rhetorically-gifted politicians, should have taken their own lessons to heart. But they wouldn't even countenance mere discussion of the only remedy which would work against international financial turbulence.

What of related economic problems which, since September, 2001, generated a series of summits allegedly aimed at addressing global inequality? The record is just as miserable:

- At the Durban World Conference Against Racism in September 2001, Mbeki shot down NGOs and African leaders demanding reparations for slavery/colonialism/apartheid. When the Jubilee South Africa movement filed lawsuits against firms which profited from apartheid, Mbeki and Erwin strongly condemned these, making it less likely that not only black South Africans, but any victims of former dictatorships anywhere, would ever recapture illegitimate profits made by banks and corporations which prosper thanks to repression.
- At the Doha World Trade Organisation ministerial in November 2001, Erwin split the African delegation so as to prevent consensus-denial by trade ministers, which had shattered the Seattle meeting in 1999. Added to ongoing US and European Union protectionism and economic decline, Africa's failure to negotiate from a position of strength worsened already fast-falling terms of trade, which in turn further depleted the continent's fragile finances to breaking point.
- In Monterrey, at the United Nations Financing for Development conference in March 2002, Manuel was summit co-chair, but he let Africa down by legitimising ongoing World Bank/IMF strategies, including debt 'relief' and undemocratic governance of the financial agencies. The cementing of the *status quo* in turn worsened most African countries' balance sheets. Africa could not even muster enough power to gain even a meagre third executive director's seat at the Bank and IMF.
- From the June 2002 G8 summit at Kananaskis, Mbeki departed with 'peanuts' (as widely interpreted), yet against all evidence to the contrary, declared that the meeting 'signifies the end of the epoch of colonialism and neo-colonialism'. The 'kneepad' strategy of begging the rich countries for more aid was discredited, and Mbeki's endorsement of Zimbabwean president Robert Mugabe's March 2002 electoral theft left the New Partnership for Africa's Development in tatters.
- At the Johannesburg World Summit on Sustainable Development in August 2002, Mbeki and Valli Moosa undermined UN democratic procedure, facilitated the privatisation of nature, and did nothing to address the plight of the world's majority. Power relations were so adverse that notwithstanding his eloquent opening speech (cited at the outset of this Afterword), the rich countries prohibited Mbeki from using the phrase 'global apartheid' in the final declaration: the obvious insults are that the term implies causality and a structured system of oppression.

Similar manifestations of Pretoria's frustrated reform strategy were evident in subsequent months:

- within Africa—for instance, Olusegun Obasanjo's blatantly corrupt

Nigerian presidential election in April 2003, and the ongoing degeneration in Zimbabwe notwithstanding increasingly futile coverups by
Mbeki and Obasanjo;

- at the 2003 Davos World Economic Forum, where Manuel and the
  African delegates were simply ignored;
- in Pretoria's high-profile – if decidedly half-hearted – anti-war stance,
  which failed to staunch the US/UK from a blatantly imperialist invasion
  of Iraq in March 2003;
- at the June 2003 Evian G8 meeting, which provided no firm commitments to halt Africa's slide;
- in a visit by George Bush to Pretoria in July 2003, which was preceded
  by the US administration cutting both its donor pledges to fight AIDS
  and military aid because Pretoria wouldn't oppose the International
  Criminal Court at The Hague; and
- in the run-up to the September 2003 Cancun WTO ministerial summit,
  which, by all accounts, was likely to fail simply because no meaningful
  concessions were on offer from the US and Europe.

There are countervailing official arguments and rationales for why
Pretoria's softly-softly approach to world political economy was so
ineffectual.[43] But it should be evident that while Mbeki and his colleagues
continued, in effect, polishing the chains of international economic slavery
at the turn of the 21st century, a growing movement – derided by Mbeki as
the 'ultraleft' – aimed to break the chains. That movement's energy and
enthusiasm grew in proportion to the futility of Mbeki's reforms. It is there,
finally, where we identify those who are genuinely against global apartheid.

Table 6: Five reactions to the global crisis

Political current	Global justice movements	Third World nationalism	Post-Washington Consensus	Washington Consensus	Resurgent right wing
Main agenda	'deglobalisation' of capital (not people) and 'globalisation-from-below'; anti-war; anti-racism; indigenous rights; women's liberation; ecology; 'decommodified' state services; participatory democracy	increased (but fairer) global integration via reform of interstate system, based on debt relief and market access; democratised global governance; regionalism; anti-imperialism	fix 'imperfect markets'; add 'sustainable development' to existing neoliberalism via global state-building; promote global Keynesianism; oppose unilateralism and militarism	rename neoliberalism (PRSPs, HIPC and PPPs) but with some provisions for 'transparency' and self-regulation; more bail-out mechanisms; general support for US-led Empire	unilateral petro-military imperialism; protectionism, tariffs, subsidies, bailouts and other crony deals; reverse globalisation of people via racism and xenophobia; intensified social control

Political current	Global justice movements	Third World nationalism	Post-Washington Consensus	Washington Consensus	Resurgent right wing
Leading institutions	social mvts; environmental justice activists; indigenous people's and autonomist groups; radical activist networks; some left labour movements; leftwing think-tanks (e.g., Focus on the Global South, FoodFirst, Global Exchange, IBASE, IFG, IPS, Nader centres, TNI); leftist media and websites (e.g. Indymedia,	Non-Aligned Movement, G77 and South Centre; self-selecting regimes: Argentina, Chile, China, Egypt, India, Libya, Malaysia, Nigeria, Pakistan, Palestine, Russia, S.Africa, Turkey, Zimbabwe with a few – like Brazil, Cuba and Venezuela – that lean left (but others	WSSD; some UN agencies (e.g., Unctad, Unicef, Unrisd); some int'l NGOs' (e.g., Care, Civicus, IUCN, Oxfam, TI); large enviro. groups (e.g., Sierra and WWF); big labour (e.g., ICFTU and AFL-CIO); liberal foundations (e.g., Carnegie, Ford, MacArthur, Mott, Open Society,	US state (Fed, Treasury, USAid); corporate media and big business; World Bank, IMF, WTO; elite clubs (Bilderburgers, Trilateral Commission, World Economic Forum); UN agencies (UNDP, Global Compact); universities and think-tanks (U.of Chicago economics department	Republican Party populist and libertarian wings; Project for New American Century; right wing think-tanks (AEI, Cato, CSIS, Heritage, Manhattan); the Christian Right; petro-military complex; Pentagon; rightwing media (Fox, *National Interest*, *Weekly Standard*, *Washington Times*); and

political current	Global justice movements	Third World nationalism	Post-Washington Consensus	Washington Consensus	Resurgent right wing
	www.zmag.org); a few semi-liberated zones (Porto Alegre, Kerala); and sectoral or local coalitions allied to World Social Forum	imperialism, e.g. E. Timor, Ecuador and Eritrea); and a few supportive NGOs (e.g. Third World Network, Seatini)	Columbia Univ. economics department; and gov'ts Canada and Scandinavia	Council on Foreign Relations, Institute of Int'l Finance, Brookings); and most EU and Japanese governments	proto-fascist European parties – but also Israel's Likud and perhaps Islamic extremism
Internal disputes	role of nation-state; party politics; fix-it v.nix-it strategies for int'l agencies; divergent interests (e.g. North-South); gender and racial power relations; and tactics (especially merits of symbolic property destruction)	degree of militancy against North; divergent regional interests; religion; egos and internecine rivalries	some look leftward (for broader alliances) while others look right to Washington Consensus (resources, legitimacy)	differing reactions to US empire due to divergent national-capitalist interests and domestic political dynamics	conflict over extent of US imperial reach and protecting national power, cultural traditions and patriarchy

Political current	Global justice movements	Third World nationalism	Post-Washington Consensus	Washington Consensus	Resurgent right wing
Noted personalities	M.Albert T.Ali	Y.Arafat	Y.Akyuz	T.Blair	E.Abrams
	S.Amin	J.Aristide	K.Annan	G.Brown	J.Aznar
	C.Augiton	F.Castro	L.Axworthy Bono	M.Camdessus	S.Berlusconi
	M.Barlow	H.Chavez	G.Brundtland	J.Chirac	O.Bin Laden
	D.Barsamian	M.Gaddafi	S.Byers	B.Clinton	C.Black
	H.Belafonte	H.Jintao	B.Cassen	A.Erwin	P.Buchanan
	W.Bello	M.Khor	J.Chretien	S.Fischer	G.Bush
	A.Bendana	N.Kirshner	P.Eigen	M.Friedman	D.Cheney
	F.Betto J.Bove	R.Lagos Lula	J.Fischer	T.Friedman	N.Gingrich
	J.Brecher	Mahathir	A.Giddens	A.Greenspan	J.Haider
	R.Brenner	N.Mandela	W.Hutton	S.Harbinson	R.Kagan
	D.Brutus	T.Mbeki	P.Krugman	H.Köhler	H.Kissinger
	N.Bullard	R.Mugabe	W.Maathai	A.Krueger	W.Kristol
	A.Buzgalin	O.Obasanjo	P.Martin	P.Lamy	J.M.le Pen
	L.Cagan	D.Ortega	T.Mkandawire	M.Malloch Brown	R.Limbaugh
	A.Callinicos	V.Putin	M.Moody-Stuart	T.Manuel	R.Murdoch
	L.Cassarini	Y.Tandon	K.Naidoo	R.Prodi	J.Negroponte
	J.Cavanagh		T.Palley	K.Rogoff	M.Peretz
	C.Chalmers		J.Persson	R.Rubin	R.Perle
	N.Chomsky		John Paul II	G.Schroeder	N.Podhoretz
	A.Choudry		M.Robinson	Supachai	O.Reich
	A.Cockburn		D.Rodrik	P.J.Snow	C.Rice
	T.Clarke		J.Sachs	L.Summers	D.Rumsfeld
	K.Danaher		W.Sachs	J.Taylor	A.Scalia
	A.Escobar		A.Sen	J.Wolfensohn	A.Sharon
	E.Galeano				
	S.George				
	D.Glover				
	A.Grubacic				

Political current	Global justice movements	Third World nationalism	Post-Washington Consensus	Washington Consensus	Resurgent right wing
	D.Harvey		G.Soros J.Stiglitz	E.Zedillo	P.Wolfowitz
	D.Henwood		P.Sweeney	R.Zoellick	J.Woolsey
	J.Holloway		G.Verhofstadt		
	B.Kagarlitsky		E.von Weizaecher		
	P.Kingsnorth		K.Watkins		
	N.Klein M.Lowy				
	Marcos A.Mittal				
	G.Mcnbiot				
	M.Moore				
	E.Morales				
	R.Nader				
	V.Navarro				
	A.Negri				
	T.Ngwane				
	N.Njehu G.Palast				
	M.Patkar J.Pilger				
	A.Roy E.Said				
	J.Sen V.Shiva				
	J.Singh B.Sousa				
	Santos A.Starr				
	J.Stecile				
	T.Teivainen,				
	V.Vargas G.Vidal				
	H.Wainwright				
	L.Wallach				
	M.Weisbrot				
	R.Weissman				
	H.Zinn				

Notes

1. Mbeki, T. (2002), 'Address by President Mbeki at the Welcome Ceremony of the WSSD,' Johannesburg, 25 August.
2. My forthcoming effort is provisionally entitled *Sustaining Global Apartheid: South Africa's Frustrated International Reforms*.
3. Myburgh Commission (2002), *Commission of Inquiry into the Rapid Depreciation of the Exchange Rate of the Rand and Related Matters*, Pretoria, 30 June.
4. *Business Day*, 2 August 2002. Qunta's contribution is interesting merely because she took allegations about Deutsche Bank seriously, and because she invoked lessons about East Asian exchange controls that were recounted in Chapter Twelve.
5. Myburgh Commission, *Inquiry into the Rapid Depreciation*, Summary, 165.
6. The use of 'ethics' in the report was merely a codeword for the most venal forms of currency trading: gambling, personal account trading, misinformation, rumours, insider trading and breaches of confidentiality. Actual currency 'shorting'—sales of the rand not in the dealer's possession, based on the risk that the currency will indeed fall—was not 'unethical' in Myburgh/Gantsho's book.
7. Myburgh Commission, *Inquiry into the Rapid Depreciation*, Summary, 127,156. The rest of the paragraph is startling in its inaccuracy and anti-social implications: 'The events of late 2001 were one of the times. In following a gradual approach to capital account liberalisation, the Government has had to make a number of macroeconomic policy decisions to avoid potential economic instability and rising inequality. These decisions include following a flexible exchange rate to act as a shock absorber against global developments. Exchange rate adjustments help cushion the economy from external trade and capital flow shocks and mitigate the impact of economic contraction, especially in respect of the poor.' As discussed below, the poor, in fact, were hardest hit because the currency crash very quickly translated into much higher consumer prices, not just of imports.
8. There is not even an estimate of the amount of flight since liberation. As for the 1998-99 rush of SA's largest firms to London for relisting, Myburgh/Gantsho repeated the KPMG consultants' simplistic argument that, 'off-shore listings by South African companies are often a consequence of the limitations on off-shore investments' (Myburgh Commission, *Inquiry into the Rapid Depreciation*, Summary, 148).
9. Because the off-shore/off-shore transactions were, by Myburgh/Gantsho's own choice, removed from his Commission's field of study, the two simply failed to mention the readily available antidote to such financial transactions: the Malaysian prohibition on external currency holdings. As noted in Chapter Twelve, these worked perfectly well to prevent further shorting of the Malaysian ringgit.
10. One can't only blame Myburgh/Gantsho; if Mbeki, Manuel and Mboweni set the terms of reference, they were exquisitely surgical in avoiding those two questions. The closest they got were that Myburgh/Gantsho should 'enquire into and report on whether between 1 January and 31 December 2001 any person or any other juristic entity, directly or indirectly, entered into, concluded or caused any transactions which contributed or gave rise to the rapid depreciation of the value of the rand during the relevant period relative to other currencies, and whether any such transactions were illegal or unethical; any of the transactions in question involved collusion and resulted in any improper gain or avoided loss.' The terms of reference continued with detailed specifications about whether 'existing regulations and/or

restrictions on the export of capital from South Africa were contravened' and 'the effectiveness of the current administrative system of ensuring adherence to exchange controls and other regulatory measures in guarding against the occurrence of such transactions; and possible action that could be taken against any person or juristic entity identified as having participated in any such transactions.'.

Thus the possibility of promoting any new capital controls was completely off the agenda, from the outset. And the failure to define 'ethical' or 'improper' meant that the big questions were reduced to technicist discourses about which kind of sleazy financiers engage in currency 'short' sales—i.e., anticipating a currency will fall and hence betting against it, by promising to buy that currency in the future (when it costs less). All in all, the Commission appears to have been set up to *fail* to ask the only questions that would help provide answers as to why the rand crashed. At least *Business Day* helped by mentioning the street gossip periodically in late 2001.

11. This was much as I experienced it a year earlier, within the economics profession, as documented above on p.xxii.
12. *Business Day*, 15 January 2002.
13. There are essentially two views of speculation. The neoliberal perspective comes most forcefully from followers of Milton Friedman, and the view that there are important differences between the 'real' and 'money' economies derives in part from John Maynard Keynes. The first position was articulated well by former Reserve Bank governor Chris Stals: 'The speculator has an important part to play in an effective price discovery mechanism, based on the principles of demand and supply operating in an amorphous market' (Myburgh Commission, *Inquiry into the Rapid Depreciation*, Stals, Expert Bundle 177).

I am sympathetic, ironically, to the Investec definition of a speculator, which distinguishes between the financial and real economy: 'anyone who uses the market to gain from a position with or without there being any other underlying transaction. The decision to hedge or not to hedge an underlying exposure is in itself speculative. Speculators provide the liquidity necessary to ensure that whenever a hedger requires a hedge position, the market is able to absorb his trade without undue disturbance to the current price. Speculators are confined mainly to professional traders' (Myburgh Commission, *Inquiry into the Rapid Depreciation*, Evidence of De Villiers, Investec Bundle 34-35).

In the same spirit, testifying to Myburgh/Gantsho, even Treasury director-general Maria Ramos cited Keynes' *General Theory*: 'Speculators may do no harm as bubbles on a steady stream of enterprise. But the position is serious when enterprise becomes the bubble on a whirlpool of speculation.' According to the Commission's final report, Ramos added that it is a matter of balance: 'Speculators can help make a liquid market while there is a healthy demand for and supply of assets or currency, and where the burden of the spread is tight. The deeper [and] the more liquid the market, the more likely it will be that speculators will be bubbles on a steady stream. However, in thin markets or in one-sided markets, as was the case in the rand market in November [2001] and particularly in December, speculators will have a greater impact, even with very small transactions' (Myburgh Commission, *Inquiry into the Rapid Depreciation*, Ramos, Record 718).

The logical conclusion—namely, preventing speculators such an opening—was rigorously avoided by the judge and the banker.
14. Mboweni, T. and T.Manuel (2001), 'Joint Press Statement', Reserve Bank and Ministry of Finance, Pretoria, December 21.
15. *Business Day*, 2 August 2002.

16. *Business Day*, 30 July 2002. Nevertheless, in his submission to the Myburgh Commission, Morrison was in denial, as Myburgh/Gantsho reported: 'Deutsche Bank is not aware of any transactions that contravened exchange controls during 2001' (Myburgh Commission, *Inquiry into the Rapid Depreciation*, Evidence of Morrison, Deutsche Bank Bundle 10, and Myburgh Commission, s.15.32). Moreover, reflecting the 'moral hazard' problem (i.e., when a bank's risky and/or anti-social behaviour is rewarded by governments), Morrison could brag that Deutsche's choice—by his former ANC boss, Manuel—to coordinate an off-shore bond offering in 2003, vindicated his institution. But there was, at least, considerable damage to the bank's brand name during 2002, when the financial sleaze bubbled to the surface.

17. Myburgh Commission, *Inquiry into the Rapid Depreciation*, D.14.4.

18. *Business Day*, 16 October 2001.

19. *Business Day*, 23 November 2001.

20. *Business Day*, 26 November 2003. At that point, referring to the *Economist* Big Mac index of currency values, the editorialists remarked, 'SA could make Big Macs here and airfreight them in bulk to an expensive country like Denmark and still provide the Danes with cheaper cholesterol than they could themselves.'

21. Testifying to Myburgh/Gantsho, Standard Chartered Merchant Bank included the factor, 'Press comment on the outflow of dividends from South African companies listed off-shore' in October-November 2001, as one of the reasons for the rand's crash (Myburgh Commission, *Inquiry into the Rapid Depreciation*, D.39).

22. Foreign direct investment went from a third quarter inflow of R3.6 billion to an outflow of R7.3 billion in the fourth quarter. Net portfolio capital flight totalled R3.4 billion in the fourth quarter.

23. Myburgh Commission, *Inquiry into the Rapid Depreciation*, C.5.4.

24. Technically, this refers to income payments and receipts, such as dividends, interest and employee compensation, transportation fees for goods and passengers, travel services and other services.

25. http://www.cosatu.org.za

26. Myburgh Commission, *Inquiry into the Rapid Depreciation*, D.5.8.2.

27. Malherbe, P. (2003), 'The Danger of High Interest Rates', *Sane Views*, 3, 20, June.

28. Demonstrating the system's irrationality, that simple remark (which logically should have strengthened the currency), was responsible, according to the *Cape Times* (20 May 2003), for a 4% drop in the rand immediately afterwards.

29. *Business Day*, 29 May 2003.

30. *Financial Times*, 6 June 2003.

31. *Business Day*, 16 October 2001. The paper explained why the current system of bank-authorised forex allocations was not helping: 'Local banks have to provide documentary evidence for each foreign currency deal specifying what the underlying transaction is. For billions of dollars a day, that's a lot of paperwork. An army of clever bureaucrats with an eye for small print is needed to vet the currency deals properly.' Instead, as Malaysia did successfully in 1998 when facing a similar degree of capital flight, the solution would have been to internalise these functions in the Reserve Bank.

32. *Business Day*, 15 October 2001. Shortly afterwards, the neoliberal publisher of the paper, Peter Bruce, argued, without any convincing new information, on behalf of a 'big-bang' liberalisation of the few remaining currency controls. To his credit, he permitted a rebuttal from former Baring currency trader Michael Power: 'Your paper has orchestrated a well-argued campaign for total abolition of exchange controls by SA. My advice is: be careful what you wish for. Your philosophy may

reflect self-interested wisdom, but lacks the unqualified support of even the International Monetary Fund. Don't open your door fully when most of the airflow through it will be only one way. You must substantially equalise the air pressure on both sides first' (*Business Day*, 21 December 2001).

33. Myburgh Commission, *Inquiry into the Rapid Depreciation*, D.16.4.
34. Myburgh Commission, *Inquiry into the Rapid Depreciation*, Bundle SARB (7) 34-35 21 Mboweni Bundle SARB (7) 35.
35. Myburgh Commission, *Inquiry into the Rapid Depreciation*, D.6.6.
36. Myburgh Commission, *Inquiry into the Rapid Depreciation*, Summary, 156.
37. Bruce was at least honest about power relations: 'Right now, though, we are on a hiding to nothing. Black fat cats are as bad at creating jobs as white fat cats. Gosh, what a surprise! The government is utterly seduced by big business, and cannot see beyond its immediate interests' (*Business Day*, 4 June 2003).
38. Legum, M. (2002), *It Doesn't have to be Like This!: A New Economy for South Africa and the World*, Cape Town, Ampersand Press. Legum's other suggestions for concrete financial-sector reform all merit far more discussion amongst South African policy wonks, but as a first priority it remains for these ideas to be fused with grass-roots initiatives, such as Jubilee's reparations movement and anti-privatisation campaigning.
39. Myburgh Commission, *Inquiry into the Rapid Depreciation*, Evidence of Manuel, National Treasury Bundle (1) 83-84.
40. Myburgh Commission, *Inquiry into the Rapid Depreciation*, Evidence of Ms Ramos, National Treasury Bundle 59.
41. Myburgh Commission, *Inquiry into the Rapid Depreciation*, B.1.2.1. It is not clear who offered this information, but the prior footnote was from 'Stals Expert bundle 170,171'.
42. Bruce of *Business Day* was cited above. According to testimony by the representative of JP Morgan, 'The events of the fourth quarter of 2001 demonstrate the real difficulties of enforcing and managing exchange control, particularly in relation to off-shore participants in the rand market. JP Morgan endorses the stated position of the National Treasury and Exchange Control in favour of the expeditious but phased relaxation of exchange controls' (Myburgh Commission, *Inquiry into the Rapid Depreciation*, Evidence of Mr JJ Coulter, JP Morgan Bundle 18). This was backed up by Morrison of Deutsche Bank: 'It is important that South Africa strives for a fully convertible currency' (Myburgh Commission, *Inquiry into the Rapid Depreciation*, Evidence of Morrison, Deutsche Bank Bundle 13).
43. See *Sustaining Global Apartheid* for more of Pretoria's justifications, and critiques thereof, than space allows in the above lists.

Index

Boland, Lois 163
Bolivia, water privatisation crisis 206
Bombelles, Tom 167
Bono 106, 108
Boswell, Terry 207, 208
Botha, P.W. 35, 37
Brady: Bond 14; Plan 5
Brady, Nicholas 96
Bretton Woods 101, 282, 284
  conference 100
  institutions 67, 68, 142, 143, 197
  system 10, 57–61
  US withdrawal from 58–9
Bristol-Myers Squibb 164, 169, 170, 178, 188
British South Africa Company (BSAC) 34, 62
Brown, Gordon 14, 96
Bruce, Peter 303
Brutus, Dennis 56
Buchanan, Pat 97, 98
Burnside, Craig 82
Bush: George 96; George W. 93
Business Day 83, 84, 284–5

Camdessus, Michel 14, 15, 68, 96, 108, 129
Cameron, Edwin 177
Cape Colony 254, 255
Cape Commercial Bank 255
capital account 278
capital controls 225, 241, 242, 273–4, 282,294, 296, 297, 300-304
  comparative 243–52
  historical precedents 243–5
  mandated by UNCTAD 275–6
  Malaysian 246–9, 276–7
capitalist crisis 284
capitalist development, uneven 31
Castro, Fidel 105
catalytic converters 123–6
Cato Institute 97
Centre for Strategic and International Studies 141
Cesan, Raul 170
Chad-Cameroon pipeline 235
Chamber of Mines 35, 259

Chang, John 82
Chase-Dunn, Chris 207, 208
Chavez, Hugo 105
Chidzero, Bernard 28, 56, 70, 71
Chikane, Frank 84
Chile, capital controls 249
Chiluba, Frederick 46, 296
Chissano, Joaqim 74
cholera 23, 220
Chomsky, Noam 109
civil war 39
Clark, John 252
Clarke: Duncan 252; Simon 270
Clinton, Bill 12, 14, 80, 83, 96, 118, 144, 147, 194
Coates, Thomas 181
Cockburn, Alexander 203
Cold War 18, 19
Columbus Steel 126
Commission of Inquiry into the Rapid Depreciation of the Exchange Rate of the Rand and Related Matters 294-297, 302, 304
Committee on the Transfer of Real Resources to the Developing Countries 56
Common Market of Eastern and Southern Africa 50
Common Monetary Union 50
Commonwealth 135
  Development Corporation 63
  Heads of Government Meeting 130
Communist Party, South African (SACP) 3, 36, 47, 56, 119, 264, 280, 281–2
community-based organisations (CBOs) 229
Congress:
  of Democrats 46
  of Non-European Trade Unions 36
  of South African Trade Unions (Cosatu) 3, 37, 47, 119, 130, 188, 203, 280, 281–2, 284
Connally, John 59
Consumer Project on Technology 157, 187
Cooper, Fred 45
corporatism 47